Climbing the Mountain

Climbing the Mountain

Bible Study for Those Who "Hear"

by
J. Cline-McCrary

© **1996** Joan Cline McCrary

11/97

Library of Congress Catalog Card Number: 96-92377

ISBN 0-9623541-3-9

First Edition

Contents

Acknowledgments

This book became a reality only because of the patience of my husband, Ron, and my daughters, Kathryn and Margaret. Its basis lies in the teachings from my family, now all passed beyond. This book acknowledges that the teaching is there for us all. Some call it *grace*. All we have to do is *acknowledge* it.

But *grace* gives us things of this world, too. For the offerings of this world, I am also grateful. The reference material was available when needed. I give thanks for Norlin Library at the University of Colorado, which had the needed art work, and the Divine Science Church of Truth in Denver, which had a copy of the Holman Bible. I thank Ron Franklin for photography, Mary Brinkopf for proofreading; Arthur Vergara for editing points, and Ram Sundaresan for graphics. Thanks, too, to Mary McClure, Doral McKee, Alice Painter Gross, and Kristen & Joe Uveges for their encouragement.

Carlo Suarès: *The Cipher of Genesis* (York Beach, ME: Samuel Weiser Inc., 1992). MATERIAL USED BY PERMISSION.

Portions of *The Torah* and *The Prophets,* MATERIAL USED BY PERMISSSION from The Jewish Publication Society.

Bibliography

Alder, Vera Stanley. *The Finding of the Third Eye.* 1993. York Beach, ME 03910: Samuel Weiser, Inc.
Alexander, gen. ed. *The Jerusalem Bible.* 1966. Garden City, NY: Doubleday & Co., Inc.
Asimov, Isaac. *Asimov's Guide to the Bible.* 1981. New York: Avenel.
Ausubel, Nathan. *The Book of Jewish Knowledge.* 1964. New York: Crown Pub.
    Pictoral History of the Jewish People. 1956. New York: Crown Pub.
Bishop, Jim. *The Day Christ Died.* 1957. New York: Harper.
Davis, John D. *Dictionary of the Bible.* 1898. rev. by Henry Snyder Gehman, 1944. Princeton, NJ: The Trustees of the Presbyterian Board of Publications and Sabbath-school Work.
Dawkins, Peter. *The Great Vision.* 1985. Coventry, England: Francis Bacon Research Trust, Coventry Printers.
Encyclopedia Americana. 1949. New York: Americana Corporation.
Fillmore, Charles. *Metaphysical Bible Dictionary.* 1931. Unity Village, MO: Unity School of Christianity.
Furst, Jeffrey, ed. *Edgar Cayce's Story of Jesus.* 1969. New York: Coward-McCann, Inc.
Gaskell, G.A. *Dictionary of All Scriptures and Myths.* 1960. New York: Avenel.
Haich, Elizabeth. *Initiation.* 1974. Garberville, CA: Seed Center.
Hall, Manly P. *Journey in Truth.* 1945. Los Angeles, CA: Philosophical Research Society.
    The Mystical Christ. 1975.
    The Secret Teachings of All Ages:An Encyclopedic Outline of Masonic, Hermetic, Qabbalistic and Rosicrucian Philosophy. 1975.
Heline, Corinne. *New Age Bible Interpretation, Vol. I.* 1985. New Age Bible & Philosophy Center.
Jones/Wake. *The Lost Books of the Bible.* 1979. New York: Bell.
Krajenke, Robert W. *Edgar Cayce's Story of the Old Testament.* 1973. Edgar Cayce Foundation.
Lamsa, George M. *Holy Bible:From Ancient Eastern Manuscripts.* 1967. Philadelphia: A.J. Holman.
CompanyMorgan, Marlo. *Mutant MessageDown Under.* 1994. New York: Harper Collins, Pub.
Suarès, Carlo. *The Cipher of Genesis:The Original Code of the Qabala as Applied to the Scriptures.* 1978. York Beach, ME 03910-0612: Samuel Weiser, Inc.
Guillaumont, et.al. translators. *The Gospel According to Thomas.* 1959. New York: Harper & Row, Pub.
The New Strong's Exhaustive Concordance of the Bible. 1984. Nashville: Thomas Nelson Pub.
The Torah. 1962. Philadelphia: Jewish Publication Society of America.
*The Prophets.*1978. Philadelphia: Jewish Publication Society of America.
Troward, Thomas. *Bible Mystery and Bible Meaning.* 1913. New York: Dodd, Mead & Company.
Young, Robert. *Analytical Concordance to the Bible.* 1936. New York: Funk & Wagnalls Company.
Webster's New Universal Unabridged Dictionary. 1979. USA: Dorset and Baber.

Illustrations

Sources:

Davis, John D. *Westminster Dictionary of the Bible.* 1898. Presbyterian Board of Publication

Encyclopedia of Religious Knowledge:Illustrated with Maps and Engravings. 1837. Brattleboro, Vermont: Fessenden & Co.

Holman's Edition, The Holy Bible. 1880. Philadelphia: A.J. Holman & Co. Courtesy of The Divine Science Church of Truth, Denver, Colorado

Leonardo Da Vinci:Selected Works. Planet Art CD Rom.

March, Rev. Daniel, D.D. *Night Scenes in the Bible.* 1869. Philadelphia: Zeigler, McCurdy & Co.

Michelangelo: Selected Works. Planet Art CD Rom.

*Masters in Art: A Series of Illustrated Monographs,*10 Volumes. 1900-1909. Boston: Bates and Guild Company. Courtesy of Norlin Library, University of Colorado, Boulder, Colorado

Illustrations:

Illustrations continued:

Illustrations continued:

Before we begin, a statement must be made. Since the beginning of time, the subject of this book has been the focus of most of the world's thought. How presumptuous to think we can even begin to touch the Truth. Yet, my intuition tells me that the greatest Truth is that which truly "reaches" the essence of us – it is that which our internal being **"hears."**

But to "hear" we must listen, and listening requires careful attention. To test our dedication and attention, indulge me by cutting an apple in half, horizontally. Now carefully observe what you "see." What you "see" represents *Truth.*

The late Carlo Suarès, a Jewish mystic, admonished that only through a life-time of study and complete comprehension of Hebrew could Truth be broached. However, few of us are skilled in Hebrew. Consequently, we must rely on the tools which we have. We must look for our own truths in the Scriptures we have available to us. My "hearing" says that those truths which are needed by me (or by you) are provided at the proper time.

If we happen to read and comprehend Hebrew, that is fabulous; if we happen to read and comprehend English, that, too is fabulous. **If we happen to cut an apple in half horizontally and see and comprehend the perfect and symbolic symmetry therein...**

... that is fabulous!

Introduction

When science has climbed to its highest mountain, it will find religion already there, sitting in repose. Albert Einstein

The Mountain nicely represents our life-experience, and mountain climbing is a fine metaphor for what the Bible calls the *righteous life*. Mountain climbing requires great dedication, great strength, great agility, great perseverance; it requires vision and understanding. So does the righteous life. The reader is invited to direct the same dedication, strength, agility, perseverance toward life as he or she would direct toward mountain climbing.

But *Climbing the Mountain* is not about mountain climbing. It is a lesson book for Bible study. It is a lesson book for going through life. It is not to be memorized or learned; it is to be freely modified by each reader. Moreover, it is not to be regarded as the definitive work on the Bible, for at its core is the premise that there can be no definitive work on the Bible. In fact, the title might be more revealing if expanded to *Lessons for Climbing the Mountain as I Have Heard Them for Myself.* Although excessive in length, the expanded title subtly reveals an important truth: each of us is an individual who has a direct and personal relationship with what we call God, whether we recognize it or not. Each of us is on the way to becoming a *righteous* person; consequently each of us is climbing the Mountain. Each of us is developing this relationship with what we call God. "To what end?" To the end which Jesus personified – to perfecting this relationship until we, too, know that we are the beloved child of the living God.

But this Bible study is not for everyone. It is of such a nature that it will have meaning only to those who are already "hearing." It is for those who "hear" that this is the *time*! This is the year 1996, and regardless of one's views, within four years we will reach the year 2000. Some pessimists anticipate the "last days" as already in process. Optimists, on the other hand, anticipate a flowering in a new millennium. Possibly, both views are correct. Mankind may be progressing to a condition that is truly a "flowering," but before it can take place mankind must first "hear" that the time is NOW.

The Bible offers the promise of a "flowering." This is the "good news" that we can read if we know how. But the reader has to know "how" to climb the Mountain. Obviously, this is a metaphor. The difficulty with metaphors, however, is that we're never quite sure what is being said. That's where the Bible comes in. If read correctly, the Bible allows us to decipher the metaphor. But this may be the problem with our current times. Too many have restricted the Bible to what we call religion, thus limiting its universality. At the same time, too many "others" have rejected the Bible entirely – cutting themselves off from its message.

Those who reject the instructions have varied excuses. Some say the Bible is a remnant of an antiquated morality. Others say that its teachings are related to things of the past and meaningless for now – and definitely meaningless for the age to come. Within this 20th Century, millions have totally rejected the Bible and its teachings, remarking that Truth is found only in science and the intellect.[1] They say that they have no need for a book tied to a religion they no longer accept as true.

---

[1] As the findings of the *Higher Criticism* of the 19th Century brought into question the "correctness" of particular translations, the entire Bible began to be challenged for its authenticity and (therefore) for its authority.

Some even say that for more than fifty years God has been dead! Some hear the shallowest voices. On the other hand, there have always been a few who heard a higher voice. The Bible gives expression to this higher voice. It tells us the story of those who successfully climbed the Mountain. It

Some Individuals Have Heard A "Higher" Voice

is now – as science approaches the top of the mountain (just as Einstein predicted) – that mankind most desperately needs these stories. The difficulty, however, is that time and habit have obscured the lessons of the stories – or maybe we are just misreading the metaphoric message we have been given.

One wonders if we can see the analogy. It's as though we think we can learn mountain climbing by reading a book. Mountain climbing can begin with intellectual instruction, but true mastery comes as we intuit our way up the face of the cliff – making adjustments as they seem to be proper to make – using both our intellect and our intuition. If we mindfully explore what the Old Testament and the New Testament are trying to teach us, we – along with Moses and Jesus – can climb the mountain where the highest science is now finding religion *in repose*.

It is not the Bible that is out of date; it is the tendency of mankind to try to restrict a vital, living book – a *mystical* Bible – by a literal, authoritarian approach to its wisdom. The Bible's critics, those who would deny the Bible and hold only to science, have only placed science in place of literalism. They have not replaced the habitual literal, authoritarian approach. They have not killed "God." They never found "God" to kill "Him." Those who speak so have not progressed beyond those who cast a golden calf to honor Baal while Moses was on the Mountain.

I'm reminded of a story one of my teachers told of his first year as an Episcopal priest. His predecessor had always used the King James version of the Bible, but one Sunday my teacher decided to use The Revised Standard Version for his sermon text. After the service he was accosted by a little Victorian lady, brandishing her umbrella. Shaking the umbrella in his face, she shouted, "Young man, the King James version was good enough for Jesus, it's good enough for you!" [2]

How like us to assume that the tools we have used are the only tools for understanding; how like us to accept as the full picture the little view of our limited vision. With just a few additions to our "climbing tools," with just a few of the traditions of the Hebrew discipline, we will find that the New Testament "finishes off" the promise and tradition of the Old. We will find that we have an incomparable book of "instructions" for living life – for climbing the Mountain. If we view the Bible as something alive, something having a vitality and life which allows it to divulge truth and wisdom to mankind – regardless of time and place – it will speak to us. Unfortunately, just as the Pharisees and Sadducees held to the Law rather than the spirit of the Law, many Christians hold to the Bible as an irrefutable book rather than holding to the irrefutable "spirit" of the Bible. Some Christians even restrict themselves entirely to the New Testament; they consider the Old Testament as a collection of stories and sayings, rather than as supreme spiritual guidance.

This point came home to me several years ago following a Sunday service in which I had focused on the Gospel of John. A member of my congregation congratulated me on the sermon, saying, "... all we ever need

---

[2] Most scholars agree that the earliest Greek translation of the Hebrew texts was the *Septuagint* of 3rd Century B.C.. This was followed by the *Vulgate* of St. Jerome (4th Cent. A.D.), which became the official version for the Roman Catholic Church. The *King James Authorized Version* of 1611, although not the first (nor only) English translation, became the most popular and in many ways (along with Shakespeare) formed the standard English language. *The Revised Standard Version* was finished in 1885.

to hear from is the New Testament." At the time I took her comment as a compliment; but in the ensuing years I have come to strongly disagree with this viewpoint. In fact, the deepest understanding of the New Testament only comes with an understanding and appreciation of the Old Testament's *instructions*. Without the basic understanding and foundation that Jesus and the disciples and apostles shared, the importance of the New Testament is lost.

Modern man has neglected this foundation. Consequently, we (both Jews and Christians) should take a closer look at the hidden jewels of tradition, for they can add untold richness to our understanding. The earliest Christians did not have to be reminded of the mystical tenets of the Old Testament; they were Jews themselves and as such based their understanding on the hidden instructions that were given.[3] Therefore, in their writings (which eventually became the New Testament) there was no need to elaborate on such an understanding. However, since the mystical tenets were not written down, most of mankind has forgotten this understanding and the instructions for living that were part of it. If we will only acknowledge some of the clues found in the Old Testament, we will find that the Bible gives instructions and understandings that can bring greater wisdom for conquering the Mountain.

Part of the understanding comes in recognizing the mystical mind that established the form for both the Old and New Testaments. Part of the understanding comes in admitting that the Bible is written on many different levels – partially literal prose, partially symbolic poetry, partially esoteric symbolism, what we can call *mysticism*. Part of the understanding comes in recognizing that the most important

---

[3] As a point of clarification: *Hebrews* is the term for the descendants of Jacob. Of the ten tribes, only two supposedly remain. *Jews* is the term for those remaining people, relating them to one of Jacob's sons, Judah. *Hebrew* is now considered a language.

material was presented in an *esoteric* manner.[4] Because of these three factors, the instructions are not as clear as they might be. They don't quite fit into our scientific, intellectual, 20th-century mindset.

We can handle the literal prose. It is the symbolic poetry and esoteric symbolism that give us a problem, for any symbolism is of a *mystical* nature. However, we cannot escape the symbolism and the mysticism; all scripture of all religions is *mystical.*[5] All scripture must be approached with the intuitive mind as well as with the intellectual mind. It is this *flexibility* which enables climbing of the Mountain.

Many modern day climbers simply rely on their own insight, discarding the Bible as a source of direction. Nevertheless, we have been given a superb collection of information for living life – in the Bible.[6] It is the Judeo-Christian Bible that is particularly suited for the edification of Western mankind. Of all of the world's wisdom, it is the Judeo-Christian Bible which offers the *authoritarian* (the intellectual mindset) in balance with the *spiritual* (the intuitive mindset). Of all of the world's wisdom, only the Judeo-

---

[4] *Esoteric* is defined as *those ideas and doctrines taught only to a select number and not intended for the general body of disciples; designed for and understood only by the initiated.*

[5] *Mystical* is defined as *spiritually significant or symbolic; allegorical.* The word mystic comes from the Greek *mystës,* meaning *one initiated.* The mystical view has always existed. Aldous Huxley called it *The Perennial Philosophy;* Christians can call it *mystical Christianity.* The Jews have called it *the Qabala.*

Carlo Suarès has written: "Frequently, over the centuries, the Qabala has been lost and rediscovered. ...[It] was alive with Mosheh (Moses); ... we find it with Abram; in still more remote ages, it disappears from the sight of enquirers, but not from the perception of those who have inherited that most ancient of ancient knowledge. All through history its transmission has been kept secret." See Carlo Suarès, *The Cipher of Genesis: The Original Code of the Qabala as Applied to the Scriptures,* Shambhala Pub., 1978, p.19.

[6] Official Councils (gatherings of official representatives) categorized and judged "spiritual" works as either authentic or of questionable value. Finally, they established what is called the **canon** – *the official accepted literature of Christendom.* The **canon** of what we call the Bible was established between the 4th and 6th Centuries, with *Revelation* being the last book to find favor.

Christian Bible represents the scriptures of two religions; only the Bible presents the wisdom of both the intellectual mind and the intuitive mind. This unified approach to the Bible

The Bible Is A "Mystical" Creation

brings answers where there were questions; it brings understanding where there was only repetition of the teachings. Moreover, if we can accept this new mindset (with the intellect and the intuition balanced), we will find instructions for our lives.

Look back at the apple. Do you see the perfection and the symbols of God's creation? It is this balance to which the Scriptures direct us. **Mankind must be balanced.** Mankind must be balanced to be what Jesus called *the righteous man.* Mankind must be balanced to **be** as he/she is intended to be. Mankind must be balanced to conquer the Mountain.

"Hear" about the Pomegranate! This tree and its fruit symbolize the potential of our lives: it has a hard, red rind, filled with innumerable seeds enveloped in bright red pulp which is "refreshing to the taste." It is a tree between 12 and 15 feet high which produces fruit about the size of an orange. Pomegranates of blue, purple and scarlet (alternating with bells of gold) adorned the high priest's robe. Pomegranates – two rows of 100 pomegranates each – embellished the two pillars at the porch of Solomon's temple.

8

Adam and Eve and the Tree of the Knowledge of Good and Evil, Michelangelo's Sistine Chapel.

Chapter One

Patriarchal Patterns

*And it shall come to pass in the last days, that **the mountain of the Lord's house shall be established in the top of the mountains,** and shall be exalted above the hills; and all nations shall flow unto it. And many people shall go and say, Come ye, and let us go up to the mountain of the LORD, to the house of the God of Jacob; and **he will teach us of his ways, and we will walk in his paths: for out of Zion shall go forth the law, and the word of the LORD from Jerusalem.** And he shall judge among the nations, and shall rebuke many people: and they shall beat their swords into plowshares, and their spears into pruning hooks: **nation shall not lift up sword against nation, neither shall they learn war any more.** O house of Jacob, come ye, and **let us walk in the light of the LORD.** Isaiah 2:2-5.*

You may ask if this *Climbing the Mountain* is about "the last days." The answer is "No," at least not now. It is about the Mountain, and it is the Mountain to which Isaiah refers. Although we have always placed more importance on the latter part of the prophecy, i.e., *and they shall beat their swords into plowshares, and their spears into pruning hooks...,* the greater importance lies in the beginning of the statement. The basis of the prophecy is: *the mountain of the Lord's house shall be established in the top of the mountains, and shall be exalted above the hills; and all nations shall flow unto it.*

Careful reading establishes that the longed-for peace cannot and will not take place until the former has been accomplished – until the *"mountain...shall be established."* Careful reading reveals that the understanding represented by the Mountain must be internalized. If this is so, then eventually each one of us will have to climb the Mountain. Isn't that the implication of the line? The question then is what is meant by the Mountain? To me the Mountain symbolizes the process by which mankind realizes who and what he/she is. It is the process whereby each individual progresses from "Adam's" expression to the "Christ's."

Through its characters, stories, symbolism and organization, the Bible gives "instruction" for following the process; it is the instruction for climbing the Mountain. The instruction begins immediately with the scheme established in the book of Genesis.

Holy scriptures, regardless of to whom they belong, are intended for a purpose. What is that purpose? Listen to Paul's insight: *All scripture is given by inspiration of God, and is profitable for doctrine, for reproof, for correction, for instruction in righteousness: That the man of God may be perfect, thoroughly furnished unto all good works.* 2 Tim 3:16-17.

But what does that mean to us? How does it relate to Isaiah's prognosis? And what does it have to do with climbing the Mountain? Notice that Paul states the purpose of all which we call religion – doctrine, reproof, correction, instruction in righteousness – to be to enable the man of God *to be perfect* (complete) *and thoroughly furnished* (equipped) *unto all good works* (whatever comes his/her way). But few see mankind as "perfect" or even potentially "perfect." Why such a discrepancy?

The late 20th Century has resurrected a word that may give us some insight about this "to be perfect..." The word is *paradigm* (from the Greek *paradigm*), meaning "a scheme for understanding and explaining certain aspects of reality."[1] Apparently a major paradigm (mindset) – that of mankind's perceiving itself as imperfect – has been in place (possibly) from the beginning of mankind's history.

Isn't it this "imperfection" that we accept as the message of Genesis? Isn't it this that we read into the story of Adam's fall? In fact, isn't it this which we call "the fall"? The trouble is that operating under this mindset of "imperfection," mankind has considered itself as separated from the whole. It has seen itself as something that is not

---

[1] Marilyn Ferguson, *The Aquarian Conspiracy: Personal and Social Transformation in the 1980's;* J.P.Tarcher, Inc., 1980, p. 26.

quite right. Moreover, under this mindset, mankind has continually sought atonement from what it perceives as an angry "God" by making (outer) sacrifices.[2] Isn't this how many of us see our lives and what we call God? Many of us feel we are imperfect; we expect to suffer in life. Many of us feel that we must make a sacrifice to protect ourselves from the punishment that we anticipate.

I must confess, here; the greatest mistake I made in rearing my children was that when they were very young and crying for not getting their way, I would say, "Well, life's tough." For many years, since I made this statement into unsuspecting ears, I have tried to correct my mistaken teaching; but, likely, it will be my children's personal Mountain climbing that will make the correction, just as it has been mine. I wonder if I heard my mother say the same thing when I was too young to dismiss it; I wonder, too if my mother heard the same thing in her babyhood.

Most of us have accepted this mistaken mindset (paradigm), and so to us "life's tough." And the intellect takes Genesis literally and *judges* that mankind will forever have to sacrifice to "God" for having "disobeyed."[3] Even enlightened Christianity presents a holy, perfect Jesus as a sacrifice, intended to "buy" our salvation. But we have misread Genesis! We have ignored the tradition that sets the mindset straight.

Primitive mankind, on the other hand, sometimes retains the mindset of "tradition." A recent presentation, Dr. Marlo Morgan's *Mutant Message, Down Under,* ascribes to Australian Aborigines a different mindset from that of modern mankind. Morgan portrays the Aborigines as acknowledging a "oneness of all" and seeing themselves as

---

[2] Webster's *Dictionary* defines atonement with: reconciliation, reparation, and satisfaction and Christian Science's **at-one-ment.**

[3] The word **judges** is highlighted to point out that **judgment** is of a different nature from **righteous judgment.**

a part of "this oneness." They see themselves only as part of the whole. Never having been "separated," they have no need of at-one-ment.[4]

This is the mindset of one who has climbed the Mountain – continually to be in atonement. As with the Australian Aborigines' positive view of themselves, the Old Testament's Mountain offers a positive view of mankind, life, "God" and "God's requirements." We are repeatedly told in Genesis 1 – to the point that we become tired of hearing it – "... **And God saw that it was good.**"

The entire Old Testament presents a scheme that all but the most enlightened have ignored. In place of a mind-set which establishes an "imperfect mankind" requiring sacrifices to placate God, the Old Testament provides a paradigm of a creature which has been created perfect – but which must consciously become aware that he/she is perfect. With this paradigm in place, any sacrifice is of "self" and intended to reveal this awareness. Under this mindset, mankind knows itself to be *perfect* and only has to recognize and exercise this perfection.

The Apostle Paul calls this awareness *righteousness,* and he tells us that whatever comes to an individual is his/her *instruction in righteousness.* This instruction is in order that the individual (man/woman of God) may be a perfect expression, completely able to be as is

Instruction In Righteousness intended for this created creature to be – a glorification of God. But our 20th-century ears may not quite understand *instruction in righteousness.* Webster defines *righteousness* as "upright; virtuous; acting in a just, upright manner." However, this definition doesn't carry the fullness presented

---

[4] See *Mutant Message, Down Under,* by Marlo Morgan; (Harper Collins). Although Morgan's assessment of the Australian Aborigines with whom she was associated is that they remain in this condition of "atonement," it may be incorrect to assume that all primitive cultures are or were at this level of expression.

by the Scriptures. If we open-mindedly look at the word *righteousness*, it means viewing "God" correctly – using a righteous paradigm. With a righteous paradigm in place, mankind's whole outlook is changed. In the first two chapters of Genesis, the Old Testament presents a "righteous paradigm" – a far different mindset than mankind has accepted for the last several thousand years.

For the "mystic" who knows the "symbolism," the entire Bible shows those steps which mankind will take on its journey to climb the Mountain to its own perfection. Jesus recognized mankind's ultimate perfection. He said, *"Be ye therefore perfect, even as your Father which is in heaven is perfect."* Mat 5:48 But how many of us think it is possible to be perfect? Yet, it is just this – how to reach perfection – that the Bible is teaching us. But for us to understand the teaching, we must have a "mystical" approach to both Testaments. Only then will we be led to a new understanding.

The history of the mystical approach reveals why we must be retaught. Although the Roman Catholic priesthood may have been taught "mystical Christianity" and the mystical meaning of the Bible, the knowledge was not extended to the laity; consequently, the mystical message did not become part of the social fabric. It is no wonder that during the Reformation, even though Protestantism opened the Bible to a "priesthood of believers," the mystical message was neglected. Even access to the Scriptures after they were put into common languages did not reveal *mysticism,* because it is hidden.[5] Mystical Christianity has always been the pursuit of only a few nonconformists.

On one hand, it is the necessity for translation in

---

[5] Aramaic was the language of Jesus; but according to one scholar writing in the 1930's, the writings were translated into Greek almost immediately after the crucifixion. (C.C. Torrey, *The Four Gospels, A New Translation,* 1933.) According to this theory, the source writings dated within 20 years of the death of Jesus. Since much of this is speculation and pertinent only to the intellectual mind, the reader is invited to check any questionable statement for its Aramaic version. See: *Holy Bible: From Ancient Eastern Manuscripts,* George M. Lamsa; (A.J.Holman Company).

14

To trace *mysticism* in Western thought, we have to go to sources which scholars often see as suspect: For instance, while Masonic tradition traces its history back to the building of Solomon's temple, the *Encyclopedia Americana* says that "The majority of modern opinion holds that Freemasonry of the present day ... had its origin in the British Isles, probably in medieval times."

So, too, a second source of Western mysticism, the Jewish Cabalistic teaching, although scholastically placed at an earlier day than Freemasonry, still is seldom credited with its most ancient beginnings. The *Encyclopedia Americana* at least acknowledges that part of Genesis and part of Ezekiel "were held in early Talmudic records to hide **esoteric knowledge within the reach of the chosen few who of mature age and proper degree of wisdom might venture to unravel their occult suggestions.**"

which the difficulty lies, for both Hebrew (the language of the Old Testament) and Greek (the translated language of the New Testament) are unknown to most Bible readers. Even with access to the Hebrew, Greek and Aramaic, the esoteric teachings may not be readily perceived or understood by most people. As a result, they have relegated these esoteric teachings to the occult. We must define "occult." Webster defines it as *hidden* or *concealed;* it is with this hidden tradition that we are concerned.

Through the ages, many spiritual systems have used numbers and letters to convey sacred teachings. According to Manly Hall, "Pythagoras taught an esoteric science of numbers which he learned from the Egyptian priests, who represented their gods by mathematical formulas and symmetrical geometric solids." Whether or not related to the ancient system, the Hebraic system where **letters allude to numbers** establishes symbolic meaning to the names of persons and place, and it leads us to a mystical understanding of the Scriptures.[6]

This system makes the Old Testament a work of symbols and hidden meanings as well as a work of "literal history" of the Hebrews, a particular "nation" of Semites. Whether the Egyptian "symbolism" is the source of Hebrew symbolism and was "imported" by Moses, or whether the

---

[6] The finest work I have found on mysticism and the numeric/alphabetic symbolism is *The Cipher of Genesis: The Original Code of the Qabala as Applied to the Scriptures,* by Carlo Suarès.

Hebrew system predates Moses, I can't say.[7] Certainly the argument that Moses imported the code is logical, but the Hebrews seem to have added an element not found in Pythagorean symbolism.The Hebraic system seems to dictate that the **observer** must remain **flexible**. The Hebraic system subtly insists that the observer must remain centered and open in his/her interpretation to whatever comes.[8]

This point of flexibility may be emphasized by the three spellings for Qabala. The usual Anglicized spelling is **C**abala; apparently the modern Jewish spelling is **K**abbalah. Suarès uses **Q**abala to denote the highest mystical interpretation.[9] Notice: the initial capital letters are in a sequence (**C, K, Q**), which emphasizes the heightening of understanding. As with the Bible, nothing in the word points this out to us; rather it is something which our intuition must observe. Our observation must utilize the *intellect*; but it is the *intuition* which brings understanding.

Suarès writes that when the Septuagint came out "it was a time of great sorrow and mourning for the rabbis who knew that **the text cannot be translated."** We might be saying that that which is revealed to intuition cannot be translated; but then how are we to understand?[10]   A loose

---

[7] Manly Palmer Hall, *Journey in Truth,* Philosophical Research Society, Los Angeles, 2nd Ed. Hall sees Moses as establishing the "occult" system of numbers and letters in the Old Testament. Tradition credits Moses with authorship of the first five books of the Old Testament.

[8] I would not claim to be schooled in the Qabala; rather, my *intuition* tells me that this conclusion is what the Qabala is trying to convey. I came to this conclusion while teaching a class using *Honey from the Rock: Ten Gates to Jewish Mysticism,* by Lawrence Kushner. Available from Jewish Lights, Woodstock, VT. Original copyright, 1977.

[9] However, when speaking of the *cabalistic tradition,* Suarès uses the "C." Intuition tells me that this usage denotes the level of understanding Suarès ascribes to that which is expressed, particularly that which is expressed to the exoteric world.

[10] Suarès, *The Cipher of Genesis;* p. 45. The "Septuagint" is the translation of the various books comprising the Hebraic "library" into Greek, circa. 3rd Century B.C., thus creating the "Old Testament."

16

symbology helps us along; consequently, the Scriptures include a great many numbers. The following numerical symbology works nicely, although care must be taken not to make its form dogmatic and hardened.[11]

1 is indivisible; it is the *monad;* it is *the **totality**.*
2 is **one** plus its **opposite**; it represents **duality.**
3 is **equilibrium**; one thing, plus its opposite, plus synthesis.
4 is equilibrium plus the monad, i.e. the **perfection of nature.**
5 represents the worldly view, i.e., the **view of senses**.
6 represents ½ of the full portion; two times equilibrium.
7 represents physical completion (perfection); the sacred full one.
8 represents *plumpness;* a surplus above the perfect seven.
9 represents *a turn to the next;* a turn to ten.
10 represents **Earthly** *accumulation.*
11 is just **short of spiritual perfection**; the beginning of change.
12 is spiritual **perfection**; but it is a perfection that can "grow."
13 added to perfection.
14 two levels of earthly completion.
16 two levels of *surplus;* four levels of *equilibrium.*
17 **"receiving"** dependent on *seeing* and *saying.*
30 accumulated equilibrium.
31 equilibrium (on three planes) plus one; undivisible.
40 natural order (end) to Earthly accumulation.
Each 0 indicates ... a glorified level (therefore, 10 is one level above 1).
1000 a supreme power: all pervading, timeless, unthinkable.
5000 *unthinkable power,* the *transformed* senses.

In the esoteric scheme, numbers and letters indicate both quantity and quality; the numbers bring a greater fullness of understanding.[12] The meaningful name of a character is added to by his/her numerical designation. Moreover, it is done so cleverly that we read the numbers as historical information. Following the same scheme, the

[11] Just as the "gods" of pagan peoples related to "celestial orbs," apparently, part of the symbology of numbers also comes from simple observation of the physical. As we can all see, there is **one** "body" upon which we are all dependent – the sun. Similarly, there is **one smaller** body (the moon) and **five** more bodies (visible planets) to be seen in the night sky. Is it any wonder that **seven** represents the ultimate of the physical? Moreover, the body has **five** openings that **sense.**

[12] For other presentations of the Biblical *code,* see Northrop Frye's *The Great Code: The Bible and Literature;* Harcourt, Brace, Janov Pub. or Edward Hoffman's *The Way of Splendor: Jewish Mysticism and Modern Psychology,* Jason Aronson Inc., Northvale, NJ.

compilers of the New Testament utilized the symbolism of numbers in the stories and parables, thus giving an "importance rating."[13]

To test the system, let's return to *Be ye therefore perfect, even as your Father which is in heaven is perfect.* Mt. 5:48. The line is number 48, which is 4x12. Its placement as number 48 establishes great importance.[14] Moreover, it is the last line in a chapter that carries the Sermon on the Mount, and it is immediately preceded by 31 statements which follow Jesus' statement: *Think not that I have come to abolish the law and the prophets; I have come not to abolish them but to fulfill them.* Few lines are such attention getters as is line #48. It becomes the #32nd statement, a statement following a prime number (a number which cannot be divided) and the product of 8 x 4. In addition, the Greek meaning of the word *perfect* is completeness. But, notice what we have done...

By focusing on the symbolism of numbers and of names and places, we've deserted the intuition and gone back to the intellect. We've centered our attention on assessing numbers and names, and we've become inflexible. We've returned to the worldly

> The science of numbers in the Bible is a study in itself. Carlo Suarès begins his work with the explanation that the "twenty-two graphs which are used as letters in the Hebrew alphabet at twenty-two (22) proper names **originally used to designate different states or structures of the ONE Cosmic Energy, which is essence and semblance, of all that is.**" Suarès, p. 12.

---

[13] Symbology largely depends on the English translation of the Hebrew (or Greek or Aramaic) and differs according to who is interpreting the symbols, but there seems to be a fair amount of agreement. Strong's *Concordance* represents the accepted explanation current at the turn of the last century, as does Young's. Fillmore's *Metaphysical Bible Dictionary* adds another element, as does Gaskel's *Dictionary of All Scriptures and Myths*.

[14] The Preface to the current revision of *The Torah* distinguishes between chapter and verse divisions in the Bible, saying: Chapter divisions "are neither ancient nor Jewish, but medieval Christian." On the other hand, the Preface says that **verse divisions are "considerably older and of Jewish origin."** (1962) 2nd Ed., Jewish Publication Society of America.

mindset, thus ignoring the most important tradition – that which takes precedence over the symbolism of numbers and letters – that of "flexibility."

We might think of this flexibility with a term which comes to us from surfers – **hang loose**. You may question the use of slang in a Bible study, but think of what the term means. As a surfer climbs "into" a wave, he/she is called upon to react in compliance with that wave. Nothing in the surfer's actions can be absolute. The "intellect" is of some help, but it must comply with the "intuition." While experiencing the various waves that come, the surfer must be entirely flexible and listen to the "intuition."

Another analogy for this "flexibility" would be "riding a see-saw." Here, one climbs to the center of the see-saw then balances by varying the weight on either leg – as it seems right to do. This is *balance*. The mystical tradition of the Bible presents the challenge to balance the intellect with the intuition. It is this mystical tradition which modern man's understanding lacks.

Maintaining this tradition of symbolism and mysticism lends an entirely different paradigm to the understanding of the Bible. It requires that the observer must remain balanced and open to whatever comes. Therefore, **the observer must consider the "whole" presentation.**[15]

The Bible is not a scientific thesis, placing logical point upon logical point for a proven premise; it is a work of poetry, adding *precept upon precept.*Is. 28:10.The proven premise comes only at the end, after all the *precepts* and *lines* have been put together and *intuition* has perceived what was to be perceived – and this perception may "see" differently with each individual. As with the surfer riding the wave, *intuition* utilizes the information which *intellect* provides to it; at the same time, "intellect" uses the perception which "intuition" gives it.

---

[15] Suarès uses the term *Indetermination* to describe the process. See *Cipher of Genesis,* p.143.

For the most part, this soon-to-be-closed millennium has concentrated on the intellectual mindset. It is the intellect which has occupied Western culture, and the Western culture has spread its concentration to the rest of the world. It has been 1000 years of material development. As such, this millennium has seen a mindset that mans armies, develops weapons, builds buildings, feeds unnumbered millions, harnesses many forms of nature, gains access to space beyond Earth and even creates machines that rival its own capabilities. But the period has entertained an authoritative mindset; it has supported a mindset that expects to control. Only now is it beginning to respect the intuitive mindset that complements the intellectual side.

Take Bible as a Whole

My daughter recently took a class that is just now being taught in college; it is called the Philosophy of Biology. The professor described the class as a new paradigm for the study of biology. In this new paradigm, mankind no longer sees itself as conquering and controlling nature; mankind sees itself as anticipating and cooperating with nature – to the benefit of both mankind and nature.

The Old Testament says it nicely: *The Lord God took the man and put him in the garden of Eden **to till it and keep it**.* Yet, since it has been the authoritarian mindset which has interpreted this line, we have read it as saying that man is to bend nature to his/her will. Admittedly, this could be the meaning of Genesis 1:28, but Genesis 2:15 seems to have a different attitude.[16] Biblical scholars have long explained the differences between the first two chapters of Genesis by attributing each chapter to different times and different translations, basing their reasoning on Genesis 1's use of *God*

---

[16] Compare the two verses. Gen. 1:28: "Be fruitful and multiply, and fill the earth and subdue it; and have dominion over the fish of the sea and over the birds of the air and over every living thing that moves upon the earth." and Gen. 2:15: "And the LORD God took the man, and put him into the garden of Eden to dress it and to keep it."

and Genesis 2's use of *LORD*. [17] However, since our new
paradigm insists that we use the Bible as a whole for our
"instructions in righteousness," the **whole** gives us a different
mindset. *To have dominion* means to have the power to rule;
it does not mean "to dictate to." Moreover, when we use
both verses, we get a different view of mankind's obligation.
With the entire set of lines working together (the intellect
remaining flexible, the intuition in action), mankind is given
the power to rule the earth and all on it – *in order* to **till the
Garden and keep it.**   It is this taking the entire
Bible as a whole that shows the way for climbing the
Mountain. The way is given to us from the beginning – in
Genesis.[18] It focuses the instructions, and its form continues
through *Revelation*. If we ignore it, we can't follow the
instructions for the climb.

| In The "Beginning" |

We can at least get a start on our
understanding with attention to the *motif* of
Genesis. The new Jewish translation suggests
the paradigm by how it chooses to begin. The Jewish text
begins: **When God began to create the heavens and the earth** – *the earth
being unformed and void, with darkness over the surface of the deep and a
wind from God sweeping over the water – God said, "Let there be light"; and
there was light. God saw that the light was good, and God separated the light
from the darkness. God called the light Day, and the darkness He called Night.
And there was evening and there was morning, a first day.*[19]

A footnote in the new translation acknowledges that
another possible translation is the traditional *In the*

---

[17] This book neither claims nor desires to be a definitive work. This is the
intuition's view of the Bible, not the intellect's. However, the supposed
"discrepancy" can be explained in a different way than standard "criticism" explains
it. I support the view that the Bible presents a scheme which covers both Jehovah
and Elohim, each being different aspects of what we conveniently call *GOD*. See
pages 43-45.

[18] Carlo Suarès postulates that Genesis can be read on four different levels: 1.
anecdotally; 2. symbolically; 3. ontologically (*being* or that which *is*); and 4.
transcendently (that which cannot be communicated). See *The Cipher of Genesis:
The Original Code of the Qabala as Applied to The Scriptures*, p. 164.

[19] Genesis 1:1-5; *Torah,* op. cit., p. 3.

beginning; but notice the difference the new translation makes. With the new translation there is a sense of *ongoing creation.* Now we can "see" that all of the information that follows, i.e., the entire Bible, is related to an **ongoing process – not** a **single** *creation.* As an ongoing process, there is reason for the Bible's stories and characters (each character facing his/her own challenges), for they form a pattern which directs mankind as he/she progresses. Even though the ongoing process is never clearly stated for the intellectual mind, it is there for the intuition to perceive. The progression is suggested to us by the Qabala.[20] It is this progression that is the "ongoing creation." Moreover, somewhere there is a whispered *"So listen!"*

> Chapter One of Genesis sets up the paradigm. Chapter Two elaborates on it – still stating that everything is "good." The new Jewish translation affirms this "goodness" as it begins Chapter Three with verse twenty-five (25). *The two of them were naked, the man and his wife, yet they felt no shame.*

The direction for this "different" understanding comes with the "word" found in Hebrew letters at the beginning of Genesis. I have seen the translated "word" in very old Christian Bibles, but it seems to have been eliminated from newer versions. It is the first sequence of letters in Genesis – *Bereshyt.* בראשית The King James version translates it as *In the beginning;* but the whole Bible only works as a complete unit if it is viewed as a code that establishes how we are to approach the whole. Each of the letters בראשית has greater meaning than just being part of a word. (See Suarès, pp. 72-77.)

If we acknowledge what *Bereshyt* is proclaiming – **this ongoing creation** – then all life is in a process (only part of which is a physical existence). However, part of life **is**

---

[20] Suarès writes: "Qabala is a training of the mind that makes it so subtle and pliable as to allow it to pass through the mysterious doorway of human genesis and enter into the sphere where *life-death* and *existence* carry on their inter-play. Jointly, on both sides, the most precious gift of life is at stake: the principle of Indetermination, which allows all that can *be* to *become.*" Suarès, p. 77.

physical existence, so the next twenty-five verses of Genesis gives us a running inventory of the physical creation. (Notice: 25 is 5x5.) Finally, we get to a phrase that has been repeated with each set of creation: *And God saw that this was good* – only this time it reads: ***And God saw all that He had made, and found it very good.*** Gen. 1:31 Notice! Nowhere does this "view" suggest that mankind is evil or that he has to atone for an original misdeed; it makes the opposite point. Genesis says: *And God created man in His image, **in the image of God He created him**: male and female He created them.* Gen. 1:27.

Moreover, this statement about the "goodness" of all that God created is in verse #31, a prime number, a number which cannot be divided. To my intuition, such a designation makes a clear statement: **This is wholly true! It cannot be broken apart!** Such a "focus" establishes a paradigm which views mankind as **good and made in the image of God.** And this paradigm acts as the "control" design for everything else that will be placed in the instructions for climbing the Mountain. We could state the controlling design with one compound sentence: **Mankind is made in the image of God, and all that God has made is *good.***

With this paradigm in place, all else must comply. The next four chapters of Genesis simply set the scheme for all that comes under the paradigm. Through the end of chapter two, everything is fine and the creation manifests perfection; **but then we hit Chapter Three.** – Something interferes with our view of the paradigm. We could call it a snake or the devil or whatever. –

Traditional translations start Chapter Three with a different motif, and the *serpent* is introduced.[21] However, the new Jewish translation does something even more interesting. The last "obvious" line of Chapter Two is #24: *Hence a man leaves his father and mother and clings to his wife so that they become one flesh...* (the RSV and King James versions continue with verse #25 saying: *And the man and his wife were both naked, and were not*

---

[21] *Motif* is defined as "an influence or stimulus prompting to action."

ashamed. Gen. 2:25.) But significantly, the new Jewish translation places this verse #25 at the beginning of the next chapter.

In *The Torah's* new translation, Chapter Three – the chapter where all the trouble manifests – begins: *And the man and his wife were both naked, and were not ashamed.* Mankind is again told that God – this **Oneness** which the Jewish tradition says can be neither described nor named – has set up a perfect system; and as long as mankind "remembers" such a system, everything works nicely. However, part of the original system is that it is an ongoing process; it has to grow. Consequently, the "appearance" of all will change.

From this point on, whatever we "see" may be "true" or it may be an "appearance." From this point on, mankind's challenge is to remember that the original-perfect system is still the design. Mankind's challenge is to remember that "appearances" only reflect the participant's ability to "see" this original-perfect system – or conversely – the participant's "inability" to "see." Less than "perfect" appearances reflect the tendency of the individual to see himself/herself as apart from the original system, thereby "separate and alone."

It is chapter "three" that establishes the paradigm that brings the difficulty with "appearances." Even though in the new translation it starts out using the "true paradigm," verse seven totally reverses the original-

True Perception Changes to Misperception

perfect statement. With the worldly *seven*, Genesis states the earthly view: *... Then the eyes of both of them were opened and they perceived that they were naked...* We might add ... and they saw themselves as alone **and separated from Oneness.**[22]

---

[22] We could say that "seven" represents all of our worldly cares. An intensive computation of the numerical occurrences in the Bible was the life work of a Dr. Ivan Panin (1855-1942). Panin particularly pointed out the almost incalculable variations on schemes using the number "seven" or its forms. Contact Bible Numerics, P.O. Box 206, Waubaushene, Ontario, L0 K 2 C0.

Of course, according to this mistaken paradigm we know why there's a difference. In these few verses mankind has *eaten the fruit of the tree of the knowledge of good and evil* – that tree from which he was specifically told NOT to eat. But he/she *does* eat, and he/she can't remember what it was that he/she was supposed to "see." It will take many millennia and (in the *Revised Standard Version)*1168 pages to correct man's misperception.

But then, "God" – by definition – can't make a mistake. So, look back at Genesis 2:9: *And from the ground the* LORD *God caused to grow every tree that was pleasing to the sight and good for food, with the **tree of life** in the middle of the garden, and the **tree of the knowledge of good and evil**.* Notice, both trees exist in the Garden

Two Trees Exist in the Garden of Eden

of Eden, so the original plan requires dealing with the tree of the knowledge of good and evil. That means that the original "plan" includes the "misperception." Only when we get to Revelation 22 is the misperception corrected. In John's vision or *(Revelation)* there is only one tree. John says: *Then he showed me the river of the water of life, bright as a crystal, flowing from the throne of God and of the Lamb. In the midst of the street of the city, and **on either side of the river, was the tree of life** with its twelve kinds of fruit, yielding its fruit each month; and the leaves of the tree were for the healing of the nations.* Rev. 22:1,2.

John's vision is *true* perception; and it is the progression from misperception to true perception that is the Mountain. As soon as the tree of the "knowledge of good and evil" is gone, we have triumphed! As soon as we reach Revelation 22, the instructions for climbing the Mountain are finished. By Revelation 22 we are back at the awareness that the perfect paradigm is in effect – and always has been. It is that *the mountain of the house of the Lord shall be established as the highest of the mountains.* Is. 2:2.

Remember the old psychology test which asked the individual to describe the partially filled glass of water? The response (either half-full or half-empty) supposedly disclosed one's habitual view of life. To the intuition, this is what the Bible is disclosing to us. The original design was given to us as full-full; but almost immediately (with Chapter Three of Genesis) the appearance is changed and we're offered the choice between half-full and half-empty.

According to appearances, in the length of two short chapters, our species has gone from being judged "good" to being judged "dust." It's as though we've been placed in a game situation, to see if we can come out with the right answer (which is *full-full*). The "game" is within ourselves, and its purpose is to help us "remember" the original scheme.

Mankind Must Understand As Does the Christ After Chapter Three, Genesis becomes an instruction book for retrieving this awareness of the original scheme. If we follow the patterns found in the stories and the instructions given through them, we can begin to come out with the **full-full** answer. But to ease the process, we must see the "whole."

Genesis is probably the most important book in the Bible, for it reveals the pattern that exposes the "whole." It reveals the on-going process of creation. The first two chapters set up the original paradigm. The next nine chapters are almost like a small outline; they give the overall scheme of the process. Then, beginning with Chapter Twelve, Genesis gives us a series of scriptural "stories" to help us assess each step in our progressive climb. In fact, all of the Scriptures are intended to aid us in our climb.

My personal climb has had the added help of music in learning Scripture. One work in particular has inspired me: Georg(e) Friedrich Handel's *Messiah*. Why? Because Handel hammers down the scriptural lessons as does no one else. He

finishes with a grand *Alleluia* that says *Praise, ye, the Lord.*[23]
Alleluia is fine, but the message that has always caught my
attention comes earlier in *The Messiah*. It is a quotation from
I Corinthians: *Since by man came death....* Paul puts the whole
matter of mankind's progress quite succinctly: *For since by man
came death, by man came also the resurrection of the dead.* ***For as in Adam
all die, even so in Christ shall all be made alive.*** 1 Cor 15:21-22

You can almost hear the repetition which Handel uses
to drive the idea home! Here, in one line, is the whole scheme
for the Judeo-Christian Bible. Mankind, which begins its
understanding at the level of Adam, must eventually arrive
at understanding the "whole" as Christ understood it. Only
then is there no death; only then are we "made alive."

It's not that mankind is cursed because Adam was
"thrown out of the Garden of Eden," but that Adam was "thrown
out" in order that mankind could understand as does the Christ.
This is a completely different way of looking at the "fall."
This is in compliance with the original scheme. This goes along
with *"And God saw* **all** *that he had made, and found it* ***very good.***" The Bible
takes us from the understanding of Adam – who sees
himself/herself as dust – to that of the Christ – who recognizes
himself/herself as *the child of God*. This process begins with
a creature called Adam/Eve; it progresses through the Patriarchs;
it takes form with Moses; it proceeds through David; and it
culminates with the "Son of David," the Christed Jesus.[24]

In addition to setting the original-perfect scheme, the
story of Adam introduces us to three elements that will occur
repeatedly throughout the entire Bible. First is the element of
duality. Almost from the beginning – from the creation of
"man/woman" – there is *negative* and *positive.* And as soon
as the *fruit of the tree of the knowledge of good and evil* is eaten,

---

[23] *Allelulia* is Greek for *Hallelujah* (Praise ye Jehovah*)*.

[24] Throughout the Bible, symbolic comments are made by the use of 1. Names (both
of the masculine and the feminine), 2. Surroundings, 3. Children (that which is
produced), 4. Vocation or Possessions, and 5. Age.

mankind differentiates between them — between good and evil and between feminine and masculine.

The second element is very close to this; it is **balancing**. You may notice that I have been using he/she in place of the generic masculine pronoun "he." There is no need to add *she* to the generic indefinite pronoun; I use *he/she* for a different reason. Remember, we were told that mankind...*male and female created he them.* Gen. 1:27. Now, the intellect will probably say that this means that there are two sexes; but the intuition sees it differently. The intuition sees this as stating that mankind has **positive** (masculine) and **negative** (feminine) characteristics.

Although Eastern philosophy has always explained life with its *yang* and *yin,* western psychology has used the concept only to explain some of the "glitches" that appear in unbalanced mankind. But science has now determined that in both men and women there are two sides to the brain – one side having masculine attributes, one side having feminine attributes. Even the most functioning individual has to *balance* the two sides of himself/herself into working together.

It is this working together that is the imperative. What a lovely "hang-loose" concept. Look at all the dimensions we have uncovered. We can look at the physiological division, knowing that our physical body, mind, and soul must be ONE; we can look at the psychological division, knowing that conscious mind, subconscious mind and superconscious mind must be ONE; we can interpolate that the entire picture must also be ONE. The dictionary defines *interpolate* as "to alter or corrupt by inserting new or foreign matter." Isn't this the intellect's view?[25] The intellect fears whatever interrupts its habitual pattern. Isn't this Adam's accepting that he is "dust"? But notice what the feminine sees! Eve, the "mother of all living," rejoices: *I have gotten a man with the help of the LORD.* Gen. 4:1

---

[25] *Interpolation* is one of the few things I have retained from high school geometry; but I had to go to the unabridged dictionary (*Webster's New Universal Unabridged Dictionary*) to find the proper definition. *Interpolation* is defined:"in mathematics and physics, the operation of finding terms between any two consecutive terms of a series, which shall conform to the law of the series."

The new Jewish translation uses this verse to begin the fourth chapter of Genesis – as opposed to its finishing Chapter Three. Traditionally, the number *four* represents perfect balance, i.e., the perfection of nature.(See p.16.) It is the feminine which "intuits" the Truth. It is the feminine side of us that brings our awareness of the original paradigm. It is the feminine which is the "ready vessel."[26]

The Feminine Aspect

A note of caution must be made here. Respect and adulation of the feminine is not achieved by denigration of the masculine! Denigration of either the masculine or the feminine does just as much harm to the other side. It is not necessary to demean the masculine in order to raise the feminine to its rightful place.

Remember, too, we are considering feminine not only in the physical sense, but also in the sense of an individual's (either man's or woman's) feminine side. To me, "masculine" represents the conscious mind. On the other hand, "feminine" represents the subconscious mind; it represents that which "perceives" what is behind all that the conscious mind "sees." As the Bible presents it, the rightful place of the feminine (initially) is to lead the way – to help the masculine see the truth. The feminine side of us is for perception. However, once the feminine has brought access to the truth, it then is to submit to the masculine activity. This can explain the Bible's almost exclusive use of male prototypes.[27] The male characters refer to the masculine portion of us – the conscious mind – that runs our lives. It is the conscious mind which learns. However, know that **only as the conscious mind "listens" to its "mate," can it "hear" the *still, small voice* of God.**

---

[26] At the risk of making concrete that which is not concrete – the feminine side is thought to "house" the intuition, the emotions, the feelings, the arts and crafts, the creativity, etc. The ancients saw the "soul" as feminine. The masculine side "houses" the intellect, the conscious mind.

[27] Admittedly, the explanation could lie in a male-dominated Western culture, but I see the Eastern culture as no-less male dominated (almost the opposite); yet the Eastern culture recognizes the *yin* and *yang* elements of existence.

Anthropologists tell us that primitive cultures held women in reverence, because only women could bring forth life. So, too, in the Bible it is the feminine that brings forth life; it is the feminine that is revered. In fact, it is held in such reverence that it begins the whole presentation. The letter "B" (Bayt-ב) is given the position of greatest importance in the whole Bible, in that it **begins all** of the Hebrew Scriptures.[28]

בראשית –

"**B**"is the second letter in the Hebrew alphabet, as well as in the English and Greek alphabets; correspondingly, in esoteric traditions, #2 represents the feminine.The Hebrew presentation may be unique, however, in that despite its being #2, everything "starts" with the feminine. It may be "this" that the Bible tries to hammer home to us. "**A**"(#1) can't grow or even show itself until "B"(#2) is the "ready vessel."[29] God does not act until man is ready to receive; and this depends on man's feminine side. Throughout the Bible, the feminine side will initiate each change. Therefore, Eve begins the progress.

Paradox Abounds

The third element which must be mentioned is **paradox**. The Bible is packed with paradox; we are continually presented with paradoxical features in the stories. We are endlessly invited to recognize that our judgment must remain in a "hang-loose" mode. We are repeatedly invited to recognize that what our worldly judgment anticipates may not be in keeping with "God's intent." We are continually invited to "ride the see-saw." It begins with Eve; the feminine side begins advancement. It chooses to accept the invitation to "eat" from the tree of "the knowledge of good and evil."

---

[28] The ב (*Bayt*) (and the "B" that is its descendent) "is the archetype of all 'dwellings,' of all containers: the physical support without which nothing is." See Suarès, p. 61. As the reader will notice, the *Bayt* is the last letter in בראשית (due to the fact that Hebrew is written in the opposite direction from English).

[29] Manly Hall comments that followers of Pythagoras reputedly spat upon the ground at the mention of #2. One wonders if Greek mystical understanding was less developed than Hebrew, or if such an action had an esoteric meaning which Hall did not decipher. *The Secret Teachings of All Ages.*

The paradox is that in following *that which is forbidden*, the entire process of mankind's transformation begins. Adam/Eve is more archetype than "character," and it is this archetype that is being modified at each individual step on the climb.[30] The whole story of the Bible is *Adam/Eve's* being transformed into *the Christ*.

What then are the characteristics of archetypal mankind?

1.Name:Adam/Eve (ruddy/life-giver)[31]

2. Surroundings/Attitudes: Adam/Eve's surroundings go from the Garden of Eden, where *God caused to grow every tree that was pleasing to the sight and good for food, with the tree of life in the middle of the garden, and the tree of knowledge of good and evil.* Gen.2:8,9 to somewhere *forth from the garden of Eden, to till the ground from which he was taken.* Gen. 3:22,23. But the final affront is that they are "separated" by *cherubim, and a flaming sword which turned every way,* from the all-important *tree of life.* And what is Adam's attitude toward its feminine side? ... *And Adam said, This is now bone of my bones, and flesh of my flesh: she shall be called Woman, because she was taken out of Man. Therefore shall a man leave his father and his mother, and shall cleave unto his wife: and they shall be one flesh.* Gen. 2:22-24.

Other than Adam's awareness that his/her masculine and feminine sides are one flesh, Adam is no mental giant. In the beginning, he has little awareness. He has no clue who he is; he doesn't know that he was made in the image of God. Nor is he a moral giant. His masculine side blames the feminine side, and the feminine side blames something outside of herself (she thinks) for eating the forbidden fruit, i.e., for accepting the mind-set that sets itself apart from the whole. And what is the result of this mindset? Isn't it typical human existence?

Don't we all see ourselves in the picture of Adam/Eve? We accept the whole scenario that has been given to us by the

---

[30] *Archetype* is defined in *Webster's Seventh New Collegiate Dictionary* as "the original pattern or model of which all things of the same type are representations or copies."

[31] See Strong's Hebrew Dictionary, p. 8. *Adam* suggests a common sort of human being, a person of low degree. It can refer to the color of dirt or blood. *Eve*, p. 37.

intellect. The intellect looks around and attributes what it sees to God's displeasure. It has God tell us: *in pain you shall bring forth children ... And to Adam he said, ..."Because you have ... eaten of the tree of which I commanded you, 'You shall not eat of it,' ... in toil you shall eat of it all the days of your life; thorns and thistles it shall bring forth to you; and you shall eat the plants of the field. In the sweat of your face you shall eat bread till you return to the ground, for out of it you were taken; you are dust, and to dust you shall return."* Gen. 3:16-19.

Of all the recent declarations of science, the postulate I consider most important is this: **the observer finds what he/she expects to find**.[32] It certainly is true of our archetype. Adam has eaten of the tree of the knowledge of good and evil; consequently, that is what he gets. Moreover, as long as he judges by appearances and expects evil, he will get some evil.

Adam and Eve

But *evil* isn't what it seems. (Notice: *evil* spelled backward is *live*.) From now on – until Adam/Eve changes its mindset – the masculine side will *endlessly toil* and the feminine side will *painfully produce* all that they produce. Mankind will continue to "reap as he has sown" – as he expects to find, he will find – and things will be different only when he remembers who he is. Things will be different only when mankind remembers that he/she was created "in the image" and the likeness of God.

Adam/Eve's level of understanding is symbolized by the names and the sequence of his/her sons. Consider the first two sons, Cain (acquisition[33]) and Abel (emptiness or transitoriness[34]): *Now Adam knew Eve his wife, and she conceived and bore Cain, saying, "I have gotten a man with the help of the LORD." And again, she bore his brother Abel. Now Abel was a keeper of sheep, and Cain a tiller of the*

[32] This is a simplification of what has been called Schrodinger's Cat theory. See Michael Talbot's *Mysticism and the New Physics;* Bantam; pp. 27-41.

[33] Robert Young, LL.D., *Young's Analytical Concordance to the Bible,* Funk & Wagnalls Company, New York, 1936; p. 135.

[34] *Ibid.,* p. 3. Strong translates *Abel* as coming from a word meaning "something transitory and unsatisfactory:" op. cit., p. 32.

32

*ground. In the course of time **Cain brought** to the LORD **an offering of the fruit
of the ground,** and **Abel brought of the firstlings of his flock and of their fat
portions. And the LORD had regard for Abel and his offering, but for Cain and
his offering he had no regard.** So Cain was very angry, and his countenance fell.
The LORD said to Cain, "Why are you angry, and why has your countenance
fallen? **If you do well, will you not be accepted? And if you do not do well, sin is
couching at the door; its desire is for you, but you must master it.**" Gen. 4:1-7*

But Cain has to develop; so Cain slays Abel. Abel, *the
emptiness,* is acceptable to God; but it will have to be
eliminated for growth to take place. Cain, *the acquisition*
nature which prevails through the entire scheme and this mindset, states its fears: *Cain said to the LORD, "My punishment is greater than
I can bear. Behold, thou hast driven me this day away from the ground; and from
thy face I shall be hidden; and I shall be a fugitive and a wanderer on the earth,
and whoever finds me will slay me."* [35]

But this mindset is reassured: *"Not so! If any one slays Cain,
vengeance shall be taken on him sevenfold." And the LORD put a mark on Cain,
lest any who came upon him should kill him.* Gen. 4:13-15.

3. The archetype has **three** sons, not two: Cain
(acquisition), Abel (emptiness), and Seth (substituted).[36] Only when
he is 130 [note:13x10] does Adam become *the father of a son
in his own likeness, after his image,* Seth. Seth provides the
way for carnal mankind to evolve.

4. Archetypal man has neither possessions nor
accomplishments to prove his worth.

5. Adam/Eve's final numbers reveal that they succeed
in their assigned task. Adam/Eve continues for 800 more
years, in the end receiving the designation of 930 years.[37]

---

[35] There are volumes on God's rejection of Cain's offering.Cain's offering has no
mention of being his "first fruits" as it is mentioned about Abel's. Cain's
acquisition self (the ego) has no thought of anything other than itself. It certainly
isn't willing to give its first fruits as offering. **But, it cannot be destroyed; it will be
transformed.**

[36] Strong's, op.cit., p. 122.

[37] Notice the numbers: 13 x10; 8x100; 93x10 (93 is a prime number – that which
cannot be divided – but possibly more importantly, its digits add up to 12).
Reconsider the numbers on page 16. Adam's 930 ranks third among the patriarchs.

Only Methuselah (969), Jared (962) and Noah (950) rate more years than Adam/Eve.

While the sons of Adam/Eve say something about the archetype, they are more revealing of the process which the archetype (and carnal man) is to undergo. It is the "acquisition" nature which is to have the physical experience. Mankind will continue; and in place of the "emptiness" which man expressed, early on, man will acquire a substituted nature. Mankind will acquire a new mindset. The feminine side loses Abel, but it "sees" the appropriateness of the entire process; and Eve says: *"God has appointed for me another child instead of Abel, for Cain slew him."* Gen. 4:25

The feminine side simply acknowledges what is taking place. It does not judge it as evil; it simply observes. It is our mistaken mindset, our worldly expectation, that judges "elimination" as negative. It is our mindset that **judges** an end to "emptiness" as evil. In actuality, the end to "emptiness" is proper, and it allows the positive progression to continue. We are told: *To Seth also a son was born, and he called his name **Enosh**. At that time men began to call upon the name of the LORD.* Gen. 4:26

In fact, only as the "emptiness" is eliminated do we "begin to call upon the name of the LORD." Emptiness does not exist if we are of Cain − if we possess the *inner light*. On the other hand, if we are of Seth's lineage, we will be transformed.

Carlo Suarès offers a more esoteric explanation of Cain's "elimination" of Abel: "The immanent energy of Qa heen (Cain) is projected from the interior, or the *inner light*, and is in no way subject to time. That of Set (Seth) is concerned with the evolution of the 'containers'..."[38]

---

[38] See Suarès, p. 143.

A teacher and "healer" from the turn of the last century, Malinda Elliott Cramer, taught that there are two separate paths which mankind can follow to *enlightenment.* One path is the way of the **intuition**; it is the course taken by the one who recognizes and listens to the inner light; it is the way of the initiate. Only once in a while are there those who follow this path. Such was Enoch, for Enoch *walked with God.* Such was Melchizedek; such was he whom we call Jesus.

The second path is the way of the **intellect**; it is the way of evolution. It is the process that most of us will follow. We will perceive ourselves from time to time and "judge" our actions and our thoughts, but we will hold ourselves to our earthly expressions. Such is the way of Seth, the way of Enosh. It is the way of Abraham, Isaac, Jacob and Joseph. It is the way of Moses, the way of Saul, David and Solomon. And it is the path that will allow archetypal man to turn into the *enlightened* man/ woman.

The book of Genesis presents to us an ongoing "creation," a "creation" that is in process. The Mountain will first be climbed by Abraham, then Isaac, then Jacob, then Joseph. The climb will reach greater heights and greater understanding on the part of the participants with each character. The story will continue as we proceed through the Bible to Exodus; there the path up the Mountain will be solidified by Moses and his religion of symbols. Later the climb will be expanded by David and his son, Solomon. Finally, the Mountain will be conquered by Jesus, the Christ.

The Expulsion from Paradise
by Masaccio.

Adam and Eve in Paradise   by Albrecht Dürer (1471-1528)
The man and his wife were both naked, and were not ashamed. Gen. 2:25.

Chapter Two
Enoch and Noah

The two major patriarchs that come before the "flood" are Enoch(2) and Noah. Observing them can add some light to our understanding, for they "see" differently. Only Enoch sees the truth. While Enoch sees the glass as "full-full," Noah sees "nakedness."

These two major antediluvian characters seem to be in a class more closely related to Adam/Eve than to Abraham and those who follow. Intuition tells me that both Enoch(2) and Noah are what we might call "second-level archetypes." They seem to be intended to further define this scheme of Genesis. They are not the overall design that Adam/Eve is. Notice that their wives are not named. They are more directional than lesson-teaching. In fact, their purpose may be to reveal the truth of the possibilities of this physical plane of ours.

Possibly more than any other individual in the Bible, the second Enoch is a symbolic character.[1] Significantly marked as line **24,** Enoch's story is concluded: ***Enoch walked with God; and he was not, for God took him.*** Gen. 5:24 [2]

---

[1] (There are two Enochs. The first Enoch is the son of Cain.) The name **Enoch** translates as "to be narrow" which can be inferred as "initiate," (see footnote, p. 34). The character whom we know as Enoch is the **seventh** generation of the generations of Adam. Moreover, he is born when his father (Jared) is **162** (which adds up to **9**, a special number in initiatory symbolism). In addition, at age **65** (which adds up to **11**), he produces a son (Methuselah) who dies at **969** (higher than anyone else). Moreover, if Methuselah's individual numbers are added together, Enoch's son adds up to **24.** Not only that, but at the age of **365** (days in a year) Enoch(2) is "taken."

[2] The intellectual mindset can make all sort of scenarios out of this line. Some explanations run so far afield as to say that space ships must have picked Enoch up. Or the intellectual mindset can reason that Enoch just wandered into the desert, died and was devoured by wild animals.

Not "hearing" symbolism, the intellectual mindset seeks a physical explanation for this line; but the intuitional mindset looks beyond the physical and accepts the statement as it is. The intuitional mindset accepts that **"we are not physical beings having a spiritual experience; we are spiritual beings having a physical experience."**[3]

The two "Enochs" are close together in Genesis. Although they share the same name, they do not share the same heritage. As son of Cain and continuing the metaphor of the sons of Adam (Cain is not of the physical), the first Enoch carries with him the nature of Cain, i.e., the projection of energy from the "inner light." However, Enoch (2) is the sixth-generation descendent of Seth. Seth is tied to the physical expression, as are we. And tied to the physical expression, he "should" not possess the ability to project energy from the inner light. However, we are told that Enoch (2) walked with God and *was not.*

Sethian Enoch Ascends We are being given *hope.* There is hope for mankind to advance from being tied to the physical. After an evolutionary process that lasts seven generations, Sethian mankind (evolved to the understanding of Enoch) has developed to where it, too, expresses energy from an "inner light." Now *"Enoch walked with God; and he was not ..."*

Even though the two Enochs begin from different mindsets, they both end at the level where they are expressing their energy from an "inner light." This is emphasized by their descendants. Within five generations, Enoch (1) produces Methusael (man who is of God) who is the father of Lamech

---

[3] I don't know where this saying originates. It is found in Marlo Morgan's, *Mutant Message Down Under;* Harper Collins, Pub., NY, 1991, 1994, but I remember having heard it many years ago.

(overthrower, wildman).[4] Enoch (2), Seth's descendant, coming seven generations after Adam, produces Methuselah (man of a dart) who is the father of another Lamech. Notice, although the names "Methusael" and "Methuselah" are almost identical, Methuselah takes this "article of destruction" and combines it with an unused root which means "to extend." Through "extension" the mankind which had been tied to the physical reaches the level where he expresses his inner light. It is this extended-dart man which produces Noah, and Noah and his sons set up the scheme for all of | **Noah** | mankind. In fact, Lamech hopes that Noah: *will provide us relief from our work and from the toil of our hands, out of the very soil which the LORD placed under a curse.* Gen. 5:28

We all know the story of Noah – at least, we all know the first part of the story. We know that the LORD gets tired of the "mankind" creatures that he had created and decides to finish them off with a flood, *But Noah found favor with the LORD.* Gen.6:8 *... Besides, Noah was a righteous man; he was blameless in his age; Noah walked with God.* Gen.6:9 And after the flood, **God** tells Noah that *never again shall all flesh be cut off by the waters of a flood, and never again shall there be a flood to destroy the earth.* Gen. 9:11 [5]

Noah comes down from the Mountain | **Noah's Son "Sees" Nakedness** | and plants a vineyard; then he proceeds to get drunk on the wine! If that isn't bad enough, Noah's son, Ham, sees him lying naked! Even worse, he "looks"! Not only that, but Ham (who is the father of Canaan) has the audacity to tell his brothers, Shem and Japheth; but "without looking" they tenderly cover Noah. When Noah wakes up, he curses Canaan (the son of Ham) for what Ham

---

[4] [Methusael] Strong, p. 75. [Lamech] Young, p. 583.

[5] We can take the explanation of the text coming from different times and different writers, but *esoteric* traditions allocate differences of degree and nature to **God** as opposed to **Lord**. This is a question which each reader will have to take upon himself/herself to decipher. See pages 43-45.

40

has done. The whole set of events is ridiculous; nevertheless, the intellect still accepts the story. The intuition isn't so easily placated. The intuition wonders what the sin was. Was the sin in "drinking" or "looking" or "telling"? The story is nonsensical on the surface; so the intuition looks for the underlying meaning.

Remember... Noah, like Enoch, is a second-level archetype. His story is still instructional. With this in mind, let's look at what the sin supposedly was. I think the whole understanding here has to do with **"nakedness."** The difficulty lies in the intellect's holding to the standard definition of nakedness. If we "hang loose" and interpret **"nakedness"** as our **viewing life only on the physical level,** the story begins to make sense. Adam/Eve is the major archetype – that which originally is one with God to the point that he/she "felt no shame" at their nakedness, but this condition has changed. "Nakedness" becomes a matter of shame. It becomes a question of separation from God.

Interestingly, the word "naked" has several different interpretations. In the first few chapters of Genesis there are

> Three separate words are used to denote nakedness:
> 1. to be bare (have smoothness be crafty),
> 2. referring to the genitalia,
> 3. to loosen or expose.

three separate words used for **naked** or **nakedness.** The first and second usages come from the same primitive root which means *to be bare (to have a smoothness);* however, the second usage – after Adam/Eve accepts duality – has a connotation of craftiness which is not associated with the first usage. (The Torah's footnote, p. 6, uses the word *shrewd.*) The next usage of nakedness is with regard to Noah and carries with it the awareness of the genitalia.[6] To my intuition, this describes mankind's full acceptance of his physical nature. Only with Moses is this full acceptance of a totally physical nature challenged. With Moses, **naked** is related to a different

---

[6] See Strong, pp. 730-731.

primitive root, one which implies *to loosen* or *to expose.* Only as the second and third definitions (craftiness and the genitalia) are *loosened* and *exposed* does the awareness of the genitalia – and the shame – begin to be eliminated. Only then can we return to the original *smoothness* in which we "feel no shame." The whole scheme is a ploy for whether we accept our *smoothness, i.e. perfection,* or the *appearances* that we *see.*

I just had a good example of this lesson. I was meditating in front of a patio window, and my cat decided to come sit on my lap. Outside, the wind was blowing the wind chime, creating a moving shadow on the inside floor. My cat, perfectly happy, headed toward me, totally ignoring what was outside the window. However, apparently out of the corner of her eye she saw **something.** Startled, she jumped in the air – she was startled **by the shadow.** She could not *see* that the *shadow* was nothing.

It is the animal nature of mankind which accepts the shadows. It is the worldly mindset – that which has accepted the "knowledge of good and evil" – which sees the "nakedness" and is ashamed. It is mankind which has not yet acknowledged its inner light that truthfully "sees" shadows. In fact, Cain was warned that he had to have discernment. *"If you do well, will you not be accepted? And if you do not do well, sin is couching at the door; its desire is for you, but you must master it."*

Apparently, Noah serves a similar function to that of the second Enoch. He is the grandson of the *dart which is extended,* and he is the son of Lamech, the *overthrower, the wildman.* And Lamech, at age 182, names him "Noah" (quiet, resting place), and announces: *This one will provide us relief from our work and from the toil of our hands ...* But Noah is a little more tied to the physical expression than was Enoch. This is indicated by an excess of number 7's. His father, Lamech, lives to age 777: and Noah, himself, lives to 950 (which adds up to 14).

In fact, Noah is so tied to the physical that he is more like we are than any of the previous patriarchs. The best instance is with regard to the animals. Significantly, Adam/Eve had an implied oneness with the animals. Adam/Eve were told they were: *to rule the fish of the sea, the birds of the sky, the cattle, the whole earth, and all the creeping things ...* Gen. 1:26,

Not so with Noah. No longer are we talking about archetypes. Now there is a greater separation between mankind and the rest of nature. To Noah, God says: *The fear and the dread of you shall be upon all the beasts of the earth and upon all the birds of the sky — everything with which the earth is astir — and upon all the fish of the sea; they are given into your hand. Every creature that lives shall be yours to eat; as with the green grasses, I give you all these.* Gen. 9:2,3

Nevertheless, Noah expresses what the best of worldly mankind ever expresses. Here is the hope of mankind, that he/she will return to an existence in which there is no longer toil and work. Here is the hope to return to ONENESS with God. There's just one problem: we're so tied to this earthly plane – we're so tied to the physical. And despite God's promise to Noah that "He" won't destroy mankind again, the "paradox" is that Noah's group even increases this tie to the physical when Ham sees his father *naked*.[7] We were in bad enough shape after Adam/Eve; but with Noah's drunkenness and Ham's acceptance of appearances, we're even more mired in duality. We are convinced we're separate from God.

My grandfather used to tell me that the lesson of Noah's drunkenness was that you weren't supposed to drink (he was a teetotaller). However (all deference to my dear grandfather), it is not the condemnation of beer or wine which the symbol addresses; it is how the sons handle their father's **nakedness**. We know that Ham (hot, warm, i.e., that which is most worldly) looks straight at the "nakedness" and accepts it. On the other hand, Shem (a marked individuality implying

---

[7] I find Noah's drunkenness enlightening considering some of the recent opinions of anthropologists. The new theory is that mankind became farmers (as opposed to hunter/gatherers) in order to have the ingredients for **beer**. And obviously, this domestication – in order to raise grain (or grapes in the case of Noah) required for beer (or wine) – eventually led to civilization.

honor) and Japheth (expansion), i.e., those characteristics of an advanced humanity – even upon hearing the testimony of the world (Ham) – turn their backs on the nakedness and place a cloth over their father. Gen. 9:18-28.

What we're being told here is that as long as we keep looking at the physical expression and consider it to be the whole picture, we're in the same condition as Ham's son, Canaan. We, along with Canaan, are cursed to be slaves to the physical. As long as we remain in the mindset which is tied to the *knowledge of good and evil* – as long as mankind considers himself/herself a physical being which **may** or **may not express spiritually** – we are just that. We have the choice of covering Noah – as do Shem and Japheth – not seeing the nakedness and thus bringing relief to the physical nature; or we can react as does Ham.

Paul explains it partially. *And so it is written, **The first man Adam was made a living soul; the last Adam was made a quickening spirit.** ... The first man is of the earth, earthy: the second man is the Lord from heaven. As is the earthy, such are they also that are earthy; and as is the heavenly, such are they also that are heavenly.* I Cor. 15:44-48.

Paul perceives the glass to be full-full. Only those who understand that they are truly spiritual beings – albeit, **spiritual beings having a physical experience** – see the glass as full-full. Our characters in Genesis will "climb" the Mountain to come to that point.

We have finished the preparations for the climb, and it has been a long ordeal. But there's one more concept we must address: the difference between GOD and LORD. This is the most complex of all of the preliminary instructions, for this is the most esoteric. In fact, it should be approached only as each one feels it necessary. Traditionally, both Jews and Christians consider **God** and **LORD** as synonymous, taking the explanation of a biblical scholar, Jean Astruc (1684-1766), that Genesis came from the blending of two ancient documents

– one using **YHWH,** the other using **El** – to designate God. The Higher Criticism of the 19th Century accepted this explanation, and it is still the current view. There is another view, however, one which each reader will have to assess for himself/herself, because it cannot be easily communicated.[8]

Carlo Suarès makes a very important statement with regard to this question. He begins that the viewpoint of Genesis II "... does not belong to a Yahvic tradition different from and inconsistent with the Elohimic tradition of Genesis I (as has been stated by scholars). [Rather], **It describes the universal life-energy as seen from inside, from its essence, and no longer through its evolutionary aspect. The essence is included in the appearance, the beginning is in the end and the end is in the beginning."**[9]

At the moment, my intuition is saying it this way: **YHWH is the embodiment of the Elohim taking place.** Thus, the inclusion of both **YHWH** and **El** is for my edification – or for the edification of each one of us. "El" is the God that I intuit; **"YHWH"** is the God that I express. This seems to be the message of the entire Bible; for as we progress through Genesis and the books that follow, what earlier had been either LORD or God becomes the **LORD God.** Only when the Law's (LORD's) name (nature) is *written on our foreheads* are we expressing as the image of God. Only then is mankind expressing as is intended. As Revelation says:

---

[8] YHWH (or YHVH) was first written as *Jehovah* by Peter Gallin, the confessor of Pope Leo X, in 1518. See historical presentation in Nathan Ausubel's *The Book of Jewish Knowledge;* pp. 44,45. Suarès uses YHWH.

[9] Suarèz, pp. 103-104. On page 43, Suarès writes: **"The Qabala knows that YHWH is not a deity but an immanence which can become alive and active when the two vitalities in us, the container and the contained, fecundate each other.** Historically, those vitalities of Israel came into being when the mistaken expression, material and materializing, of the Temple and of Jerusalem, was destroyed. The Qabala, for the time being, obeyed the Law, and reciprocally the Law held the Qabala in great respect and honor." We might add: but understood it not.

Suarès writes in another place: "The schema Yod-Hay-Vav-Hay (YHWH), translated the LORD or Jehovah, which appears in Genesis II, expresses an existence fulfilled by two lives [Hay and Hay] of psyche and body mutually fecundating one another. When this happens, YHWH is alive in us."

There shall no more be anything accursed, but the throne of God and of the Lamb shall be in it, and his servants shall worship him; they shall see his face, and his name shall be on their foreheads. Rev. 22:3,4.

It's a good thing that Noah walks with God (El), because his relationship with the LORD (YHWH) needs improvement. And, for Noah's descendants, this condition will continue for the rest of the Old Testament. The entire plot and the entire series of characters and stories will be for Noah's descendants to improve the situation. Shem is an ancestor of Jesus, so the potential is there; but only with the advent of Jesus is the situation "restored."

This is why mankind must climb the Mountain. Mankind must know – as did Jesus – that he/she is the son/daughter of the living God. And mankind's journey to this understanding is climbing the Mountain. Mankind is to grow and develop. Mankind is to learn – as do the various characters in the Bible – what is The Truth. Climbing the Mountain is to come to that understanding which allows the LORD God to express.

And they that entered, male and female of all flesh, went in as God had commanded him, and the LORD shut him in. Gen. 7:16.

And Ham, the father of Canaan, saw the nakedness of his father. Gen. 9:22.

46

The Departure of Hagar, J.C. Buttre.

Chapter Three
Abram: Father of Nations

Ten generations from Noah we are introduced to he who will begin the journey to climb the Mountain; and he (and those who succeed him) will progress farther and farther away from that mankind which looked on Noah's "nakedness." He will progress farther and farther away from the tower of Babel that "confounded the speech of the whole earth." (see Gen.11:1-9) He, and those who are of his line, will progress farther and farther up the Mountain.

You may notice that he is introduced to us as Abram, rather than Abraham. He will not gain the **"ha"** of empowerment until chapter 17. Until then he will just have to blunder his way through life, much like modern mankind. However, before we proceed, an all-important statement must be made: we are not investigating the "historical" Abraham. We are investigating the "esoteric" Abraham. It is the "esoteric" which has relevance to us and to our own journey. The "historical" Abraham is long gone. Remember, the only reason for this book is for each of us to have a view of the Bible which will allow us to climb the Mountain more easily. With this established, we can proceed; but first we must check the information we are given.[1]

Name and Heritage of Abram

Abram is Ab (A [masculine] + B [feminine]) + **Ram** (high father of physical life; father of exaltation; initiate)He is from the line of Seth and the line of Shem. He is 20 generations away from Adam and 10 generations from Noah. He is the son of Terah (turning, wandering) and the grandson of Nahor (nostrils

---

[1] See Gen. 11:24-30. The reader is invited to check both Strong's *Concordance* and Young's *Concordance* for the translations of the names of people and places.

48

snorting); and he is the first of three brothers – one of which dies in Ur and one of which apparently remains in Ur. That which dies in Ur is the father of Milcah (counsel); that which remains in Ur is the husband of Milcah (counsel). Abram has no "counsel." He's married to Sarai (contention) who is barren.

Abram represents each of us as we begin our spiritual journey.[2] What have we said about ourselves? At least we are partially aware of ourselves, sufficient to take a wife (be aware of our feminine side); but we are tied to habits and ways of living that see the physical life as all important. We try to manipulate our lives so that our needs (often our fears) are met; but that means that we see ourselves as separate from what we experience. As a result (although we don't know this is the reason), we are barren. We don't produce what we would like to produce.

Then, for some reason, our situation changes.[3] This first change, or at least the first change of which we're aware, comes because of our heritage, which combines a wandering nature – an undesignated dissatisfaction with life – and an almost "snorting" determination to finish this dissatisfaction. It is this that takes us out of our comfortable (although dissatisfied) rut toward "the land that I will show you."

This comfortable rut was in Ur of the Chaldeans, a lush land, but a land where "magic" prevails. What is "magic"? Magic is the power-expression of the physical mindset. It's where if you don't like something, you "manipulate" its change. Now something tells us to move, and where are we headed? To Canaan (low, flat [to bend the knee] to bring low into subjection).

Sounds bad, doesn't it? Correct me if I'm wrong, but haven't we been "taken in" before ...? at least twice before in the previous eleven chapters of Genesis? Remember? The serpent

[2] He/she is neither masculine nor feminine; but we will henceforth refer to each character as he or she is presented in the Bible.

[3] Sometime in the future, after repeated experience, we will recognize that it is the feminine side which prompts the action; but for now we are not that aware. At least we are aware that we have a "feminine" side; but this side of us seems to disagree with us most of the time, so we don't listen to it very much.

said the "apple" would make us "like divine beings." And remember the tower of Babel? Wasn't it intended to reach us up to heaven? Now we're given another opportunity. Only this time the promise isn't so grand – and the ambition isn't on nearly so great a scale. What we're "hearing" relates to our chief admonition – Hang loose! In hang-loose terminology, we're saying **"to get high-up, you've got to go low-down."**

The discussion is academic, anyway. Abram doesn't have much choice. His wandering, turning nature sets him going from Ur, but then it pauses in Haran. Only the death of this nature (Terah dies in Haran) allows Abram and us to continue the journey.

As with Abram, our spiritual journey is seldom something we choose voluntarily. Usually, it's illness or grief or apparent disaster that prompts our activity; and how we choose to begin is different for each of us, too. Moreover, as with Abram, there probably are pausing places where we might like to linger and procrastinate; but each time we pause, something will "urge" us to move on again. I almost used the word "force," but "urge" is more accurate, for "force" is something outside of ourselves; "urge" comes from within.

Now the LORD said to Abram, "Go from your country and your kindred and your father's house to the land that I will show you. And I will make of you a great nation, and I will bless you, and make your name great, so that you will be a blessing. I will bless those who bless you, and him who curses you I will curse; and by you all the families of the earth shall bless themselves." Gen. 12:1-3

This spiritual journey is not a mass migration. We've got to leave our kindred (those supports we've relied on for so long); we've got to leave our father's house (any thinking or understanding or support that belongs to another) in order to go to the "land I will show you."

Does that mean we give up the church or the religion we were raised with? No! It means that the spiritual path we accept MUST be our own! It may end up similar to that of our family, but it must be that which WE choose. Simply by labeling

50

the true beginning of Abram's journey as Chapter 12 and

Surroundings and Attitudes of Abram

emphasizing it with Abram's age (75 which adds up to 12), Genesis tells us that this is something beyond a worldly way of being. Notice something else. Abram does not take up from Ur and follow a band of traveling spirituals. This is not a journey into "cultism." The truly spiritual journey is a lonely trek; the "groupie" way, where we're surrounded by others, is still the way of the world.[4]

Following his father, Terah (wandering ways), Abram reaches Haran (to kindle), and there his father dies. But Abram is not totally alone, he does have an entourage: his wife, Sarai (a contentious feminine side) and his nephew, Lot (concealed, a veil covering). Abram's companions reveal a great deal about him – and about us at this stage of our spiritual climb.

In the tradition of myth, at age 75, Abram is no beginner; he starts the climb with some understanding. But he is just beginning to climb the Mountain, and he has some "baggage" with him which will have to be changed or discarded. After Haran, Abram is free of at least a part of his former wandering ways. Of course, his wife is still with him. The feminine side of us is a part of us forever; but for now, it is contentious (argumentative), and we don't pay much attention to it. The nephew Lot, however, – this veiled portion of us that is not a product of ourselves, just related to us – cannot remain with us; eventually he will have to leave.

To this "encumbered" Abram, the Lord speaks; and after Abram follows the directive, the Lord actually appears to him and promises: *I will give this land to your offspring.* Gen. 12:7. Thereupon

---

[4] I am using "cult" in the sense of those groups which encourage an extreme devotion on the part of the participants either to an individual or the group itself. Admittedly, Christianity was a "cult." I should clarify what is implied here with regard to organized religion. Some might say that the truly spiritual seeker will stay away from organized religion of any sort. I disagree. There is much to be said for the support and approval found in organized religion. The difficulty with either expression lies in the cult or organized religion becoming one's focus rather than one's own spiritual journey.

Abram builds an altar and invokes the Lord by name. Finally, he journeys *by stages toward the Negeb,* i.e., toward the south, the parched land.

The author of Hebrews classifies Abram's activity as faith, and adds: *without faith it is impossible to please him (God). For whoever would draw near to God must believe that he exists and that he rewards those who seek him.* Heb. 11:6 The author gives us his definition of faith, earlier in the chapter: *Now faith is the substance of things hoped for, the evidence of things not seen.* Heb.11:1

Traditionally, the church has taught that Abram's greatest asset was "faith." But I would suggest that in our modern vocabulary the word "trust" more accurately expresses what is being conveyed. The word which is used in Hebrews is *pistis;* it indicates a conviction of religious truth, but it comes from a primitive verb, *pĕitho,* which in its passive mode means "to assent, to rely."[5]

It's nice that the concordance gave me some "real" proof to use for a left-brained argument.[6] Admittedly, for the intellect to be happy, there has to be some left-brained proof. But my intuition has no doubt that Abram's accomplishment was in listening (and assenting) to what he was hearing inside himself. Isn't this invoking the Lord by name?

Even on the surface, the story of Abram contains all of modern mankind's challenges. Abram finds that the "magic" of Ur doesn't work, so he finally leaves it; but he leaves it, mostly, just to wander around. He **Abram Goes** passes through "the land" that is supposed to be **To Egypt** "his" and even builds an altar to the LORD; but he keeps wandering. He ends up in Egypt (the land of the world, but a dry land) – not because that's where he intended to go, but because there was "famine" back in the land which he had

---

[5] See Strong, (Gr.) #4102 & #3982.

[6] An aside here. In writing this, my remembering "ears" heard something from my childhood; my "old ears" heard "lame-brained." Is it possible that anything other than the intellectual approach was so ridiculed as "lame-brained" that even 50 years later we are unable to break apart from the intellectual approach?

been promised. And once in Egypt, he does the "unforgivable."
He denies his feminine side. He's afraid that the Egyptians (the
world) will see "her beauty" and "kill him." So – because of
fear – he passes Sarai off as his sister, and she is taken into
Pharaoh's palace.

The new Jewish translation points out an important
difference in understanding from that of the King James version.
Line 16 (7) reads: *And because of her, it went well with Abram;* he acquired
sheep, oxen, asses, male and female slaves, she-asses, and camels.[7]

I'm going to make a daring statement, here: It is the
feminine side of us that **produces.** It is the feminine side of us
that **makes things go well with us. It is the feminine side that
recognizes the eternal energy that is within us.** And we must
not deny that side. If we do, eventually it will catch up with us
as it did with Abram ... *for the Lord afflicted Pharaoh and his household
with mighty plagues.* Gen.12:17 Even in the world, the one who denies
his/her feminine side cannot continue to prosper. *And Pharaoh
put men in charge of him [Abram], and they sent him off with his wife and
all that he possessed.* Gen. 12:20

Actually, Abram comes out smelling like a rose, at least
on the surface. The account reads: *Abram was very rich in cattle, silver
and gold.* Gen. 13:1. Isn't this a contradiction? No, it is just one of
the many paradoxes of life, but, notice all of these are
unimportant. He still does not have a "son." Those who deny
their feminine side may appear to do well by worldly standards;
but they will never get to the top of the Mountain doing so. Not
that Abram cares about getting to the top of the Mountain; he
is still barren. He leaves Egypt only because he is forced (urged)
to move on again. As a result, he proceeds by stages back to the
place where he had built an altar to the Lord on his first time
through "the land," and *there Abram invoked the Lord by name.*
Gen. 13:4

---

[7] *Torah,* op. cit., p. 21. (Gen. 12:16) The old King James rendering read: *And he
entreated Abram well for her sake ...* , which doesn't quite tell it all. One more item
about Sarai (Sarah) is given to us only in Gen. 20:12. There Abraham reveals that
Sarah is his father's daughter, but not his mother's.

It should be noted that the "place" for this altar is between Bethel (house of God) and Ai (the holy city of the Canaanites). In other words, at this point, Abram is not sure which mindset he will choose. His view of life falls between that of the "righteous man" and that of the Canaanites, but nevertheless, he invokes the Lord by name.

Immediately, a change takes place.[8] Abram is given the opportunity to change his nature. He is given the opportunity to be free of this veiled nature which has been accompanying him from the beginning. He is given the opportunity to "let Lot leave." Lot chooses the physical abundance and moves everything to Sodom. Only after Lot is gone does the Lord again address Abram. And the Lord says: *for I give all the land that you see to you and your offspring forever.* Gen. 13:14. (Note: 13[added] and 14[two levels of earthly completion.])

If we were making a modern movie of the narrative, this would be the appropriate place to have a "gospel choir" interject: **"Do you have the faith to *believe?*"** Abram gives us at least a little bit of a **"yes."** He moves his tent, *and came to dwell at the terebinths of Mamre which are in Hebron; and he built an altar there to the LORD.* In other words, Abram changes his mindset. He now "puts on" an attitude comparable to the terebinths (oak trees) of Mamre (vigor).[9] He is at Hebron (seat of association), and he builds his second altar to the LORD.

You'll have to excuse the alliteration; **Let's Let Lot Leave** I couldn't resist. Besides, it emphasizes that we must closely observe Lot's departure from Abram. First, this

---

[8] Genesis 13:7. Here is an example of why we get into trouble with a literal translation of the Bible. In line 7, denoting earthly completion, there is an added comment, i.e., *The Canaanites and Perizzites were then dwelling in the land.* We know that the Canaanites were (are) those who were cursed for "having viewed Noah's nakedness," (those who hold tightly to the physical). The Perizzites, however, did not exist at the time of Abraham, because they were the descendants of Judah's Perez (breaking forth, a rising light), an ancestor of Jesus. However, their "meaning" gives explanation to why Abram's cattle and Lot's cattle could not inhabit the same land. Once the light begins to break forth in us, the veiled portion of us begins to "quarrel" with the semi-enlightened portion of us.

[9] Strong's definition gives us a chance for an interesting analogy here. Mamre (#4471) relates to a verb which means to wring the neck of a chicken without tearing its head off. It's an apt analogy to how we have to deal with ourselves, isn't it?

is an amicable parting, with Abram giving Lot the choice of where to go. In other words, Abram is willing to accept what is left to him. Second, notice that even though he is officially separated from Lot, Abram will have more dealings with him.

So it is with our own veiled selves. We can't attack those things which are hidden in us; we can't demand that they leave us or even surface themselves. Only by allowing the veiled subjects to come up of their own volition can we be successful in being free of them. Moreover, simply having addressed these items and consciously having released them doesn't finish the job. Lot (the veiled, the concealed portion of us) comes back again and again. Even when we think we're free from him, his descendants remain in the "promised land."

As we climb this Mountain, time and again we will be confronted by those things which lie concealed in us. Nothing we ever experience, see, hear, smell, taste, feel – or even think – ever leaves us completely. Only a small portion of our memory is held in our conscious mind; the remainder rests in the subconscious (veiled or concealed) and comes to the surface only as the climb progresses.

There are even those who say that "the sins of the father" remain with us in the form of individual "cell" memory. While such probably can never be proven, the tendency for certain diseases to be hereditary suggests that there may be some validity to the theory. Such a theory can explain the discrepancy that although we know that the body constantly renews itself and replaces all cells within a certain amount of time, those areas which have suffered trauma often do not regain their vigor.

To the esotercist, until Abraham – totally and with *love* – lets Lot leave, he will continue to be plagued by him. Therefore, inadvertently, Lot brings the next big opportunity for Abram to continue his climb – by being "captured" during the war between the four kings and the five kings.

As with many instances in the Bible, the story of this war means little unless we "translate" the names and places.[10] Even then, it will take substantial hang-loose thinking to "see" what's going on. Apparently Abram's "senses" are being tested. That is the usual reference when the number "five" is used, so let's begin with the "five kings,"first looking at the third king.[11] He is Shinab (a father has turned), a Canaanite. Remember, Canaan was the son of Ham, he who "judged" Noah to be naked. Again we're asking what mankind "sees" as true. And what does mankind consider "true"? That which he perceives with his senses.

For the most part mankind only pays attention to his senses; that is how he judges. From birth we judge and are ruled by what we *feel, see, hear, smell,* and *taste*; **Four Kings and Five Kings** and as we age nothing changes. We only become more sophisticated in our judgment, but there's nothing redeeming in our five kings. In fact, they all come from places that are the opposite of "redeeming." Their various cities of origin can be translated as *burnt,* a *ruined heap, reddish, earthy,* and even when (as in the case of Zeboiim) there is *beauty,* it's followed by a *gulp - that which he has swallowed up.* The last line is almost prophetic; all of these "cities" will be destroyed when Sodom and Gomorrah are destroyed. But that gets ahead of the story. Before they can be destroyed, they must be made aware. (The senses are not to be destroyed; they are to be heightened.)

---

[10] Consider the following scheme: **Five Kings - relate to senses.** 1. Bera (gift)/Sodom (to scorch); 2. Birsha (with wickedness)/Gomorrah (ruined heap); 3. Shinab (a father has turned)/Admah (reddish, earthy); 4. Shemeber (splendor of heroism)/Zeboiim (prominence); 5. (No name)King/Bela (a gulp; that which he has swallowed up) or Zoar (little). **Four Kings - relate to power.** 1. Amraphel (powerful people)/Shinar (the plain of Babylon); 2. Arioch (lion-like)/ Ellazar (Babylon); 3. Ched-or-lao-mer ([a son of Shem] sheafband)/ Elam (Persia and hidden [to veil from sight]); 4. Tidal (splendor, renown)/ Goiim (nations, gentile, heathen, massing troop of animals, related to feminine). See both Strong's and Young's concordances.

[11] Five refers to the senses and, therefore, the physical world. See page 16.

The beginning of this awareness-process comes as the senses are "made war upon" by the powerful natural order.[12] The "five" kings join forces at the Valley of Siddim (extension), the Salt Sea. However, these united senses still serve Chedorlaomer (sheafband) from Elam (veiled from sight) for twelve (12, i.e., spiritual perfection) years.[13] For a minute, look back at page 39 and Methuselah; it was only through "extension" that the line from which Abram descends was able to progress. Now, at the Valley of Siddim (extension), more growth will take place.[14]

And just who is making war on our senses? The natural order and the power of the natural order. Notice that the "four kings" all have some special power, and they come from the eastern centers. *Four* represents the natural order; it is the perfection of nature, and it is "powerful..., splendor..., lion-like..., sheafband" – but also it is "flat" and "veiled from sight."

If we anticipate a heightened mankind resulting from its progress from Adam to the Christ, isn't it appropriate that those senses upon which mankind relies must become heightened? Well, the process begins in the symbolic 13th year as they rebel against the natural order. [15]

---

[12] Abraham Maslow considered *Self Actualization* as the aim of all individuals, but he saw it as possible only after the basic needs (the needs that relate to the senses) have been met.

[13] Notice: it is not 7 years, which would be only earthly perfection; also notice, that spiritual perfection (#12) also incorporates earthly perfection (#7), the balance of nature (#4), plus the monad, (#1).

[14] An appropriate aside might be to notice what happens to salt when water is added to it. It expands.

[15] Since *sheafband* is the translation of the leader of the Four Kings, it has to have a higher meaning. A *sheaf* comes from an Anglo-Saxon word meaning to collect or bundle together; the *band* is that which binds them together. The Biblical image of a *sheafband* may have referred to the binding that held individual stalks of grain together. The image of *wheat* appears time and time again in the Bible, and always has importance. (David buys the location of a *threshing floor* for the Temple.) But the importance of *sheafband* seems to be that the five senses are always bound together. They always function at the same level. If the mindset is on the physical, the senses will operate at that level. Only as the mindset is heightened do the senses operate at a heightened level, and (one of our chief paradoxes) vice-versa.

Most of us, during most of our lives, simply assume that what we see, feel, taste, hear, and smell is what is actual. It is only as we **extend** ourselves that we begin to recognize a spiritual world beyond our physical world. And as we do so, the natural order

| Rescue |
| of Lot |

(in the significant 14th year [2x7] i.e., a second level of the physical) systematically defeats some of the impediments in our way, "giants" such as Rephaim, Zuzim, Emim, and even the Horites in their "hill country." The natural order destroys what's high and what's low. As Isaiah said: *Every valley shall be exalted, and every mountain and hill shall be made low: and the crooked shall be made straight, and the rough places plain: And the glory of the LORD shall be revealed, and all flesh shall see it together: for the mouth of the LORD hath spoken it.* Is. 40:4,5

The Bible calls it *grace*, this enabling which is put in operation by the natural order, that which defeats the "giants" that are in our way. Remember, our problem is in "looking" and seeing *naked.* The natural order gets as far as Kadesh (holy) and Enmishpat (fountain of justice) before the five senses try to stop the process. However, the five senses are not as powerful as the natural order (grace); and running from what is to *be,* they throw themselves into the burning pits. It is at this point that Lot (our hidden side) gets kidnapped, and that brings Abram into action.

Remember our original sin? It was in "partaking of the tree of the knowledge of good and evil." It was in judging. Here is a prime example of the effect of judging. In Sunday School we were taught that "Lot got kidnapped and Abram had to go save him." It looks like that on the surface; but that's "judging. " In reality, the whole episode is taking place in order that Abram can grow. The whole episode is taking place to allow Abram to act. Neither we nor Abram can *rest* in our holy place under the oak trees. Enlightenment is an upward-spiral activity. We are given rest only to let things become internalized. Abram has rested. He has assimilated the strength (oak trees) and is allied to Mamre (vigor), Eshkol (cluster of grapes, i.e., productivity), and Aner (boy). Attention must be called to the inclusion of Aner.

Abram does not have full spiritual strength. He is still young in his spirituality. But he challenges the natural order, anyway, and triumphs. This triumph takes place in Chapter 14, verse 14 (four 7's). We're being told that Abram has the natural order (4) of earthly perfection. *When Abram heard that his kinsman had been taken captive, he led forth his **trained men, born in his house, three hundred and eighteen** of them, and went in pursuit as far as **Dan.*** Gen. 14:14.

There are three items for our attention, here. Abram is taking only those "portions" of himself that are truly his; moreover, when added together, they add up to 12. Therefore, with this spiritual effort (combined with the vigor he has accumulated) he pursues the enemy as far as "Dan." The definition of "Dan" is "judge." Therefore, he pursues the enemy as far as his "judgment" allows him to do so.

Isn't it interesting how we have come back to this word *judge*? Jesus uses the word, too, and he makes it all-important. He says: *Judge not, that you be not judged. For with the judgment you pronounce you will be judged, and the measure you give will be the measure you get.* Mt. 7:1,2. This is the most important concept of the Bible. It is the **LAW.**

This LAW is so important, we must repeat it.

With the judgment you pronounce you will be judged, *and* ***the measure you give will be the measure you get!***

Matthew considered it so important that he used the line to begin the chapter designated for "earthly completion." The entire Bible tries to make this point to us: at whatever level we are operating (thinking, doing, believing, trusting, etc.), that is the level of experience that will come back to us. Only when we are operating at the appropriate level for the "image of God" have we got it right! Only then does the climb become "easier."

We have the opportunity to observe Abram's level of "judgment." The narrative continues: *And he divided his forces against them by night, he and his servants, and routed them and pursued them to Hobah, north of Damascus. Then he brought back all the goods, and also brought back his kinsman Lot with his goods, and the women and the people.* Gen. 14:15,16.

Hobah comes from "to secrete oneself."[16] This whole situation has to do with that which is secreted within us, that which is hidden or veiled from us. We are being told that only that portion of us which is truly **ours** can deal with these hidden items. Often the process begins at night, and only if we are persistent will that which is secreted within allow us to access what is Beginning To Produce hidden. As any student of psychology will recognize, the night visions are dreams. Interestingly, although in Genesis we find night visions that result in blessings (as with Abram and Jacob); it is not until Joseph that the dreams are interpreted. At this level in our development (Abram), there is not more than an awareness of the night visions. Moreover, these night visions (sometimes they may be as Abram's, i.e., pursuing an enemy) begin to make us aware of some of our hidden secrets. They also give us the opportunity to "give out" that "measure" (in the dreams) that we are at the moment.

Abram's "measure" at this moment is that he has "recovered" some of his hidden portions. He rescues Lot, but he doesn't invite Lot to again join him. Lot returns to Sodom. Actually, the "hidden portions" are not nearly so important as the honor Abram receives after challenging the natural order. He is greeted by the leader of the five kings and, more importantly, by Melchizedek (king of Salem [peace] and priest of God Most High). It is notable here that the term "God" is used, rather than "LORD."[17] Abram's senses are giving him positive feedback on the physical level; and we can interpolate that, simultaneously, he is expressing at a higher level than just the physical.

This is affirmed by Melchizedek's offering of bread and wine. With his blessing, which affirms ... *God Most High, who has delivered your foes into your hand,* Melchizedek indicates that it is something more than the physical which Abram is experiencing.

---

[16] Strong.

[17] The term "God Most High" is . 'elyown:H5945 'elyown:H5945 'el:H410. If I'm correct, this is the first mention we have had of 'El since the time of Shem and chapter 10. Chapters 11-13 have only dealt with YHWH.

And Abram recognizes that it is not his own doing that has accomplished the triumph, so he gives 1/10th (one portion of earthly accumulation, his first fruits) to Melchizedek.

Acknowledgment by Melchizedek This "war" between the four kings and the five kings is one of the most symbolic sections in the Bible; for on the physical plane, nothing really happened. The four kings were not "defeated," nor were the five kings "destroyed." The only thing that really took place was that Abram (now utilizing powers which were truly his) took action.

Abram now has access to his hidden portions, and he is even able to have an appreciation of what he is "seeing," because the "senses" are working at his level, rather than Lot's. Moreover, when the king of Sodom offers him the spoils, Abram refuses to accept anything from him, declaring that he will accept only what his "servants" and those who went with him deserve. In other words, Abram recognizes that he is judged as he judges. Moreover, he gives the supreme power the credit for what he is now "seeing" and what is happening.[18] Hooray! Abram is beginning to triumph over the challenge. Abram is beginning to notice the fact that he is "made in the image of God."

Half-empty? Half-full? Full-full? Mankind seems to fall into three categories. One category (half-empty) – having seen mostly evil – expects evil and either passively takes whatever comes its way or aggressively works for its own will. Doing either, it produces more evil. A second category (half-full) – having seen mostly good – expects good and actively works for that good; however, since this category of mankind still feels the need to personally bring about the good, evil sometimes comes in.[19]

---

[18] See Gen.14:21-24. Notice what numbers are being used for the designated verse, [2x7; 3x7; 2x12]).

[19] This is a very important concept. It is an extreme paradox. If we feel a **need**, we have established in our mindset that we are **missing** whatever we're talking about.

A third category (full-full) – having no judgment of either good or bad – anticipates that its needs will all be met; it **expects such to happen** with its active participation but not with its personal activity bringing about the result. The third category trusts the natural order. It does not use the "magic" manipulation of Ur, nor does it feel it has to bring about its own good. It takes what comes, recognizing it as appropriate and expecting divine order.[20] Needless to say, it's hard to find the third category. The only one in the Bible who truly fits this category is Jesus. It certainly is not Abram.

The presentation of the four kings-vs-the five kings brings us to something that must be discussed before we can proceed any further: that is the idea of simultaneous planes of interpretation – not only of the Bible, but of life itself. In fact, the symbol of the four kings suggests as much.

We have viewed Abram with regard to his mindset. We have observed his mental position by what happens to him; and we have observed him in relation to his name, his heritage and his attitude toward his feminine side. But all of this is an over-simplification. Particularly the terms "feminine" and "masculine" are oversimplifications. The balancing between the masculine and feminine is only one layer of the balancing that takes place as the aspirant climbs the Mountain.

Simultaneous Layers of Understanding

Each of us must eventually recognize that **body, mind,** and **spirit** are **one; and all must be balanced.** Even the term "balanced" is an oversimplification, for "balanced" implies only "two" in a "dance." The balance that we are envisioning is more accurately *twelve* times *two* **in a** *dance*.

It is: **body** – physical, mental, spiritual;

mind – conscious, sub-conscious, super-conscious;

spirit – Father, Son, Holy Ghost;

transcendence – no separation.

---

[20] Apparently, the Aborigines pictured in Marlo Morgan's *Mutant Message, Down Under,* fit in this category.

And the dance? The dance takes place constantly, both in the Bible and in life. Possibly the best analogy I can think of is something that comes from science fiction. Those of you who are *Star Trek* fans will remember the three-dimensional chess set that belonged to Spock. Esoterically, we can explain climbing the Mountain as such a game. The esoteric explanation of life is that we must balance all of the above groups of three, simultaneously. To make it even harder, we must also balance the positive and negative (masculine and feminine) sides of all.

As in Spock's three-dimensional chess set, the "move" on one level affects the "pieces" on the other two levels. In Abram's case, as a change takes place on the physical level (Abram releases Lot), a corresponding change takes place on the mental level (Abram releases some "veiled" items). At the same time, a corresponding change takes place on the spiritual level. Abram recognizes that the feat is accomplished by other than himself. Therefore, he gives Melchizedek, God's representative, 1/10th of his first fruits.[21]

These simultaneous levels of understanding explain the conditions for Abram's upcoming sacrifice. In explanation, it is some time after meeting Melchizedek, and Abram is doubting the promise he has been given. He says the "promised land" makes no difference since he has no children. Suddenly, he is told to sacrifice a heifer, a she-goat, and a ram (all three years old), plus a turtle dove and a young bird. Gen.15:9,10.

Two ideas stand out. The three animals are of an age where they are ready to produce, and their ratio is two-to-one female. This is a sequence that is found time and time again: growth or added productivity comes with two female conditions and one male.

Traditionally, the she-goat is the lower feminine aspect; the heifer is the higher feminine aspect. Both are sacrificed. Even what we call the higher feminine thoughts must be transformed.

---

[21] Abram's meeting Melchizedek marks a special level of understanding, but only when the lower three levels are completely balanced – and symmetrical – can transcendence take place. Abram won't ever get to this level. Only Jesus will.

While the animal instincts must be split in two before being sacrificed, the birds (the *peace* of the turtle dove and the *flying thoughts* of the young bird) can remain as they are, according to the King James version. However, the Torah's version cuts the turtle dove in two, leaving only the young bird whole.

Abram does as instructed, and another night experience comes upon him. *As the sun was about to set, a deep sleep fell upon Abram, and a great dark dread descended upon him. And He (The LORD) said to Abram, "Know well that your offspring shall be strangers in a land not theirs, and they shall be enslaved and oppressed four hundred years; but I will execute judgment on the nation they shall serve, and in the end they shall go free with great wealth. As for you, you shall go to your fathers in peace: you shall be buried at a ripe old age. And* **they shall return here in the fourth generation, for the iniquity of the Amorites is not yet complete.** *"* Gen. 15:12-16.

Since we know that we are dealing with more than one plane, the actions and the comments take on several meanings. In the Hebraic system of symbols, numbers indicate levels of operation as well as states of consciousness. For instance, numbers in the tens (10's) indicate the physical level. Numbers in the hundreds (100's) indicate another plane, what we might call the mental plane. Numbers in the thousands (1000's) indicate a level above that, what we might call the cosmic or the spiritual plane.[22]

While the four-hundred-year "visit" can be interpreted on the mental plane to refer to the Hebrews' "sojourn" in Egypt which ended only with the Exodus, on another level it can mean something quite different. To me it says that only as we balance all three planes (and all elements on each plane) can we inhabit the "Promised Land," (the fourth plane, the plane of transcendence.)

---

[22] I have substantially oversimplified this concept. The true student should consult Carlo Suarès' *The Cipher of Genesis*, pp. 61-71. According to Suarès, the numbers from 10 to 90 describe "projections in manifestation." "The nine multiples of 100 express the exalted archetypes in their cosmic states. **The number 1000** is written with an enlarged Aleph (Aleph, in Hebrew, actually means a thousand), but it is seldom used. It **expresses a supreme power, a tremendous cosmic energy, all pervading, timeless, unthinkable.**" p. 63.

If we take the imagery of the Australian Aborigines, this idea is more easily understood. To paraphrase Marlo Morgan, the Aborigine would say: **We come from *forever*, and we go to *forever*. However, for now we are "spiritual beings having a physical experience."** And whether or not the world would "judge" us to be spiritual individuals, this physical experience includes spiritual experiences.

Abram's spiritual story is related thusly: *When the sun had gone down and it was dark, behold, a smoking fire pot and a flaming torch passed between these pieces. On that day the LORD made a covenant with Abram, saying, "To your descendants I give this land, from the river of Egypt to the great river, the river Euphrates, the land of the Kenites, the Kenizzites, the Kadmonites, the Hittites, the Perizzites, the Rephaim, the Amorites, the Canaanites, the Girgashites and the Jebusites."* Gen. 15:17-21.

Finally, we have been given a "physical" description of this "Promised Land" that our offspring are to inherit. But that's the rub, the ***Promised Land*** isn't a physical land; **it's a spiritual land.** Notice what the symbolic meanings of the various boundaries are.[23] Notice what we're being promised, at least in hang-loose thinking: **prosperity** to the point of "double prosperity," encompassing everything that we create by **extension** or that we **hunt** and (the understanding of) **they that went before.** Moreover, it is accomplished as we prostrate ourselves, keeping ourselves unprotected. For everything will be mended, healed and made whole. That which we **say** will be in compliance with true judgment (**to bend the knee**); for that is what Jah (**YHWH**) intends (**Jah has dipped**).

---

[23] Taking selected translations by Strong, the description of "the land" symbolizes: ... from the River of Egypt (**prosperity**, flooded plain; both Upper and Lower Egypt) to the Great River (Euphrates - of greater importance, **double prosperity**, river of the East). Then is seems to say that the land includes: Kenites (to create by **extension**, to procure); Kenizzites (to **hunt**); Kadmonites (Eastern ancient ones; **they that went before**); Hittites (**to prostrate**, either by violence or by confusion and fear); Perizzites (an unprotected, **unwalled village**); Rephaim (giants, related to *firstlings*, but related to **mend, heal x make whole**); Amorites (from **to say**); Canaanites (from **to bend the knee**); Jebusites (residents of Jebus [**Jah has dipped**).

The lesson of the Old Testament is the "Promised Land." On the other hand, the lesson of the New Testament is the "Kingdom of Heaven." Notice that the lesson of the Old Testament is the **possession** or **conquering** of the land, the acquiring. The lesson of the New Testament is just the opposite. It is the **relinquishment,** the letting go. Each portion of the Bible has its particular focus, but the supreme paradox is the composite lesson. **To attain the Promised Land, we must possess it; to attain the Kingdom of Heaven, we must relinquish the Promised Land.** We are simply learning to *hang loose.*

Abram hasn't learned to hang loose, yet. He is still at the level of acquiring, and he is convinced that unless he has a son he cannot get the land which was promised. Mankind hasn't changed much. We still require a physical manifestation to "prove" whatever we have hoped for has come to be. So in our "fear" and "doubt" we take things into our own hands. Conveniently, we, like Abram, can blame our feminine side. Significantly, it is the higher feminine side that suggests the action that will begin Abram's production.

Remember, we are aiming for total balance; but before the masculine and the feminine can be balanced, the two feminine expressions must be working as one – as in the earlier ratio of 2 feminine to 1 masculine being given for sacrifice. The endeavor is to allow the promise to be fulfilled. In the case of Abram, the two women must work together to enable Abram to be the *father of nations.*

The story presents this abstraction with Hagar and Sarai. Sarai is the long-time wife of Abram; Hagar is the Egyptian handmaiden of Sarai.[24] *And Sarai said to Abram, "Behold now, the LORD has prevented me from bearing children; go in to my maid; it may be that I shall obtain children by her." And Abram hearkened to the voice of Sarai. So ... Sarai, Abram's wife, took Hagar the Egyptian, her maid, and gave her to Abram her husband as a [concubine.] And he went in to Hagar, and she conceived; and when she saw that she had conceived, she looked with contempt on her mistress.* Gen. 16:2-4.

---

[24] The chapter is 16 (7), and Abram has been in Canaan for **ten** years.

In the esoteric tradition the *female* refers to those things which are not quite *stable*. The female is related to water, to emotions and passions; but at the same time, the female represents the soul. However, we are told that Abram's soul is barren. How can this be? We know that Abram is to become the father of nations; that means something has to change. What changes is that our protagonist begins to deal with this feminine side of himself, even though it is the slave-part.

This contentious feminine that we've *been connected to* for so long actually aids in our growth. Even though she is acting out of fear and mistrust, Sarai, the higher feminine, starts the action through her insistence to Abram that he lie with Hagar.[25] However, it is the lower feminine aspect that will actually bring the physical product into existence. In Abram's case it is Hagar (an Egyptian, i.e., of the world, and Sarai's handmaiden, i.e., of lesser status,) who produces the first son.

We must separate ourselves from the story for a moment, because the story pulls us down to the world's view. We're really being shown the spiritual activity that goes on in all of us. Likely, the activity will begin with less than the ideal circumstances. But at least we – like Abram – begin to produce. However, be forewarned. We may not appreciate the process that we've begun. In Abram's case, he really gets in trouble. As soon as she conceives, Hagar sees herself as greater than Sarai; and Sarai blames it all on Abram. So – in the usual habit of the conscious mind – Abram gets out of it by telling Sarai to *Deal with her as you think right.*

Needless to say, our contentious nature is not very fair. Sarai treats Hagar "harshly," and Hagar runs away. Hagar goes as far as a spring on the road to Shur, where an angel of the LORD

---

[25] A footnote in the Torah sheds some light. While Sarai says: "...perhaps I shall have a son* through her," the asterisk calls our attention to a subtle meaning for "son." The footnote explains that the expanded interpretation would add "be built up," a play on words between *ben* (son) and *banah* (build up.) p. 25. How much more meaningful it is to see the feminine as building itself through its actions.

finds her and urges her, *Go back to your mistress, and submit to her harsh treatment. ...and I will greatly increase your offspring, and they shall be too many to count.* Gen. 16:7-10.

Our lesser feminine side can get us into all sorts of apparent trouble. Because of fear or doubt or lust or jealousy or revenge or spite or anger or "whatever"... we may take the "wrong" step: we

> **Lesser Feminine Produces Ishmael**

may marry the wrong partner; we may take the unwanted job; we may conceive the unwanted child; we may contract the deadly disease; we may let loose our temper; we may say the wrong thing! And our higher feminine side is of no help. It just makes us feel worse. So, we – like Hagar – often run away toward Shur.[26] Only the urging of an angel of the LORD changes the outcome. This angel may come in the form of another person; or it may simply come from inside ourself. Regardless, it is an urging to take whatever comes and persevere – *for the LORD has paid heed to your suffering.*

In the case of Abram, the conscious mind is reassured by the birth of a son, Ishmael (God heeds). He accepts the blessing, accepting what Hagar had been told: *Ishmael will be a prolific Adam, his hand with all and the hands of all with him.*[27] Esoterically, Ishmael is not given a lesser position; his level of understanding simply is not one which will allow him to advance to the next level. Only Abram will advance. His age is 86 (14, i.e., two earthly levels). By producing a son – even through a lesser feminine expression, Abram has taken the first step toward becoming the father of nations. And the story continues.

---

[26] According to Strong, the location #7793 is in the desert, but its related definitions give a broader picture: #7791 suggests a wall going about; #7788 suggests traveling about "as a harlot or a merchant." Note that in either case, we are closed in and dependent upon others.

[27] Suarès, p. 158. The standard translation is: *"He shall be a wild ass of a man, his hand against every man and every man's hand against him; and he shall dwell over against all his kinsmen."* I accept Suarès' translation, partially, because of the numbers of the verse. Notice: it is Chapter 16 (adds up to 7), and the verse is the all-important 12. But possibly more important is Hagar's comment in verse 13: So she called the name of the LORD who spoke to her, "Thou art a God of seeing"; for she said, "Have I really seen God and remained alive after seeing him?"

> *When Abram was ninety-nine years old the LORD appeared to Abram, and said to him, "I am God Almighty;* **walk before me, and be blameless.** *And I will make my covenant between me and you, and will multiply you exceedingly." Then Abram fell on his face; and God said to him, "Behold, my covenant is with you, and you shall be the father of a multitude of nations. No longer shall your name be Abram, but your name shall be Abraham; for I have made you the father of a multitude of nations.* Gen. 17:1-5.

Further progress is likely to call for a greater sacrifice. That which will have to be sacrificed is the great attachment to the physical. It will affect him and everything that surrounds him. At this point, we have advanced. Abraham is 99, three times the level of the initiate (9+9 = 18 or 1+8), and he has now been promised even more than he was originally promised. Moreover, his higher feminine side will join in the empowerment. *As for your wife Sarai, ... her name shall be Sarah (princess).* But the whole deal depends on Abram's carrying out the dictated circumcision. And Jehovah says: *Thus shall My covenant be marked in your flesh as an everlasting pact.*

This is not a casual agreement; circumcision is an act that has repercussions on all planes. It is particularly potent on the physical level. According to Isaac Asimov it was a tradition followed by many of the peoples in the Middle East, possibly following the traditions of ancient Egypt.[28]

Aside from its symbolism, the only lucid explanation I have found for circumcision is in Carlo Suarès' *The Cipher of Genesis.* To Suarès, the effect of *circumcision* (both psychologically and physiologically) is to enable the male to establish an immediate awareness of self in order to escape the entrapment of desire for sensual pleasures after puberty. Similarly, I think the esotericist would say that only as the

---

[28] According to Isaac Asimov, *Asimov's Guide to the Bible,* Avenel, p. 199, Circumcision was not confined to the Israelites. "It was practiced among the ancient Egyptians and among most of the Semites of the western portion of the Fertile Crescent (perhaps through Egyptian cultural influence.)" Circumcision is not a sacrifice of this portion of the human anatomy. Ausubel calls it "a rite whose object it was to link each generation with all before it in the symbolic continuity of identity." Nathan Ausubel, *The Book of Jewish Knowledge,* p. 114.

individual can harness the conscious mind and keep himself/herself free from the snare of the sensual is his/her attention on the spiritual.[29]

"Israel" To Be "Circumcised" The question of circumcision brings us back to the challenge we have been given all along. Do we look at this earthly world with its senses, desires, passions and titillations – concentrating our attention on these elements? Or do we look at the earthly world and its attractions – knowing that there is something beyond these appearances? Do we look on Noah's *nakedness*, or do we walk backward and cover him over? We're determining where our concentration is. Abram, now empowered as Abraham, has taken a physical, conscious step – the covenant is marked

---

[29] Carlo Suarès writes: We believe that circumcision is an important factor in the Genesis of man (or resurrection of Aleph). ... The foreskin, in enveloping the gland, shelters it from all contact. Because of this protection, the non-circumcised child lives until the age of puberty as if that organ, as a sexual organ, did not exist – except in those momentary states of excitation to which ... the child is subject.... It is not until puberty that the gland undergoes exterior contacts sufficient to establish an active transmission throughout the whole sexual system. Until that time, the system can be compared to a dead-end street, ... inasmuch as the fixation of the centre of interest is blocked at the entrance.

Suarès continues: The practice of circumcision on the young child results in (1) a physiological shock (2) a partial desensitizing of the gland ... followed by (3) an indefinite prolongation of the sexual shock in the whole organism... The trauma of circumcision immediately introduces within that psyche a mobile element; it is ...prolonged indefinitely and radiates with in the vital centres during their formative periods.

Thus, in the non-circumcised, the psyche is crystallized around a birth trauma ... The younger the child, the more malleable he is, so that these reactions act upon him like a mold. This procedure is violently troubled by circumcision at eight days... Instead of a slow condensation of fluctuating elements determined by the surroundings, we find an active, awakened, vital centre in full process of organization, capable of transforming its reactions to the environment into purely individual elements. Not only does the individual consciousness – the "I" – construct itself more rapidly, but its foundations are laid in a living, flexible element constantly related to the development of the individual. ...

When, at the age of two or three months, the intelligent coordination of movement begins to occur, there is already, in the circumcised child, a subconscious "nucleus" around the sensorial activity which engendered it. The psychophysical exchanges become intense... Later on, when the male centrifugal force assumes its sexual character, it finds that its "enemy" (the psyche)... has proclaimed itself master of the house. What takes place psychologically is clear enough. The sensibility of the sexual organ has been dulled ... Thus sensuality becomes imaginative but does not disrupt the individual's consciousness. ... Instead of the man being carried away, his mind rules... He does not lose consciousness of himself. He cannot possibly lose this awareness during the act of coitus.

Circumcision at puberty. Quite different is the result of circumcision... at the age of thirteen ... as is the case among followers of the Moslem faith. With the violent sexual shock, at the prodrome [onset] of puberty, the sensorial perceptions suddenly become purely sexual. This drains (pulls) the masculine energy towards sex, maintaining it there in a continually erotic state. As a consequence of this practice, a stoppage of the intellectual faculties and even a regression due to sexual excess may be produced. Suarès, *Cipher of Genesis*, pp. 221-227.

70

in his *flesh as an everlasting pact* with God. Abraham is 99; his son Ishmael is 13.[30]

Circumcision symbolically represents the sensual; and speaking of the "sensual," we haven't heard from Lot for quite a while. Supposedly, he has been doing his thing in Sodom. Remember that he chose the richness of the Jordan plain when he moved away from Abram. He's been there ever since, except for the time when he was abducted by the four kings and then rescued by Abram. Now, he has a wife and several daughters, of whom the older ones are married, for he has sons-in-law. Remember, Lot's name means *a veil* or *covering*. He represents the veiled portion of us, that which is not quite out in the open, and he lives in Sodom (to scorch). Fire of any sort in the Bible refers to burning up the "sacrifice" – whether on the altar or in the process of "refining us to finest gold."

Sodom and Lot It is Chapter 18 (9), twice the number of the initiate. The promise has been given, the covenant has been made and proven by circumcision, and another son – this time from the higher feminine – is on its way. It is time for Abraham's hidden nature to be eliminated; but we're fond of it. We're attached to it, so we argue with God to spare Sodom. God finally agrees, if there are "ten" innocent ones. Of course, we know the answer. As the two angels discover, Lot is the only "innocent" in Sodom; even his sons-in-law don't believe his warning. So Sodom is to be destroyed *because the outcry against them before the Lord has become so great that the Lord has sent us to destroy it. Gen. 19:13*

Our earthly vision rebels at the thought of a "loving" God destroying anything; but, such rebellion reveals our misunderstanding. We are still operating at the post-Edenic

---

[30] Gen. 17:24,25. This explains Suarès' noticed discrepancy between Jewish circumcision at 8 days and Moslem circumcision at age 13. Ishmael often is considered the progenitor of the Arabs. However, Nathan Ausubel disagrees with Suarès, saying that Moslems also circumcise at 8 days. Ausubel, *The Book of Jewish Knowledge,* p. 226.

level. We accept "death" as a final happening; we do not remember that *we come from forever, go to forever, and are a spiritual being having a physical experience.* The physical man may undergo some destructions of one type or another, but the spiritual man will continue.

If we consider Lot as his own person, Lot and his two "innocent" daughters survive – even though the old, worn-out feminine side looks back and becomes crystallized. If we consider Lot as a hidden portion of Abraham, the "innocent things that are hidden" remain, but they are relegated to "a little place." Whichever way, we are assured... *God was mindful of Abraham and removed Lot from the midst of the upheaval.* Gen. 19:29.

We could stop the story of Lot here, but the remainder of the chapter contains a story which we should address: the story of incest between Lot and his two daughters. On the surface, the story explains the existence of two tribes of the area, the Moabites and the Ammonites, but esoterically it emphasises that even the hidden portions of us will eventually "dwell in the hill country" and will bring forth *something.* However, these "things" are conceived because of fear (the girls were afraid that they would never be approached by potential husbands, and so they get Lot drunk to lie with him); and because Lot isn't even aware of the contact, what is produced isn't on a high level. It's just *produced.* The descendants of these incests will have to be dealt with in later times as enemies of Israel. Nevertheless, their being dealt with works for good.

This brings us to something which Abraham will not understand; only the level of Jesus can understand it. Jesus says it in several different ways: *As ye judge, ye shall be judged... As ye sow, so shall ye reap ... "For no good tree bears bad fruit, nor again does a bad tree bear good fruit; for each tree is known by its own fruit. For figs are not gathered from thorns, nor are grapes picked from a bramble bush.* ***The good man out of the good treasure of his heart produces good, and the evil man out of his evil treasure produces evil;*** *for out of the abundance of the heart his mouth speaks. "* Lk. 6:43-45.

Lot is not an evil man; he is just frightened and unsure of God's love. Nor is Abraham a good man; he is just going along with what seems to be given him. When Abraham takes on the properties of Lot, i.e., when he becomes frightened and unsure, he gets in trouble – as he does with Abimelech.

Abimelech is the king of Gerar (to destroy roughly). Again we are given a symbolic story. Abraham hasn't progressed very far. He's still in the parched land, Negeb. He is not receiving as should a "child of God," and he camps (not a camp that will be permanent, but a sojourn) between Kadesh (a holy sanctuary) and Shur (a wall going about). ... And once more he passes Sarah off as his sister. As it was in Egypt, Abraham again fears that he will be killed "because of my wife." He **judges** that God's power is insufficient in **this place**. Again, he brings difficulties on those with whom he's dealing; and it makes Abimelech and his women barren.

Notice what Abraham has done. He is not trusting God; he is using his own judgment (based on the physical); then he acts out of fear. He thinks that God is "limited." He thinks God might protect him sometimes, but not this time and place. Abraham thinks he has to protect himself. He tells Abimelech: *when God caused me to wander from my father's house, I said to her, '... at every place to which we come, say of me, He is my brother.'" Gen. 20:13.*

Remember what Jesus said? *out of the abundance of the heart [a] mouth speaks.* This is what we all have to learn, and we will be in a parched place until we learn it. What we receive from life says nothing about the amount of work we've done; it says nothing about how "good" we've been. What we receive from life reveals what is in our heart, what we *expect*. OOOh! That's hard to take, isn't it?

But, if we "come clean" as Abraham does here, everything works to our benefit. If we are willing to look at ourselves and be totally honest with our surroundings and those surrounding us, we, like Abraham, will come out on top. Abimelech gives Abraham sheep and oxen, male and female slaves, and tells him, *settle wherever you please.* Abraham could not ask for more. In addition, Abimelech gives Abraham a thousand pieces of silver to *vindicate* Sarah and "to clear her before everyone." Abimelech (father + king) elevates the feminine to its rightful place. As sister, instead of wife, she is Abraham's equal.

It is interesting that Sarah is elevated to such a position. But this "higher feminine" would likely not be in this position if not for the insight of the "lower feminine," Hagar. Remember, it is Hagar who first "sees" correctly, and she says to the Lord: *Thou art a God of seeing.* For she said, *Have I really seen God and remained alive after seeing him?* Gen. 16:13.

Now, Abraham is ready for his "true" son. His feminine side is beginning to "see," and his feminine side is elevated and of one mind. – Hagar has to leave. – Only the elevated, single-minded feminine produces the son that is truly like us.

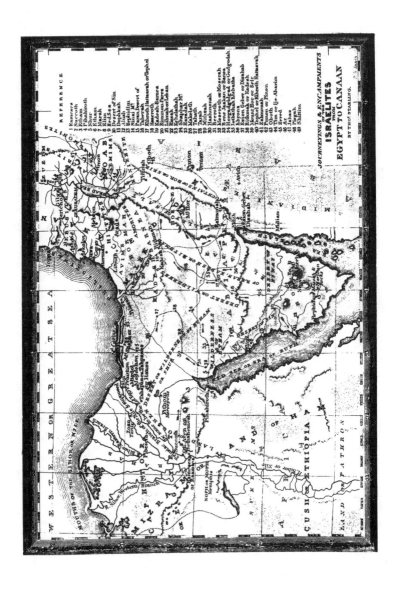

JOURNEYINGS & ENCAMPMENTS
OF THE
ISRAELITES
FROM
EGYPT TO CANAAN

BY THOS STARLING.

Chapter Four
Abraham and Isaac

*Now the LORD said to Abram, "Go from your country ... to the land that I will show you. And I will make of you a great nation, and I will bless you, and make your name great, so that you will be a blessing. **I will bless those who bless you, and him who curses you I will curse; and by you all the families of the earth shall bless themselves.**" Gen. 12:1-3.*

Although he cannot see what YHWH has promised, Abram continues on his journey; and the "fruits" of the promise increase as his understanding increases.
*When Abram was ninety-nine years old the LORD appeared to Abram, and said to him, "**I am God Almighty; walk before me, and be blameless.**¹ And I will ... multiply you exceedingly." Then Abram fell on his face; and God said to him, "Behold, my covenant is with you, and **you shall be the father of a multitude of nations.**" Gen. 17:1-4.*

Now Abram is empowered with *ha*, the Hebrew letter representing empowerment (ה). He is now Abra**ha**m and his wife is Sar**ah**.² He is a unified expression of this YHWH. Apparently Abraham knows that he is more than just a "physically bound" man, for – in keeping with the **LAW** that we are judged as we judge – he is assured he will receive more.

What is God's promise to us ? Isn't it the same as to Abraham? Jesus, perceiving it as a | Only "One" Promise | connection between Father and child, said: ... *what man of you, if his son asks him for bread, will give him a stone? Or if he asks for a fish, will give him a serpent? ... how much more will your Father who is in heaven give good things to those who ask him! So **whatever you wish that men would do to you, do so to them; for this is the law and the prophets.** Mt. 7:9-12*

---

¹ Loosely translated, the Hebrew reads:... YHWH ... said to him, "*I Am El Shaddai.*" The God which Abraham is expressing (YHWH) is saying that "He" actually possess unlimited power. "He" is *ALMIGHTY EL.* There is much more to be realized than this earthly expression. (See pages 43-45.)

²Abram means *high father;* and Abraham means *to be populous.* Sarai means *dominative,* coming from a word meaning *the head person,* while Sarah means *a female noble, princess.* Notice the inversion of the "**h**" and "**a**" between Abraham and Sarah.

But there's God's little provision in the second part of the promise that says *walk before me, and be blameless*. Jesus says the same thing in another way: *Enter by the narrow gate,* explaining:... *for the gate is wide and the way is easy, that leads to destruction, and those who enter by it are many. For the gate is narrow and the way is hard, that leads to life, and those who find it are few.* Mt. 7:13-14.

We should have a big, fancy type-face for *life*, for by *life* we mean something more than just existence. We are talking about *life* that is vital and alive, fully connected to that which created it and all other expressions of this "creator" – whether these expressions are aware or not. Even more instructive is Jesus' comment that *those who find it are few.* Notice, we have returned to the same old question. How do we judge life? We can enter through the wide gate, seeing ourselves as isolated and separated from an unknowable God or system; or we can enter through the narrow gate, being the "righteous person" – he or she who sees himself/herself as the child of God.

Abraham has progressed by way of the narrow gate; he is among the *"few."* Except for a couple of miscalculations prompted by fear, he has expressed this "righteous" mindset; and now he's given a legitimate son. This son evidences at the symbolic Chapter Twenty-one (3x7), and he is named Isaac.[3] He is to supersede Ishmael.

Ishmael and Isaac

When I was a child – since all religious questions were directed to my grandfather – I was indoctrinated with the judgmental Puritanism of the Victorian Age. To the Victorians, just the stigma of "illegitimacy" was sufficient to condemn Ishmael. But I couldn't help asking what's wrong with Ishmael; why isn't he "enough" to establish all these nations and multitudes? Abraham wonders, too. He says to this almighty God: *Oh that Ishmael might live by Your favor!* Gen. 17:18.

Don't we approach God with the same appeal? We long for the total expression – the *Promised Land* – and all the

---

[3] Strong distinguishes between *Yitschâq* (laughter, but mockery) and *Jitschak* (he laughed). See #3327 and #3446. One wonders if we are involved in a "pun" here, and we get to *judge* as we will.

blessings that come with it, but we're reluctant to let the lesser manifestation go. The difficulty lies in the fact that the appearance of the "legitimate" expression likely will mean that the lesser expression is no longer a part of us, and we're not sure we trust God to give us what He has promised. However, eventually – as with Sarah– the more intuitive part of us will insist that *the son of that slave shall not share in the inheritance with my son Isaac.* The heightened feminine side of us can distinguish between those things in our life that are of "high quality" as opposed to those of "lesser quality."

It has been my experience that when my conscious mind refuses to "let the lesser items go," some incident happens that "forces" the "letting go." Most of these "items" which my conscious mind holds on to are people and relationships or jobs and financial conditions. In both areas, I find myself reluctant to accept change. What is difficult to remember is that the lesser expression doesn't have to be "destroyed" or transformed as were the senses. The lesser expression, whether it is a disloyal friend, an unappreciative boss or an anemic bank account, will simply go its own way and continue to express at its own level.
As Hagar cries, an angel of God calls to her: *"What troubles you, Hagar? Fear not, for God has heeded the cry of the boy where he is. Come, lift up the boy and hold him by the hand, for I will make a great nation of him."* Gen. 21:17-18. And we know that Ishmael prospered, because he is credited with twelve sons all of whom camped together *opposite from Egypt.* Gen. 25:18.

It is our "fear" and our "lack of trust" that keep us from recognizing that we can "let things go." The world is not dependent on our "control" or even participation; divine order will prevail. Although the lesser side of us can function and prosper in the world, it does not produce at the highest level. Let's use the symbolism. For instance, let's say that we live with an emotional mindset of fear. This mindset will produce expressions similar to the "slave-son" Ishmael.

Job said it nicely: *For the thing which I greatly feared is come upon me, and that which I was afraid of is come unto me. I was not in safety, neither had I rest, neither was I quiet; yet trouble came.* Job 3:25,26.

Only when our feminine side becomes empowered – only when we are able to begin to recognize our fears and tell them to leave – can the "non-slave-son" Isaac inherit. Until then, the "slave-son" will remain.

Those things which are symbolized by the "slave-son" status are those things in our lives that are a "lesser expression." It is this "slave-son" which we will produce as long as we are coming from fear. Genesis evaluates Ishmael's condition with: *He lived in the wilderness of Paran; and his mother got a wife for him from the land of Egypt.* Gen. 21:21 Even though he stays in the "wilderness," he does pretty well, dying at age 137 (11).Gen. 25:17.

I'm going to make a giant leap here. Ishmael represents the first product of "we who have been promised everything." This product isn't quite up to par; in fact it's rated by the wilderness of Paran (no pun intended) which can be translated loosely as "to explain oneself." Can we see ourselves in this condition? Intellectually, we know we have been promised great things, but we are not quite convinced. We still feel we have to "explain ourselves."

> **The LAW Requires Righteous Speech**

This relates back to an obscure statement earlier in Genesis. Abram, in a night vision was again being given the "promise," but the vision ended with an enigmatic statement: "*... for the iniquity of the Amorites is not yet complete.*" Gen.15:16. (See page 64.) Abram was told that his "offspring" could (or would) not return to occupy the "Promised Land" until the "iniquity of the Amorites was complete." This makes sense only if we use a hang-loose definition. If the iniquity of the Amorites is our tendency to *speak unrighteously*, then Ishmael's fate falls in line with the iniquity of the Amorites.[4]

---

[4] Amorites refers to those living in a prominent region (such as a mountain); but the name comes from a primitive root, loosely defined as *to say.*

A parenthetical comment is appropriate here. To "speak unrighteously" is to say that which is **untrue**. For instance, knowing that the truth about us is that we are "made in the image of God," any statement such as I am evil, I am sick, I am poor, etc. – which denies our true nature – is untrue. It is unrighteous speech. Conversely, any statement – such as "I am a child of God" – which affirms our true nature and our true relationship with the Divine is **righteous speech.**

Matthew has Jesus state it unequivocally.[5] *"... I tell you, on the day of judgment men will render account for every careless word they utter; for by your words you will be justified, and by your words you will be condemned."* Mt. 12:36,37.

This is the **LAW!**[6] *...with the judgment you pronounce (speak) you will be judged!*

Abraham (and we, as we begin to climb the Mountain,) are just beginning to recognize the **LAW**; and until we hold to this knowledge, the climb will not progress. Moreover, we will be tested time and time again (often with similar situations and personalities involved), each instance giving us the opportunity to prove our knowledge of the LAW. At Chapter Twenty-one, verse 22, Abraham is given a chance to prove his knowledge of the LAW. We have already met the "personality" that will test Abraham's knowledge. It is Abimelech, this time accompanied by the chief of his troops, Phicol. The meaning of the names is very important here. Abimelech combines the *ab* (father) with *mâlak* which can be interpreted to mean *to induct into royalty*. Phicol's name shows that he's here to see if Abraham has learned his lesson or if he is just "full of hot air."[7]

---

[5] Notice what Matthew says by the placement of these two lines. The first line is Chapter 12, verse 36 (3 x 12); the second line is 37, a prime number which adds up to 10. The statement cannot be broken apart ... *by your words you will be justified, and by your words you will be condemned.*

[6] Check back to page 59.

[7] Strong. Ab (1) + mâlak from *to induct into royalty*. Phicol is from *the mouth as means of blowing.*

Abimelech tells Abraham: *God is with you in all that you do; now therefore swear to me here by God that you will not deal falsely with me or with my offspring or with my posterity, but as I have dealt loyally with you, you will deal with me and with the land where you have sojourned.* Gen. 21:22,23.

Abraham Usually Follows The LAW   This could be the world's testing of our virtue. The world can see that we are producing (one way or another), and it wants reassurance that we won't try to "cheat" again. Abraham says, *I swear it.* But simultaneously, he challenges Abimelech for that which Abraham claims to be his, i.e., the well which Abimelech's servants had appropriated. Abraham still cares for the world's opinion. However, the suggestion that this is "induction into royalty" puts the test on a higher level. The test is more for ourselves than for the world. At this moment Abraham is beginning to invoke his "sonship."

The "well" for which Abraham challenges Abimelech is the "spring" to which Hagar fled. In other words, it is not a well (which requires labor to produce); it is a natural occurrence. It is easy for us to expect reward for our labor, but it requires a higher mindset to recognize the fruits of God as ours.

However, Abraham isn't quite as confident as he might be; he still feels that he needs to establish his right to what he considers his. Consequently, he gives Abimelech seven ewes to agree that he, Abraham, "dug this well." (As we *climb* at the lower levels of the Mountain, we may still feel we have to convince the world that what we are given is rightly ours.).[8]

The place where all this activity takes place is called Beer-sheba (well of oath), and there Abraham plants a tamarisk bush. Abraham's confidence in his sonship is not sufficient to warrant an oak (a tree requiring a great source of water); he can handle only a desert bush that requires little water. And we are

---

[8] Does this mean that those who take without laboring are operating at a higher mindset? I don't think so. The test is the difference between the person who labors because of fear that he/she will not be provided for– **as opposed to the person who labors to the glory of God, knowing that he/she will be provided for.**

told that Abraham resided (RSV uses *sojourned*) in the land of the Philistines for a long time.[9]

We are almost finished with Abraham. We're almost finished with this first stage of our climb. We have only the final test for this level of the Mountain; and when God calls, Abraham answers, "Here I Am."

Abraham's Final Test

Again I'm going to do some hang-loose reasoning. Whether or not the lessons (all that has happened since Chapter Twelve of Genesis) have been learned is going to be proven in one test.[10] The Elohim tells Abraham to take that which is most precious to him – his son, Isaac – and go to the land of *Moriah* ("to see" Jah) and *offer him there as a burnt offering on one of the heights.* It's probably not the "answer" Abraham expected when he said, "Here I Am."

Abraham's "Here I AM" has greater implication than what appears on the surface. Loosely, the passage implies that the Elohim is testing whether Abraham's "speech" (what he "says" is his mindset) is what he "sees."[11] This I Am opportunity will come to us numerous times in our climb. Of all biblical phrases, it is the most esoteric, but we will understand it only as we progress through the climb.

Here I Am

At this point, this is the first time the Bible has allowed an individual to use the phrase. (All the other instances have had "God" saying it.) It was reversed by Cain who questioned God, *Am I my brother's keeper?* Cain (the original form – which was powered by an *inner light*) didn't quite have it right. My intuition tells me that the entire purpose of the climb is to come to the place where we can say *I AM*, knowing that we produce (say) what we hold in our mindset (what we see).

---

[9] Philistines comes from an ancient root *to roll (wallow) oneself.*

[10] The Torah reads: *God put Abraham to the test.* p. 35.

[11] *Moriah* comes from *to see (to perceive)* plus the "iah" ending which is a contraction for Jah, *Lord most vehement.*

Abraham proceeds through the test, even to the point of binding Isaac and placing him on top of the firewood. Just as he picks up the knife to "slay his son," an angel of YHWH calls to him. Again he answers "Here *I AM*."

As a child, I was horrified by the story of Isaac. I could not accept that this father was willing to sacrifice his child. It is only as a parent that I understand the story. Abraham places absolutely nothing above his obedience to God, even that which is most precious to him. Fortunately, we are not called upon to destroy those things which are most dear to us; we are called upon simply to be willing to "let them go." And, if you are like me, the most difficult example of this test is with regard to my children. Yet, like Abraham, we will be given a test (or tests, until we comply) to allow us to "let go," – to release our children (or whatever we hold so important) into God's hands.

This sounds simplistic, doesn't it. I remember many years ago I used to scorn strong believers when they said this; but numerous "tests" that I have been given have convinced me that the only way to deal with life's challenges is to "let go" – to stop thinking we, ourselves, have to "create life." Isn't this the challenge that Abraham is facing at this moment? Isn't this the test of whether we have learned what is given to mankind to learn? The question is whether we are willing to sacrifice "the world" to attain the "Promised Land?" Abraham's test is mostly symbolic, even though it relates to the custom of human sacrifice practiced by some at the time. If the story is literal, then God intervenes in a potential human sacrifice, following the admonition given earlier that: *Whoever sheds the blood of man, by man shall his blood be shed; for God made man in his own image.* Gen. 9:6.

But I don't think this is intended as a literal sacrifice;

it is a test of "willingness." Significantly, God says: *"Do not lay your hand on the lad or do anything to him; for now I know that you fear God, seeing you have not withheld your son, your only son, from me." And Abraham lifted up his eyes and looked, and behold, behind him was a ram, caught in a thicket by his horns; and Abraham went and took the ram, and offered it up as a burnt offering instead of his son. So Abraham called the name of that place The LORD will provide; as it is said to this day, "**On the mount of the LORD it shall be provided.**"* Gen. 22:12-14.

And Abraham lifted up his eyes and looked, and behold, behind him was a ram, caught in a thicket by his horns; and Abraham went and took the ram, and offered it up as a burnt offering instead of his son. Gen. 22:13.

Do you notice Abraham's present mind-set: **"On the mount** of the LORD **it shall be provided."** Abraham has finally triumphed. What a supreme paradox. We are not required to eliminate that which is so precious to us; we simply must be *willing* to do so. Then, *it shall be provided.* Each of us, as we climb the Mountain, will learn this truth.

Abraham has learned the truth, and he has learned the lesson! The representative of God calls to him again and once again increases the promise: *"By myself I have sworn, says the LORD, because you have done this, and have not withheld your son, your only son, I will indeed bless you, and I will multiply your descendants as the stars of heaven and as the sand which is on the seashore. And your descendants shall possess the gate of their enemies, and by your descendants shall all the nations of the earth bless themselves, **because you have obeyed my voice.**" So Abraham returned to his [servants], and they arose and went together to Beer-sheba; and Abraham dwelt at Beer-sheba.* Gen. 22:15-19.

Because he "sees" as he "speaks," Abraham (every aspect of him) is to be blessed without measure; and by what he produces (his sons), all the nations will bless themselves.

Abraham Passes The Test

With each major character which the Bible presents to us, the sons (in a few cases, daughters) represent spiritual growth in the individual. Of all of the sons, the name most difficult to interpret is "Isaac," for Isaac means *he who laughs*. As mentioned (fn.3), there are two implications for the meaning. One implies a mockery; the other implies a reflection, a devotion. Using our hang-loose approach, Isaac (the heightened Abraham) – this consciousness that is just beginning the actual climb of the Mountain – may be expressing both implications. In the light of "mockery," he doesn't totally believe the promise that was given to his father. In the light of "devotion," he continues to reflect on the promise, having no other choice since he is his father's son.

The son, Isaac, (the fruits of the individual Abraham) is to thrive; but – as with all triumphs in life – Abraham's achievement brings change. What changes is that the new masculine expression – Isaac – will require a higher feminine aspect. Therefore, at age 127, it is time for Sarah to die.

Even the "heightened" feminine expression must be replaced by a higher expression. This emotional (feminine) side of us began as Sarai (dominative or contentious), and gained empowerment as Sarah; but even with the name change, it is still **contention,** something which brings difficulties to the conscious portion of us.

This "contention" has helped Abraham reach the numeration designating the initiate and the third plane (100); but Sarah, herself has reached the level of 1000.[12] Never-theless, Sarah dies at 127, which added together comes to 10 (a new beginning).[13] But first, the old emotional nature has to be "buried," as the King James version says, *"...out of my sight."*

---

[12] To Sarah [Abimelech] said, "Behold, I have given your brother **a thousand pieces of silver**; it is **your vindication** in the eyes of all who are with you; and **before every one you are righted."** Gen. 20:16. See pp. 63-64, fn. 22 regarding #1000.

[13] The new feminine side of us will be akin to Milcah and Nahor (see page 46). Milcah indicates *counsel;* Nahor indicates *snorting nostrils (determination).*

We Westerners are so "hung up" on death and burial that this incident in the story of Abraham never seems to get the scrutiny it deserves.[14] Remember that the "righteous" Jew is not to touch a "dead" body.[15] Even Jesus made the enigmatic statement: *Let the dead bury the dead.* Using an esoteric explanation, the attitude toward "dead" bodies makes sense.

Esoterically, "the dead" refers to those things which have outlived their time, those things which are the opposite of "live." It is those things which are no longer vital. It is those habits, those connections, those reactions, – even those "fruits"– which are no longer beneficial in our

> **Bury Sarah**
> **Out of Sight**

lives. And like dead bodies, *the dead* cannot be retained. Like "dead bodies" they become "poisonous" if they are allowed to lie around. Consequently, they must be buried "out of our sight."

If we were of the consciousness of Jesus, we could say, *Let the dead bury the dead*; we could just walk away and know that the habit, the connection ... the whatever... was "buried" for good. But at the Abraham level of consciousness, he (and we) must take care that the whole "burial" is accomplished. And, like Abraham, we must take care that the "burial ground" is proper and is properly paid for.

Consequently: *[Abraham] said to them, "If you are willing that I should **bury my dead out of my sight,** hear me, and entreat for me Ephron the son of Zohar, that he may give me the cave of Machpelah, which he owns; it is at the end of his field. For the full price let him give it to me... as a possession for a burying place." Now Ephron ... answered Abraham in the hearing of the Hittites, ..., "No, my lord, **hear me**; I give you the field, and I give you the cave that is in it... bury your dead." Then Abraham bowed down before the people of the land. And he said to Ephron in the hearing of the people of the land, "But if you will, **hear me**; I will give the price*

---

[14] It is interesting that the new translation of the Torah eliminates a phrase that is found in both the RSV and King James, i.e. *that I may bury my dead out of my sight.* But the Hebrew has two similar words right next to each other. It is almost as though it is saying: "... bury the dead in a sepulchre ... or anywhere ... just bury the dead."

If I'm correct, "hung up" is also a *surfers'* term. It is a derogative verb which refers to mounting a wave that is too big, or unmanageable; thus one does not proceed. That's a fairly good description of our attitude toward death, isn't it?

[15] If we accept the *esoteric* meaning for "dead," we may be nearing accepting and understanding the *esoteric* meaning for "righteous."

of the field; accept it from me, that I may bury my dead there." Ephron answered Abraham, "My lord, listen to me; a piece of land worth four hundred shekels of silver, what is that between you and me? Bury your dead." Abraham agreed with Ephron; and ... weighed out... the silver which he had named..., four hundred shekels of silver,....So the field of Ephron in Machpelah, which was to the east of Mamre, the field with the cave which was in it and all the trees that were in the field, throughout its whole area, was made over to Abraham as a possession in the presence of the Hittites,....., Abraham buried Sarah his wife in the cave of the field of Machpelah east of Mamre (that is, Hebron) in the land of Canaan. The field and the cave that is in it were made over to Abraham as a possession for a burying place by the Hittites.
Gen. 23:8-20

Unless interpreted esoterically, Abraham's actions are a pompous show of pride; but with an esoteric interpretation, Abraham's actions represent what happens to us as we climb the Mountain. Repeatedly through our climb, it will be necessary for us to "bury our dead." It will be necessary for us to totally eliminate certain portions of our lives. It will be necessary to deal with Ephron, the Hittite. "Ephron" means fawn-like. In other words, that with which we're dealing appears gentle and timid; but we know (and feel) the terror implied by the fact that he's a Hittite.[16] Moreover, the entire transaction takes place within the sight and hearing of the Hittite people. Possibly this means that we must "bury our dead" within full sight of that or those of whom we are so afraid. We must be willing to "publicly" face the "terror" which we feel.

Being human isn't terribly complicated. Although the hidden portions of us sometimes bring "glitches," most of the time the conscious mind runs the show; and the conscious mind is organized by habits which it follows. We establish habits for thinking, breathing, speaking, eating, eliminating; we establish habits for reactions, for relationships. At this point, the conscious mind – Abraham – is changing a habit.

---

[16] The Hittites were an Indo-European sea people (possibly Minoan survivors of the explosion on Crete). They may have been related to the Hyksos Kings who ruled Egypt for a time and may have been Joseph's Pharaoh. They invaded Palestine as well as all lands next to the Mediterranean; their presence prompted terror because they had iron and chariots – two things which the Hebrews lacked at this time.

Even though "terror" offers the land for free, Abraham must pay the full price. Notice he pays with a second level of the natural order, i.e., 400; but he is not paying with the most valuable commodity. He pays with silver, not gold. Moreover, the land which is purchased (both literally and symbolically) contains more than just a cave for a single burial. It is in *Machpelah* (to fold together, to repeat) facing Mamre (vigor); and it includes *the field with its cave and all the trees anywhere within the confines of the field.*

Be reminded that there were **oaks** at Mamre; therefore, **oaks** are a possibility. Each time we're faced with a challenge, we're getting a little braver – a little more confident. These challenges "fold together and repeat" themselves; and since they do, we can learn new habits that will eventually allow us to triumph over the challenges. Someday, we will plant an **oak** instead of a tamarisk. But the planting of *oaks* is for a higher level of consciousness. The present time is for heightening the feminine expression. It is time for Isaac (the fruits of Abraham) to take a wife, not from among the daughters of the Canaanites (those who see only the physical expression), but from a higher expression (those who know there is more than just the physical). *You shall go to my father's house, to my kindred, and get a wife for my son.* Gen. 24:38.

Nahor (determination) was the brother of Abraham, married to their niece Milcah (counsel), supposedly sister of Lot (veiled). They produced a son, Bethuel.[17] It is he who is the father of Rebekah (fettered by beauty), sister to Laban (shining thoughts). Finally, in place of contention, the Abraham consciousness (now through Isaac, its higher expression) will be joined to a feminine expression that comes from *counsel* and *determination*. United with this expression, Isaac will produce more than Abraham did.

---

[17] Bethuel is called (Gen. 25:19) *the Aramean of Paddan-aram.* The name Bethu'el implies being "broken in pieces" by God, and *Aramean* (and *aram)* comes from a root meaning *to be elevated. Paddan* comes from a root which means *to extend.* Paddan-aram then is *a plateau of this elevated land.*

On the surface Isaac appears to be the most unimportant of the patriarchs. He does nothing of any note to the world. He allows himself to be sacrificed – almost – then he goes about re-digging wells. Moreover, each time he re-digs a well, he's challenged by outside forces – and he moves on. Isaac's tendency to "move on" doesn't speak well for him. Yet, when he is observed esoterically, his level of consciousness is essential for the development that is taking place. Isaac internalizes the lessons learned by Abraham. If the climb is to continue – if the development of our consciousness is to progress from the nature of those who have gone before, i.e., Adam, Noah, Abram, Abraham – Isaac must survive and must re-dig his father's wells (a total of seven). But first, he must unite with this higher feminine – Rebekah. Not the highest form of the feminine, Rebekah, nevertheless, is an advancement over Sarah.

Isaac Marries Rebekah

Her name (fettered by beauty) indicates that she has some drawbacks, and certainly her actions when her two sons are grown bring question to her level of expression. However, she is necessary. Why? The counsel, determination, and beauty (slightly tarnished, but beauty, nevertheless,) are necessary for us to progress to the next level of consciousness. At this point, Isaac is 40 years old, and (having "inherited" the attributes of his father) is an *initiate*.[18] But, since we know that Isaac is going to pass the accomplishments of his father, we can infer that true spiritual development requires development beyond primary *initiation*. *Now Isaac had come from Beerlahairoi, and was dwelling in the Negeb. And **Isaac went out to meditate** in the field in the evening; and **he lifted up his eyes** and looked, and behold, there were camels coming. And **Rebekah lifted up her eyes, and when she saw Isaac, she alighted from the camel**, and said to the servant, "Who is the man yonder, walking in the field to meet us?" The servant said, "It is my master." ... And the servant told Isaac all the things that he had done. Then Isaac brought her into the tent, and took Rebekah, and she became his wife; and he loved her. So Isaac was comforted after his mother's death. Gen. 24:62-67.*

---

[18] Varying according to the culture, *initiation* is a formalized bestowal of the higher wisdom accepted by that culture. It is not available to everyone, only to those who have served an apprenticeship and passed the *tests*. In some ways, Isaac's near sacrifice resembles certain initiatory ceremonies.

Notice the numbers involved here. It is Chapter Twenty-four **(2x12)** of Genesis, and the verses are **62** through **67**. The numbers used are particularly interesting in light of the fact that this Genesis 24 has double the number of verses found in each of the preceding chapters.[19] Consequently, we're being told that something special is taking place.

My intuition sees it this way: We are at the second sequence of perfection, and at this point the initiate is given greater blessings (#8-plumpness) which can ultimately expand to that which extends beyond (#13-added to perfection).

We are told that Isaac is settled in Negeb. Do you remember Negeb? It means "wilderness," and many years earlier Abraham started out for it. Esoterically, "the wilderness" always precedes spiritual development. Moses had to wander in the "wilderness" for 40 years. Jesus was in the "wilderness" for 40 days. Isaac lives in the wilderness, and at this point – when he meets the new feminine expression – has just come back from the vicinity of Beer-lahai-roi. Simply because of the numbers involved, I suspect that we are being told something quite different from what appears on the surface of this narration. Again, let's try some hang-loose thinking. "Beer-lahai-roi" is translated as "well of a living (One) my seer," but the words suggest more.[20] My hang-loose thinking says it this way: We are evaluating Isaac's "expression." Isaac isn't much different from his half-brother Ishmael; but instead of parched land, he "sees." He is different in that he has "dug" and found something "alive" in himself.

---

[19] Don't you find it strange that this chapter of Genesis is so long? The designated verses in chapter 24 (2x12) of Genesis are far greater than in any of the other chapters. Interestingly, this last quotation begins with 62 (8) and ends with 67 (13). In "hang loose" thinking, the designation puts Isaac where he is getting the "beginning of plumpness," and he progresses to that "added above perfection."

[20] Using the sounds, verse 62 reads: Isaac *bow bow* to come, to go *be'er* from primitive root *to dig; also to explain* be'er_la-chay_ro'iy *to dig + living + seer (vision)* yashab *to dwell or remain* negeb 'erets *parched land.* Isaac expresses as in a parched land, but also still has a remnant of "explaining." He is not very far from Ishmael's expression.

If you remember, Ishmael's expression is *explaining himself*. He speaks "unrighteously." Moreover, he is still under the influence of a "lesser" feminine expression; his mother gets him a wife *from the land of Egypt,* (from the world). On the other hand, Isaac has "dug" inside himself and found something "alive." His father's servant brings him a feminine expression that combines *counsel* and *determination*.

There isn't much obvious difference between Ishmael and Isaac. There isn't much obvious difference between our "lesser expression" and our "greater expression." We may still lose our tempers, we may still indulge in unhealthy habits, we may still produce less than the "Promised Land." Moreover, we're probably living in a wilderness of some sort; but it is possible for our conscious mind – whether it believes what it's saying or not – to find us a new emotional support. It can be something as simple as consciously saying **"I'm perfect, whole and complete,"** or even what most of us were taught as children, **"Jesus loves me, this I know."**

Abraham affirmed his "Here I Am!" He produced more sons, but he *willed all that he owned to Isaac.* Abraham died at 175 years. *His sons Isaac and Ishmael buried him in the cave of Machpelah in the field of Ephron son of Zohar the Hittite, facing Mamre, the field that Abraham had bought from the Hittites ...[with] Sarah his wife. After the death of Abraham, God blessed his son Isaac. And Isaac settled near Beer-lahai-roi.* Gen. 25:9-11.

Like his father before him, Isaac is barren **Rebekah Bears Twins** at the beginning. Finally, after Isaac appeals to YHWH, Rebekah conceives. *The children struggled together within her... And the LORD said to her, "Two nations are in your womb, and two peoples, born of you, shall be divided; the one shall be stronger than the other, the elder shall serve the younger." When her days to be delivered were fulfilled, behold, there were twins in her womb. The first came forth red, all his body like a hairy mantle; so they called his name Esau. Afterward his brother came forth, and his hand had taken hold of Esau's heel; so his name was called Jacob. Isaac was sixty years old when she bore them. When the boys grew up, Esau was a skillful hunter, a man of the field, while Jacob was a quiet man, dwelling in tents. Isaac loved Esau, because he ate of his game; but Rebekah loved Jacob.* Gen. 25:22-28.

As proven by the nature of his twin sons, Isaac has a divided nature. One part of him is worldly, in fact, so worldly that it places its physical desires over its spiritual heritage. One part of him is quiet and "dwelling in tents." But Isaac– the conscious awareness – has little attention for this side of himself. Isaac loves Esau better than Jacob. Isaac is divided within himself. His masculine / feminine sides are not working together. Eventually, he will become blind; he will not be able to "see." But at the moment, Isaac's attention is on strictly physical conditions. "Famine is in the land."

Here we thought we had progressed on our climb; but Isaac gets the same "tests" Abraham had to face. Now he's faced with "famine," apparently a famine adding to the famine that was faced by Abraham. But, unlike Abraham, Isaac is told *"Do not go down to Egypt; stay in the land which I point out to you. Reside in this land, and I will be with you and bless you ... fulfilling the oath that I swore to your father Abraham."* Gen. 26:2-3. As a result of this admonition, Isaac goes to Abimelech, king of the Philistines, in Gerar.

Symbolically this presents something often faced by he/she who is on the spiritual path. Even though we think we've made some spiritual progress, life at the level of Isaac may appear more difficult than it did at the level of Abraham. What we seem to be experiencing (particularly in the physical world) simply adds to the problems we had before. Earlier we would have "escaped" to the physical world (Egypt), but we're led not to do that this time; and so we "consult" something or someone that we consider to have greater understanding. But, just as we were at the earlier level, we are not totally honest, even with ourselves.

Like Abraham before him, Isaac presents his feminine side as his "sister." *When the men of the place asked him about his wife, he said, "She is my sister"; for he feared to say, "My wife," thinking, "lest the men of the place should kill me for the sake of Rebekah"; because she was fair to look upon. When he had been there a long time, Abimelech king of the Philistines looked out of a window and saw Isaac fondling Rebekah his wife. So Abimelech called Isaac, and said, "Behold, she is your wife; how then could you say, 'She is my sister'?" Isaac said to him, "Because I thought, 'Lest I die because of her.'"* Gen. 26:7-9.

You may remember that after Abraham's similar fiasco, his confession to Abimelech placed Sarah at a higher level. It is not presenting Rebekah as "sister" that is the "mistake," it is the **"fear"** that is **"unrighteousness."** Isaac is just as fearful of recognizing his feminine side as was Abraham.

At this stage, we are fearful to totally "speak" and "see" righteously. For such requires total acceptance of our feminine side, and we feel that this leaves us vulnerable. "Righteousness" requires total trust that we are truly "made in the image." Only when we get to the place where we are completely willing to "turn the other cheek" and "forgive seven times seventy" have we accepted our feminine side. Only then have we stopped denying the feminine. Total acceptance of the feminine side of us is quite distant from Isaac's position on the climb.

At least Isaac recognizes his "mistake," and he prospers; however, Isaac becomes so prosperous that the Philistines become envious, *stopping up all the wells which his father's servants had dug in the days of his father Abraham, filling them with earth.* Gen. 26:15.

Remember the **LAW**? Sometimes it's called the "law of cause and effect;" sometimes it's called the "law of judgment." It doesn't matter what it's called; it means **"as we sow, so shall we reap."** It means that for every "difficulty" we encounter, we have sown it. In this case, all the "digging" that Abraham did, will have to be done again.

Since the LAW is always in operation, the explanation for Isaac's problems has to be that the "difficulty" is still there. The "earth" is still in the well. And Isaac again digs *the wells of water which had been dug in the days of Abraham his father; for the Philistines had stopped them after the death of Abraham;* and Isaac gives *them the names which his father had given them.* Gen.26:18.

Not only are there "old wells" to *re-dig*; there are new ones to *dig*, too. But as with Isaac's discovery of a "spring" which he names Esek (to strive with), likely, the Philistines (the world which "wallows itself") will claim it as theirs. Even if we "move on" to another well, as with Sitnah (harassment), the Philistines will follow. It's as though we're "damned if we do, and damned if we don't." We can't please the "Philistines."

If we are like Isaac, we simply move on to Rehoboth (from "to become thin"*),* saying: *Now at last the Lord has granted us ample space to increase in the land.* Gen. 26:22.

Don't count on it! Remember what Jesus said: ***Do not think that I have come to bring peace on earth***, *I have not come to bring peace, but a sword. For I have come to set a man against his father, and a daughter against her mother, and a daughter-in-law against her mother-in-law; and a man's foes will be those of his own household. He who loves father or mother more than me is not worthy of me; and he who loves son or daughter more than me is not worthy of me; and he who does not take his cross and follow me is not worthy of me. **He who finds his life will lose it, and he who loses his life for my sake will find it.*** Mt. 10:34.

Jesus experienced the turmoil that the spiritual climb brings. The climb brings change, and change brings turmoil. Just as we experience turmoil, so does Isaac. This spiritual climb most likely will require everything from us that Isaac had to find in his lifetime. It requires willingness to be sacrificed; it requires uniting with a higher feminine expression.

Caution here: this does not mean "getting divorced" to find a "higher" mate; it means finding a less emotional, more caring person *within ourselves*! Then it requires acknowledging that expression. It requires "re-digging" what we thought was already "dug"; and it requires dealing with the turmoil that comes with all of these endeavors.

The Isaac expression makes no great strides in the climb, but the challenges it encounters are apparently necessary for the climb to proceed. These challenges are not necessary because of the need for punishment or chastisement; these challenges are necessary to "deliver" us to that mindset where we "speak" and "see" righteously.

Jacob's Night at Bethel by Doré.

Chapter Five
Jacob and Esau

Strive for peace with all men, and for the holiness without which no one will see the Lord. **See to it that no one** *fail to obtain the grace of God; that no "root of bitterness" spring up and cause trouble, and by it the many become defiled; that no one* **be immoral or irreligious like Esau,** *who sold his birthright for a single meal. For you know that* **afterward,** *when he desired to inherit the blessing,* **he was rejected,** *for he found no chance to repent,* **though he sought it with tears.** Heb. 12:14-17.

P

oor Esau, through countless ages he's been maligned, all because his "mother liked Jacob better." In fact, if we read the story literally, Jacob certainly comes out less than a hero. He appears to be a "mamma's boy," he appears to be a cheat, and he appears to be a coward. That's not too good for the one who is supposedly climbing the Mountain to the next stage. The only way Jacob comes out positive is if we view him symbolically; for symbolically, both sons make a statement about their father Isaac.

Therefore, let's return to Isaac for a moment. At age 40 he marries Rebekah; however, she is barren. So he pleads with the Lord, and the Lord responds, but *the children struggled in her womb.*[1] The Lord explains to Rebekah: *Two nations are in your womb, two separate peoples shall issue from your body; one people shall be mightier than the other, and the older shall serve the younger.* And at age 60, Isaac becomes the father of twins. *The first came forth red, all his body like a hairy mantle: so they called his name Esau. Afterward his brother came forth ... his hand had taken hold of Esau's heel: so his name was called Jacob.* Gen. 25:23-26.[2]

---

[1] Gen. 25:21-22. Interestingly, *The Torah* separates the story of Isaac from the rest of Chapter 25 with a space and a "title" of תולדת. Using the numerical value of each letter, as suggested by Suarès, the "title" adds up to 840 (which makes **12**).

[2] According to *The Torah*, Esau is a play on the Hebrew word for "hair." Jacob is a play on the Hebrew word for "heel."

In hang-loose symbology we're being told that each of us has two natures (nations) which struggle within us. We're also told that the "younger" side of us will eventually rule the "older."[3] Actually, we should look at this as a promise that we will become more enlightened. The "older" side of us "comes forth *red.*" It is similar to Adam, but it is to be "supplanted" by a different nature.

In addition to being a pun on the word **Esau** "hair," the name *Esau* comes from a verb which refers to "handling, roughly" (sensibly, felt).[4] Esau's characteristics are of a more primitive nature. He is "a skillful hunter, a man of the outdoors." He has "a taste for game," and this is why he is nicknamed "Edom."[5] It is this nature that says: *Give me some of that red stuff to gulp down, for I am famished. ... I am at the point of death, so of what use is my birthright to me?* Gen. 25:30. Esau places all importance on the physical and a sensual appreciation of the physical. Further, he accentuates this physical tie, at the age of 40, when he marries two Hittite women, *and they were a source of bitterness to Isaac and Rebekah.* Gen. 25:34. [6]

Esau is that portion of us which holds to the senses as the source of sustenance and of "seeing." This point is emphasized by the Bible's form. Between the birth of the twins and Esau's marriage is a complete chapter in which Isaac's major problem is that the Philistines keep filling "his wells" with "earth." It is no coincidence that the "wells" (looking within

---

[3] Isaac Asimov, in *Asimov's Guide to the Bible,* (Avenel, 1981), p. 93, points out that the Edomites (descendants of Esau) were well established on the outskirts of Canaan when the Israelites entered; therefore, the Israelites as a tribe were "younger," but "through the centuries that followed the rise of David, the Israelites ruled over the Edomites."

[4] See Strong, #H6215.

[5] *The Torah*, p. 43. "Edom" is a play on the Hebraic *'adom* (red).

[6] Traditionally, Esau's marriage to two Hittite women is given as evidence of his unworthiness. However, the names of the wives are such that they would have been assets – if they had not been related to "terror." One wife is Judith (Jewess), daughter of Berri (a pit or a well); the second is Basmath (fragrance – the same name given to a daughter of Solomon), daughter of Elon (an oak grove).

ourselves) are repeatedly filled with "earth" by the Philistines (to wallow oneself); this will likely be the experience of anyone who climbs the Mountain.

As we increasingly attempt to hold to the remembrance that we are truly the child of God, we will encounter – time and time again – happenings that will pull our attention back to "earthly" concerns. We may be concerned for our physical safety or health or the safety of a loved one, our financial stability, our relationships – all sorts of things that in our "sensual" mindset "reveal" our assessment of ourself and our connection to "God." In fact, we may be so fearful about an "earthly" concern that we experience "terror." It's no wonder that Isaac and Rebekah find Esau's Hittite wives a "source of bitterness."

This "physically oriented" side of us may even attempt to change its ways. After Jacob is given the blessing, Esau realizes that his wives "displease" his father, so he marries again, this time a daughter of Ishmael. Esau has joined himself to a closer relative, but an offspring of Ishmael is still on the "sensual" level. Esau fails to recognize that the "outer" cannot be reoriented until the "inner" is changed. Whether his wives are Hittite or Ishmaelite, they are of the physical mindset. This doesn't make Esau evil. The only trouble with Esau is his "unholiness."

By the symbols of his sons, we're told that the trouble with Isaac (he who is climbing the Mountain) is his lack of "wholeness." He's not *whole*. He's divided; he's not single-minded. And as James warns: *A double-minded man, unstable in all his ways, will receive nothing from the Lord.* Ja. 1:7,8.

Isaac does not follow Paul's admonition to "strive for *holiness*." As a result, his | **Isaac's Eyes Become Dim** | eyes become "too dim to see." He will be "supplanted" by a nature that knows the value of its "birthright." Only he who values his "birthright" receives the "blessing." Jacob will continue the climb.

98

The name "Jacob" means "heel catcher" or "supplanter." His birth order makes him #2, and his nature is more of the feminine than that of Esau. He is described as a "mild
Jacob man, who stayed in camp." Even more importantly, Jacob acknowledges that "Esau is a hairy man and **I am smooth skinned.**"[7] It is this "smooth" side that listens to the feminine voice, and the feminine advises Jacob to "go to the flock and fetch me two choice kids." Notice, while Esau must go outside of his surroundings to "hunt game" for the dish which will obtain the blessing, Jacob is told to make it out of something which is "near at hand."

We might remember the example that Jesus gives of the ten virgins who awaited the "bridegroom." Jesus likened the "Kingdom of Heaven" to the five "wise" virgins who both trimmed their lamps and had their oil with them. It is they who meet the "bridegroom." The five "foolish" virgins, who must "go out" to acquire oil, find the "door shut" when they return.[8]

Esau, too, is "shut out" from the heir's "blessing." Instead, according to *The Torah*, (p. 48) Isaac says: *"See, your abode shall enjoy the fat of the earth and the dew of heaven above. Yet by your sword you shall live, and you shall serve your brother; but when you grow restive, you shall break his yoke from your neck."* [9]

---

[7] Gen. 27:11. Again we run into the allusion to "smooth." See page 40. While Adam/Eve in the Garden saw **not** their "nakedness," the word for "nakedness" alluded to "smoothness." After their acceptance of the "knowledge of good and evil," the word for "nakedness" becomes "craftiness." Finally, here with Jacob, we are returning to "smoothness."

[8] See Matthew 21:1-14.

[9] The traditional wording is: *Esau said to his father, "Have you but one blessing, my father? Bless me, even me also, ..." And Esau lifted up his voice and wept. Then Isaac his father answered him: "Behold, **away** from the fatness of the earth shall your dwelling be, and **away** from the dew of heaven on high. By your sword you shall live, and you shall serve your brother; but when you break loose you shall break his yoke from your neck." Now Esau hated Jacob because of the blessing ..., and Esau said to himself, "The days of mourning for my father are approaching; then I will kill my brother Jacob."* Gen. 27:38-41.

We think of Esau as not being *blessed* by Isaac's blessing, but *The Torah's* wording says something different. In *The Torah's* version, Esau, like Jacob, is also to have the "fat of the earth and the dew of heaven;" but he will have to live in a confrontational world.[10] And he will have to serve his brother until he "grow(s) restive." Only the *King James* version has the wording I think is implied here. It reads: *...by thy sword shalt thou live, and shalt serve thy brother; and it shall come to pass **when thou shalt have the dominion**, that thou shalt break his yoke from off thy neck.*

If we read carefully, we will see that in truth Isaac's riches stay with Esau. Therefore, something else is being given here. The physical mindset is told that it will not be free from this confrontational world until it has **the dominion,** and only then will it be "free" of "thy brother."

Here's another paradox. Although the "younger" is to rule, as soon as "the older" gains the **dominion**, the older is free.[11] This sequence, i.e., the younger superseding the elder, is proper. The "heightened feminine," the "enlightened soul," is to lead the entity to the understanding that it is *one with God*, only then does the "confrontational world" and any sort of domination cease.

But Esau is of the physical mindset; he has no "heightened feminine," and he wants it all right now. So he resents the fact that he has "to climb," and he hates the side which is necessary to make "the climb." The feminine side recognizes this and tells Jacob: *Obey my voice; arise, flee to Laban my brother in Haran, and stay with him a while, until your brother's fury turns away; until your brother's anger turns away, and he forgets what you have done to him; then I will send, and fetch you from there. Why should I be bereft of you both in one day?"* Gen. 27:43-45.

---

[10] One of my teachers, Mary Beth Olson, pointed out that since *primogeniture* was the accepted Hebrew practice, Isaac's blessing of Jacob– plus the birth right which had been conferred earlier– bestowed all of Isaac's property to Jacob, as opposed to delivering it to Esau, who (in fact) was the elder son and rightful heir.

[11] *Webster's* defines **dominion** as: supreme authority; sovereignty; domain. Interestingly, it also lists: *an angel of the fourth highest rank.*

We need not fear; we will lose neither side of us. It is only that the development will most likely come first through the activities of that side of us which is less tied to the physical mindset. And likely, as with Jacob, this side will first begin to understand as it "sees" night visions.[12]

Jacob Sees The Climb *Jacob left Beer-sheba, and went toward Haran. And he came to a certain place, and stayed there that night, because the sun had set. **Taking one of the stones of the place,** he put it under his head and lay down in that place to sleep. And **he dreamed that there was a ladder set up on the earth, and the top of it reached to heaven; and behold, the angels of God were ascending and descending on it!** And behold, the LORD stood above it and said, "I am the LORD, the God of Abraham your father and the God of Isaac; the land on which you lie I will give to you and to your descendants; and your descendants shall be like the dust of the earth, and you shall spread abroad to the west and to the east and to the north and to the south; and by you and your descendants shall all the families of the earth bless themselves. Behold, I am with you and will keep you wherever you go, and will bring you back to this land; for **I will not leave you until I have done that of which I have spoken to you.**" Then Jacob awoke from his sleep and said, "Surely the LORD is in this place; and I did not know it." And he was afraid, and said, "**How awesome is this place! This is none other than the house of God, and this is the gate of heaven.**"* Gen. 28-10-17.

Needless to say, there are many possible interpretations of Jacob's "ladder." It can be seen as indicating a connection between heaven and earth. *The Torah's* wording suggests such an interpretation. The ladder is called a "stairway" or a "ramp." The passage reads: *How awesome is this place! **This is none other than the abode of God,** and that is **the gateway to heaven.**"*[13] If we consider the ramp to be a "stairway," angels of God climb up and down to minister to the earth. However, if we consider it as a "ladder," it suggests that "access" to the heavenly condition consists of "movement" up and down. Hence, mankind's journey is not consistently "up." But, as with our many interpretations, Jacob cannot analyze what he sees. It

---

[12] Again *The Torah* divides the narrative. Jacob's story is interrupted, and the "title" ויצא is inserted. Using Suarès' values, this adds up to 107. We have risen another layer of understanding, but we are just at the beginning.

[13] *The Torah,* Gen. 28:17.

is sufficient that he "sees," and he sets the stone that he had used for a pillow as a pillar; and he anoints it with oil.[14]

Some items must be noticed, here. First, the "one" promise has again been increased. We will now be like the dust, covering all directions: and the Lord promises not to leave **until all is accomplished.** Jacob "sees" the Lord more clearly than did either Abraham or Isaac; but like Abraham and Isaac, Jacob is "fearful." His "fear" is not of God, but of his relationship with God. While he recognizes the Lord's presence, he does not accept his own "sonship." He even puts conditions on his acceptance of "God" as his protector, saying: *If God remains with me, if He protects me..., and if I return safe to my father's house – the Lord shall be my God.* Gen. 28:20-21. Even now, Jacob is not pure "hero."

Secondly, notice the four place-names in the story. Jacob leaves Beer-sheba (the "spring" at which Hagar "saw" God and Abraham's well of an oath, which Isaac had to re-dig) heading toward Haran (literally, *to glow* or *to burn*; figuratively, *to show passion*), stopping at "a certain place," Luz (place of bending, curve). Here Jacob begins to "see," and he names this "certain place" Bethel (house of El.)

These place-names will require some "hang-loose" logic. Something monumental has happened in Jacob's life. He has newly acquired a state of mind similar to Hagar's "opened eyes," an understanding that somewhat "sees." But he leaves this place in a passionate condition heading for Haran. This is the same Haran where Abraham's father (wandering ways) died and where Abraham procrastinated for a time. It is really not the place to procrastinate for too long; because, while it can "glow," it also can "burn."

---

[14] Any anointing with oil implies a "dedication." The usual esoteric interpretation of "stone" is "understanding." It is "understanding" upon which Jacob "sleeps," and it is this which he sets up as a tribute (and dedicates) to "God."

We can all surely remember times when something "monumental" happened to us that literally made us feel as though we were "burning." Apparently this is the physiological effect of extreme emotion. This is apparently what Jacob is experiencing, but on his way he stops at a place of "bending." He stops not because he thinks something will happen, but because the "sun went down."

Again, isn't this what happens in our lives? It is not our decisions or our "doings" that bring opportunities for change into our lives. Usually, it just "happens." It's what the Bible calls "grace." And this "grace" allows Jacob to perceive what had previously eluded him. *Surely the Lord is present in this place, and **I did not know it!** ... How awesome is this place! This is none other than the abode of God, and that is the gateway to heaven.* [15] Once again, as with Abraham, there should be a gospel choir interjecting *Praise the Lord* into the narrative.

Jacob is approaching the prime directive. – And what is the prime directive? – That mankind should "see" and "say" as the "righteous man," for only the "righteous man" *sees* and *says* that the LORD GOD is all-powerful, all-knowing, everywhere present, and (therefore) accessible.[16] Only the "righteous man" concedes that previously he/she *did not know it.* Only the "righteous man" understands that *that in which the LORD (YHWH) is present* is "none other than the abode of God (El or the 'elohim) and... the gateway to heaven." Jacob is becoming the "righteous man."

The LORD God Is Omnipresent Omnipotent Omniscient

Let's stop for a minute. Have we, like Jacob, ever found ourself embroiled in a situation where even though we

---

[15] Notice that both **Lord** and **God** (YHWH and El) are included in these two verses.

[16] Nineteenth Century writers expressed it as: Omnipotent, Omniscient, and Omnipresent. "Accessibility" is obvious since there is no separation from God.

know there is a "God" which is in charge – even though we do what seems to be appropriate – the whole thing ends up with us emotionally burning – even if we turn the other cheek, even if we run away from the physical situation?

How easy it is to be like Job and excuse ourselves, explaining the whole thing as the presence of a force contrary to the will of God, declaring that we have not sinned and have held to our "righteousness."[17] How much more difficult it is to see the whole incident as part of whatever the plan is for us; how much more difficult it is to accept that we are the "child of God" and **are "receiving"** as such **despite all appearances.**

How much more difficult it is to agree that all that which evidences on earth (YHWH) is the abode of El and "gateway to heaven." How much more difficult it is to "take our eyes" from the physical (the appearances) and announce that we are under the rule and law of God. Instead we "judge" the appearances, "seeing" incorrectly and "saying" inaccurately. Jacob, on the other hand, "judges" correctly and "resumes his journey."[18]

Supposedly, in order to protect this "fledgling" understanding from a feminine side that could retie it to the physical (as has

Jacob's New Feminine Expression

taken place with Esau), Rebekah sends Jacob to her brother Laban (shining thoughts) to find the proper feminine expression. Approaching Laban's abode, Jacob finds "a well in the open," and he "sees" Rachel, Laban's daughter. However, those who surround the "open well" are those coming from Haran (the mindset of the passions), and they say that Rachel cannot water her flock until all of the flocks are

---

[17] Only after much suffering does Job comment: *"I have uttered what I did not understand, things too wonderful for me, which I did not know."* Job 42:3.

[18] *The Torah,* p. 50, gives the secondary definition as "lifted up his feet." The esoteric symbolism of "feet" is "understanding." So Jacob "lifted up his understanding."

104

gathered up. Although only partially "enlightened," Jacob knows this to be "incorrect," so he ... *rolled the stone off the mouth of the well, and watered the flock of his uncle Laban. Then Jacob kissed Rachel, and broke into tears.* Gen. 29:1-11.[19]

Isn't this what happens to us? Even when we know that the feminine expression (the spiritual understanding) that we're perceiving is appropriate for us, the "physical rules" say we're wrong. Whether it's the "outside" world or our "inside" selves, this thinking says we can't be *whole* until we've got the whole thing together. Sometimes we're even told that we're all "sinners" in the sight of God. It's implied, therefore, we can't "water our flocks." But he who is "climbing" disregards those who know not, and waters the flocks of the appropriate feminine. In so doing, he earns the attention of the "shining thoughts."

Of course, the "shining thoughts" is our own ability to hold ourself to what we know to be true – that "this is an awesome place" and the "gateway to heaven." Naively we expect this "shining thoughts" to immediately implement our desires. The problem is that although we "intellectually" know that "this is an awesome place" and the "gateway to heaven," we have not yet "internalized" this knowledge. Consequently, we are given the story of Jacob and Laban.

I assume we all know the story of the relationship between Jacob and Laban. On the physical level, Laban mistreats Jacob by tricking him into "serving" him longer than Jacob thinks necessary. He has to serve 7 years for Leah before he can serve the 7 years for Rachel. To Jacob that's

---

[19] There are those who say it is impossible to "see" and "say" until we have mastered the whole "thing," i.e., until we have 12x12. It is this that the outer world tells Jacob ... *Rachel's flock can't be watered until all of the flocks are "gathered."* Notice that Jacob's answer is to proceed, despite the world's curtailment. But notice the numbers of the verse. It is Chapter 27 (# 9, number of the initiate), verse 11 (beginning of fruition). This is much more than most of the world ever comes close to... So proceed! Roll the stone away!

excessive time for what he wants – the higher feminine expression and the fruits that come with it. And we all agree, because we think the same about our own rewards.

There is a little joke that applies here. In many ways we all unsuspectingly express it, so we must listen with hang-loose hearing. It goes: Lord, give me "patience," and give it to me **right now!** Or it can be Lord give me "riches"... or Lord give me "understanding," but **make it quick!** And what's the answer?

In the vernacular: **No Way!** is it going to happen! ... not because we're denied "patience" or "riches" or "understanding," but because the "temporal" demand shows that none of these things are yet a part of ourselves. Therefore, despite any number of "shining thoughts," the challenge is for Jacob **to become** "patient," "rich," and "understanding." Consequently, he ends up "serving" Laban for

Jacob and Laban

almost twenty-one (21) years, i.e., three (3) times the earthly measure of mastery (7) – until he has developed the necessary ingredients in himself.

Just as we try to give the Lord a "temporal" limit, Jacob gives Laban a temporal limit. Jacob figures he'll work seven years for Rachel; and then he'll be all set to reap the rewards. But, unexpectedly, Jacob ends up being married first to Rachel's elder sister, Leah (weary, exhausted, weak eyes). Laban explains: *It is not the practice in our place to marry off the younger before the older.* In other words, **we can't receive the higher rewards until we have mastered the lower challenges.** It requires another agreement of another seven years to acquire Rachel (lamb, migrating ewe) as wife, too. But apparently we will start to get some of what we want, even though we haven't totally triumphed. In fact, we may get more than we bargained for, because each wife comes equipped with a maidservant, a feminine of lesser degree.

Can you "imagine" Jacob's "blessings"? In a literal interpretation, he now has four women to support. Symbolically, his feminine side expresses itself in four different ways. The lower feminine (Leah) isn't very strong, but she initially produces four sons in a row. Then Leah's maidservant, Zilpah (extracting an essence, dripping tears, bitterness) also produces. Higher on the feminine scale, Rachel produces nothing for many years, but at least she has a maidservant, Bilhah (bashfulness, timidity, tenderness), who produces in between the "production" of Leah and Zilpah. Only after ten (10) sons and one daughter does the heightened feminine produce the"true expression."

Remember, Jacob is climbing the Mountain, and the "Jacob" level of the climb brings great "change" as well as "productivity" in our lives. We now recognize there is a LORD, God. But notice what else we're seeing. Jacob now knows that where he "is" is the LORD's abode. He comes to this understanding not because of any action he takes, but because it is there for him. Now he'll begin to produce his own characteristics. No longer is he just Isaac's son; now he will produce for himself.

However, the feminine side (the productive side) is not fully joined to him – and it is not unified. His feminine side doesn't "see" too well, and it even comes "from tears and bitterness." Moreover, its higher expression keeps "migrating" around, jumping from thing to thing and not really producing anything – being "bashful and timid" (although also tender). Yet Jacob's feminine side does bring changes about in him.

Despite the inadequacies of Jacob and his feminine side, while he is living with "shining thoughts" at Paddan-aram (a broad, level plain) and working for greater understanding, he begins to produce. And what does he produce? He produces ten sons in a row.

Let's consider the children of Jacob, esoterically.[20] Through the "weak eyed" Leah, Jacob produces: 1. Reuben (behold [sight] a son); 2. Simeon (who hears, obeys, i.e., **hearing)**; 3. Levi (joined to, attached, uniting, **loving**); and 4. Judah (**praise YHWH**); and Leah ceases bearing. But Rachel, becoming envious of her sister, gives Jacob her maid Bilhah *as concubine, and Jacob cohabited with her.* Through Bilhah, Jacob produces and Rachel names: 5. Dan (rule of righteous **judgment**) and 6. Naphtali (with mighty wrestling [strength] ... with my sister, I have prevailed). But sisterly rivalry continues. Having ceased to bear for a time, Leah gives Jacob her maid, Zilpah; and through Zilpah Jacob produces and Leah names: 7. Gad (good fortune, **abundance)** and 8. Asher (straight, straight forward, **happiness**).

Next comes a strange little story where Rachel asks Leah for some mandrakes that Leah's son, Reuben, had gathered. Leah answers: *...was it not enough for you to take away my husband, that you would also take my son's mandrakes?* Even identifying "mandrakes" as an aphrodisiac ("love apples" according to Young) makes the story petty. But the esoteric message may be more important. Just as Sarai is replaced by Sarah, and Sarah is replaced by Rebekah, and Rebekah is replaced by Rachel and the others, the feminine side of us must continue to grow to allow the masculine side of us to "produce." But this growth may bring some friction to our "household."

---

[20] See Gen. 29:31-35, Gen. 30:1-24, and Gen. 35:18. The sons of Jacob are probably the strongest teaching tools of the Old Testament. They symbolize the characteristics of Israel (the name of the "developed" Jacob), he who climbs the Mountain. These characteristics are reiterated by Jacob as he is dying and later by Moses. They constitute the twelve tribes of Israel which symbolically enter "the Promised Land."

The most insightful view of them can be found in the work of Charles Fillmore. Apparently following the teaching of Malinda E. Cramer, who taught daily classes (which Fillmore attended) on Genesis in Kansas City for more than six weeks during the spring of 1891, Fillmore later elaborated on the meaning of the names of the twelve tribes. He presents the sons of Jacob, not only as characteristics of the "enlightened" initiate, but as esoteric references to different parts of the body. The consumate student is directed to Fillmore's *Metaphysical Bible Dictionary* and to his *Twelve Powers of Man*, which extends the metaphor to the twelve disciples.

For instance, let's say that our emotional side has always been somewhat fearful; but, despite our fearfulness, we are given substantial spiritual fruits. Consciously, we know that we must eliminate this fearfulness, and we may for a time; but then we question whether we can produce (Rachel asks for an aphrodisiac), again allowing this lesser feminine nature access to the conscious mind which produces some more.

Jacob produces:
1. Reuben (**sight**)
2. Simeon (**hearing**)
3. Levi (**loving**)
4. Judah (**praise** YHWH)
5. Dan (**righteous judgment**)
6. Naphtali (**strength**)
7. Gad (**abundance**)
8. Asher (**happiness**)
9. Issachar (**reward**)
10. Zebulun (**order**)
Dinah (**feminine of justice**)
Finally Rachel bears
11. Joseph (**perfection**)
And after Jacob grows
12. Benjamin (**power**)

Rachel agrees that Jacob can again lie with Leah; and Leah conceives and bears 9. Issachar (who brings hire, there is **reward**), 10. Zebulun (God has given me a choice gift [**order**] plus an unnumbered daughter, Dinah (feminine expression of justice).[21] The production is not bad, in fact it's good; but it's not the level of production that we desire. Only the highest feminine nature can produce that for which we long.

The Torah reads: *Now God remembered Rachel; God heeded her and opened her womb. She conceived and bore a son, and said, "God has taken away my disgrace." So she named him Joseph, which is to say, "May the Lord add another son for me."* Gen. 30:24.

This passage introduces the new climber, #11. Joseph (progressive increase, **perfection unto perfection**). However, read literally, the passage which subtly condemns the childless does great harm. Just because of this passage alone, I imagine many women have been convinced that it is a "disgrace" not to bear children. But as with most things that misdirected mankind chooses to stigmatize, the worldly view is "inaccurate." It is Jacob's inability to "see clearly" that turns

---

[21] It is interesting that Rachel agrees only for Jacob to lie with Leah that one night, yet we have a multiple of three times one night's activity. How true it is that just one loosening of our higher feminine expression produces more than just one thing.

"grace" to a negative. *Disgrace* says more than we might think. The "grace" is always there; the negative is Jacob's.

Only after he has several more important experiences will Jacob grow sufficiently so that Rachel's desire for another son can be fulfilled, but it will mean the elimination of the heightened feminine. Rachel will die with the birth of her second son, 12. Benjamin (son of the right hand). Benjamin comes only after Jacob reaches another level on the climb. By that time, the feminine will be united with the masculine, and Jacob no longer will be on the broad, level plateau.

Let's break the metaphor into more recognizable parts. The total progeny of Jacob comes from "four" women, hence it is of the "natural order." But the greatest portion of it comes from "weak-eyed" Leah, who produces seven (7) sons and one daughter. Dinah eventually makes the number of Jacob's progeny thirteen (13), a very special number.[22] However, **Jacob As Metaphor**
Leah's **first five sons** – *sight, hearing, loving, praise, and righteous judgment* – precede what we might think of as "fruits." These **are the five heightened "senses" that we've been looking for** – those senses which are directed toward the spiritual rather than the physical.

Esoterically, even though Jacob does not yet "see" with strength, he improves his "sight" and "hearing" and begins to "love." Moreover, he "praises" all the while and maintains "righteous judgment." He recognizes that he is a child of God. It is in this understanding that Jacob possesses "strength," "abundance," and "happiness." Only in this understanding does one who is still "in hire" (not yet on the mastership level) receive "reward" and "order." Jacob's life takes on an order and a balance that it needed. This is the "justice" (female, not fully empowered) that comes to he/she who

---

[22] The only other #13 is Jesus, when added to the disciples.

110

climbs the Mountain this far. After this point, he/she who climbs experiences "from perfection to perfection." Everything just keeps getting better and better, until he/she is **acting (seeing/saying)** and receiving as the "son of the right hand" – he/she who wields the power.

This esoteric synopsis is what mankind's true life is! This is the story of Jacob and the story of all mankind on the climb; but we have mentioned the "added son" too soon. Jacob/Rachel cannot receive Benjamin until more changes take place. So, let's return to the story of Jacob. He's still on a "broad plateau," living with "shining thoughts," with four "wives," eleven "sons," and one "daughter." It is time for him to continue the climb, so he asks Laban to *"give me leave to go back to my homeland"* with my wives and children, *"for whom I have served you."* Gen. 30:25,26.

Using hang-loose thinking, we can see ourselves at a certain place on the climb. Much of our internal work is finished. We "see," we "hear," we "love." We are even receiving strength, abundance, order, etc., and everything is going from "perfection to perfection" within ourselves. We have passed the second level of earthly "perfection" (14), and now we feel it's time to leave this "flat" place where we've been for "20 years." It's time to continue the climb, taking with us all these attributes that we've accumulated; but we're stuck on a plateau, and "shining thoughts" is reluctant to give up control.[23]

Jacob has yet to trust fully, for he asks, "When shall I make provision for my own household?" Not having the absolute knowledge of "righteous judgment" that God will

---

[23] I wonder if this is the level of "treasure mapping," where the individual states what he/she desires from the universe, then "visualizes" it into manifestation. In many ways, this state of mind is not too far removed from the "magic" of the Chaldeans.

provide, Jacob still carries the worries of the physical plane. So he makes another "deal" with Laban, agreeing to take care of the flocks if Laban will "pay him wages" in the form of the "dark sheep" and the "spotted and speckled goats." He tells Laban *"... let me pass through all your flock today, removing from it every speckled and spotted sheep and every black lamb, and the spotted and speckled among the goats; and such shall be my wages."* Gen. 30:32.

On the surface, Laban agrees, but for the third time he "cheats" Jacob, by taking all of the "dark sheep" and the "spotted and speckled goats" out of Jacob's flocks – even though he tells Jacob *"... **Let it be as you say.**"*

Again, the lesson is a paradox. It's like the admonition against "hope." If we have to "hope" for something, we have **"said"** that we do **not** have it. As long as Jacob feels it necessary to bargain and plead for what is due him, he doesn't have it. He is "saying" he doesn't have it; and **so it "is."** But, finally, Jacob spiritually produces the solution. *Then Jacob took fresh rods of poplar and almond and plane, and peeled white streaks in them, exposing the white of the rods. He set the rods which he had peeled in front of the flocks in ... the watering troughs, where the flocks came to drink. And since they bred when they came to drink, ... the flocks brought forth striped, speckled, and spotted. And Jacob separated the lambs, and set the faces of the flocks toward the striped and all the black in the flock of Laban; and he put his own droves apart, and did not put them with Laban's flock. Whenever the stronger of the flock were breeding Jacob laid the rods in the runnels before the eyes of the flock, that they might breed among the rods, but for the feebler of the flock he did not lay them there; so the feebler were Laban's, and the stronger Jacob's.* Gen. 30:37-42. [24]

Operating under this new mindset, Jacob *grew exceedingly rich, and had large flocks, maidservants and menservants, and camels and asses.* The "fruiting" defies physical laws; but

---

[24] I have yet to determine a literal explanation for this part of the story. The problem may be that there is no "physical" explanation; its understanding immediately switches us to the esoteric. One of the great spiritual thinkers of the last century, Thomas Troward, attempted to give "physical" credence to the science of "seeing" and "saying" producing the physical manifestation. According to Troward, mankind is made in the image of God and produces in the same way. In this light and with this understanding, because Jacob proceeds "seeing" and "saying" that the "peeled rods" will produce the flocks that he desires, **it is accomplished.**

112

esoterically it makes sense. Making a sort of fence of striped poles in itself will not produce spotted and striped goats. It must be that **the poles allow that which is desired to be separated from that which is not desired – then it is that**

Producing Our Own Wages

that from which we "drink" is what we produce; but this is only true with the lesser "fruits," the goats. As for the sheep, the higher "fruits," they are produced by "facing" *the streaked or wholly dark-colored animals in Laban's flock.* "Facing something" relates to what one "sees." (Remember, all along we've been saying that what we "see" and "say" is what we get, and so it is with Jacob.) *And so he produced special flocks for himself: **which he did not put with Laban's flocks.*** Gen. 30:40.

The number given to this verse tells us to pay attention. Jacob is producing the "rewards," the "wages" that he deserves; but, having done so, he then keeps them separate. This applies to those of us on the climb. We must hold what we produce, i.e., our understanding, separate from that which will pollute it; and we must separate that which is the strongest to produce even more.

Climbing the Mountain is not a simple task, nor is it a joint effort. At this "Jacob" level, we may find that we have to separate ourselves and "our production" from those who have helped in our development. At least for a time we may have to leave the teachers and the institutions or the friends which have helped us to grow.

Just as Laban has regard for Jacob only as it applies to himself, even those who are on the path oftentimes will see our development and what we "produce" in light of themselves. As a result, they – like Laban – may delay our departure from the plateau if we continue to mix our flocks with theirs. The problem lies in our recognizing our true "sonship." Only when we are able to "see" clearly that the production is God's "doing" with our activity, do we have the internal confidence to proceed.

Now Jacob heard that the sons of Laban were saying, "Jacob has taken all that was our father's; and from what was our father's he has gained all this wealth." And Jacob saw that Laban did not regard him with favor as before. Then the LORD said to Jacob, "Return to the land of your fathers and to your kindred, and I will be with you."

So Jacob sent and called Rachel and Leah into the field where his flock was, and said ... "I see that your father does not regard me with favor as he did before. But the God of my father has been with me. You know that I have served your father with all my strength; yet your father has cheated me and changed my wages ten times, but God did not permit him to harm me. If he said, 'The spotted shall be your wages,' then all the flock bore spotted; and if he said, 'The striped shall be your wages,' then all the flock bore striped. Thus God has taken away the cattle of your father, and given them to me." Gen. 31:1-9

The aspirant who keeps "the high watch" receives from the Lord and is encouraged to continue. Jacob says: *"In the mating season of the flock I lifted up my eyes, and saw in a dream that the he-goats which leaped upon the flock were striped, spotted, and mottled. Then the angel of God said to me in the dream, 'Jacob,' and I said, **'Here I am!'** And he said, 'Lift up your eyes and see, all the goats that leap upon the flock are striped, spotted, and mottled; for I have seen all that Laban is doing to you. I am the God of Bethel, where you anointed a pillar and made a vow to me. Now arise, go forth from this land, and return to the land of your birth.'"* Gen. 31:10-13.

Jacob has recognized his "sonship." Jesus said the same thing a different way when he was told to silence his followers. *He answered: "I tell you, if these were silent, the very stones would cry out."* Luke 19:40. To he/she who has "recovered sight" to the point of knowing his/her "sonship" with God, all things come to be. This is the ultimate "grace," and it returns us to the "land of our birth." And the feminine side recognizes that what we have received "belongs to us and to our children."

*Then Rachel and Leah answered him, "Is there any portion or inheritance left to us in our father's house? Are we not regarded by him as foreigners? For he has sold us, and he has been using up the money given for us. All the property which God has taken away from our father belongs to us and to our children; now then, **whatever God has said to you, do.**"* Gen. 31:14-16.

Jacob in the house of Laban.

Chapter Six
Jacob Is Renamed Israel

T raditionally, "named" implies having that "nature," and "Jacob" means the "supplanter." This level is to supplant, to replace, what has gone before; but when it "supplants," it will be renamed "Israel." We often forget that Jacob and Israel are the same person; instead, we almost always think of Israel as the "nation." But "the nation" is correctly that which issues from Jacob. "Israel" [1] ישראל (i.e., ruling with God) is that which produces the greater expression, the nation which retains the knowledge. However, before Jacob is renamed Israel, several incidents take place that have no great importance in the "literal" world, only in the symbolic. Since they relate to the "renaming," we must look at them.

First is the activity that takes place as Jacob leaves Laban. Jacob sneaks away while Laban is off shearing sheep. In fact it takes three days before Laban knows that Jacob has gone; and it takes seven more days for Laban to catch

> **Rachel Steals Her Father's Household Gods**

up with Jacob, at Gilead, on a "height."[2] But Laban had had a dream the previous night where he was warned against "attempting anything with Jacob, good or bad." So

---

[1] Suarès, page 181, deciphers "Israel" as 10·300·200·1·30 (reading from right to left) which added together comes to 541 which adds up to **10.** The reader can do as he will with these numbers. It is presumptuous for me to suggest what the Qabala means. This presentation, *Climbing the Mountain,* is by necessity far short of the "greater" understanding; it is just a "beginning." The student with "greater" understanding should become acquainted with Suarès' work.

[2] *Gilead* comes from two words, one originating from a verb *to roll, to wallow,* and the second referring to *a recorder (a prince).* See Strong's *Concordance.*

Laban doesn't do anything except look for his "household gods." Laban, most likely, would not have cared whether Jacob and his daughters left, except that his "gods" are missing. Eventually, we find out that Rachel (unbeknownst to Jacob) took them and is hiding them on the saddle of her camel, from which she says she cannot get down because "it is the way of women with her." Finding nothing, Laban is still out of sorts, but Jacob "becomes incensed and takes up his grievance with Laban."

The whole story takes thirty-five verses, and the only thing that happens is that Jacob and Laban build a rock monument which they call Mizpah, *because he [Laban] said, "May the Lord watch between you and me, when we are out of sight of each other. If you ill-treat my daughters or take other wives besides my daughters – though no one else be about, remember, God Himself will be witness between you and me."* Gen. 31:49, 50. [3] They agree never to cross the "mound and this pillar" with hostile intent, and "*May the God of Abraham and the god of Nahor*" – their respective ancestral deities – "*judge between us.*" Gen. 31:53.[4]

Let's hang loose.[5] Remember, Abraham's first altar was between Bethel (house of God) and Ai (the holy city of the Canaanites (see page 53). But Jacob has grown (as evidenced by the names of his children, etc.) and this time the "mound and pillar" of Jacob is between the God of Abraham (YHWH) and the god of Nahor (snorting nostrils, determination). Can we be saying that Jacob, who somewhat recognizes his sonship, is somewhere in between fully "taking on the mantle" of YHWH and relying on the "snorting nostrils" of his own ego? Can the "shining

---

[3] Laban said, "The daughters are my daughters, the children are my children, and the flocks are my flocks; all that you see is mine. Yet what can I do now about my daughters or the children they have borne? Come... let us make a pact, you and I, that there may be a witness between you and me." Gen. 31:43,44.

[4] *The Torah,* pp. 57,58.

[5] Notice that the chapter is 31, a prime number (that which cannot be taken apart) and the first verse quoted is 49 (7x7); the second verse quoted is 53, again a prime number this time adding up to 8 (plumpness). So something is up, here.

thoughts" that have been taking advantage of us all this time, simply be the "rantings" of our own ego that is "determined" to be in control?

Certainly, the ego sees "all" as belonging to "itself." Certainly, the ego sees "itself" as totally independent, not part of a "whole." On the other hand, "sonship" has different connotations. While "sonship" brings protection, abundance, etc., it also means relinquishing personal control. "Sonship" implies conceding to the will of God.

Rachel did well in taking Laban's household "gods." Only attention to the feminine side will lessen the power of the "lower" ego over the conscious mind. And Laban kisses his "sons and daughters" and bids them goodbye. Jacob, too, goes "on his way," *and angels of God encountered him.*

We have here a partially "new" man, and *The Torah* interjects another "title."[6] וישלח Now it is time for an even greater "challenge." Jacob must make peace with his brother.

Reconciliation With Esau

Esau's easy to find; he's in the land of Seir, the country of Edom (hair, red) – in other words, he hasn't changed. Nevertheless, Jacob sends him a message saying: *" I stayed with Laban... until now; I have acquired cattle, asses, sheep, and male and female slaves; and I send this message to my lord in the hope of gaining your favor. "* And the messenger returns saying that *"Esau, himself, is coming to meet you, and there are four hundred men with him. "* Gen. 32:4-8.

Great! Just what we needed! But ...

Somewhere... sometime... on the climb, the aspirant is going to have to make peace with his/her "brother." Mythology presents it as the "monster or dweller on the threshold." Here is that which "terrorizes" Jacob most, because (if you remember), twenty-one years ago Esau was

---

[6] According to Suarès' values, 8·30·300·10·6 (reading from left to right) = 354 = 12.

out to "kill" Jacob. And now we're told he's coming with 400 men. Up to this time, Jacob hasn't been challenged. Laban was no real threat to Jacob, because Jacob had made his flocks thrive; but Jacob had dealt "poorly" with Esau. Jacob "sinned" against Esau, and this "sin" is going to have to be addressed.[7]

Writing in I John, the disciple John says: *See what love the Father has given us, that we should be called children of God; and so we are. ... Beloved, we are God's children now; it does not yet appear what we shall be, but we know that when he appears we shall be like him, for we shall see him as he is. And every one who thus hopes in him purifies himself as he is pure. Every one who commits sin is guilty of lawlessness; **sin is lawlessness**. You know that he appeared to take away sins, and in him there is no sin. No one who abides in him sins; no one who sins has either seen him or known him.* John 3:1-6.

Jacob is just beginning "to know him," and now he will "purify" himself by meeting Esau, against whom he sinned. In one way or another, we are all "sinners." The word comes from an obscure root which means "to miss." The current explanation is that it is an archery term that means to "miss the mark." Notice what we're saying, both about Jacob and about our own actions. Oftentimes we "miss the mark." We know that we, like Jacob, sometimes misuse others, sometimes bring the "blessing" to ourselves rather than letting it lie where it is supposed to be. But in so doing, the "blessing" becomes a curse. Fortunately, we find that God's intent was for us to prosper, regardless.

I experience such a challenge. During college, I had belonged to a sorority; and my "sisters" meant a great deal to me.[8] But I began to feel unwanted and unaccepted. Consequently, I pulled myself away and "pouted." Through the next ten or fifteen years I regularly

---

[7] I have to make an aside here. I just took a break and was watching the *Opra Winfrey Show*, and someone was talking and excusing their "sin" because ----- such and such had been "done" to them. Notice, Jacob makes no excuses! He does not blame his "mother," he does not blame his "father," nor does he blame his "brother." He simply is ready to restore the relationship. If he were "blaming," he would not be at this #12 consciousness.

[8] One of the vows taken is to deal honorably with your "sisters" for a lifetime.

experienced bad dreams where I was still unaccepted, even though I was long past college. Finally, my mother's death heightened my reaction to everything, until I couldn't cope with the world; and the dreams got stronger. That's when I started meditating. Simply this "focusing" my attention on the spiritual made all the difference. Eventually, I felt impelled to rectify the "sin" I had committed so many years earlier; and finally, after several years of letters of apology, I saw each of those whom I felt I had "offended," and each meeting was preceded by a burning, "emotional terror."

Interestingly, none of these women had held anything against me. The "sin" had been in my own mind; and it was from there that it had to be eradicated.

Earlier, Jacob's attention was caught when he saw that "ladder" with angels; and by his numbers and his rewards (including his children), we know that he has been (somewhat) paying attention to the spiritual. He's even got the "household gods" that once belonged to Laban. Besides, God has been saying "Return to the land of your birth." **But !** To do this, Jacob must meet Esau. Needless to say, *Jacob was greatly frightened; in his anxiety, he divided the people with him, and the flocks and herds and camels, into two camps, thinking "If Esau comes to the one camp and attacks it, the other camp may yet escape."* Gen. 32:8,9.

Our champion on the climb hasn't learned the lesson yet. Remember what John said, *Sin is lawlessness.* And do we remember what the LAW is? (See page 79.) **The LAW is:** *with the judgment you pronounce you will be judged.*

What is Jacob's **judgment?** Jacob prays: *"I am not worthy ... of all the steadfast love and all the faithfulness which thou hast shown to thy servant, **for with only my staff I crossed this Jordan; and now I have become two companies.** Deliver me... from the hand of my brother... Esau, for I fear him, lest he come and slay us all, the mothers with the children. But thou didst say, 'I will do you good, and make your descendants as the sand of the sea...'"* So he lodged there that night, and took from what he had with him a present for his brother Esau, two hundred she-goats and twenty he-goats, two hundred ewes and twenty rams, thirty milch camels and their colts, forty cows and ten bulls, twenty she-asses and ten he-asses. Gen. 32:10-16.

Only he/she who accedes to the LAW is **righteous.** We might think that Jacob is far from such designation, but there is one line that indicates differently. Jacob says: ... *with only my staff I crossed this Jordan.* It doesn't sound very important, but this is the first time "staff" has been used. Eventually, *staff* will become more important. Esoterically *staff* refers to something other than what it sounds like. *Staff* comes from a root word meaning to "germinate." In clearer terms, it is something that is "productive," and eventually, Aaron's "budded" staff is one of the items to be placed in the Ark of the Covenant.[9] We can hang loose and guess that the opposite of having a "staff" in hand, would be having a "sword," in hand. Remember, that was one of the differences in the "blessing." Esau was to be a man of war ... until he reached dominion. Jacob was never to be a man of war, so it would be improper for him to have a sword.[10]

Are you sufficiently hanging loose? Little innuendoes are being thrown at us left and right.

| Are You "Hanging Loose?" |

Now, we come to the question of what "war" is. Esau was told: ... *by thy sword shalt thou live...,* and eventually David will be denied building the Temple because he was a man of war; so "war" must mean something other than what is obvious.

---

[9] *Staff* also likely refers to the "spinal cord" which has been "opened," thus activating the "inner light." Eastern disciplines refer to it as the *Kundalini,* as do those who call themselves Metaphysicians. I have attempted to stay apart from strict *metaphysics* in this work, but in this instance some readers will receive much needed "light" by reading the works of the late Corine Heline. Particularly enlightening are the several volumes of the *New Age Bible Interpretation.*

[10] A second hidden mystical reference is the *divided into two camps.* This one is really hidden, and the only way it came into my mind was that I was verifying the spelling of *Kundalini,* and I was forced to check with *Bible Interpretation.* At this level of Jacob, the aspirant is not only gaining in his/her awareness of his/her relationship with the Supreme; he/she is likely undergoing what the Eastern disciplines call the "opening of the chakras and the activating of the Kundalini." It means that the mechanism which truly empowers the Christed man is beginning to function. Eventually, we will refer to these two camps as Joachim and Boaz, the two pillars of the Temple; for now we will describe it as "two camps."

Remember, it is not the intellect that climbs the Mountain! The Bible is not to be "learned." The Bible is for teaching the unified "mind" to "**see**," to "**hear**," to "**say**," and to "hang loose"! Until we learn this, we are still *living by the sword*; we are still "men of war."

As with all *mystery* writing, all mythology and all legends, the aspirant must "finish off" his world of war by finally facing the "dweller on the threshold." So, too, is it with Jacob. As it is in all symbolic literature, he must confront that which is most like him – his twin brother – the other side of himself.[11] Now Jacob selects presents for Esau: 200 she-goats/20 he-goats; 200 ewes/20 rams; 30 milch (milk) camels with colts; 40 cows/10 bulls; 20 she-asses/10 he-asses.

As presented, this just sounds like a bunch of animals; but let's hang loose for a moment. There are several ways to consider Jacob's presentation. First, let's consider the type of animal. We are offering goats and sheep, camels and cows, and asses. (See page 63 regarding Abraham's animal sacrifice.) Second, only the camel colts are young; all others are mature. Third, notice the balance between male and female animals.

Goats and sheep, traditionally, represent the difference between the spiritual and the non-spiritual. Each year, the nation of Israel celebrated the "scape-goat," the one (of two sacrificial goats) that was spared the fire and sent out into the desert, thus carrying all the sins of Israel. Both goats and sheep were sacrificed in the later religious sacrifices. Of these, Jacob is giving Esau an equal amount – 200 females and 20 males, all mature.[12]

---

[11] A surprisingly profound presentation of this was made in the George Lucas *Star Wars* series (in *The Empire Strikes Back),* as Luke Skywalker, now under the tuteledge of the Jedi Master, Yoda, confronts what he thinks is his most dreaded enemy, Darth Vader. After decapitating the enemy, Luke peers into the helmet, only to find a reflection of his own face.

[12] Interestingly, the ratio is **not** 2 to 1 as Abraham's sacrifice was. Now the ratio is 1/10, the level expected for "tribute."

> ## Animal Lexicon
> **Wool, Meat, Milk Producers**
> goat- hair, milk, meat, stubborn,
>   self-willed
> sheep-wool, meat, placid, manageable,
>   dumb
>
> **Hide, Meat, Milk Producers**
> cattle - larger, but hide requires slaughter
>   can be herded fairly easily
>
> **Beasts of Labor and Burden**
> oxen–large bovine, castrated bull,
>   obedient, strong
> camel – stamina, carries great load,
>   stubborn
>
> **Beasts of Burden for Man**
> ass - carries both burdens and mankind,
>   somewhat managable, more surefooted
>   than horse, survives on barest vege-
>   tation., great perseverance
>   When bred with horse, it produces a
>   superior draft animal, smart and
>   sure – but sterile.
>
> horse - fast, for kings, for war, smart
>
> **Wild Beasts**
> lion - king of beasts, strong, smart, mate for life,
>   communal animal, uncontrolled by man
> snake - closest to ground (no legs)
>
> **Birds**
> eagle - king of birds, swift, strong, smart
> sparrow - innumerable, "worthless," tiny
> "turtle" dove - peace, beauty, contentment,
>   ground nester, evidences good water

The larger animals are intended as a "strong" statement. Jacob sends 40 cows and 10 bulls. Cows produce mostly milk, something for infants. But the most valuable milk-producer is the camel, for it is noted for endurance. Since these give milk, they are female. Colts usually refers to male young, and here the ratio is even – 30 milk camels and their colts. Lastly, Jacob sends 20/10 asses, with the ratio of 2 to 1 female.

Jacob tells his servants to deliver all of the animals, drove by drove, with space in between each drove. Esau isn't going to see all that he's being given in tribute until it all arrives. Jacob thinks, *"If I propitiate him with presents in advance, and then face him, perhaps he will show me favor."* And Jacob sends his peace offering.

All of these animals added together come to a total of 580, with 490 females and 90 males. Can we possibly be saying that this is a declaration of the aspirant's level at this point? Symbolically, the "feminine," intuitive side is

7x7x10;the "intellectual" is 9x10, the level of the initiate's advance. The "feminine" side has reached the fullness of "earthly completion." The intellectual side, the conscious mind, is now to progress in the initiatory process. Interestingly, the 580 number gives us 2x29x10. I'm speculating, but wasn't it at #11 that the ancestors produced? Now Jacob is at a second level of 11 (2+9) ready for a new beginning.

I must admit, I find all these numbers distracting. I would prefer not being tied to the intellectual analysis so much. I'm sure it was given as supplementary information, but full attention to it detracts from the intuitive message. So, let's return to other symbolic information. Notice that the fewest animals are those which "cannot" be eaten.[13] Only part of what is being sent to Esau can be consumed; but it is the greatest part. Notice also, that Jacob is sending the present to "propitiate" Esau. Jacob is not at the point of expecting good. Even though he's ready for initiatory progress, he still questions what he'll receive.

Supposedly, there remain a few descriptions of the initiatory process of some of the mystery schools, and at least one of the levels of initiation included a "night-long"

---

[13] The list of "clean" and "unclean" animals is found in Leviticus, Chapter 11 and Deuteronomy, Chapter 14. "Whatever **parts the hoof and is cloven-footed and chews the cud,** ... **you may eat.** Nevertheless among those that chew the cud or part the hoof, **you shall not eat these**: The **camel,** because it chews the cud but does not part the hoof, is unclean to you. And the **rock badger,** because it chews the cud but does not part the hoof, is unclean to you. And the **hare,** because it chews the cud but does not part the hoof, is unclean to you. And the **swine,** because it parts the hoof and is cloven-footed but does not chew the cud, is unclean to you. Of their flesh you shall not eat, and their carcasses you shall not touch; **they are unclean to you. These you may eat, of all that are in the waters. Everything in the waters that has fins and scales, whether in the seas or in the rivers, you may eat.** ... **Everything in the waters that has not fins and scales is an abomination to you.** And these you shall have in abomination **among the birds, they shall not be eaten, they are an abomination**: the **eagle, the vulture, the osprey, the kite, the falcon ...,** every **raven** according to its **kind, the ostrich, the nighthawk, the sea gull, the hawk** according to its kind, **the owl, the cormorant, the ibis, the water hen, the pelican, the carrion vulture, the stork, the heron** according to its kind, the **hoopoe, and the bat.** All **winged insects that go upon all fours are an abomination** to you. Yet **among the winged insects that go on all fours you may eat those which have legs above their feet, with which to leap on the earth.** Of them **you may eat: the locust** according to its kind, **the bald locust** according to its kind, **the cricket** according to its kind, and **the grasshopper** according to its kind. But all other winged insects which have four feet are an abomination to you." Lev. 11:1-22.

session where the aspirant, somehow, "wrestled" with a "challenge." Many of those reading this *Climbing the Mountain* may have experienced such an occurrence in their "sleep." These "night visions" have a clarity that normal "dream time" lacks, and they carry an intensity that not only is "overwhelming" at the time but lingers into the daylight hours. Sometimes these encounters are with the "dweller on the threshold." Regardless of the oponent, the encounters are so intense that we're never again the same. Such is Jacob's experience.

> *The same night he arose and took his two wives, his two maids, and his eleven children, and crossed the ford of the Jabbok. He took them and sent them across the stream, and likewise everything that he had. And **Jacob was left alone; and a man wrestled with him until the breaking of the day.***
>
> *When the man saw that he did not prevail against Jacob, he touched the hollow of his thigh; and Jacob's thigh was put out of joint as he wrestled with him. Then he said, "Let me go, for the day is breaking." But Jacob said, "**I will not let you go, unless you bless me.**" And he said to him, "What is your name?" And he said, "Jacob." Then he said, "**Your name shall no more be called Jacob, but Israel, for you have striven with God and with men, and have prevailed.**" Then Jacob asked him, "Tell me, I pray, your name." But he said, "Why is it that you ask my name?" **And there he blessed him.** So Jacob called the name of the place **Peniel**, saying, "**For I have seen God face to face, and yet my life is preserved.**" The sun rose upon him as he passed Penuel, limping because of his thigh. That is why the children of Israel ... do not eat the thigh muscle that is on the socket of the hip, since Jacob's hip socket was wrenched at the thigh muscle.* Gen. 32:22-32. [14]

Did you notice the two words which are so close in spelling – *Peniel* ("face of God") and Penuel? *The Torah* utilizes both spellings, too; and yet, the definition for both

---

[14] Physically, the "thigh can refer to the "sciatic" nerve which runs through it and which connects to all parts of the lower body. The "Higher Criticism" of the Nineteenth Century saw the "thigh"as a euphemism for sexual prowess.

The above quote (and the numbers for the verses) was taken from the RSV. What I assume is a symbolic variance between the RSV and *The Torah* is the numbering of the verses. *The Torah* begins Chapter 32 with the last verse of 31 (according to the RSV); by so doing, it ends with verse 33. This would mean nothing to me except that Jesus supposedly died at the age of 33; therefore, it seems to have some symbolic importance. Moreover, the next chapter is 33, so the whole sequence emphasizes the importance of Chapter 33. Rather than just dealing with Jacob and indicating that it applies to what came earlier; 32 begins with Laban kissing his "sons and daughters."

words is the same. Can the two "spellings" possibly indicate a difference between the *spiritual* occurrence and the *physical* "reality." With hang-loose logic we can see that the all-important "**el**" finishes off both names. *The Torah* uses the term "**a divine being**" in place of "God"; nevertheless, the Hebraic **El**ohim provides the "el" portion of the name *Israel*. However we say it, "el" is joining YHWH in this encounter. Jacob's "encounter" with the "dweller on the threshold" is more important than just a psychological confrontation with the "darkest" part of himself; it is an "encounter" that changes Jacob to the point that it reestablishes Jacob's connection to the divine.

Notice, Jacob is entirely alone. We already knew that the climb was a singular experience, but Jacob even sends all of his belongings over the Jabbok. Jabbok is a smaller stream of water than the Jordan, and it lies **east** of the Jordan. Its name is related to a primitive root which means to "pour out," "to empty." Therefore, it is an "empty" vessel, Jacob, which wrestles with the "divine being" and therefore triumphs. So is it with us all.

But Jacob is not "empty" because of weakness. He has triumphed several times to get to this place; he is "empty" because he voluntarily sets himself aside from his family and his possessions.[15] Admittedly, part of his action is because of the fear of Esau; nevertheless, it is a voluntary "emptying," and it provides a great "**opportunity**."

Sometimes we may have to "leap frog" to "hang loose." The location where Jacob wrestles the "being" for a blessing is at Peniel, which *The Torah* footnotes as "face

---

[15] Physically, the pineal body (gland) is a "small conical reddish body ... attached to the posterior cerebral commissure." It once was believed to have been a "vestigial sense-organ, probably an eye." Current thought ascribes to it glandular functions, due to its secretions. "It appears to be connected with growth, both physical and mental." From the *Encyclopedia Americana*.

Esoterically, it is the center, when activated in conjunction with the pituitary center, which leads to the "opening of the third eye."

of God."[16] The spelling is so close to "pineal"that I have always assumed that the two relate to each other. According to Descartes: "In man, soul and body touch each other, only at one single point, the pineal gland in the brain." [17]

The intellectual world may not agree,but I think the esoteric world will. It is at our biblical "Peniel" that Jacob experiences this joining of soul and body as he **"sees"** the face of God. He perceives part of the nature of God; thus he is prepared to meet his brother. *And Jacob lifted up his eyes and looked, and behold, Esau was coming, and four hundred men with him. So he divided the children among Leah and Rachel and the two maids. And he put the maids with their children in front, then Leah with her children, and Rachel and Joseph last of all. He himself went on before them, bowing himself to the ground seven times, until he came near to his brother. But Esau ran to meet him, and embraced him, and fell on his neck and kissed him, and they wept.*

And when Esau raised his eyes and saw the women and children, he said, "Who are these with you?" Jacob said, "The children whom God has graciously given your servant." ... Esau said, "What do you mean by all this company which I met?" Jacob answered, "To find favor in the sight of my lord." But Esau said, "I have enough, my brother; keep what you have for yourself." Jacob said, "No, I pray you, if I have found favor in your sight, then accept my present from my hand; for truly to see your face is like seeing the face of God, with such favor have you received me. Accept, I pray you, my gift that is brought to you, because God has dealt graciously with me, and because I have enough." Thus he urged him, and he took it. Then Esau said, "Let us journey on our way, and I will go before you." But Jacob said to him, "My lord knows that the children are frail, and that the flocks and herds giving suck are a care to me; and if they are overdriven for one day, all the flocks will die. Let my lord pass on before his servant, and I will lead on slowly, according to the pace of the cattle which are before me and according to the pace of the children, until I come to my lord in Seir." So Esau said, "Let me leave with you some of the men who are with me." But he said, "What need is there? Let me find favor in the sight of my lord." Gen. 33:1-15.

Jacob is sufficiently wise to know that he can't again join himself to Esau. Meeting one's brother doesn't necessitate reunification. Separation from that which has no

---

[16] *The Torah*, p. 60.

[17] G.A. Gaskell, *Dictionary of all Scriptures and Myths,* Avenel Books, N.Y., (1960), p. 576. Gaskell explains: "The pineal gland and the pituitary body are means for detecting vibrations subtler than science ordinarily recognizes ...[and] are used to some extent as a means of educating the soul through the physical body."

regard for its "birthright" is mandatory for one on the climb.
*So Esau returned that day on his way to Seir. But **Jacob journeyed to Succoth, and built himself a house, and made booths for his cattle; ...** And Jacob came safely to the city of Shechem, which is in the land of Canaan, on his way from Paddan-aram; and he camped before the city. And from the sons of Hamor, Shechem's father, he bought for a hundred pieces of money the piece of land on which he had pitched his tent. There he erected an altar and called it El-Elohe-Israel.* Gen. 33:16-20.

We must be observant here. First, we're at Chapter 33 (3x11), and immediately upon concluding the "wrestling match" with the divine being, Jacob **lifts up his eyes and looks,** and he **sees his brother.**

The New Consciousness Must Find Its Own Way

Notice also that whether we like it or not, Esau is prepared for war, if necessary; but Jacob makes obeisance – bowing to the ground seven times. The result is that Esau *ran to meet him, and embraced him, and fell on his neck and kissed him, and they wept.* When all is in divine order, *sin* is immediately forgiven.

Any earthly challenge that confronts us must be dealt with on the earthly plane as well as the spiritual. Jacob bows to the earth seven times (earthly completion). Even Jesus had to "deal" with his earthly challenge. He had to face and endure "crucifixion." Even "the Christ" cannot just sit in his cave and chant "Krishna," expecting that the Pharisees and the Sadducees will go away. To do so would be close to the "magic" mindset of the Chaldeans; we left that long ago.

Peace must be made within ourselves to effect peace with the outer challenge. Jacob now **sees** his outer challenge differently than he had before: *truly to see your face is like seeing the face of God, with such favor have you received me.*

This "new awareness" **sees** that everything is of God. But Jacob is also smart enough to know that he cannot again become entangled in the relationship. Though it would be easy to fall in "behind" Esau, Jacob **sees** that it would be unwise; and even though Esau "generously" offers the protection of his men, Jacob must decline.

It sounds like an excuse to say that *the children are frail, and ...the flocks and herds giving suck are a care ...; and if they are overdriven for one day, all the flocks will die,* but it's true. This "new consciousness" cannot be retied to the old challenge and survive; it cannot be "driven hard" without its being killed. This "new awareness" must be handled gently, with time for it to progress. So Jacob "pulls up his tent pins" and journeys to a place where he can build a "tabernacle" (booths), a place where these "milch camels" and flocks can become strong and self reliant.

Esau returns to Seir. The name Seir means "rough," but it comes from a root meaning "to be horribly afraid." (An aside is that otherwise Esau would not have come with an large contingent.) Can it be that the intellectual world's fear necessitates its armies and "endless" warfare?

On the other hand, the change that just came about Jacob is a substantial change which we can all experience. Part of the difference in our lives will be that where we were previously "horribly afraid," we no longer are quite so fearful. In fact, by recalling this "horrible fear," we can tell when (from time to time) we return to the Esau nature.

We are still climbing the Mountain (Seir refers to a "rough" mountain), and the "roughness" is this fear that is part of Esau's state of mind. But Jacob has a new state of mind, and he "journeys" to **Succoth** (booths, i.e. huts of entwined boughs, tabernacle).

Apparently the designation of "tabernacle" comes from "anything" being constructed of upright pieces of wood and being obvious from a distance (prominent).[18] As do David and Solomon, later, Jacob builds himself a house first; then he builds the tabernacle. Our own expression must first be established. Notice that Jacob's tabernacle is not for the LORD; it is for cattle, but it is a "tabernacle."

---

[18] Strong lists two different words for "tabernacle." One implies its construction from "pillars" of wood; the second implies its having a "prominent" exposure.

Jacob has followed a certain course. His journey began at Beer-sheba (well of an oath) with his father Isaac, but because of "fear" Jacob leaves (spending the night at Bethel [house of God]) and heads for Laban at Paddan-aram, a "plateau" where little change takes place for 20 years. Eventually, at the Lord's urging he leaves, crossing the Jordan, to return to Canaan (to bend the knee). He has a night vision at Peniel, and he is "renamed" (has a new "nature"). But now he is "camping" before the city of Shechem ("a ridge," coming from "the neck which carries burdens"), and he even buys the land where he has pitched his "tent" from Hamor (a male ass; coming from a root meaning to "boil up with scum," to glow with redness). Sounds pretty bad, doesn't it? Maybe Jacob's fallen off the Mountain – but we know he's still climbing.

The Climb Is Always A "Process"

Let's hang loose for a minute. We know Jacob is expressing at the level of the initiate, and just a short time ago he felt as though he had actually seen "God;" yet here he is placing himself in front of a city that represents "a neck" that is bowed down because of the burdens it carries. Not only that, but he even gives this "redness" 100 "pieces of money" [notice neither silver nor gold]. There is nothing redeeming about either the city or the people here. In fact, it is described as a place that is "guarded" or "walled in." We wonder, how does a fellow who has just "seen God" find himself in such a "place?"

What we don't recognize is that finding ourselves in this "place" of "redness" and "burdens" is part of the process Jacob is undergoing – part of our process, too. Remember what Jesus said: *"Do you think that I have come to give peace on earth? No, I tell you, but rather division; for henceforth **in one house there will be five divided, three against two and two against three;** they will be divided, father against son and son against father, mother against daughter and daughter against her mother, mother-in-law against her daughter-in-law and daughter-in-law against her mother-in-law."* Luke 12:51-53.

130

For some reason, our western civilization has a "make it quick" habit. Not only do we expect instant gratification, we expect immediate "peace" as soon as we become "slightly spiritual."[19] However, if the life of Jesus is any indication, we can expect the climb to involve numerous "opportunities" to check our "competency." It's all a test to see if we can recognize that our spiritual power is "as we say." Jesus tells us it isn't going to be a "make it quick" happening, and he warns that we'd better settle with our "accuser" for we'll *never get out till [we've] paid the very last copper*. So it is with Jacob. He's still "in the process." But, at least, he has some understanding. He builds an altar and "calls out" El-Elohe-Israel.[20]

Jacob (we've got to **learn** to call him Israel) has built an altar (a place of tribute) right in front of this walled city that feels its burdens so greatly and comes from "redness;" and he **declares** El (strength), Elohe (all aspects of God) with his name (Israel). And he declares it twice.[21] Now he'll be "tested."

*Now **Dinah the daughter of Leah**... went out to visit the women of the land; and **when Shechem** the son of Hamor the Hivite, **the prince of the land, saw her, he seized her and lay with her and humbled her**. And his soul was drawn to Dinah the daughter of Jacob; he loved the maiden and spoke tenderly to her. So Shechem spoke to his father Hamor, saying, "Get me this maiden for my wife."*

*Now Jacob heard that he had defiled his daughter Dinah; but **his sons were with his cattle in the field, so Jacob held his peace until they came**. And Hamor the father of Shechem went out to Jacob to speak with him. The sons of Jacob came in*

---

[19] Jesus continues this teaching with a slightly different focus. *He also said to the multitudes, "When you see a cloud rising in the west, **you say** at once, 'A shower is coming'; and so **it happens**. And when you see the south wind blowing, **you say**, 'There will be scorching heat'; and **it happens**. You hypocrites! You know how to interpret the appearance of earth and sky; but why do you not know how to interpret the present time? "And why do you not **judge for yourselves what is right**? As you go with **your accuser** before the magistrate, **make an effort to settle with him on the way**, lest he drag you to the judge, and the judge hand you over to the officer, and the officer put you in prison. I tell you, you will never get out till you have paid the very last copper."* Luke 12:53-59.

[20] *The Torah* and the other sources translate that this is Jacob (now Israel) calling the altar El-elohe-yisrael (according to *The Torah*, El, God of Israel.) How much more important it is, if Israel is **declaring** this as a fact.

[21] See the Hebrew, Greek Dictionary.

*from the field when they heard of it; and the men were indignant and very angry, because **he had wrought folly in Israel** by lying with Jacob's daughter, for such a thing ought not to be done. But Hamor spoke with them, saying, "The soul of my son Shechem longs for your daughter; I pray you, give her to him in marriage. Make marriages with us; give your daughters to us, and take our daughters for yourselves. You shall dwell with us; and the land shall be open to you; dwell and trade in it, and get property in it." Shechem also said to her father and to her brothers, "Let me find favor in your eyes, and whatever you say to me I will give. Ask of me ever so much as marriage present and gift, and I will give according as you say to me; only give me the maiden to be my wife."*

*The **sons of Jacob answered** Shechem and his father Hamor **deceitfully**,... They said to them, "We cannot... give our sister to one who is uncircumcised, for that would be a disgrace to us. Only ... [if] **you will become as we are and every male of you be circumcised**... will [we] give our daughters to you, and we will take your daughters to ourselves, and we will dwell with you and become one people. But if you will not listen to us and be circumcised, then we will take our daughter, and we will be gone." Their words pleased Hamor and Hamor's son Shechem. And the young man did not delay to do the thing, because he had delight in Jacob's daughter. Now he was the most honored of all his family. So Hamor and his son Shechem ... spoke to their fellow townsmen, saying ... "Only on this condition will the men agree to dwell with us, to become one people: that every male among us be circumcised as they are circumcised. Will not their cattle, their property and all their beasts be ours? Only let us agree with them, and they will dwell with us."*

*... **and every male was circumcised**, all who went out of the gate of his city. **On the third day,** when they were sore, two of the sons of Jacob, **Simeon and Levi, Dinah's brothers, took their swords and came upon the city unawares, and killed all the males. They slew Hamor and his son Shechem with the sword, and took Dinah out of Shechem's house, and went away.** And the sons of Jacob came upon the slain, and plundered the city, because their sister had been defiled; they took their flocks and their herds, their asses, and whatever was in the city and in the field; all their wealth, all their little ones and their wives, all that was in the houses, they captured and made their prey.*

*Then **Jacob said to Simeon and Levi, "You have brought trouble on me by making me odious to the inhabitants of the land,** the Canaanites and the Perizzites; my numbers are few, and if they gather themselves against me and attack me, I shall be destroyed, both I and my household." But they said, "Should he treat our sister as a harlot?"* Gen. 34:1-31.

This enigmatic story is more palatable if we see it as a symbolic statement. Dinah (feminine of Justice) is the feminine expression of weak-eyed Leah. She is "justice," but justice that does not "see" clearly. And she's raped by that which feels itself bent over by the world's burdens. I'm sure we can all see ourselves in this picture. We're outraged by the world's treatment of "justice." We're ready to strike out for the "weak" and "misused." We're so enraged that we're ready to revert to the "warlike" nature of Esau; and it's particularly our Simon (hearing) and Levi (love) parts that become enraged. Only that which we "love" can elicit sufficient emotion to move us. But "hearing" without "seeing" lacks the Truth which *seeing* and *hearing* brings.

Certainly, there is no question that our "worldly" burden-feeling nature must be circumcised (cleansed, purified, dedicated), and the circumcision weakens this nature sufficiently that its male nature (conscious mind) can be wiped out. Notice the paradox. We're supposed to be loving and gentle; but if we see "burden-bending" circumstances, we're not supposed to accept it as true. Remember the lesson with "hope"? If we "hope," we're saying we're lacking that which we hope for. Here, if we acknowledge this "burden bending" nature, we are accepting it as true. Therefore it must be wiped out for "justice" to prevail. And JUSTICE does prevail. Dinah goes with all the rest of Israel to Egypt. She's one of the **33** members of Israel.[22]

To this point, except when he sent everything over the Jabbok, Jacob has had Laban's "household idols" with him. To us this makes no difference. We know that figures of stone or wood or metal have no power.

Rid Yourselves Of Alien "Gods" In Your Midst

We're schooled in the laws of physics, so we know that no physical "god" can make any difference in our lives. We do know this, don't we? ...Maybe we don't. We're fearful that "such and such" will make us sick ... or destroy our lives ... or make us impoverished. We're fearful that "whatever powers we ascribe to physical phenomenon" will affect us. But, these are *alien gods*; they have no power. Jacob is told: *"Arise! Go up to Bethel (house of God [El]) and remain there; and build an altar there to the God who appeared to you when you were fleeing from your brother, Esau."* Jacob is consolidating the growth he has

---

[22] See *The Torah*, Gen. 46:15.

made; it is time to unequivocally declare the truth. Jacob tells his household: *"Rid yourselves of the alien gods in your midst, purify yourselves, and change your clothes."* Gen. 35:2

You and I have numerous alien "gods" in our midst! The term "god" implies something that has power over us. We allow lack or plenty to "control our lives." We allow habits to be our "gods;" we allow relationships to be our "gods;" we allow past experiences to hinder us. We allow all sorts of "alien gods" to have sway over us. Soon, Moses will give us the definitive commandment. **I am the LORD, thy God! Thou shalt have no other "gods" before me!**

For Jacob there is only ONE God, *"the God who answered me when I was in distress and who has been with me wherever I have gone."* Gen. 35:3. So Jacob's entire "household," i.e. absolutely every cell and thought (both conscious and unconscious) of Jacob, takes the "alien gods" and the "rings" in their ears (the outer manifestations – even if they appear to be gold) and buries them under the oak tree (greatest strength) at that place where the neck bends because of the burdens carried by the shoulders. Isn't it appropriate that all these "alien gods" and their mindset are buried at Shechem? Now only the God which Jacob recognizes accompanies him. And the retribution Jacob expects from the other cities never materializes; for a *"terror from God"* falls on the them so that they do *"not pursue the sons of Jacob."*

One wonders if
1. having seen "God" and
2. having prevailed,
3. having received a "new name,"
4. having acknowledged "God" as El Shaddai (God, Almighty),
5. having eliminated those "elements" which feel "burdened,"
6. having buried our parents' "alien gods," rid ourselves of any other alien gods in our midst, purified ourselves, and changed our clothes (outer expression),
7. we have reached earthly completion where the mind of Job (where *that which I most feared has come upon me!*) has been **set right.**

Now we can receive at the level of Jacob; now we must function at the level of Jesus, who says: *"Hereafter I will not talk much ...: for the prince of this world cometh, and* **hath nothing in me.** *But that the world may know that I love the Father; and as the Father [commands], even so I do."* Jn. 14:30-31.

134

Remember, Jesus tells us that he "brings division" on earth – *in one house there will be five divided.* It is the "senses," that which interprets the world for us that must be divided to be made spiritual. Then we recognize that whatever happens in this world is for the fruition of the spiritual world, for the two are ever ONE.

Let's look at Jacob again. Jacob has done everything he was supposed to do (whether we judge it so or not). He has even buried the "alien gods" as he was told, and he has built an altar at the place where he first met God, Bethel. Now we would think everything would be peaceful and full of "fruit." But, remember, we judge with the judgment of the world, and two more "worldly" happenings take place.

First, Jacob and his family set out from Bethel (house of God) for Bethlehem (house of bread), i.e., Ephrath (fruitfulness); but before reaching "fruit-fulness," Rachel goes into labor, bringing forth her second son. As Rachel is dying, she names him Benoai (son of my strength or suffering). The female side may keep seeing "suffering" longer than does the masculine; for Jacob renames him Benjamin (son of the right hand), i.e. "the power is now with Jacob." And the feminine that is like a "wandering ewe" dies and is buried on the road to "fruitfulness." This feminine expression has not been "sure;" it has not "said" *fruitfulness,* so it dies.[23]

Rachel Dies Short of Fruitfulness

Unlike Isaac who had only the feminine expression of "fettered by beauty," Jacob has had two legitimate feminine expressions: this "ewe" and weak-eyed Leah. Leah will remain and will eventually be buried beside Rebekah and Sarah, Abraham's wife. But the "ewe"

---

[23] See Genesis 49:31 (Note: 7x7 + prime number which adds up to 4.) It is interesting that Genesis uses "journeyed on." "Rachel" can mean "journey," so a (probably) intentional "pun" sees this feminine remaining with us. It is always active and alive within us.

(feminine and mature of "lamb") nature is buried on the way to "fruitfulness."

There is one last story, here. It begins:*Israel journeyed on, and pitched his tent beyond Migdal-eder.* Gen. 35:21. It may just be a continuation of the point being made by the death of Rachel and the renaming of Benjamin. But this story is so esoteric, that it is only a one-verse, one-sentence enigma. *While Israel stayed in that land, Reuben went and lay with Bilhah, his father's concubine; and Israel found out.* Gen. 35:22. If you remember, Bilhah means "timid," but also "tenderness." And this story finds Bilhah "lying" with Reuben (sight).

Let's try a hang-loose approach to the story. Let's say that Jacob is at a place of assessment of his life. We know all of his attributes; they are found in the list of his sons (see page 108); but it is his first son, Reuben (sight), that is the most necessary to be functioning adequately. This "sight" "lies" with "timidity," and Israel recognizes it. Once having recognized this "timidity" and the pun in the whole statement, this feminine expression can provide its higher aspect; it can provide tenderness; "timidity" is gone.

To "see" properly, we can have no "timidity." Nor can we "lie." Properly tied to Jacob (Israel), this "tenderness" produces Dan (righteous judgment) and Naphtali (strength). There is no longer the earlier "timidity" in us. Only now can we finish off the earlier masculine expression. *And Jacob came to his father Isaac at Mamre, or Kiriatharba (that is, Hebron), where Abraham and Isaac had sojourned. Now the days of Isaac were a hundred and eighty years. And Isaac breathed his last; and he died and was gathered to his people, old and full of days; and his sons Esau and Jacob buried him.* Gen. 35:27-29.

Genesis summarizes so that we don't get lost. Both sides produce; both Esau and Jacob have numerous children. Chapter 36 (12x3) lists the accomplishments (the progeny) of Esau, and within the first line of Chapter 37, there is a new expression. It is **Joseph**. The progeny of the spiritual side, Israel, will continue the climb.

Joseph before Pharaoh.

Chapter Seven

Joseph: the Increaser

*Jacob dwelt in the land of his father's sojourning, in the land of Canaan. ... Joseph, being **seventeen** years old, was shepherding the flock with his brothers; he was a [helper] with the sons of Bilhah and Zilpah ... and Joseph brought an ill report of them to their father.   **Now Israel loved Joseph more than any other of his children,** because he was the son of his old age; and he made him a long robe with sleeves. But when his brothers saw that their father loved him more than all his brothers, they hated him, and could not speak peaceably to him. Now Joseph had a dream, and when he told it to his brothers they only hated him the more. He said to them, "Hear this dream ...: behold, we were binding sheaves in the field, and lo, my sheaf arose and stood upright; and behold, your sheaves gathered round it, and bowed down to my sheaf."   **His brothers said** to him, "... **are you** indeed **to have dominion** over us?" So they hated him yet more for his dreams and for his words. Then he dreamed another dream, and told it to his brothers, and said, "Behold, ... the sun, the moon, and eleven stars were bowing down to me." But when he told it to his father and to his brothers, **his father rebuked him, and said to him, "... Shall I and your mother and your brothers indeed come to bow ourselves to the ground before you?"** And his brothers were jealous of him, but his father kept the saying in mind. Now his brothers went to pasture their father's flock near Shechem. And Israel said to Joseph, "Are not your brothers pasturing the flock at Shechem? Come, I will send you to them." **And he said** to him, **"Here I am."** Gen. 37: 1-13.*

The story of Joseph begins in Chapter 37 of Genesis, and *The Torah* uses וישב as a signpost.[1] We are told that Jacob has taken up residence in Canaan (to humble self, bend the knee), in the valley of Hebron (a society, but also a "spell") where his father had only "sojourned" (a moderate visit). All his sons are with him, but Jacob (Israel) *loved Joseph best of all.* At the moment, Joseph is at Jacob's level of expression; but eventually he will go to a higher level. However, for now he's dealing principally with Dan (righteous judgment), Naphtali (strength), Gad (abundance), and Asher (happiness) [page 108]; but he "speaks" poorly of them. That's a problem. Haven't we said that the "righteous man" must learn to "see" and to "say" correctly? Jacob may have learned

---

[1] Using Suarès' formula, this adds up to 318, i.e. 12; but notice that Jacob's 12 (see page 117) was derived from a larger number.

to "see," but Joseph will be the one to learn "to say." So far he's not doing too well.

Our climber of the Mountain speaks poorly of those fruits that come to the "righteous man." It is the sons of Bilhah and Zilpah (servants to Rachel and Leah) to whom Joseph is assigned as helper. Correctly viewed, they are the fruits of right expression; but Joseph is "saying" ill of them. At least he is not "bad mouthing" those "brothers" that are so essential to right expression, i.e. sight, hearing, loving, praise, reward, and order (all sons of Leah).

Having declared "Here I Am," Joseph searches for his brothers: leaving Hebron, going to Shechem (bowed neck because of burdens), and proceeding to Dothan (Chaldaizing, dual) where he finds them. These sons of Jacob have returned to the mindset that Abraham left in the first place, and now here comes this "dreamer" to chastise them. No wonder they're ready to kill him and throw him into the pit.

As we climb the Mountain, we will likely find that some of our old habits and ways of thinking conflict with our new awareness. Sometimes we even find this Joseph portion of us chastising us when we succumb to the old **Joseph Sold Into Egypt** ways of thinking. The old ways of thinking and acting would rather go unchallenged, and so they pose a danger to our new ways. They may even conspire to eliminate the new nature. But Reuben (sight) intends to save Joseph; and Judah (praise), also trying to save Joseph's life, suggests that Joseph be sold to Ishmaelites coming from Gilead (a spring of water). This will end with the Midianites (brawling and contention) finally selling Joseph to Potiphar, a courtier and Pharaoh's chief steward.

However it is that our personal lives tell the story, it's likely that our "Mountain climbing" selves will sometime be in Egypt. For *out of Egypt* came Abram, Jacob, Joseph, Moses and Jesus; so, too, must we "come out of Egypt."

Even to today's mind, Egypt is awesome. It seems ageless, encompassing an ancient time we cannot even approach and yet still touching our Roman ancestors. Moreover, in monuments that saw Abraham, Joseph, Moses and Jesus, its silence says more than words. We see the gold of King Tut's tomb on display and wonder at such riches coming from what we think of as a primitive people. But Egypt also offers "hidden" lessons. We may even perceive the symbolism of the statuary of Ramses II and question the spirituality of those whom we regard as "pagans." So we go to "Egypt" where we will stay for "400 years." [2]

Papyrus, pyramids, and crane.

As quickly as it began, the story of Joseph is interrupted by Genesis 38, an enigmatic story about Judah. On the surface, the story has little value other than to explain the parentage of two tribes in the vicinity. Interestingly, the story also provides explanation of one of the ancestors of Jesus, Perez (See Gen.46:12 and Mt. 3:33). I'm going to "hang loose" and speculate that before all of Israel goes to Egypt, something momentous has to take place. Joseph needs strength to deal with Pharaoh. This strength is to come from Judah, that

---

[2] Strong's *Concordance* uses the Hebrew *Mitsrayim* – indicating both Upper and Lower Egypt and coming from a word which means *a hemming in, a limitation, i.e., the border of Palestine,* and relating to an **unused root referring to the forehead.** Remember, *Know well that your offspring shall be strangers in a land not theirs, and they shall be enslaved and oppressed four hundred years ... in the end they shall go free with great wealth.* Gen. 15:13,14 (See page 63).

> The elements of the story found in Genesis 38:
> Judah **(praise)** is near Hirah (to wax pale in the sense of splendor) and joins the daughter of Shua (to cry aloud for freedom), a Canaanite. With her he **has three sons:**
> 1. Er (from be *bare*, be *naked* and related to **"opening the eyes, wake, lift up self"**),
> 2. Onan **(strong)**, and
> 3. Shelah **(to request, to demand)**.
> Judah gets a wife for Er. Her name is **Tamar (to be erect, a palm tree)**. But Er *was displeasing to the LORD, and the LORD took his life.* So was it with Onan who next was joined to Tamar. Then Judah promises Tamar that she will wed Shelah when he is old enough, but Judah ignores his promise and weds Shelah to another. Therefore, Tamar **tricks Judah into "lying" with her, thus producing twins, Perez (breaking forth, gap) and Zerah (a rising of light).**

characteristic of Jacob called *praise,* that tribe from which the Jewish people come, that tribe which will eventually be almost the whole of Israel. No other son of Jacob can claim this. Of all the characteristics of Jacob, Judah is the most important. The translations for Judah's sons' names expose his level of expression, for praise must be completely "upright;" it must include "opening the eyes" and "strength" and having the ability "to demand." However, Judah's sons are not up to their role.

Again, as in the past, it will be the feminine that will take things into its own hands. The masculine side doesn't have the integrity to follow through with its promise; so the feminine side, Tamar – this "upright tree" (not the strength or quality of an oak, but standing tall, nevertheless,) accomplishes what needs to be accomplished – "breaking forth" with "a rising of light." [3]

Now we can go down into Egypt, and we again have our significant **#12,** for we are at Genesis 39. We are almost finished with Genesis! Joseph and his sons are the fruition of the process that began with Abram. But the entire process will not be concluded until mankind reaches *Revelation* and the

---

[3] A point should be made here. Notice that the "son" of Judah which emerges first (the one designated by a crimson thread) is Zerah (a rising light); yet, that which is born first is Perez (breaking forth). There is a place on the "climb" where we seem to be given "light" and "inspiration," and we're likely to take some "pride" and pleasure in it. However, it is not that which simply "emerges" for a moment that becomes the ancestor of Jesus; it is that which finishes the process first – that which is "born" or "reborn" which accomplishes the fulfilment.

fulfillment of the Christed one. Only as that which began as Adam becomes the reigning Christ shall "all be made alive." Only then is Cain's mark, the mark in their forehead which has "limited" them, transformed; only then will they *see his face, and his name shall be on their foreheads.* Rev. 22:4. But recognition of the Christ is several thousand years away, so back to Joseph.

Yet, in some ways, the story of Joseph is an older version of Jesus' parable of the good servant. Upon examining the "performance" of the servant, the master says: *Well done, good and faithful servant; you have been faithful over a little, I will set you over much; enter into the joy of your master.* Mt. 25:21.

> *Well done, good and faithful servant; you have been faithful over a little, I will set you over much; enter into the joy of your master.* Isn't this the reason for climbing the Mountain, to enter into the joy of our master?
> ...and what is Joseph's message to us? "God intends it for good!"

Eventually, this will be the nature of Joseph's experience in Egypt, but not until Joseph undergoes some challenges. We all know Joseph's story. He gets sold into slavery. Not a pleasant thing to happen to a 17-year-old boy, but Joseph's no "run-of-the-mill" fellow; he has the LORD with him. Fortuitously, he is purchased by Pharaoh's chief steward, Potiphar. That's the equivalent of being the slave of the fellow who "runs" the White House. It's a good "job," but Joseph's still a slave. Nevertheless, he seems to do well, for *his master saw that the LORD was with him, and that the LORD caused all that he did to prosper in his hands. So Joseph found favor in his sight and attended him, and he made him overseer of his house and put him in charge of all that he had.* Gen. 39:3,4. And as happened with Sarai, *the Lord blessed his house for Joseph's sake...* Well, we could probably stay a slave like this forever. Joseph has ultimate power; his boss doesn't even check on him, and he's got the fat of the land of Egypt to live on.

Joseph and Potiphar

In this physical world, it's fairly easy to find persons who are experiencing life at Joseph's level of the climb. They're fairly prosperous; they have all their physical needs met, and even their "desires" satisfied. In the world of Egypt they should be happy. And we find Joseph happy; he's not even complaining that he's a slave. To the intellect, he's got everything going for him, except for this "slavery" thing, but the intellect doesn't worry about that anyway; so on the surface eveything's all right. Of course, we know that things can't stay like this; so here comes CHANGE – again because of the feminine.

There are those who see "questionable" biblical women as evil. They always blame the "fall" on Eve; they point to Lot's wife as "disobeying." They see the Queen of Sheba as "worshiper of false gods." They denounce Herod's wife as an adulteress and murderer of John the Baptist; and they see Potiphar's wife as a "seducer of boys." What they don't see is that "God works in mysterious ways." We've already dealt with Eve and Lot's wife; we have yet to deal with the Queen of Sheba and Herod's wife. Now let's look at Potiphar's wife. But to begin, we must look at Potiphar (Egypt, i.e, worshiper of Ra).[4] *Now Joseph was taken down to Egypt, and Potiphar, an officer of Pharaoh, the captain of the guard, an Egyptian, bought him from the Ishmaelites who had brought him down there.* Gen. 39:1.

We're going to have to hang loose on this. Throughout the Bible, Egypt is used as a somewhat "positive" presentation of the world. Unlike Babylon, which carries its "evil" connotations, Egypt is used as a place to come to "to be saved" if you "get in trouble" in the "promised land." And in this case, Joseph is brought to this "place" by the descendents of Ishmael, he who represents the "natural man" (see pages 67, 76-78), he who believes in God to the point of being "circumcised" but who still "explains himself." In other words, Joseph ends up in "Egypt" – that which worships the natural world (ruled by the sun) – because he is brought there by the fact that he does not yet "say" correctly. And he ends up enslaved to Potiphar, who "manages" the whole scene.

---

[4] Neither Strong or Young has a translation of Potiphar, other than relating him to Egypt. Fillmore (p.534) relates being of Egypt to worshipping Ra, the sun god.

We need to clarify something. You will notice that the above quotation identifies Potiphar as the *captain of the guard.* It is this designation that is found in both the King James and Revised Standard versions. However, *The Torah* specifies: Potiphar, *a courtier of Pharaoh and **his chief steward.*** It means more in the wording of *The Torah.* The captain of the guard is only over military matters; he's still at the "sword" level. The chief steward is over the entire operation; he is the ultimate manager of the life of Egypt. And it is the feminine side of this which tries to seduce Joseph. But Joseph answers:

There is none greater in this house than I; neither hath he kept back any thing from me but thee, because thou art his wife: how then can I do this great wickedness, and sin against God? Gen. 39:9.

It's quite easy to be seduced by the world. We become convinced that our jobs are the most important thing in life, and we "short" our families of the attention they deserve. We become convinced that whatever comes to us (riches, fame, adulation, friendship) is necessary for our continuation. We become convinced that that which has importance in our lives is located outside of ourselves. Potiphar's wife's demands are "Spirit's" way of allowing Joseph to continue the climb. Joseph doesn't accept the temptations of the world. He knows who he is; he "sees." But his rejection of the "world" puts him "prison," where to all "appearances" things are "bad."

To our non-righteous judgment, Joseph has ended up worse off than before. – **Wrong!** Joseph is climbing. *But the LORD was with Joseph and showed him steadfast love, and gave him favor in the sight of the keeper of the prison. **And the keeper of the prison committed to Joseph's care all the prisoners who were in the prison; and whatever was done there, he was the doer of it;** the keeper of the prison paid no heed to anything that was in Joseph's care, because the LORD was with him; and whatever he did, the LORD made it prosper.* Gen. 39:21-23.

Hang Loose, Observe the "Paradox" Of Life

Remember what we established as we started this climb? We agreed to "hang loose" and observe the "paradox" of life? We are really challenged here. How can the Bible say

144

whatever he did, the LORD made it prosper when Joseph is locked up in prison? Are we willing to hang loose and observe the paradoxes? The first "paradox" is that Joseph simply said "Here I Am" and he ends up in Egypt. The second "paradox" is that Joseph held to a "moral" position, and yet he ends up in prison, no longer living off the fat of Egypt.

Remember what Jesus said? ... *Blessed are those who hunger and thirst for righteousness, for they shall be satisfied. ...Blessed are they which are persecuted for righteousness' sake: for theirs is the kingdom of heaven. Blessed are ye, when men shall revile you, and persecute you, and shall say all manner of evil against you falsely, for my sake. ... For truly, I say to you, till heaven and earth pass away, not an iota, not a dot, will pass from the law until all is accomplished.* Mt 5:6,10,11, 18.

And what is this **LAW**? ... *with the judgment you pronounce you will be judged!* (See pages 78,79.) What is all this paradox to accomplish? That Joseph (and mankind) will both "see" and "say" with "righteous judgment." Consequently, Joseph has been placed in a situation where all of this can be brought about. It goes without saying that we are still in the world. The world still worships Ra (the sun), and Pharaoh has absolute control of the world. And the drama continues.

Now Pharaoh gets angry with his chief cupbearer and chief baker and confines them *"in the house of the chief steward, in the same prison house where Joseph [is] confined. The chief steward assign[s] Joseph to them, and he attend[s] them."*[5] Actually, our situation hasn't changed much since we first got to Egypt. We've progressed from slavery to prison, but we're still under the "spell" of that which "manages" Egypt. All of this time we've been close to Pharaoh's representatives, but now we're moving closer to Pharaoh himself.

---

[5] The wording of the Revised Standard Version makes more sense to our Western intellectual mind: *"...and he put them in custody in the house of the captain of the guard, in the prison where Joseph was confined. The captain of the guard charged Joseph with them, and he waited on them; and they continued for some time in custody."* Here it makes sense for Potiphar to still be associated with Joseph, because Potiphar is in charge of the prison, too.

Just as Jacob is defined by his "sons," Pharaoh is defined by his courtiers. He has a steward, a baker and a cupbearer. He becomes angry with the baker and the cupbearer and puts them in the "keeping" of the steward. Now, in hang-loose thinking, Pharaoh is that which dictates to this "world," and the "baker" makes bread; he provides Pharaoh (i.e. that which dictates) with sustenance. But Jesus tells us *"thou shalt not live by bread alone,"* so we know that the baker is not essential to Pharaoh. The "cupbearer," however, is the one who tests the cup before it is given to Pharaoh; he is invaluable.[6] As you know, Joseph's interpretation of the baker's dream is that he will be beheaded within three days; the interpretation of the cupbearer's dream is that he will be restored to his post.

Considering the Hebraic joy of "double *entendre,"* we may have another reason for the baker's demise and the cupbearer's salvation. *The Torah's* wording is significant. *On the third day ... Pharaoh singled out* (lit. lifted the head) *of his chief cupbearer and his chief baker from among his officials. He restored the chief cupbearer to his cupbearing, and he placed the cup in Pharaoh's hand, but the chief baker he impaled.* Gen. 40:20-22.

Joseph must eventually let the "sustenance" level go; eventually he must operate only at the level which accepts the "cup" and the "wine" in it, taking no thought of self.[7] Moreover, the cupbearer's survival assures that our "climber" will make it to Pharaoh's court – although for now it makes no difference, for *the chief cupbearer did not think of Joseph; he forgot him.* Gen. 40:23.

And *The Torah* give us a signpost:[8]   מקץ

---

[6] The King James and Revised Standard editions use "butler" for "cupbearer," but Western custom seldom required an official "tester." Poisoning of the ruler was a habit of the East, not the West.

[7] Lamsa's translation says the baker is "crucified."

[8] Using Suarès' values, מקץ (reading from left to right) is 900 · 100 · 40 or 1040 = 5, but notice that we have advanced to the third level of numbers, i.e. 1000.

146

Ideally, to our mind, the climb should be an easy walk up a hill, accompanied by wild flowers and shady resting places. Yet, here is Joseph, through no fault of his own, in prison – still we say he's on the climb. Not only that, but it takes two more years before the scene changes. Is it any wonder few finish the climb? Most individuals rely on

Both the Baker and the Cupbearer Have Dreams

"seeing" as the world "sees." But what the world "sees" is far from what is taking place.

The world "sees" these "interruptions" as times of inactivity. Jacob's "interruption" was with Laban, at the flatland of Padan-aram, and there he labored for 20 years. But Joseph is at a higher level than was Jacob; he cuts the time by 10 times. He stays in prison only **2 more** years.

*After two whole years, **Pharaoh dreamed that he was standing by the Nile,** and behold, there came up **out of the Nile seven cows sleek and fat,** and they fed in the reed grass. And behold, **seven other cows, gaunt and thin,** came up out of the Nile after them, and stood by the other cows on the bank of the Nile. And **the gaunt and thin cows ate up the seven sleek and fat cows.** And Pharaoh awoke. And he fell asleep and **dreamed a second time; and behold, seven ears of grain, plump and good, were growing on one stalk.** And behold, after them sprouted **seven ears, thin and blighted by the east wind. And the thin ears swallowed up the seven plump and full ears.** And Pharaoh awoke, and behold, it was a dream.*

*So in the morning his spirit was troubled; and he sent and called for all the magicians of Egypt and all its wise men; and Pharaoh told them his dream, but there was none who could interpret it to Pharaoh. Then the chief butler [cupbearer] said to Pharaoh, "... When Pharaoh was angry with his servants, and put me and the chief baker in custody in the house of the captain of the guard [chief steward], we dreamed on the same night, he and I, each having a dream with its own meaning. **A young Hebrew** was there with us, a servant of the captain ... [steward]; and when we told him, he **interpreted our dreams to us, giving an interpretation to each man according to his dream. And as he Interpreted to us, so it came to pass;** I was restored to my office, and the baker was hanged* [or impaled, depending on the translation]." Gen. 41:1-13.

Appropriately, at verse 14 (2x7), *The Torah* reads:
Thereupon Pharaoh sent for Joseph, and he was rushed from the dungeon. He had his hair cut and changed his clothes, and he appeared before Pharaoh.

As with Jacob's "change of clothes" (page 133), Joseph, too, changes the "outer" before entering the court of "he who totally controls this land which worships Ra" – before entering the presence of the mindset which accepts the physical picture as *truth*. Knowing that the *outer* will not change until the *inner* has changed, we recognize that "something" has changed inside Joseph.[9] I use the word *internalization*. Joseph has "internalized" – totally accepted as true – what he has been receiving all along... *and whatever was done there, he was the doer of it; the keeper of the prison paid no heed to anything that was in Joseph's care, because the LORD was with him; and whatever he did, the LORD made it prosper.* Gen. 39:22,23.

Now Joseph is released from "the dungeon." The metaphor of "a dungeon" applies to us, too. As long as we "see" ourselves at the mercy of a capricious "fate," we are in "a dungeon," where we cannot "see the light." Only as we recognize that the LORD is with us and makes *everything* prosper for us do we "see." Then we can

Pharoah's Need for Interpretation Frees Joseph

face Pharaoh. *And Pharaoh said to Joseph, "I have had a dream, and there is no one who can interpret it; and I have heard it said of you that when you hear a dream you can interpret it." Joseph answered [and said to Pharaoh, **Do you think... that without God I am able to give Pharaoh an answer that everthing will be well?**]* [10] Gen..41:15,16. *... Pharaoh's spirit was troubled; and he sent and called for all the magicians of Egypt and all its wise men; ... but there was none who could interpret it to Pharaoh.*

As I read this line, *Humpty-Dumpty* comes to mind ... *and all the King's horses and all the King's men couldn't put Humpty-Dumpty together again.* The trouble is that the magicians, Egypt's wise men, and "all the King's horses and all the King's men" are all mindsets of the intellect. They see and interpret what the eyes "see" as the "whole." But Joseph knows the truth: there is only **GOD;** and *without* God he

---

[9] The King James Version, The RSV, and even Lamsa translate that ... *he shaved himself.* You will notice that the frontplate for this chapter shows a clean-shaven Joseph. The "discrepancy" is of no value except for the esoteric meaning. A good Jew does not shave; the beard is the sign of wisdom. But according to Gaskell the hair of the head is a symbol of "faith, intuition of truth, or the highest qualities of the lower mind." (P.334) Possibly we're hearing that Joseph renews this "faith & intuition of truth" just as he renews the outside of him, his clothes.

[10] The brackets indicate that portion of the quote taken from *The Torah.*

cannot give Pharaoh an answer that everything will be well. This is a double negative, so let's reverse the statement: i.e. **with** God, everything **will be** well – we're back to our "full-full" glass.

What Jacob "sees" in his night vision and what Joseph interprets from Pharaoh's dream are similar. Jacob sees a ladder (both up and down) as the

"Full-full" Glass Has Ups & Downs expression of life. In a way, Joseph, too is "seeing" both "up" and "down" as the expression of life. He is "seeing" both

"plenty" and "lack." What makes Joseph different from the majority of mankind is that he "listens" to what he is "told." He is "told" how to deal with the "down" times, i.e., to plan for the "down" times by good management during the "up" times, all the while knowing that the ultimate scheme is "full-full."

Joseph concludes his interpretation: *"As for Pharaoh having had the same dream twice, it means that the matter has been determined by God and that God will soon carry it out. Accordingly, **let Pharaoh find a man of discernment and wisdom, and set him over the land of Egypt**. ... and organize the land of Egypt in the seven years of plenty."* Gen. 41:32-34.

This story of Pharaoh and Joseph is the challenge we all face. We "see" both "ups" and "downs" in our lives. Even if we hold to the understanding that we are made in the image of God, we're likely to have some "bad" things come into our lives. The disciples, too, questioned this fact. In passing the beggar who had been blind from birth, they questioned Jesus: *"Rabbi, who sinned, this man or his parents, that he was born blind?"* John 9:1,2. To all appearances this man was receiving "bad" from life, but Jesus answers: *"It was not that this man sinned, or his parents, but **that the works of God might be made manifest in him**. We must work the works of him who sent me, while it is day; night comes, when no one can work. As long as I am in the world, I am the light of the world."* John 9:3-5.

Too often we take this incident with the blind man and ascribe Jesus' answer only to his healing that man, but the end of the chapter says more. The Pharisees are questioning the man who was healed of blindness, trying to get him to condemn Jesus, and they say: *"We know that God has spoken to Moses, but as for this man, we do not know where he comes from." The man answered, "Why, this is a marvel! You do not know where he comes from, and yet **he opened my eyes. We know that God does not listen to sinners, but if any one is a worshiper of God and does his will, God listens to him.** Never since the world began has it been heard that any one opened the eyes of a man born blind. **If this man were not from God, he could do nothing."** They answered him, "You were born in utter sin, and would you teach us?" And they cast him out. Jesus heard that they had cast him out, and having found him he said, **"Do you believe in the Son of man?"** He answered, "And who is he, sir, that I may believe in him?" Jesus said to him, "You have seen him, and it is he who speaks to you." He said, "Lord, I believe"; and he worshiped him. Jesus said, **"For judgment I came into this world, that those who do not see may see, and that those who see may become blind."** Some of the Pharisees near him heard this, and they said to him, "Are we also blind?" Jesus said to them, **"If you were blind, you would have no guilt; but now that you say, 'We see,' your guilt remains."** John 9: 29-41.*

It is "seeing" that is all important. Jesus' earlier comment might be expanded: ... *that the works of God might be seen – by him (the blind man) – and made manifest in him.* If this is the case, then all that we "think" we experience is for the same reason, i.e., that the "kingdom of God come upon the earth." It is in "seeing" incorrectly that we become "guilty." It is in judging "unrighteously" that we sin. Judging "righteously" we "see" that we are the "light of the world," for at another time Jesus said: *"You are the light of the world. A city set on a hill cannot be hid."* Mt. 5:14.

Joseph does not try to "hide" himself. He acts as the "light" of the world, and Pharaoh says, *"... there is none so discerning and wise as you. You shall be in charge of my court, and by your command shall all my people be directed [order themselves]; only with respect to the throne shall I be superior to you."* Gen. 41:39,40.
Regardless of our expression, whatever we consider to be Pharaoh or Caesar or King is just that. The diagram on the following page indicates why they are all-powerful. They wear a crown that indicates their "wholeness." Pharaoh's crown establishes his "saying" that he controls all of Egypt.

150

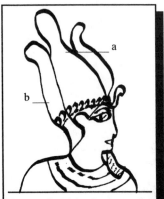

Esoterically, Pharaoh wears such a headdress, symbolizing (a)[white] upper Egypt and (b)[red] lower Egypt [upper and lower powers]. Pharaoh possesses the "serpent" protection and the beard of rank and maturity. In addition, his "eye" is open and he "sees."

One of the most important symbols in the entire Bible is that of Pharaoh (or King or Cæsar at later dates), for Pharaoh represents that which "rules" the physical world.[11] At this point Pharaoh is granting to Joseph command over all the court and all the people – control over all facets of the physical life – short of totally releasing the physical. And Pharaoh says: *"I am Pharaoh; yet without you, no one shall lift up hand or foot in all the land of Egypt."* [12]

At the level of Joseph, the physical world may "appear" to be at our feet, but eventually we will find the physical world not nearly so compliant. And Israel will have to leave Egypt and be "led" away from *worldly rule.* Even a physical separation will not accomplish the break; the final break from "worldly rule" will be accomplished only by the Christed Jesus – and then only on the spiritual plane. As for now, he who is "climbing" is second in command of all Egypt and brings the "order" necessary to ensure sufficient provisions to "feed" the entire world.

---

[11] The accumulated statuary of the Ramses II collection is particularly interesting if viewed esoterically. Ramses is shown in successive statues and attributes: (1) as young Ramses (with his finger over his lips) protected by a standing falcon, (2) as warrior, (3) as architect, (4) as scribe, (5) as priest, (6) as Sphinx, (7) as Pharaoh and (8) as Collosus (with massive, unproportioned legs [understanding] and a hole in the top of its head) – stating that Ramses II attained all levels of understanding.

[12] Esoterically, this statement has great importance. The world supposes that only the fully "enlightened" man, only Jesus could "direct" the physical – only Jesus could walk on water. But metaphysicians have long maintained that each of us – by what we "see" and "say"– directs our physical manifestation. *The good man out of the good treasure of his heart produces good, and the evil man out of his evil treasure produces evil; for out of the abundance of the heart his mouth speaks.* Luke 6:45.

*And Pharaoh called Joseph's name Zaphenathpaneah; and he gave him in marriage Asenath, the daughter of Potiphera priest of On. **So Joseph went out over the land of Egypt. Joseph was thirty years old when he entered the service of Pharaoh king of Egypt. And Joseph went out from the presence of Pharaoh, and went through all the land of Egypt.** During the seven plenteous years the earth brought forth abundantly, and he gathered up all the food of the seven years when there was plenty in the land of Egypt, and stored up food ...in every city the food from the fields around it. And Joseph stored up grain in great abundance, like the sand of the sea, until he ceased to measure it, for it could not be measured. Before the year of famine came, **Joseph had two sons,** whom Asenath, the daughter of Potiphera priest of On, bore to him. **Joseph called the name of the first-born Manasseh, "For," he said, "God has made me forget all my hardship and all my father's house."** The name of the second he called **Ephraim, "For God has made me fruitful in the land of my affliction."** The seven years of plenty that prevailed in the land of Egypt came to an end; and the seven years of famine began to come, as Joseph had said. **There was famine in all lands; but in all the land of Egypt there was bread.** When all the land of Egypt was famished, the people cried to Pharaoh for bread; and Pharaoh said to all the Egyptians, "Go to Joseph; what he says to you, do." So when the famine had spread over all the land, Joseph opened all the storehouses, and sold to the Egyptians, for the famine was severe in the land of Egypt. Moreover, **all the earth came to Egypt to Joseph to buy grain, because the famine was severe over all the earth.** Gen. 41: 45-57.*

In order to assess "he who is climbing and now rules Egypt" we must "see" what is being said about him. He is thirty years old, he is given an Egyptian name, and he marries an Egyptian woman who is daughter to the priest of On. On the surface, Joseph is at the highest level of earthly expression, and twice we are told: *And Joseph went out from the presence of Pharaoh, and went through all the land of Egypt.*[13]

Admittedly, Joseph is fully "in" the world; and he is in charge of it. Moreover, he has "forgotten" how he came to Egypt and is very prosperous, as evidenced by his two sons, Manasseh (to forget) and Ephraim (2 x fruitfulness).

Symbolism is difficult at best. You will notice that throughout this book much is left unsaid. Only the intellect is in need of a definitive presentation. The intuition does better when much is left unsaid. Certainly this is true of Pharaoh, but Joseph is not Pharaoh. Don't think that the individual on the climb ends up as Pharaoh; for we are "in" our "place" for

---

[13] Supposedly Ramses II went around Egypt four times, denoting his total control. One wonders if Joseph's two trips denote only ½ control?

the additional "light" that will come to us, not to control the world. Joseph has triumphed in the world in order that he may conclude unfinished business. Now he can meet those who sold him – his brothers.

We all know the story. *When Jacob saw that there were food rations to be had in Egypt, he said to his sons, "... Go down and procure rations for us there, that we may live and not die."* And so all of the brothers, except Benjamin, go to Egypt. And, since Joseph is in charge of dispensing all food, they come into his presence. Not revealing himself, Joseph proceeds to test them and their sincerity; consequently, he demands that they bring the youngest brother, Benjamin, to Egypt to him to prove that they are not spies. *Then they said to one another, "In truth we are guilty concerning our brother, in that we saw the distress of his soul, when he besought us and we would not listen; therefore is this distress come upon us." And Reuben* [sight] *answered them, "Did I not tell you not to sin against the lad? But you would not listen. So now there comes a reckoning for his blood." They did not know that Joseph understood them, for there was an interpreter between them.* Gen. 42:21-23. And Joseph weeps; nevertheless, he continues the "test," taking Simeon captive.

It's a good story however you look at it. It's an even better story if we look beneath the surface. For quite some time, Joseph has been the one climbing the Mountain. He has been successful for quite a while. He may be in Egypt, but Egypt's actually better in "physical rewards" than Canaan was. Canaan (bending the knee) really didn't have much going for it, and his life has actually improved since being away from Canaan – even if he had to be a slave and then in jail for a time. The whole process has only taken thirteen (13) years.[14]

But remember, we're looking at the symbolism. What are we saying about this step in the climb? It is Reuben (sight) who "sees" the truth. And what is the truth? The truth is that their previous state of mind brought about the present

---

[14] Caution! Thirteen does not refer to a period of time, but rather to a level of accomplishment. It means that we have triumphed over all things which we needed to triumph over, i.e. ourselves. It is #12; then one more is added.

situation. Moreover, it is Simeon (hearing) which Joseph keeps for ransom; and as the other brothers return to Jacob and tell their story, the Jacob consciousness is distraught and fears that the worst will happen if Benjamin goes to Egypt. We didn't realize that this Jacob consciousness had so little faith. Even though he wrestled with a   representative of God – even though he made peace with his brother – Jacob does not have Joseph's trust in God.   Joseph, on the other hand, has found out that God will bless him regardless of appearances, and he apparently intends to enlighten his brothers and us to this truth. Upon the return of the brothers, Joseph "tricks" them for a second time, planting a goblet in Benjamin's bag and saying:
"Only he in whose possession the goblet was found shall be my slave; the rest of you go back in peace to your father." Gen. 44:17.

Here *The Torah* again interrupts the narrative with a "signpost."[15]   וַיִּגַּשׁ   And immediately Judah speaks.   Just think, all these years and pages that we

Judah (Praise) Honors JVHV Instead of Self

(the Jacob consciousness) have had Judah (praiseYHWH) with us, he's never expressed as he should.   In fact, the last time we were dealing with him was Chapter 38, and he was producing "breaking forth" and "a rising light." (See p. 140.) Now what he "says" reveals that he has grown.   Thirteen years ago, when some of the brothers might have wanted to kill Joseph, Judah pointed out that killing him would not benefit them. He urged "selling" him instead. Judah's "praise" was not at the highest level. (See Gen. 37:26-27.) But now Judah tells Joseph that he is obligated to take care of Benjamin; and selflessly, he offers himself: *"... let your servant, ... remain instead of the lad as a slave to my lord; and let the lad go back with his brothers. ...   how can I go back to my father if the lad is not with me? I fear to see the evil that would come upon my father."* Gen. 44:32-34.

It matters not what we profess until we are willing to be "selfless;" only then are we "praising YHWH." And

---

[15] Using Suarès' formula,   וַיִּגַּשׁ   adds up to 319, which adds up to 13.

Judah's act brings an end to the "tests." Joseph reveals himself to his brothers, saying: *"I am your brother, Joseph, whom you sold into Egypt. ... do not be distressed, or angry with yourselves, because you sold me here; for God sent me before you to preserve life. For the famine has been in the land these two years; and there are yet five years in which there will be neither plowing nor harvest. And God sent me before you to preserve for you a remnant on earth, and to keep alive for you many survivors. So **it was not you who sent me here, but God; and he has made me a father to Pharaoh, and lord of all his house and ruler over all the land of Egypt.** Make haste and go up to my father and say to him, 'Thus says your son Joseph, **God has made me lord of all Egypt; come down to me, do not tarry;** you shall dwell in the land of Goshen, and you shall be near me, you and your children and your children's children, and your flocks, your herds, and all that you have; and there I will provide for you, for there are yet five years of famine to come; lest you and your household, and all that you have, come to poverty.' **And now your eyes see, and the eyes of my brother Benjamin see, that it is my mouth that speaks to you.** You must tell my father of all my splendor in Egypt, and of all that you have seen. Make haste and bring my father down here."* Gen. 45:5-13.

Notice that several segments of this passage are repeated. It could be the Hebraic habit of overstatement, but likely there is an esoteric meaning. Here and in a few later lines the writer emphasizes that there will be five (5) more years of famine. If the number seven (7) refers to "earthly completion," possibly the greatest part of "earthly completion" is control over the "five" – over the senses. Joseph, now reunited with "Israel," has balanced ("two") and now will deal with "five." The whole of Israel will be saved, 70 persons in all (including Jacob and Joseph and Joseph's two sons). However, Joseph cautions Jacob to tell Pharaoh that the family are *"breeders of livestock. ... For all shepherds are abhorrent to Egyptians."* Gen. 45:34 And all of "Israel" is "settled" in Goshen and given *holdings in the choicest part of the land of Egypt, in the region of Rameses, as Pharaoh had commanded.* **Joseph sustained his father, and his brothers, and all his father's household with bread,** *down to the little ones.* Gen. 47:11,12.

What are we saying about ourselves at this point on the Mountain climb? We have been signposted as at #13, but the previous signpost was an "elevated" #5. We know that we are greatly rewarded by God. We now have even made peace with things in our lives that might have encumbered the rest of our climb, for we recognize it was not "outer" actions that brought us to "Egypt," but God. In fact when these "outer" actions appologize to us, we forgive them *saying* "*... you meant evil against me; but God meant it for good, to bring it about that many people should be kept alive, as they are today. So do not fear; I will provide for you and your little ones." Thus he reassured them and comforted them.* Gen. 50:20,21.

Most important, our "perfection" is "sustaining" **sight, hearing, loving, praise, righteous judgment, strength, abundance, happiness, reward, order, power, and justice**; and we have been given "**forgetfulness**" and "**rising light**."

Even though we are producing as is intended, we are still "strangers" in a strange land. We are not in the "Promised Land," and we are not totally in control of our own destiny. We are not Pharaoh. Before we can become King, we must return to that "place" of the "bended knee." But for now we will live and die in "Egypt."

> **"God" Intends All For Good**

Appropriately, Jacob will die in Egypt. Jacob was 130 when he arrived in Egypt, expressing 13 on two planes. He lives for 17 more years; and, finally, he calls Joseph to him asking him to *"place your hand under my thigh as a pledge of your steadfast loyalty: please do not bury me in Egypt. ... take me up from Egypt and bury me in their [my fathers'] burial place."* Gen. 47:29.

Jacob's early announcement may be necessary to accomodate the esoteric.[16] Finally (at 147 [12]) it is time for

---

[16] According to Suarès, (see Suarès, p. 25) Israel "transfers his power to Joseph" by this occurrence. To Suarès, a slightly later occurrence (Gen. 48:22) is Jacob's delivery of "a second portion (or mountain) that came from 'a hand that speaks,'" i.e. the Qabala, to Joseph's control. Some mystics see the Arcane knowledge as having been carried out of Egypt with Jacob's body and having been stored in the desert, thus necessitating Moses' visit to Midian before gaining special powers. Some see it as being carried out with Joseph's bones when the Israelites leave Egypt. Regardless of what the scenario was, it seems reasonable to "say" that while the "mystical knowledge" can be conveyed in writing, only one who has incorporated the "mystical knowledge" into himself/herself can use it. Therefore, only with Moses has the time passed when "the iniquity of the Amorites is complete." See Gen. 15:16. Only with Moses does the "hand that speaks" again speak. See page 78.

156

Israel (Jacob) to die, so Joseph takes Manasseh and Ephraim to Jacob for Jacob's blessing. Despite Joseph's placing Ephraim on the left, Jacob blesses Ephriam (double fruit) with his right hand, thereby putting Ephriam before Manasseh.[17]   To Joseph's protest, Jacob responds: *"I know, my son, I know; he also shall become a people, and he also shall be great; nevertheless his younger brother shall be greater than he, and his descendants shall become a multitude of nations." So he blessed them that day, saying, "By you Israel will pronounce blessings, saying, 'God make you as Ephraim and as Manasseh'"; and thus he put Ephraim before Manasseh.* Gen. 48:19-20.

In our lives, it is likely that Manasseh (forgetfulness) will have to precede our receiving the "double fruit," because "forgetfulness" seems to be necessary to allow us to place the "world" in its rightful place. Only the spiritual is important; the "world" will follow the spiritual. That is the lesson of the LAW. When we "speak" spiritually – when we "speak" righteously – the "world" falls in line. Remember: *With the judgment you pronounce you will be judged!*

Jacob knows this; and before he dies he "blesses" his sons, telling "what is to befall [them] in days to come."
1. Reuben **(sight)** - Unstable as water, you shall excel no longer, for when you mounted your father's bed, you brought disgrace.
2. Simeon **(hearing)** & 3. Levi **(loving)** - Simeon and Levi are a pair; their weapons are tools of lawlessness. ... I will divide them in Jacob; I will scatter them in Israel.
4. Judah **(praise YHWH)** - The scepter shall not depart from Judah.
5. Zebulun **(order)** - Zebulun shall dwell by the seashore; he shall be a haven for ships. [Notice: was born #10]
6. Issachar **(who brings hire, ... reward)** - Issachar, a strong-boned ass ... bent his shoulder to the burden, and became a toiling serf.
7. Dan **(righteous judgment)** - Dan shall be a serpent by the road, that bites the horse's heels so that his rider is thrown backward.[18]
8. Gad **(abundance)** - He shall be raided ..., but he shall raid at their heels.

---

[17] This is the fifth time this has occurred: with Cain and Abel, with Ishmael and Isaac, with Esau and Jacob, with Zerah and Perez, and now with Manasseh and Ephraim. In each case, the first-born is superceded by the second-born. It implies that he/she who climbs the Mountain must be "born" again. Only these "second-born" characters are ancestors of Jesus. (See Mt. 1:1-17 and Luke 3:23-38.)

[18] A "rider on horseback" is one who is "of the world."

9. Asher **(straight, happiness)** - Asher's bread shall be rich, and he shall yield royal dainties.
10. Naphtali **(strength)** - Naphtali is a hind (male deer) let loose, which yields lovely fawns.
11. Joseph **(whom Jehovah will add to)** - Joseph is a fruitful bough, a fruitful bough by a spring ... the elect of his brothers.
12. Benjamin **(son of the right hand)** - [He] is a ravenous wolf; in the morning he consumes the foe, in the evening he divides the spoil.

Only hang-loose logic gives us explanation: We cannot rely on our physical "sight." Physical sight gives us *appearances*; it is unstable. Physical sight tries to take the place that the "spiritual man/woman" is to take, i.e. of discerning Truth. Nor are physical "hearing" or "loving" reliable; they will be scattered. However, "praise" of the Lord will always rule. And "order" will provide safe haven for those on the unstable "waters."[19] "Righteous judgment" will bring us back to our "way," and we will find abundance. Even if our abundance is "raided," we will again find it. He/she who maintains this "straight" (unswerving "mind") held on "happiness" will produce "royal dainties." And he/she will have the "strength" of the loose male deer, unbelievably joyous and producing beauty. And he/she will be "added to," perfection upon perfection. He/she will have complete "power," defeating whatever challenges come before him/her and reaping the rewards after the challenge is met.

Jacob Knows the Truth of Our "Parts"

Jacob "says" what is appropriate for each facet of our nature; then he instructs that he be buried *"... with my fathers in the cave which is in the field of Ephron the Hittite, the cave which is in the field of Machpelah [to fold together], facing Mamre [vigor], in the land of Canaan [bend the knee], the field that Abraham bought from Ephron[fawn-like] the Hittite [terror] for a burial site – there Abraham and his wife Sarah were buried; there Isaac and his wife Rebekah were buried, and there I buried Leah – the field and the cave in it, bought from the Hittites." When Jacob finished his instructions to his sons, he drew his feet into the bed and, breathing his last, he was gathered to his people.* Gen. 49:29-33. See pages 84 - 86.

[19] Water may be "unstable" but it is absolutely necessary for life. Again we have a paradox. But "order" makes us men/women of discernment, fully able to decide what is Truth and what is not.

158

The Jacob level of consciousness is still tied to "terror," but it has triumphed over it. His earthly remains are accompanied by the dignitaries of Egypt, together with "all of Joseph's household, his brothers, and his father's household; only the children, the flocks, and the herds were left in Goshen." This is a show of triumph over the world; even chariots and horsemen accompany the body. And at the "threshing floor of" Goren ha-Atad there is a "very great and solemn lamentation" and seven days mourning. Then his twelve sons carry him to the land of Canaan and do as he had requested. "Terror" is no longer the challenge. Now the threshing floor will be the challenge of the "world." It is the "threshing floor" that will separate "chaff" from "wheat."

For the time being, Israel (now a nation) will remain in Egypt. Joseph's position has cemented a place for them in the Egyptian society. For a time they will prosper. Joseph lives to see the children of the third generation of Ephraim and Manasseh, his sons. Finally, at age 110 (his birth order [11] raised another level), Joseph tells his brothers: *"I am about to die; but God will visit you, and bring you up out of this land to the land which he swore to Abraham, to Isaac, and to Jacob." Then Joseph took an oath of the sons of Israel, saying, "God will visit you, and you shall carry up my bones from here." ... and [Joseph] he was embalmed and placed in a coffin in Egypt.* Gen. 50:24-26.

The Pyramids of Tizeh, looking East from the Nile, showing the site of the Sphinx.

This ends *Genesis*, that which began: ***When God began to create....*** We are far beyond the early beginnings of the process; the process continues almost on its own with just the urgings of the LORD which indicate needed change.

What began with בראשית (1213 [7] *ongoing* "earthly completion") concludes with חזק (115)[7] this time just one level of earthly completion. This portion of the climb is finished.

Restored front of the Great Rock Temple at Ibsambul, on the Nile. (Now at the Aswan Dam.)

Moses
is drawn
"from
the waters."

Chapter Eight
Moses: Drawn from the Waters

"Hebrew women are not like the Egyptian women; for they are vigorous and are delivered before the midwife comes to them." [1]

Ll of us – both male and female – are symbolized by "Hebrew women in travail." We are all bringing forth this "rebirth" in ourselves. Whether we intend it or not, we are all climbing the Mountain. But the last time we saw "ourselves," we were "embalmed" and lying in a coffin in Egypt. However, we are not like "Egyptians"; we are more vigorous and will "be delivered" more readily – by the LAW.

---

[1] *These are the names of the sons of Israel who came to Egypt with Jacob, each with his household: Reuben, Simeon, Levi, and Judah, Issachar, Zebulun, and Benjamin, Dan and Naphtali, Gad and Asher. All the offspring of Jacob were seventy persons; Joseph was already in Egypt. Then Joseph died, and all his brothers, and all that generation. But the descendants of Israel were fruitful and increased greatly; they multiplied and grew exceedingly strong; so that the land was filled with them.*
__Now there arose a new king over Egypt, who did not know Joseph.__ And he said to his people, "Behold, the people of Israel are too many and too mighty for us. Come, let us deal shrewdly with them, lest they multiply, and, if war befall us, they join our enemies and fight against us and escape from the land." Therefore they set taskmasters over them to afflict them with heavy burdens; and they built for Pharaoh store-cities, Pithom and Raamses. But the more they were oppressed, the more they multiplied and the more they spread abroad. And the Egyptians were in dread of the people of Israel. So they made the people of Israel serve with rigor, and __made their lives bitter with hard service__, in mortar and brick, and in all kinds of work in the field; __in all their work they made them serve with rigor.__
Then the king of Egypt said to the Hebrew midwives, one of whom was named Shiphrah and the other Puah, "When you serve as midwife to the Hebrew women, and see them upon the birthstool, if it is a son, you shall kill him; but if it is a daughter, she shall live." But the midwives feared God, and did not do as the king of Egypt commanded them, but let the male children live. So the king of Egypt called the midwives, and said to them, "Why have you done this, and let the male children live?"
The midwives said to Pharaoh, __"Because the Hebrew women are not like the Egyptian women; for they are vigorous and are delivered before the midwife comes to them."__ So God dealt well with the midwives; and the people multiplied and grew very strong. And because the midwives feared God he gave them families. Ex. 1:1-21.

Fortunately, the intuitional mind can understand multiple metaphors. Now, in addition to my metaphor of the climb and the Bible's metaphor of "birth" and "rebirth," the book of Exodus gives us the metaphor of "being drawn out of the Nile." Pharaoh, representing the governing mind of the "world," commands: *"Every son that is born to the Hebrews you shall cast into the Nile, but you shall let every daughter live."* Ex. 1:22.

Let's "hang loose" for a minute. We know that the "masculine" part of us refers to the intellectual mind. We know that the "feminine" part of us refers to the intuitional mind and to the feeling side of us. We know that Egypt refers to the "physical world," and we know that the Nile is the "life blood" of Egypt. In addition, "he" who was climbing the Mountain, i.e., Joseph, is lying "embalmed" in a coffin in Egypt. Moreover, now the King of Egypt, Pharaoh, dictates that our intellectual self be thrown into the Nile, and remember Jacob's comment about Reuben? It was *unstable as water*. So this Nile that we're to be thrown into has endless "dangers." Well, it can't get much worse! Our chance of climbing the Mountain looks pretty dim. We may be in Egypt forever.

It's like the "cliff-hanger" at the end of the week's silent film episode. The heroine is lying tied on the tracks, waiting for the train to run over her; but the hero has just been caught in the villain's trap. What can be done to free the hero in time? That's the paradox. While we know we are the "beloved children" of the LORD, it "appears" that we're always in life-threatening situations. So how do we get free of appearances? We climb the Mountain.

Therefore, he who will continue the climb must be placed in a "wicker basket," a smaller form of Jacob's tabernacle-styled animal pens (see p. 128). But Moses' basket is caulked with bitumen and pitch (what has been *burned*), and it is "plucked" from the "waters" of the Nile by Pharaoh's daughter (the feminine side of the "world" mind) and Moses is "nursed" (given milk [beginning knowledge]) by his own

"Hebrew" mother. Only when the child is grown is he made
"Pharaoh's daughter's" son and named Moses.[2] It is Moses
who will put the LAW into a form that we can understand. It
is Moses who will lead us out of the land of Egypt, so that we
can get back to the "Promised Land."

At the significant verse 11 the process begins. *One day,
when Moses had grown up, he went out to his people and looked on their
burdens; and he saw an Egyptian beating a Hebrew, one of his people.* **He
looked this way and that, and seeing no one he killed the Egyptian and
hid him in the sand.** *When he went out the next day, behold, two Hebrews
were struggling together; and he said to the man that did the wrong, "Why
do you strike your fellow?"*

*He answered, "Who made you a prince and a judge over us? Do you
mean to kill me as you killed the Egyptian?"* **Then Moses was afraid,** *and
thought, "Surely the thing is known."* *When* **Pharaoh** *heard of it, he*
sought to kill Moses. *But Moses fled from Pharaoh, and [settled] in the
land of Midian; and he sat down by a well.* Ex. 2:11-15.

In Midian the same scenario takes place that took place
with Jacob.[3] (See p.104.) Only this time 7 "daughters" are
trying to water their father's flock and being prevented by
shepherds from doing so. And *Moses rose to their defense,
and he watered their flock.*

The "physical world" "sees" itself as the center of
everything; it tries to keep our attention. The world always
keeps trying to keep us from what is "ours," and for a time on
the climb we have to keep "demanding" that the "flocks get
watered." Moses is still at a point where he is challenged, and
he still has to resort to "war" to bring about what needs to be
brought about. But by so insisting, he is brought to Reuel (a
pasture, related to hunger and famine), priest of Midian who gives

---

[2] According to *The Torah*, p. 100, fn. *Moses* is the Heb. *Mosheh* from the Egyptian
for "born of" and is "associated" with *mashah* meaning "drawn out." According to
Manly Hall, Manetho (Egyptian historian quoted by Josephus) says Moses was a
priest of Heliopolis. Hall also says that MOSES is a cabalistic rearrangement of
three Hebrew letters which refers to the sun.

[3] *Midian* comes from a root that means *to judge,* but at this point the "judging"
means *contention* and *quarreling.* Although these Midianites are descendants of
Abraham, they have not progressed as far as has Moses, son of those who have been
on the climb.

him his daughter Zipporah (little bird, in the sense of hopping about) as wife.[4] Here is "paradox," for the definitions are all dependent on one's perspective. He who is supposed to climb the Mountain must **discern** the truth about others and himself. As with everything in life, it depends on how you "see."

You may cry **foul!** We didn't think we had to choose what we "see." We expected the climb to be a constant movement upward. But remember what Jacob saw at Bethel? The stairway was not an "up" escalator! It had both "ups" and "downs" on it. So for us to go "up" again, we're going to have to "see" better. We're going to have to have greater understanding. We're going to have to notice "where" we are. And Moses gets a son, Gershom (a stranger there), and Moses says, *I have been a stranger in a foreign land.*

A *stranger* has two characteristics: A *stranger* is one who is *not at home*, but also one who is *not recognized.* And Moses "sees" himself as *in a foreign land,* a land that is totally unlike himself. If you are on the climb, you may find yourself at this same juncture. It's nice that Moses recognizes that Midian is unlike himself. But notice the tense that is used. Moses says: *I have been...* This refers to Egypt as much as to Midian. Moses was *unrecognized* and *not at home* in Egypt just as much as in Midian.

We, too, are *strangers in a foreign land.* Remember... we are "spiritual beings" having a "physical experience." Only when we recognize this can we proceed. It probably will not be "instant" advancement. Exodus says: *A long time after that, the king of Egypt died. ...* and *God looked upon the Israelites, and God took notice of them.* Now the process continues. The stage is set for a change in our hero.

---

[4] Suarès, p. 31, translates the names differently. Suarès says *Reuel* means *Elohim's shepherd.* Suarès says that according to Qabala, Reuel has been guarding the Qabala; when he releases it to Moses, he becomes Jethro. *Zipporah* is *little bird*, but it refers to the chirping of birds, the "call of morning," an arising.

*Now Moses was keeping the flock of his father-in-law, Jethro, the priest of Midian; and he led his flock to the west side of the wilderness, and came to Horeb, the mountain of God. And the angel of the LORD appeared to him in a **flame of fire out of the midst of a bush; and he looked,** and lo, the bush was burning, yet it was not consumed. And **Moses said,** "I will turn aside and see this great sight, why the bush is not burnt." When the LORD saw that **he turned aside to see,** God called to him out of the bush, "Moses, Moses!" And he said, "Here am I."* Ex.2:1-4.

Let's check the names and places. Notice, the father-in-law is now Jethro (*to exceed; his excellence);* that's an improvement over the earlier definition.[5] And Moses goes to the west side (from *to roar [as with waves][that which faces East])* of the wilderness, to Horeb (parched) which is called the mountain of God, and it is here that he **"sees"** the burning bush and **"says"** *I will turn aside and see.*

Needless to say, we've run into this "wilderness" before, and we'll run into it several more times. To our minds, it is a contradiction. We think that "growth" should be indicated by "water" and "green" and "fruitfulness." "Wilderness" is just the opposite. What we're forgetting is that "something" has to get us to the point of growth. That's the "wilderness." It's usually a "low point" in our lives; but, in Truth, it is a "high point" – for we're told it's the Mountain of God. Moreover, the name of the Mountain indicates that "burning" is taking place; however, we are told that even though the bush (that which is growing there) is on fire, it is not "burned up."

I don't know about you, but I've certainly had times in my life where I felt as though I was in the wilderness, seldom "seeing" it as the Mountain, and feeling the fire – even to the point of a burning sensation – and not even having the blessing of being consumed by the fire. I was still there, whether I

---

[5] Suarès and other esotericists have suggested that Moses came to Midian to retrieve the Qabala which the Israelites had carried out of Egypt with Jacob's body. Having delivered the "power" to Moses, Reuel changes to Jethro. Apparently, it is the "understanding" of the "initiate" Moses, prince of Egypt, when added to the Qabala, which "extends and exalts" the priest of Midian.

wanted to be or not. The change in me took place when I "turned aside." So it is with Moses. It is written: *When the LORD saw that he had turned aside to look, God called to him out of the bush...*

Correct me if I'm wrong, but isn't this the first time we've had the LORD and "God" working together in the individual?[6] We are beginning to get to the place where the individual is expressing the *LORD God.* We might have expected that a new expression was taking place, for Exodus began with another sign post.[7] Exodus is preceded by שמות (10+7 = 17, totaling 8). We have gone up one level from Joseph, and we are at a point of growth. But this growth comes only as we "turn aside to look." And God says: "Moses! Moses!" And Moses answers: "Here Am I."

The "Place" On Which We Stand Is "Holy Ground"

God replies: *"Do not come closer. Remove your sandals from your feet, for the place on which you stand is holy ground. I am," He said, "the God of your father, the God of Abraham, the God of Isaac, and the God of Jacob." And Moses hid his face, for he was afraid to look at God.* Ex. 3: 5,6.

The "place" on which we stand is ALWAYS holy ground! But we in the almost 21st Century don't understand this pronouncement any more than Moses does. It is just as true now as it was then; but, like Moses, we hide our faces, "afraid to look at God." The "face" has great importance in the esoteric; for the "face" determines what and how the individual "sees." Since he hides his face, Moses cannot fully "see," but at least he's "hearing."

And what is he hearing? He hears the LORD saying: *"I have seen the affliction of my people who are in Egypt and have heeded their outcry because of their taskmasters ... and I have come down to deliver them out*

---

[6] See pages 44 and 45; esoterically there's a distinction between God and LORD. But clear definition forces us into the intellectual approach. Suarès writes, the intellectual approach such as taken by the Jews in the first three centuries of our era "worshiped a deity which cannot but be anthropomorphized when it is prayed to." He explains the other view: **"The Qabala knows that YHWH is not a deity but an immanence which can become alive and active when the two vitalities in us, the container and the contained, fecundate each other."** Suarès, p. 43.

[7] See *The Torah*, p. 99.

*of the hand of the Egyptians, and to bring them up out of that land to a good and broad land, a land flowing with milk and honey, **to the place of the Canaanites, the Hittites, the Amorites, the Perizzites, the Hivites, and the Jebusites.** ... Come, I will send you to Pharaoh that you may bring forth my people, the sons of Israel, out of Egypt." But Moses said to God, "Who am I that I should go to Pharaoh, and bring the sons of Israel out of Egypt?" He said, "But I will be with you; and this shall be the sign for you, that I have sent you: when you have brought forth the people out of Egypt, you shall serve God upon this mountain."* Ex. 3:7-12.

Great! We're promised that the Lord will be with us.[8] Then we're told that the "sign" won't be given until **after** we've brought the people out of Egypt, and then the sign is that we'll "serve God upon this mountain." Doesn't sound like a very good "deal," does it? Not only that, but the land we're supposed to go to – although it's got all sorts of "goodies" in it – is the land of several alien tribes.[9] Obviously, in this land of "milk and honey" we will have to "bend low" (Canaanites), we will have to deal with "terror" (Hittites) and "saying" (Amorites). There will be "a rising light" (Perizzites), but we will be "measured" (Hivites [sew a string as a measuring tape]) and placed on the "threshing floor" (Jebusites). This land that the voice "promises" can't be worth all that.

Moses is no novice; he's "a prince of Egypt,"and his Hebrew parents are even from the prestigious house of Levi (loving). But he does wonder about this voice that is "speaking" to him; so he asks its name. And God answers: *Ehyeh-Asher-Ehyeh, (I am that I Am). Thus shall you say to the Israelites,*

---

[8] The first line of this quote is verse 7. Somehow, through our work so far we have repeatedly run into the word *paniym*, which relates to "the face" (as the *part* that *turns)*. Here in verse 7 we find the word followed by *nagas* (related to "harass") and then *yada* (to know by seeing). One wonders if verse 7 (related to "earthly perfection") is suggesting that the "difficulties" of Israel (standing for each of us) is still – as it has been through Genesis – because our "turn of face" does not allow us to "know by **seeing.**" Now, we must not only "leave" Egypt, we must enter a land filled with these various tribes – tribes with which our ancestor Abraham contended.

[9] See page 64, fn. 24. Abraham had to deal with the same "tribes." The only difference is that some of the tribes have disappeared. Those who have gone are the Kenites, Kenizzites, Kadmonites, Raphaim, and Girgashites.

*'Ehyeh (I Am) sent me to you.' ... **Thus shall you speak** to the Israelites: **The LORD**,[10] the God of your fathers, the God of Abraham, the God of Isaac, and the God of Jacob, **has sent me to you**: This shall be My name forever, this My appellation for all eternity.[11] Ex. 3:14-16.*

It is this I Am that in structs Moses.[12] He is to go to "his people" and tell them "who" has sent him and take "them" out of Egypt. And he is assured: *Yet I know that the king of Egypt will let you go only because of a greater might. So I will stretch out My hand and smite Egypt with various wonders which I will work upon them; after that he shall let you go. And I will dispose the Egyptians favorably toward this people, so that when you go, you will not go away empty-handed. **Each woman shall borrow from her neighbor and the lodger in her house objects of silver and gold, and clothing**, and you shall put these on your sons and daughters, thus stripping the Egyptians.* Ex. 3:19-22.

This last line has always bothered me. To my way of thinking "borrowing" with intent to "steal" is "stealing." I cannot ascribe such suggestions to God; therefore, there must be a different interpretation to the whole. Hang-loose thinking eliminates the moral problem, but notice that it is the **"woman"** who is instructed. Let's assume that, as with everything and everyone we have encountered so far, **the Bible is giving instruction to each man/woman as to the process to follow to climb the Mountain**, but the instruction is to the feminine side of us all. This is what has been happening all along. The only trouble is – and isn't this always the case – how easy it is for us to get bogged down in the "literal" story. We could say it another way – how difficult it is for us to "hang loose." So let's see exactly "where" we are.

---

[10] According to *The Torah*, YHWH or YHVH (traditionally read *Adonai* "the Lord"), is associated with the root *hayah* **"to be."** See *The Torah*, p. 102.

[11] *The Torah*, p. 102.

[12] According to Thomas Troward, *Bible Mystery and Bible Meaning*, p. 77, the words *Nuk pu Nuk* (I Am that I Am) appeared on the walls of every Egyptian temple.

"Where" We Are

We know we are "children" of that "God" which created all; but we also know that we don't always remember this truth. Furthermore, we know that we were created "in the image" of this "God"; therefore, whatever we "see" and "speak" is what takes place on this earthly plane. Consequently, a process "begins-and-continues" that will eventually bring us to constant awareness of this truth. Eventually, we will have "righteous judgment." But not until certain changes take place.

The "changes" take place from "time to time" and seem to be "steps" to different levels. The first few "levels" of this continuous process find us being "promised" a physical existence (we think) that will have no problems, so we keep climbing in our "awareness." We make one trip to "Egypt" (full emersion in the world), but we come back to a flat land, mostly because what rules "Egypt" couldn't trust us.

Most of our time is spent in attaining perception in this flat land. We do become aware of our "senses" and the fact that we can't completely trust them to tell us the truth. We do produce "children" or thoughts that are increasingly like our true self, but these "young" aspects of our nature haven't been tested. Therefore, we must go to "Egypt" to be tested; so that's where we end up.

At first we're slaves, but then we find that we're almost in charge. However, as we become more enmeshed in Egypt, we find that we really are "slaves." In other words, the world keeps telling us what to do and how to do it. That was always the case, we just didn't fully recognize that "Pharaoh" was boss.

Then something happens. We take a stand that the "world" doesn't like. We react, and then, likely, we run away. But somehow the "Lord" catches our attention, and we turn aside to look at what "truly" IS, only to find that we have something to do. We have to take ourself – and all that is in us and all that is ours and all that we borrow – away from the control of Pharaoh. We have to leave the world's domination.

The trouble is that we've produced so many thoughts and characteristics in the time we've been "of the world," that the difficulties in "pulling us out" of Egypt are tremendous. But the "Lord" says "he's" with us. Moreover, every excuse that we can find gets "shot down." This "Lord" that says his name is I Am makes it so there's really no other way for us to behave. We have to do what we've been "told" to do. And what is that? We've been told to go to Pharaoh ... to tell him to **"Let my people go!"**

We will go neither "empty-handed" nor "alone." We will proceed on the climb, not only with what is truly ours, i.e., what we have internalized, but with what we have "borrowed" from a neighbor or a lodger. It is not physical "gold and silver" that we borrow; it is **spiritual** "gold and silver." We are assured that we will have what we need to accomplish the task. We will be given "associates" and individual "powers" for our individual climbs. Moses is given his brother Aaron to speak for him *...he shall serve as your spokesman, with you playing the role of God to him. And take with you this rod, with which you shall perform the signs.* Ex. 4:16,17. Moreover, he is shown that what he "says" comes to fruition; he throws down his "rod" and it becomes a snake.[13]

Although the climb is a singular "feat," it is not a "singular" journey. Each of us will find that we have particular talents that will help, but possibly more important will be the associates who will (from time to time) accompany us on the climb. Likely, they will not be present for the entire duration, likely they will contribute only what is needed at a particular moment. I know that I have found many "neighbors" and "lodgers" from whom I have borrowed "gold and silver," sometimes from direct contact, sometimes from their written works. The "borrowings" will have to be internalized, acknowledging that because of the "riches" of the associates are we enhanced.

But YHWH adds*: ... see that you perform before Pharaoh all the marvels that I have put within your power. I, **however, will stiffen his heart so that he will not let the people go.** Ex. 4:21.

Haven't you always wondered about this? If YHWH is so anxious for Moses to rescue the people of Israel, why isn't he "softening" Pharaoh's heart? Can it be that the entire exercise is for Moses, rather than for the people? The problem is between the literal and the esoteric meaning of what's going

---

[13] Esotericists have long seen Moses' "rod" (or Aaron's rod) as the "spinal cord," which when "activated" becomes the empowered kundalini (a snake). It is this "rod" which buds and is "stored" in the Ark of the Covenant. However, when the Ark is opened, only the tablets of the Law remain.

on. Moses is that portion of us which finally says to the world and to the worldly "ego" which rules it, "Let ME go that I may 'worship.'" But this is not just a surface change in us. For it to be accomplished, there must be a **total change.** And eventually – if we are to be a spiritual person as opposed to a worldly person – it must be an irreversible change. Therefore, our "first-born son" – our worldly mindset, our present "paradigm" – has to be slain. Only against a "stiffened" heart is one sufficiently adamant to effect irreversible change.

Moses, now accompanied by Aaron, goes to the people of Israel, ... *and they bow low in homage.* But when they approach Pharaoh, Moses and Aaron are reprimanded for distracting the people from their labors. Pharaoh admits that *Even now they are more numerous than the people of the land.* [14] In retaliation, Pharaoh adds to the Israelites' burdens, requiring that they gather their own straw for the making of bricks.[15]

Making bricks
in Egypt.

[14] The line is a Samaritan usage, quoted as a footnote in *The Torah,* p. 105.

[15] The king of the "worldly us" admits that the spiritual portions of us are overtaking in numbers the "worldly" portions of us. Only as more and more of our thoughts are directed to the "spiritual" do we gain enough strength to be of the level of Moses and challenge Pharaoh. And likely, situations will take place that will "tempt" us to "stay" in Egypt. Our burdens may even increase as we pass through this period.

It is particularly interesting that **straw comes after the wheat has been cut and after it has been threshed –on the threshing floor.** We have to "solidify" and place into bricks anything in our lives that is other than "wheat." Nevertheless, this activity strengthens us and more rapidly brings the time when we can leave this carnal condition which we call "Egypt."

And the people complain, so Moses appeals to YHWH: *Why did You bring harm upon this people? ...Ever since I came to Pharaoh to speak in Your name, he has dealt worse with the people; and still You have not delivered Your people.* Ex. 5:22,23.

Do not be deceived. The spiritual climb is not a peaceful journey. From what I have experienced and from what I have observed in the lives of others, just the opposite is likely to be the case. We are greatly "tied" to the world; separation from it takes a massive effort. YHWH says to Moses: *You shall soon see what I will do to Pharaoh: he shall let them go because of a greater might; indeed, because of a greater might **he shall drive them from his land.*** Ex. 6:1. And *The Torah* gives us another signpost.[16]   **וארא**

Those who are climbing at the level of Moses are at a level above the earlier patriarchs. For God says to Moses: *"I am the LORD. **I appeared to Abraham, to Isaac, and to Jacob, as El Shaddai, but I did not make Myself known to them by My name** יהוה.* [17] *I also established my covenant with them, to give them the land of Canaan, the land in which they lived as sojourners. I have heard the moaning of the Israelites because the Egyptians are holding them in bondage ... Say therefore '...I will free you from the burdens of the Egyptians, and deliver you from their bondage. **I will redeem you with an outstretched arm and through extraordinary chastisements.** And I will take you to be My people, and I will be your God. And you shall know that I, the LORD, am your God who freed you out from the labors of the Egyptians. I will bring you into the land which I swore to give to Abraham, Isaac, and Jacob, and I will give it to you for a possession. I the LORD.'"* But when Moses told this to the Israelites, they would not listen to Moses, their spirits crushed by cruel bondage. Ex. 6:2-9.

It is easy to dismiss this narrative as meaningless to us; yet it applies to us just as much as it did to the Israelites in the story – and just as much as it did to the Jews at the time of Jesus. They and we are being told that we can "live" in a "promised land" and be "freed from the labors of the Egyptians." But, like the Hebrews, our spirits are crushed by "cruel bondage," and we don't listen.

---

[16] **וארא** (1·200·1·6 = 208= 10), i.e., earthly accumulation and completion.

[17] See page 168. fn. #10.

We're bound by our conviction that we are susceptible to all sorts of diseases and pestilences and accidents and "natural" disasters. Even those who claim to be on the spiritual path "see" themselves growing older, "feel" the pains of disease, "bind" themselves to the pronouncements of doctors. That's okay! Neither we nor the Israelites are at the level of Christ, yet. Even though the Israelites "leave" Egypt, mankind doesn't change much.

You know how the story goes with Pharaoh. Moses and Aaron keep demanding – keep performing signs that should convince him – but Pharaoh's a stubborn fellow.[18] *Then the LORD said to Moses, "**Pharaoh will not listen to you; that my wonders may be multiplied in the land of Egypt."** Moses and Aaron did all these wonders before Pharaoh; and **the LORD hardened Pharaoh's heart**,...* Ex. 11:9,10.

Can it be that our difficulties in freeing ourselves from Pharaoh are necessary for the anticipated development to take place in us? Interestingly, this ends the chapter, making it an unusually short chapter, and it brings us to the all-important number **12** which says: *The LORD said to Moses and Aaron in the land of Egypt, "This month shall be for you the beginning of months; **it shall be the first month of the year for you."** Ex. 12:1,2.* And the Lord gives Moses and Aaron instructions for the *Passover*.[19]

---

[18] Exodus 11:9 catches my eye. *"Pharaoh will not listen to you; [in order] that my wonders may be multiplied in the land of Egypt."* Notice the similarity to Jesus' answer to his disciples in response to whether the blind man was "born" blind because he had "sinned," or his parents. Jesus answered that the man had been "born blind' in order *that the works of God might be made manifest in him.* John 9:1-3.

[19] *Tell **all the congregation of Israel** that on the **tenth** day of this month they shall take... a **lamb** for a household;...**according to what each can eat...** Your lamb shall be **without blemish, a male a year old;** you shall take it from the **sheep or** from the **goats;** and you shall keep it **until the fourteenth day** of this month, when the **whole assembly** of the congregation of Israel **shall kill their lambs in the evening**. Then they shall take some of the **blood,** and put it **on the two doorposts and the lintel of the houses in which they eat them**. They shall **eat the flesh that night, roasted;** with **unleavened bread** and **bitter herbs** they shall eat it. Do **not** eat any of it **raw or boiled** with water, but **roasted, its head with its legs and its inner parts**. And you shall let none of it remain until the morning, **anything that remains until the morning you shall burn**. In this manner you shall eat it: your **loins girded, your sandals on your feet, and your staff in your hand; and you shall eat it in haste.** It is the Lord's Passover. For I will pass through the land of Egypt that night, and I will smite all the first-born in the land of Egypt, both man and beast; and on all the gods of Egypt I will execute judgments: I am the LORD. Ex. 12:3-13.*

Christians neglect the lessons of "Passover," yet herein lies the secret of release from the bondage of Egypt, for we must be in the "right mind" to leave Egypt. The difficulty lies

Passover in the fact that symbolism does not offer a solid "grasp." In fact, just the opposite – it invites a "loose" hold. The "intellectual" mind sees the above instructions either as applying to this one particular time in history or as a symbolic repetition of the historical event. Even then, the intellect knows that "painting" blood around a doorway offers no physical protection against *whatever* took the "first-born of Egypt." Then, unless the Bible is a number of meaningless stories, this has a deeper meaning.

To me, the "Passover" instructions direct our attention to what is going on within us at this point of the climb. Until the level of Moses, we may have listened to what we call "God," but we still saw God as something "outside of ourselves." Now, we find "God" is that which says "I Am." And this I Am tells us that that which has been our first expression has to be **"burned" out of us with "fire."**[20] And then it must be **totally consumed**. It is to be accompanied by "bread" (physical sustenance) which has no leavening (**nothing making it larger than itself**) and "bitter" (**unpleasant to the physical senses**) herbs. It is to be eaten "hurriedly" (**without thought**), with "loins girded" (**the life-force retained**), with "sandals on our feet" (**separated from the earthly [also accepting wisdom]**), and our "staff" (**rod, Kundalini power**) in our hand (**directed**). Anything left is to be **burned**. And this process is to be undertaken each "year" (at the end of 12 [spiritual completion] periods). [21]

---

[20] Vera Stanley Alder, writing in the early part of this century, wrote: "Fire can burn up anything of lower vibration than itself." *The Finding of the Third Eye,* p. 54. Samuel Weiser, Inc., York Beach, Maine.

[21] Mary Baker Eddy, founder of the Christian Science Church, always spoke of the *carnal mind* as the mindset which separates mankind from its "perfection." It is the "carnal mind" – that mindset which "sees" itself as separate from God – that Egypt represents. And if Pharaoh will not allow this carnal mind to be released, **life** will "burn" it up and consume it for us. The "carnal mind" must be released.

The recurring cleansings are important, but they cannot take place in Egypt. Separation from Egypt is necessary, and it is the mission of Moses and Aaron to lead "the people" out of Egypt, with their *dough before it is leavened and their kneading bowls wrapped in their cloaks upon their shoulders. The people of Israel ... had asked of the Egyptians jewelry of silver and of gold, and clothing; and the LORD had given the people favor in the sight of the Egyptians, so that they let them have what they asked. Thus they despoiled the Egyptians. And the people of Israel journeyed from Raameses to Succoth,* **about six hundred thousand men on foot, besides women and children. A mixed multitude also went up with them, and very many cattle, both flocks and herds.** *And* **they baked unleavened cakes** *of the dough which they had brought out of Egypt, for it was not leavened, because* **they** *were thrust out of Egypt and* **could not tarry,** *neither had they prepared for themselves any provisions.* **The time** *that the people of Israel dwelt* **in Egypt was four hundred and thirty years.** *And at the end of four hundred and thirty years, on that very day, all the hosts of the LORD went out from the land of Egypt.* **It was a night of watching by the LORD, to bring them out of the land of Egypt;** *so this same night is a night of watching kept to the LORD by all the people of Israel throughout their generations.* Ex. 12: 34-42.

It is this "night of watching" that is the Passover, and it is to be celebrated by "the people" each year, through all generations. But there are some different provisions for the generations. Traditionally, the Passover Seder service includes a teaching device where the youngest child or participant asks the father-celebrant "why ceremonial customs are different on the Seder night from other nights of the year." The father replies: "Slaves were we unto Pharaoh in Egypt."

What is it then, which makes this "watching night?" If we interpolate that *Israel* alludes to the individual, then the "sacrifice" and the "consumption of it" must be undertaken by the "whole." It is our

1. The **whole assembly** of Israel **shall offer it.**
2. **No bone** shall be **broken** of it.
3. It must be **eaten in one house**.
4. **No foreigner** may eat of it.
5. No resident **"hireling"** may eat of it.
6. No **"uncircumcised" person** may eat of it.
   A male slave must first be "circumcised."
   A stranger, and his male associates, must first be "circumcised."
7. **There shall be** ONE **law** for the citizen and the stranger who dwells among you. **Ex. 12:43-49**

whole self that must participate – our innermost thoughts and secret selves that must take part in the endeavor. But our *bones*, our basic structure, shall not be broken. Moreover, it is an undertaking just for each individual, not for groups of individuals. However, it is not for those whose mindset is not of the LORD'S, nor for those who are just at that mindset because they were "hired for a short time." It is confined to those who are circumcised – having "cut off" the world – and who have dedicated themselves to God. For there is only **one** LAW...*as ye judge, ye shall be judged*; and it applies whether or not the individual knows he/she is a child of God.

There are those who claim that the "stand-apart" attitude of the Hebrews is an "elitism," thinking themselves to be on a higher level than others. But the intuitional mind perceives the hidden meanings. Seen in hang-loose terms, only the "circumcised" (he/she who has dedicated himself/herself to "God" and has "cut off" the physical obstacles to a higher expression) can climb to another level – and only he/she who has climbed to the next level can pull the "the people" up.[22] For the same "LAW" applies to "citizen" and "stranger"...***with the judgment you pronounce you will be judged.***

Only the intellectual mind searches for proofs to substantiate the "symbolic," but, then, the intellectual mind does not do well with symbolism. So Exodus clarifies what might not be clear from symbolic ritual. *The Lord said to Moses, "Consecrate to me all the first-born; whatever is the first to open the womb among the people of Israel, both of man and of beast, is mine."* Ex. 13:1,2.

Traditionally, this "first-born" is taken to be the eldest son, but another meaning is "firstling," that which first opens the "fissure." It is as Paul said (see p. 43): *The first man is ... earthy;* therefore, "that which opens the fissure" of mankind must be redeemed.

---

[22] "In the view of some scholars, the possibility is not ruled out that the sacrifice of the paschal lamb and the blood-rite which accompanied it had a much greater antiquity than the Bondage in Egypt. But over the course of the primeval centuries, it was absorbed, like the Festival of Abib and the Festival of Unleavened Bread, into the historical concept of Passover. Still, of all this no positive proof can be brought forward; these are merely logical inferences and conjectures." Ausubel, *op. cit.,* p.326.

And Exodus continues: *And Moses said to the people, "Remember this day, ... for by strength of hand the LORD brought you out from this place; no leavened bread shall be eaten. This day you are to go forth, in the month of Abib. ...Seven days you shall eat unleavened bread, and on the seventh day there shall be a feast to the LORD. ... And you shall tell your son on that day, 'It is because of what the LORD did for me when I came out of Egypt.' And **it shall be to you as a sign on your hand** and as a memorial **between your eyes, that the law of the LORD may be in your mouth;** for with a strong hand the LORD has brought you out of Egypt. ... And when the LORD brings you into the land of the Canaanites,... **you shall set apart to the LORD all that first opens the womb.** All the firstlings of your cattle that are males shall be the Lord's. Every firstling of an ass you shall redeem with a lamb, or if you will not redeem it you shall break its neck. **Every first-born of man** among your sons **you shall redeem.** ... It shall be as a mark on your hand [and as a symbol on your forehead that with a mighty hand the LORD freed us from Egypt.]"* Ex. 13:1-16.

We are to "redeem" the spiritual man from the earthy man; we are to "redeem" that which opened the "fissure" from that man which is of the earth.[23] Like "first-born," **redeem** means more than our current definition.[24] What catches my eye is **to release.** Each of us has "opened the fissure" and each of us must "be released." Each of us must be released from this *earthy* expression; each of us must be released from Egypt. And it is the LORD that does the releasing. It is that which calls itself I Am which acts with a mighty hand to free us from Egypt – not "earthy" man. And *The Torah* gives another signpost. בשלח [25]

We might have thought that "release from Egypt" meant we were finished with the climb; but quite the opposite is true. Even though we're gaining, we're still clearly the earthly expression. We haven't even made it to the "promised land." In fact, protecting us from "seeing" "war," God leads us in a round-about way. Even though the land of the Philis-

---

[23] Notice that the "ass" (a "stubborn"beast of burden) is to be redeemed by the "lamb," or else its neck is to be "broken."

[24] Strong defines *padah* as a primitive root meaning *to sever, to ransom, to release.*

[25] בשלח translates as 8·30·300·2 and equals 340 = 7, but 7 coming from three levels.

178

tines is "nearer," God leads us "by way of the wilderness at the Sea of Reeds."[26]

Let's stop for a minute. If we hold to the literal interpretation, we can get lost. It's even more devastating to our understanding if we "see" Charlton Heston as Moses, directing unnumbered Israelites through a "pulled back" Red Sea which eventually drowns Pharaoh's army.

Numerous apologists have postulated that the "Red Sea" was actually a "Reed Sea," a swampy area south of Goshen. In such an environment, Moses' special intuition would do well finding a safe path. Other apologists have suggested that a natural occurrence such as a tidal wave could have pulled the "sea" back. Some others have even suggested that this happened as Atlantis was exploding and sinking, thus creating a giant tidal wave which pulled the waters back. However, if we simply use hang-loose reasoning, there's no need for all this speculation. In fact, the story nicely portrays what we will experience on the climb.

"Leaving" Egypt is the easy part; it simply takes some willpower. We just have to have enough willpower to tell Pharaoh "we're going!" as we "kill" the *first born*. It's *staying departed* that's hard; Pharaoh's army will follow.

Pharaoh's Army Threatens Our Escape from Egypt I remember my early attempts to quit smoking. My "spiritual self" was agreeable, and numerous times I quit; but "Pharaoh's army" was quickly in pursuit. Before long, I'd find myself back in the world where it was comfortable to smoke; and again I'd be smoking. *Smoking* is like taking a small group of Israelites out of Egypt – but we've got 600,000+ people following us.

This isn't eliminating one habit. This is 600,000 – one-half the full portion, times three levels, and times the "ultimate spiritual" – this is a tremendous undertaking. But the hardest part is in keeping our resolve "to leave Egypt." **Not being**

---

[26] Ex. 13:17,18. *The Torah*, p. 122.

retaken by Pharaoh's troops is our greatest challenge. But remember, we're led by a "pillar of cloud by day and the pillar of fire by night" – and we're carrying Joseph's bones with us. We've got a lot of help.

Then YHWH tells Moses *to turn back and camp before Pi-hahiroth, between Migdol and the sea, facing Baal-zephon.*[27] YHWH never seems to "pull his punches." If you read the footnote, you'll see that we are truly "camping" between "the devil and the deep, blue sea" – the "unstable waters" – the passions that can defeat us.

YHWH's instructions are intended to accomplish the final break. We are to be facing Baal-zephon. We are to face this "master" *Typhon* – these passions that have ruled us for so long. We have to "face" them to "see" what they truly are. Moreover, we're given a "tower" to use. (Not as good, nor as high, as a Mountain, but a beginning.) And all of this location relates to our

We Must Face Our Passions

ability **to say** (accented by the repeated *paniym, paniym*). And here come Pharaoh and his army. Moses tells the people: *"Have no fear! Stand by, and witness the deliverance which the Lord will work for you today; for the Egyptians whom you see today you will never see again. The Lord will battle for you; you hold your peace." Ex. 14:13,14.*

The LORD does the work; we are to hold our peace. We're not good at holding our "peace," are we? On the surface we put on a show of "speaking" righteously, particularly when others are near. But, like Moses, we're not too sure

---

[27] *Turn back and camp* doesn't quite translate, because it contains our old friend *paniym* (face, mouth). See page 167, text and footnote. *Pi-hahiyroth* includes the root of "prepare for future"+ mouth for blowing (speech) + a cavity. *Migdol* stands for "tower." Then the verse reads: *"paniym, paniym Baal-zephon." Baal-zephon* is *Baal* (master) + *zephon* (Typhon, the Egyptian "god," which is the "destroyer.")

According to Gaskell, "Typhon (Set) is the part of the soul that is subject to the passions... it signifies 'that which tyrannizes and constrains by force.'" "The more learned among the priests call the sea *Typhon.*" - Plutarch, *Isis and Osiris,* quoted by Gaskell, *op.cit.,* p. 773. *Set* is the "personification of darkness, and the mighty antagonist of Horus, by whom he was slain."- Budge in the *Book of the Dead* Gaskell, p. 679.

we can escape the Egyptians. Then the LORD says: *"Tell the people of Israel to go forward. Lift up your rod, and stretch out your hand over the sea and divide it, that the people of Israel may go on dry ground through the sea."* Ex. 14:15,16. Suddenly, a cloud separates us from Pharaoh for the "night."

It is during the "day" (with our conscious mind) that *our* work must be done, but the *LORD's* work often occurs at

Moses Must Use "Rod" and Arm

night. Moses holds up his arm; and during the night, the LORD *drove the sea back by a strong east wind all night, and* **made the sea dry land**, *and the* **waters were divided.** Ex. 14:20,21.

This is a "night vision." Those of you who have dedicated yourselves to the climb have probably experienced one or more. Abraham had a night vision and saw angels and heard that he would have a son. Jacob had one night vision which gave him greater understanding (the stairway) and another in which he had to "wrestle something" to be blessed. Joseph's visions gave him future "knowledge." Moses' "night vision" requires more of him. He has to remain determined to go to another mindset. He has to remain determined to "leave Egypt," and he has to keep this determination regardless of the emotions that threaten to come upon him. Because of his "determination," the *sea* (those untrustworthy waters) is split. He holds up his "rod" in his right hand, and he holds up his "arm." He is totally ONE in his determination.

And the people of Israel went into the midst of the sea on dry ground, the waters being a wall to them on their right hand and on their left. The Egyptians pursued, and went in after them into the midst of the sea, all Pharaoh's horses, his chariots, and his horsemen. ... in the morning ... the LORD in the pillar of fire and of cloud ... discomfited the host of the Egyptians, clogging their chariot wheels so that they drove heavily; and the Egyptians said, "Let us flee from before Israel; for the LORD fights for them against the Egyptians." Ex. 14:22-25.

Then the LORD said to Moses, "Stretch out your hand over the sea, that the water may come back upon the Egyptians, upon their chariots, and upon their horsemen." So **Moses stretched forth his hand** *over the sea, and the* **sea returned to its wonted flow when the morning appeared;** *and the Egyptians fled into it, and the LORD routed the Egyptians in the midst of the sea.* **The waters returned and covered the chariots and the horsemen and all the host of Pharaoh** *that had followed them into the sea;* **not so much as one of them remained.**

> *But the people of Israel walked on dry ground through the sea, the waters being a wall to them on their right hand and on their left. Thus the LORD saved Israel that day from the hand of the Egyptians;* **and Israel saw the Egyptians dead upon the seashore.** *And Israel saw the great work which the LORD did against the Egyptians,* **and the people feared the LORD; and they believed in the LORD and in his servant Moses.** Ex. 14:25-31.

A "night" of such triumph produces great euphoria; Moses and the Israelites sing a song that foreshadows David's dancing in the streets centuries later. It is a "heady" joy. We may even think we've finished climbing the Mountain, but don't get carried away. There are more lessons. In fact, Psalm **111** makes it clear that the *"fear" of the Lord is the* **beginning** *of wisdom; a good understanding have all those who practice it.* But the use of the word "fear" requires a "righteous" translation. *To fear*, properly translated, means to "revere" – to have ultimate respect for. It is this that is the **beginning** of wisdom. All the portions of Moses are on the "path." All of Moses "respects" the LORD and has faith in the LORD and in Moses.

The waters returned and covered the chariots and the horsemen and all the host of Pharaoh that had followed them into the sea; not so much as one of them remained. Ex. 14:28.

182

And the people stood afar off, while Moses drew near to the thick darkness where God was. And the LORD said to Moses, "Thus you shall say to the people of Israel: '... You shall not make gods of silver to be with me, nor shall you make for yourselves gods of gold. **An altar of earth you shall make for me and sacrifice on it your burnt offerings and your peace offerings, your sheep and your oxen; in every place where I cause my name to be remembered I will come to you and bless you.'"** Ex. 20:21-24.

Chapter Nine

Moses: Lawgiver

In Your love You lead the people You redeemed:
In your strength You guide them to Your holy abode. ...
You will bring them and plant them in Your own mountain,
The place You made to dwell in, O LORD,
The sanctuary, O LORD, which Your hands established.
The LORD will reign for ever and ever! Ex. 15:13-18. [1]

It is the LORD which has done the work. And as a result, that consciousness which was "drawn out of the waters" has escaped the "waters;" but Moses is 40 years from the border of the "Promised Land." Accompanied by "a pillar of fire and a pillar of cloud" and assisted by his brother Aaron (illumined, enlightener, mountaineer) and his sister Miriam (rebellion, bitterness), the prophetess, he is followed by "the People," some 600,000 "men." [2] But that "place" for which he is headed is a "long-walk-through-the-wilderness" away. Nevertheless, a substantial change has taken place in the whole endeavor, for a change has taken place in Moses.

Prior to this point, all activities that have taken place have been described with *...Then the LORD caused ......x...... to ...y.....* For instance, in getting out of Egypt the LORD "caused" the action to take place. In fact, with all of the characters we have

---

[1] *The Torah*, p.126.

[2] At the level of Moses, we are past the division between the negative and the positive sides of us. The role of woman is elevated to equality. Remember it was Miriam who communicated with Pharaoh's daughter. It is the "heightened feminine" side of us that keeps its "eyes" open, that makes things easier for our "conscious mind" to operate. It is the "heightened feminine" that acts as prophetess; but like Sarah before her, she is bitter. She will have to change to become "Mary" and produce the Christ child. However, at this point, Miriam leads the women in dancing with timbrels. Chanting: *Sing to the LORD, for He has triumphed gloriously;* **Horse and driver He has hurled into the sea.** The feminine side recognizes that the "worldly" mindset which used to be in control has been conquered. A new mindset now directs Israel.

184

observed in Genesis – as well as Moses in the early part of Exodus – it has taken the LORD's specific intervention and activity to accomplish the undertaking.

So it is with us – until we willingly challenge "Pharaoh" and willingly hold up "both rod and arms" – until that time, the LORD does **all** of the work. But Moses is willing; he holds up "both rod and arms" all night long, and *Then Moses caused Israel to set out from the Sea of Reeds.*[3] Exodus 15:22 The difference lies in Moses' acceptance of responsibility. The climber has become the **"instrument"** through which the LORD'S work will be accomplished.

During this last century, "Psychology" has studied this phenomenon. The difference between the "freed" Moses and the Patriarchs might be seen as that point in individual development which Abraham Maslow calls "self-actualization," the point which Carl Jung calls "individuation." This

| **Moses at Level of "Self-actualization" & "Individuation"** |

is the point at which the world would probably "see" an individual as "successful" and "happy" and "understanding" himself."[4] The world may see this as the ultimate accomplishment, but the Bible sees the individual as still on the climb.

Exodus continues: *They went on into the wilderness of Shur; they traveled three days in the wilderness and found no water.* We are told much by the wording. Moses moves from the Sea of Reeds into the wilderness of Shur (a walled area), where after three days they find no water until they come to Marah

---

[3] Strong defines "reeds" as "papyrus," which is particularly interesting in light of the Egyptians' use of the "papyrus blossom" as symbolic of prosperity and plenty. In this way, we can be saying that Moses and Israel leave the "sea" of "prosperity and plenty" into the wilderness of "being walled about;" and the emotions (water) and substance (water) that they find comes in just a "trickle." Needless to say, this might produce "bitterness."

[4] See page 56. A convenient presentation of Jung is found in *The Portable Jung*, Joseph Campbell, ed., Penguin Books.

(bitterness, a trickle); but they cannot drink because of the bitterness of the water. However, the LORD "shows" Moses a piece of wood to throw into the water; when Moses throws it into the water, the water becomes sweet.

Unless there is some chemical reaction of which modern man is unaware, this means something more. Moreover, this segment – isolated as it is between Miriam's "dancing" and Israel's arriving where there are "**twelve** springs of water" and "**seventy** palm trees" – must have a greater meaning than how the words have been translated. So, let's hang loose for a moment.

We, as well as Moses, have just "escaped" from the control of Pharaoh (the carnal mindset). Very little of our climb so far has been a conscious journey. On reflection, our lives seem to have taken us from point to point, regardless of our intent and our plans. However, finally, we've come to the conclusion that the course of events has been the LORD'S doing; and we've decided that I Am, not Pharaoh, is "running the show." Pharaoh has drowned; things are different.

> There are several places where a "difference" comes. There was a "difference" at the level of Abraham, at the level of Isaac, at the level of Jacob, at the level of Joseph. By this calculation, Moses is the "**fifth**" difference.

But for a moment we feel as though we don't have what we need. And even when we find something that appears to be what we need, it has a bitterness about it. In truth, we've become determined to act as this I Am that we recently discovered could work "miracles," but now we're not finding "water" and the "people" are complaining. We feel undirected and at loose ends; so we cry out to the LORD, and the LORD shows us a piece of **wood.** As with Jacob's "tabernacle" for the animals and Moses' "basket of wood" – and as with the cross that is to come – "wood" will put everything in perspective.

"Wood" is a strong, natural element – not as strong as stone, but coming from a "living" thing. And when this element is thrown into the water (that which we **must** have), the water becomes sweet. The Hebrew wording seems to suggest that the "wood" is **what we "accept"** as the answer; then **we "declare"** that **it** is **"so,"**... **and it IS**. It seems that we're back to the "**LAW**."

From my observations and my personal experience, this level of the climb is dangerous. Some who "escape Pharaoh's army" don't recognize that they have done so. Some recognize the accomplishment, but are so embittered by the "bitter waters" they experience that they stop climbing. Some become so enamored with themselves that they stop "listening." Some are so befuddled by the "bitter waters" that they can not "see" the "wood." Not so with Moses.

Moses "hears" and throws the "wood" in the water and gives "the people" a "fixed rule," putting them to the test. He says: *If you will **heed the LORD your GOD diligently**, **doing** what is **upright in His sight**, **giving ear** to His **commandments** and **keeping** all His **laws**, then I will not bring upon you any of the diseases that I brought upon the Egyptians, for **I the LORD am your healer**.* Ex. 14:25,26.[5] This pronouncement is either "grammatically" mistranslated or – as I suspect– esoteric. Esoterically, each of us must be willing to give "our people" a fixed rule and put "them" to the test. Our whole "being" must **diligently "heed" the LORD our God.** Our whole "being" must **listen** to the commandments; our whole "being" must **keep all His laws.** Only then do we escape the Egyptian *diseases*; only then are we "healed." Only then do we express the truth of the I Am. Only then do we arrive at Elim (plural of

---

[5] I doubt if the editors of *The Torah* get the same interpretation as I do, for they split line 25 and create a new paragraph, using "He"(indicating the LORD) as the subject of the sentence. So, too, do the King James and RSV translations, there actually using "The LORD" as the new subject. Actually, this paragraph is an English teacher's delight as an example of an "indefinite pronoun." Possibly, this is a prime example of "paradox." Compare the wording of Genesis 22:16-19, where the pronoun is clear. There, too, Abraham finds a "ram" after "passing the test."

"strength" [related to **ram** and **oak**]) *where there were **twelve springs of water** and **seventy palm trees**; and they encamped there beside the water.* Ex. 15:27

Moses has changed; he has greater confidence. He is expressing the I Am; what he "says" **is**. But this is not the Promised Land, and neither Moses nor we are finished!

This "place of strength" would be a nice place to stay, but we're always prodded to keep moving. This time the "prod" comes from the people; everybody's complaining, saying the LORD should have killed them in Egypt, *when we sat by the fleshpots, when we ate our fill of bread!* Our "people" have not progressed very much, despite the difference in Moses. They're still concerned with physical food. Their "physical bodies" still rule. And the LORD says to Moses: *"I will rain down bread ...from the sky, and the people shall go out and gather each day that day's portion – that I may thus test them, to see whether they will follow My instructions or not. But on the sixth day,... it shall prove to be double the amount they gather each day."* Ex. 16:4-5. *The Torah.*

Moses and Aaron know what's going on. They tell the Israelites: *"By evening you shall know it was the LORD who brought you out from the land of Egypt; and in the morning you shall behold the Presence [glory] of the LORD, who will give you flesh to eat in the evening and bread in the morning to the full, because the LORD has heard the grumblings you utter against Him... Your grumbling is not against us, but against the LORD!"* Ex. 16:6-8. *Ibid.*

Do we recognize that our "grumbling" is against the LORD? The *test* is of ourselves. We are "trained" by the "tests" that we go through. At least Moses and Aaron recognize that what is going on in the physical plane is the LORD'S "doing." *Then Moses said to Aaron, "Say to the whole Israelite community: Advance toward the LORD, for He has heard your grumbling." And as Aaron spoke to the whole ... they turned toward the wilderness, and there, in a cloud, appeared the Presence of the LORD.* Ex. 16:9,10. *Ibid.*

The LORD's Presence will test our understanding – first with regard to this "bread" called "manna." It is a "test" with which we still have difficulty. If we have sufficient "vision" we *see* that **All is provided; but take only what you need. All else will spoil!** That's what happens, whether we recognize it or not. It is the **LAW**; in both recognizing and following it, we "judge righteously."

"Change" Makes "Tests" Necessary

The intent of all "tests" is that each of us *shall know that I Am the Lord your God.* Without this knowledge we are "earthly creatures" ruled by the carnal mindset. With this knowledge we can climb the Mountain. Learning this lesson, we **know** that we'll be provided for – **regardless!**

Learning this lesson, we have no need for anything. All is provided! But each must hold to the knowledge and act accordingly. Each must **know** that any excess will "rot." Each must **know** that what is needed must be taken when the opportunity comes. For "as the sun grows hot," the "manna" will melt; and it will disappear.

This is only the first test; the second is the requirement of the **Sabbath.** However, *Sabbath* means more than just "not working" on either Saturday or Sunday. It is the full measure of the law of "manna." It is recognition – by cessation of labor – that the LORD provides. It's like saying ... **And so *it is.***

Only those who ***doubt that the LORD provides*** have the desire to "gather" when they are to be "resting." They'll find nothing, anyway.

And the LORD says: *"How long will you men refuse to obey My commandments and My teachings? Mark that the LORD has given you the sabbath; therefore He gives you two day's food on the sixth day. Let everyone remain where he is: let no man leave his place on the seventh day."* Ex. 16:28,29.

"At twilight you shall eat flesh, and in the morning you shall be filled with bread; then you shall know that I am the LORD your God." In the evening quails came up and covered the camp; and in the morning dew lay round about the camp. And when the dew had gone up, there was on the face of the wilderness a fine, flake-like thing, fine as hoarfrost on the ground. ... The people of Israel... said to one another, "What is it?" ... And Moses said to them, "It is the bread which the LORD has given you to eat. This is what the LORD has commanded: 'Gather of it ... as much as [you] can eat; you shall take an omer apiece, according to the number of the persons whom each of you has in his tent.'" And the people of Israel did so; they gathered, some more, some less. But when they measured it with an omer, he that gathered much had nothing over, and he that gathered little had no lack; each gathered according to what he could eat. And Moses said to them, "Let no man leave any of it till the morning." But they did not listen to Moses; some left part of it till the morning, and it bred worms and became foul;... Morning by morning they gathered it, each as much as he could eat; but when the sun grew hot, it melted. Ex. 16:11-21.

The "seventh" day is the ***sabbath***; but there is a deeper meaning. The word means *an intermission,* and it is an intensive form of a root which means *to repose.* Thus, **sabbath** is a "time" dedicated to God which is to follow the completion of each "earthly" task; it is the number "7."

But radical adherence to the definition of seven days misinterprets the rule's purpose. Jesus exposed the misinterpretation of the rule. He told the Pharisees, *"Have you never read what David did, when he was in need and was hungry... how he entered the house of God, when Abiathar was high priest, and ate the bread of the Presence, which it is not lawful for any but the priests to eat, and also gave it to those who were with him?"* And he said to them, ***"The sabbath was made for man,*** *not man for the sabbath;* ***so the Son of man is lord even of the sabbath."*** Mark 2:25-28.

> *On the sixth day they gathered twice as much bread, two omers apiece; ... Moses ... said ... "This is what the LORD has commanded: 'Tomorrow is a day of solemn rest, a holy sabbath to the LORD; bake what you will bake and boil what you will boil, and all that is left over lay by to be kept till the morning.'" So they laid it by till the morning, as Moses bade them; and it did not become foul, and there were no worms in it. Moses said, "Eat it today, for today is a sabbath to the LORD; today you will not find it in the field. Six days you shall gather it; but on the seventh day, which is a sabbath, there will be none." On the seventh day some of the people went out to gather, and they found none.* Ex. 16:22-26.

If (as Jesus does) we see the LORD God as "father," the design of this world – including the requirement of the sabbath – encourages our bringing "order" to our portion of the world. Both "tests" offer the Israelites the chance to establish "order" in "the people." Symbolically, both "tests" offer "order" to the individual's approach to life; they invite adherence to the LAW – they invite the individual to "see" and "speak" and then "rest" in the knowledge.

Aren't we just like the whole of the Israelites? Our "spiritual self" (Moses) knows that the LORD is directing our whole life and that the LORD can be trusted to provide our every need – even to the level of supplying the choice item (manna) in the morning and providing both "meat and bread" (a variation). Most of the time our "intellectual self" (Aaron)

Is Our "Intellectual Self" In Accordance with the Teachings & Commandments?

190

observes and judges and says it's okay and assures the people that it's okay.⁶ But there are some people (parts of us that we may not even recognize) that don't "trust." Because of some sort of "fear," they try to gather "extra manna." We may find ourselves desirous (greedy) for anything – **desiring** more and more money, possessions, love, attention, etc. – but, as with "manna," we find that that which we gather that is more than we need **spoils and gets worms.**

Buddhists see "desire" as inhibiting enlightenment; so does the Old Testament. Only "fear" of some sort can account for "desire." If we truly "know" that **the LORD God provides all we need,** there is no "fear." Thus, we are given this "test," to teach us this truth – once we've learned the truth, "desire" is eliminated.

We often fail the test of manna; but the "test" of the **sabbath** may be our greater failure. The "spiritual self" knows that the physical mind and body need a regular period of "oneness" with the "LORD." The intellectual self probably agrees, but it seldom insists that the "time" be made available. Consequently, the "sabbath" is neglected. Even if the sabbath is observed, the "intellectual self" seldom participates whole heartedly. The intellectual self likes to be in control, and the sabbath honors I Am. In fact, it may be that the "tests" are principally for the "intellectual self," the conscious mind. Notice that the Pharisees, who often represent this approach, fail to understand the true meaning of the sabbath. Only the climber will "understand." He/she learns through trial and error and finally begins to follow the rules.

---

⁶ Some esoterists see Aaron as the mental aspect of Moses. It is he who "speaks" for Moses, and we were told earlier that Moses would be his "god." Unquestionably, our mental side is all-important. Notice, as he speaks to the "whole," they turn and "feel" the Presence of the LORD. At the level of Moses, we are led by our mental faculties. The emotions (represented by Miriam) usually follow in line, and our mental self and our higher self seem to work as a unit, directing the "people" as the higher self perceives to be correct. But during this time, we also seem to get "tested" to check whether the "whole" will comply with the LORD'S instructions.

Our "spiritual self" tells us: This is what the LORD has commanded: *Gather as much ... as each of you requires to eat. ... and remain inactive on the seventh day* [the day of completion]. Until all the *"the men of war that came out of Egypt,"* pass the test, we will be faced with the tests of "manna."[7]

To help our "recognition" of the truths connected to "manna," **one tenth** of a measure is placed before the LORD, *to be kept throughout the ages.* It will be placed in the Ark with Aaron's budded "rod" and the Tablets of the Law. "Manna" is among those symbols most important for our understanding.

We may properly ask for explanation of the supposed contents of the Ark and for the "Ark" itself. There are three "arks" in the Bible: Noah's ark (for animals); Moses' ark of bull-rushes (for man's animal nature); and the Ark of the Covenant (Ex. 25:10) which symbolizes "realized" power – and to which man's most important symbols are assigned.

In this very "physical" decade of the late 20th Century, there are those who speculate that the Ark of the Covenant housed some sort of "power source" which gave the Israelites superiority over their enemies. While these "speculators" most likely will not understand the *mystical* significance of their idea, they are close to the truth; for the contents of the Ark of the Covenant represent the truths from which the initiate manifests his/her power.

The writer of Hebrews describes the Ark as *covered on all sides* with *gold, [and containing] a golden urn holding the manna, and Aaron's rod that budded, and the tables of the covenant.* Heb. 9:4,5

On our climb, the initiate first may recognize Aaron's "budded" rod, the enhanced physical expression of the mental aspects, which is accomplished by "clearing" all the "centers" of concern and activating that power which is within us. Notice that "Aaron" is not even introduced until we (as symbolized by

---

[7] The continuation of the quote is that the men of war "had to perish" *because they did not harken to the voice of the Lord.* Jsh. 5:6. The "trek" is going to take "40" years, and the Israelites will make "44" stops.

Abraham, Isaac, Jacob and Joseph) have **accomplished** all that is in Genesis to be accomplished and until Moses has **"turned"** and **"recognized"** LORD and God as I Am. Only then does the "rod" of the mental aspect begin *to bud.*

Second to be realized is the test of the "manna," the **internalization** of the knowledge that God provides **all that we need**, both to survive and to thrive. Companion to it, but having no physical form, is the **sabbath**, revitalizing the individual. Third, is the "tables of the covenant," i.e., the Tablets of the Commandments, which establish in physical form the understanding and discipline that must be internalized. It is only through discipline and order that mankind can continue the climb; and until all have internalized the Ten Commandments, the LAW is "superimposed Law." Some forty generations from Moses, Jesus will say: *The law and the prophets were until John; since then the good news of the kingdom of God is preached, and everyone enters it violently. But **it is easier for heaven and earth to pass away, than for one dot of the law to become void.*** Lk.16:16,17. When Solomon opens the Ark(1Kings 8:9.), only the Tablets remain. The Law which must be superimposed on mankind will be with us until it is written in our foreheads; Law accedes only to LAW.

Understanding the Ten Commandments, i.e., the Law, is easier if it is compartmentalized. There are three parts to the "superimposed" Law. – The first part, the foundation upon which all else stands and containing commandments (1&2), concerns our relationship with God. Is our attention, love and loyalty toward God; do we see "God" as "Father?"

The second part reveals how we see this understanding in relation to ourselves. (3) Do we expect to receive an answer when we make a declaration, or do we "take the name of the Lord *in vain*, expecting nothing? (4) Do we take the time to reunite ourselves consciously with this "Oneness," or do we continually remain "scattered," decrying our "separation" from God? (5) Do we "honor" the masculine and the feminine from which we originate, or do we dishonor that "couple" by acts such as disrespect to our earthly parents? Only as we are balanced will we *long endure on the land which the Lord God is giving [us].* But the true measure of our compliance with the previous five commandments lies in our ability to follow the remaining five commandments, for they reveal how we express this understanding in relation to others. Do we recognize others as part of the "whole," too? Do we see that *how we act* and *how we think* returns to us multiplied?

We are not to "murder," but do we recognize that (6)"Killing" by words is just as destructive as in deed; (7)"adultery" in the mind is just as destructive as in deed; (8)"stealing" in any sense is destructive, for it establishes that we have *lack*; (9)"lying" reveals cowardice and fear; and (10)"coveting" is the final proof that we have **no** understanding.

If we undertake any of these "forbidden" activities, the thought or the action pronounces clearly that **we do NOT love** the LORD, our God! Certainly, this is the major test which we are given – whether we "love" the LORD our God and are willing to act in accordance. Every test and admonition comes down to what we *see* and *say*, i.e., our *vision* of the LORD.

The Ten Commandments

"I am the LORD your God, who brought you out of the land of Egypt, out of the house of bondage. You shall have no other gods before me. You shall not make for yourself a graven image, or any likeness of anything that is in heaven above, or that is in the earth beneath, or that is in the water under the earth; you shall not bow down to them or serve them; for I the LORD your God am a jealous God, visiting the iniquity of the fathers upon the children to the third and the fourth generation of those who hate me, but showing steadfast love to the thousandth generation of those who love Me and keep My commandments..

You shall not take the name of the LORD your God in vain; for the LORD will not hold him guiltless who takes his name in vain.

Remember the sabbath day, to keep it holy. Six days you shall labor, and do all your work; but the seventh day is a sabbath to the LORD your God; in it you shall not do any work, you, or your son, or your daughter, your manservant, or your maidservant, or your cattle, or the sojourner who is within your gates; for in six days the LORD made heaven and earth, the sea, and all that is in them, and rested the seventh day; therefore the LORD blessed the sabbath day and hallowed it.

Honor your father and your mother, that you may long endure on the land which the LORD your God is giving you.

You shall not kill.

You shall not commit adultery.

You shall not steal.

You shall not bear false witness against your neighbor.

You shall not covet your neighbor's house; you shall not covet your neighbor's wife, or his manservant, or his maidservant, or his ox, or his ass, or anything that is your neighbor's."

Ex. 20.2-14.

And *the LORD said to Moses: "Thus shall you say to the Israelites: ... you shall not make any gods of silver, nor ... of gold.* **Make for Me an altar of earth and sacrifice on it your burnt offerings and your sacrifices of well-being,** *your sheep and your oxen; in every place where I cause My name to be mentioned I will come to you and bless you. And if you make for Me an altar of stones, do not build it of hewn stones; for by wielding your tool upon them you have profaned them.* **Do not ascend My altar by steps, that your nakedness may not be exposed upon it."** Ex. 20:19-23.

From a literal interpretation, these admonitions simply refer to physical restrictions, but the esoteric viewpoint means more. Can it be that *any "gods" of silver or gold or any "altars" of hewn stones* refers to those things in the physical life that require our attention to accomplish? Rather, we are to use things of the earth, placing our full attention with the LORD. Moreover, ascension is not to be by steps, for our "purposeful" climbing exposes our nakedness. "Steps" indicate thought being taken, rather than "knowing" that one has ascended. And as it is written: The "people" say, *"Let not God speak to us, lest we die." So the people remained at a distance while Moses approached the thick cloud where God was.*

Again we have a paradox. After Eden, when the people are "separated" from God, they feel naked. But the climber – in this case Moses – does not ascend the altar by "steps; and the nakedness which Moses will find will no longer be the *pouring out*, the *emptying* which brings embarrassment. The *nakedness* of Moses returns to Eden's *smoothness*.

And *The Torah* gives a new signpost.[8] משפטים The signpost is for the "spiritual self." It is for he/she who has fully accepted "being" the child of God, he/she who is "seeing" and

> **We Are God's Holy Nation**

"saying" righteously. The "spiritual self" hears the LORD's intent: *You have seen what I did to the Egyptians, and how I bore you on eagles' wings and brought you to myself. Now therefore, if you will obey my voice and keep my covenant, you shall be my own possession among all peoples; for all the earth is mine, and* **you shall be to me a kingdom of priests and a holy nation.** Ex. 19:4-6.

---

[8] משפטים in Suarès' figures would be 600·10·9·80·300·40 = 1039 = 13. Apparently, we are advancing. This is the first time we have been over 1000, and we are at 1000 plus a prime number (39) which adds to 12.

Our Western, intellectual mind expects a literal statement to define *the covenant*; but then, the intellect can't fully understand an intangible – and the covenant is an "intangible." The Eastern mind, on the other hand, can deal with intangibles; and the East comes fairly close to encompassing the *covenant* with its perceived *cause and effect*, the law of "Karma." It is this "Karma" in which all life must account for any deviance – or causing deviation for another– from the pattern designed for it.

And what is the pattern designed for us? It is to express this "Oneness" that is the basis of all. That's pretty nebulous, isn't it. That doesn't tell us how to keep from deviating from the pattern. The Commandments are general directives, establishing a mindset that *sees* itself as part of the whole – a *whole* that is perfect and complete. But the Commandments don't specify answers to the nitty-gritty encounters of every-day life, so the LORD gives Moses many "ordinances" to particularize the Law. Esoterically read, they reveal the "intent" of the LAW on the physical, mental and spiritual levels. Esoterically read, they expand our understanding of the LAW.

Hanging loose we see the Truths represented by the Commandments. On the physical level these Commandments and their "ordinances" impose *righteousness* on selfish mankind. They require the individual to take responsibility for his own thoughts and actions.[9] For life reveals quite clearly that each happening has a *cause* and each action or thought has an *effect*. The Old Testament makes it clear in its overstated wording of "an eye for an eye" that the LAW is ever in operation, and it emphasizes *cause* and *effect*.

---

[9] Giving the esoteric view, Corinne Heline notes that unlike the Decalogue, the "diverse laws and regulations...are specifically applicable to the particular people to whom they were given and for the stage of development through which they were then passing." *New Age Bible Interpretation: Old Testament, Vol. I*, p. 238. Interestingly, slavery proponents, during that period in the United States, used the Old Testament's admonitions regarding slaves to justify their institution; in addition, the rules in Exodus became statutes for slave laws, at least when it benefited owners.

The origin of the saying reads: *When men fight, and one of them pushes a pregnant woman and a miscarriage results, but no other damage ensues, the one responsible shall be fined according as the woman's husband may exact from him, the payment to be based on reckoning [as the judges determine].* ***But if other damage ensues, the penalty shall be life for life, eye for eye, tooth for tooth, hand for hand, foot for foot, burn for burn, wound for wound, bruise for bruise.*** Ex. 21:22-25.

This is earthly **law,** designed for "men still at *war.*" On the mental level according to the "ordinances," each "injury" is repaid by a multiplied reimbursement – particularly in the case of neglect or intent to injure. But, "warring" mankind can defend itself without punishment. For example: *... If the thief is seized while tunneling [under a house for housebreaking], and he is beaten to death, there is no blood guilt in his case. ... But if what he stole – whether ox or ass or sheep – is found alive in his possession, he shall pay double.* [If he kills it, the penalty is four or five times the value, depending on the animal.]Ex. 21:37 & 22:1-3.

But on the spiritual level, more is expected of the individual. On the spiritual level, the individual "sees" and "says" righteously; then he/she "acts" righteously. *You shall be men holy to Me... you shall not join hands with the guilty... neither side with the mighty to do wrong... When you encounter **your enemy's ox or ass** wandering, **you must take it back to him.** When **you see the ass of your enemy** lying under its burden **and would refrain from raising it, you must nevertheless raise it with him.*** Ex. 22:30, 23:1,3,4-5.

It is taught that Moses wrote the first five books of the Old Testament (*The Torah),* which sets the Law in place which will mold the "nation."[10] But there are two chapters which I have neglected. Actually, they precede the giving of the Law; in fact, their understanding may be necessary for the Law to be understood. They are Exodus 17 and 18; and they are separated by another signpost יתרו.[11]

Chapter 17 is only 16 verses long. In the first half the people are again **"quarreling"** with Moses. Again there's no

---

[10] I have placed "nation" in quotes, because of the double meaning which it has. "Nation" applies to the historic Hebrew nation, which considers itself children of Moses. But esoterically, "nation" refers to the individual "entirety.""Entirety" would mean (body, mind, soul) or (conscious, unconscious, super-conscious) or (Father, Son, Holy Ghost) ... whatever you want to use to describe the "whole" realized.

[11] According to Suarès' formula יתרו represents 6·200·400·10 (616 =13=4).

water, so the LORD tells Moses to take the "elders" and the "rod" and to strike the rock (mountain) at Horeb. And Moses obeys, and **"in sight of the elders"** he gets water for the people to drink. There is no problem with it, this time. Without a transition (only a space), a second incident takes place. Amalek (a **descendent of Esau**) wars with Israel at Rephidim (from a root which implies *comfort*). For the first time we meet Joshua (eventual heir to the power of Moses), whom Moses tells to choose some men and go out and "do battle" with Amalek. Moses' contribution will be to stand at the *top of the hill, with the rod of God in my hand.* With him go Aaron (illumined) and Hur (white linen). The two men, representing illumined understanding, place Moses on a "stone" and "uphold" his hands when he tires; thus, *his hands remained steady until the sun set. And Joshua overwhelmed the people of Amalek with the sword.* Ex.17:12,13. Then the Lord tells Moses to (forever) notify Joshua that *I will utterly blot out the memory of Amalek from under heaven!* And Moses builds an altar and names it Adonai-nissi (the Lord is my banner.) Ex. 17:14-16. The segment concludes *"The Lord will be at war with Amalek throughout the ages."*

That consciousness which will replace *that which has been drawn from the water* has to be trained. And its first lesson is that the LORD and Amalek (that which has descended from the "earthy" Esau) cannot occupy the same space.[12] In other words: if we are *expressing* the LORD, we cannot still be expressing with an "earthy" nature! This must be remembered *forever*. Joshua apparently remembers the lesson; for forty years later, Joshua will say: "*And if you be unwilling to serve the LORD,* **choose this day whom you will serve,** *whether the gods your fathers served in the region beyond the River, or the gods of the Amorites in whose land you dwell; but* **as for me and my house, we will serve the LORD.**"Jsh. 24:15.

There's one more item here that we shouldn't ignore: Moses' hands remained steady **until the sun set**. To the intellect

---

[12] The Amalekites *(warlike, dwellers in the vale)* without provocation attack the rear of the Israelites. The earthy habits come upon us, without provocation (we think). Until we learn "to say" properly, we are still expressing at the level of Esau.

this probably says no more than that the battle took place in the day time. If this chapter were a normal chapter, I might agree; but this chapter and that which follows seem to be for esoteric "training." Those who recognize the esoteric tone have probably experienced the difference between their "daytime" experiences and their "night visions."

We have already spoken of Moses' "night vision." The last time Moses got tested was during the "Red" Sea incident, when he had to hold up his "rod" and his arms for an entire night. (See 179.) While he was doing so, the LORD did the work. But this time, the incident takes place in the daytime; and Moses requires a stone (understanding) to sit on and two (initiates) to hold up his hands.

Esotericists contend that we undergo training both during the day and at night. However, likely those who cannot control their passions and remain disciplined at night – when the discipline is not noticeable to others – will likely not be given increased challenges for the daytime. At the same time, those who are not willing to be disciplined during the day will receive lesser instruction at night. But, then, the incident with Amelek may be saying that the greater stress is during the daytime exercises. For, when we "see" the physical so "obviously" right in front of us, it is difficult to keep from being like Esau. So we have to be aided by the "stone" and by Aaron (illumined) and Hur (white linen - of the initiate.) And we are given יתרו 6·200·400·10 (616 =13= 4).   But we have something else to learn, and Jethro, priest of Midian, is reintroduced.[13] After hearing all that has ensued since he last saw Moses, *Jethro rejoiced over all the kindness that the Lord had shown Israel... and brought a burnt offering and sacrifices for God; and Aaron came with all the elders of Israel to partake of the meal before God with Moses' father-in-law.* Ex. 18:7-12.

---

[13] Chapter 18 begins and ends with Jethro, father-in-law to Moses. Jethro (his excellence) brings Moses' wife Zipporah and sons to him *in the wilderness, where he was encamped at the mountain of God.* We met Gershom ("I have been a stranger in a foreign land") earlier, but there is now a second son, Eliezer ("the God of my father was my help, and He delivered me from the sword of Pharaoh.")

But as Jethro observes Moses' daily activities, he asks why Moses is having to "sit as magistrate" from morning to evening all by himself. He suggests to Moses: *"You represent the people before God: you bring the disputes before God, and enjoin upon them the laws and the teachings, and make known to them the way they are to go, and the practices they are to follow. You shall also seek out from among all the people capable men who fear God, trustworthy men who spurn ill-gotten gain. Set these over them as chiefs of thousands, hundreds, fifties, and tens, and let them judge the people at all times.* **Have them bring every major dispute to you, but let them decide every minor dispute themselves.** *... Let them share the burden with you. If you do this – and God so commands you – you will be able to bear up; and all these people too will go home unwearied."* Ex. 18:1-23.

The implication for the physical level is quite clear with this chapter; but what about the spiritual level? Can it be that we are to establish "habits" that will easily take care of most of our physical decisions. If we establish habits that keep us on the narrow path, then the conscious mind only has to make decisions now and then; it only has to make decisions on the major questions. But notice, the "habits" must be "men" who fear God and spurn ill-gotten gain. Once we accept the "narrow path" as our way for the climb, we have fewer decision to make on a regular basis. If we follow the Commandments and the ordinances (keeping their ramifications in mind) we have fewer decisions to make and "all the people can go home, unwearied."

Unlike earthy mankind, Jesus was unwearied by the Commandments. When asked which Commandment was the most important, he made the whole thing simple: *"The first is, 'Hear, O Israel: The LORD our God, is ONE LORD, and you shall love the LORD your God with all your heart, and with all your soul, and with all your mind, and with all your strength.' The second is like unto it, 'You shall love your neighbor as yourself.' There is no other commandment greater than these."* Mk. 12:29-31.

But before we can achieve the simplicity of Jesus' understanding, we have to learn more. One thing we must learn is that **the Lord will make our way easier**, and the lesson is given before Moses ascends the Mountain. We are told: *Behold, I send an angel before you, to guard you on the way and to bring you to the place* *which I have prepared. Give heed to him and hearken to his voice,* **do not rebel against him, for he will not pardon your transgression;** *for my name is in him. But if you...* *do all that I say, then I will be an enemy to your enemies and an adversary to your adversaries.* **When** *my angel goes before you, and brings you in to the Amorites...* *Hittites...Perizzites... Canaanites... Hivites... Jebusites, and* **I blot them out, you shall not bow down to their gods, nor serve them, nor do according to their works, but you shall utterly overthrow them and break their pillars in pieces.** *... and I will bless your bread and your water; and I will take sickness away from the midst of you. None shall cast her young or be barren in your land; I will fulfil the number of your days. I will ... throw into confusion all the people against whom you shall come, and* **I will make all your enemies turn their backs to you.** *And I will send hornets before you, which shall drive out Hivite, Canaanite, and Hittite from before you.* **I will not drive them out from before you in one year, lest the land become desolate and the wild beasts multiply against you. Little by little I will drive them out from before you, until you are increased and possess the land.** Ex. 23:20-30.

The LORD continues: *And I will set your bounds from the Red Sea to the sea of the Philistines, and from the wilderness to the Euphrates; for I will deliver the inhabitants of the land into your hand, and you shall drive them out before you. You shall make no covenant with them or with their gods.* **They shall not dwell in your land, lest they make you sin against me;** *for if you serve their gods, it will surely be a snare to you.* Ex.23:30-33.

But the way will not be "cleared" all at once. It takes time for us to become accustomed to our new habits and ways. Those "enemies" that will be eliminated will be the Hivites (*thorn*, desc. from Canaan), Canaan (*humiliated* desc. of Ham who "saw" and "told of" Noah's nakedness), and Hittites (*terror*). The Amorites (to say) and Perizzites (light breaking) will still be among us. But the LORD will restore to us the Promised Land.[14] And the Lord says: *"Come up to the Lord, with Aaron, Nadab and Abihu, and seventy elders of Israel, and bow low from afar. But only Moses shall come near the Lord. The others shall not come near; and the people shall not come up with him at all."* Ex. 24:1,2.

When Moses had told the people all the commands of the Lord and all the rules, *all the people answered with one voice, saying, "All the things that the Lord has commanded we will do!"* Moses has been "given" the Ten Commandments, but they are not yet **"inscribed"** in the **stone** tablets. So Moses and Aaron, Nadab (*to offer freely*, son of Aaron), and Abihu (*possessor of majesty*, son of Aaron) and

---

[14] See page 53 for definitions; and see page 65 fn. for the borders and meaning.

seventy elders ascend the mountain and even though God has forbidden their presence, ...*they behold God, and they eat and drink.* And Moses ascends the Mountain, and he remains on the mountain forty days and forty nights. (See Ex. 24:3-18.)

Mount Sinai

And we are given another signpost. תרומה [15]

---

[15] תרומה in Suarès' formula is 5·40·6·200·400 = 651 = 12. Notice the difference between this sign post and the previous signpost. (See fn. 14). The previous signpost יתרו added up to 616 (4). Only as "all directions" are covered does Moses "climb" the Mountain. The difference between the two is 35 (½ of the earthly 70). Though not complete (with four sides), we are at the spiritual 12.

The High Priest, the Ark of the Covenant, the Shew-bread Table, the Altar of Incense, the lampstand and vessels for worship in the Tabernacle.

Chapter Ten
Moses' Religion of Symbols

*Hear, O Israel: **The LORD our God is one LORD**: And **thou shalt love the LORD thy God with all thine heart, and with all thy soul, and with all thy might. And these words**, which I command thee this day, **shall be in thine heart**: And **thou shalt teach them** diligently unto thy children, **and shalt talk of them** when thou sittest in thine house, and when thou walkest by the way, and when thou liest down, and when thou risest up. And **thou shalt bind them** for a sign **upon thine hand**, and they shall be **as frontlets between thine eyes**. And thou shalt write them **upon the posts of thy house**, and on **thy gates**. And it shall be, **when the LORD thy God shall have brought thee into the land which he sware unto thy fathers** ..., to give thee great and goodly cities, which thou buildedst not, And houses full of all good things, which thou filledst not, and wells digged, which thou diggedst not, vineyards and olive trees, which thou plantedst not. **When thou shalt have eaten and be full, thenbeware lest thou forget the LORD, which brought thee forth out of the land of Egypt, from** the house of bondage.* Dt. 6:4-12.

The year 1996 marks three-thousand (3000) years since David brought the Ark of the Covenant to Jerusalem. The Jewish people have a right to celebrate. Few religions can claim such a heritage. Few religions have kept the message available for so long. In fact, the form which Moses established to provide order to worship has survived even beyond all its physical vehicles. The physical appointments are long gone. Some say the Ark of the Covenant was taken by Pharaoh Shishak when he carried off Rehoboam, King of Judah.[1] Some say it never survived Nebuchadnezzar's destruction of Solomon's Temple (586 B.C.). The only physical remnant of the old establishment is a portion of Herod's Temple, what present-day Jews call the "wailing wall," all that remained after the Romans squelched rebellion by destroying Jerusalem in A.D 70. But the physical form is unimportant; the symbology of Moses' religion lives.

---

[1] Ausubel, *Pictorial History...*, p. 34. *The Jerusalem Bible* has the spelling as Sheshonk and gives the date as approximately 926 B.C. (1Kings 14:25 fn.)

At this place in our study, the form for the religion has yet to be put in place. We just left Moses on the Mountain where he is being "given" the particulars of the form. He is being given requirements for the **Tabernacle**, requirements for the **ritual** that will take place in it, and requirements for the **"priesthood"** that will perform the ritual. On the surface, Moses will set up a *religion*, but that religion will also provide the symbols that those who "see" can use to complete their learning. Symbols are being solidified; but paradoxically, they are intended to teach us to "hang loose."

Esoterically, Moses is being told what is necessary for each of us to advance on our climb. He is being told what "steps" are necessary for true "worship." **The Tabernacle**, like the Temple that follows, **brings order** to the worship of the LORD. Esoterically, all that is associated with it – its form, its furnishings, its procedures, even its colors and costumes – symbolize steps in man's advancement up the Mountain. Moreover, Moses, our spiritual self, is just about to descend from the Mountain, carrying the Commandments "etched in stone." Only when the Commandments are "solid" in us can we hang loose.

This is a crucial segment of the climb. Soon Aaron, the mental aspect of us, will give in to the fears that come upon the people as they experience the absence of their spiritual leader. And when they demand that Aaron "make" a god that will go before them, he complies.

The intellect often joins the portions of ourselves that don't understand what is going on in our lives – those portions that demand a **physical presence** to lead them. Aaron will craft the golden calf – not even the full grown bull of the Babylonians – for the people to worship, and he will use the resources that should have been saved for the Tabernacle. The unenlightened hope they will find completion in the golden calf, but esotericists teach that completion comes only as all elements (Earth, Air, Water, Fire) converge – only as all "directions" (East, South, West, North) are covered – in other words, as all elements have been learned. We have just been told that we are ½ way there. But part of "completion" lies in our recognizing that **in right-eousness there is no ½; there is no division.**

It is difficult to see this truth in the revelation that is given to Moses, but it is there. It is in the **form** of the Tabernacle. It is in the **proportions** and **numbers** given for the various items used for worship. It is in the form which the **worship** takes. It is in the **require-ments** placed on those who are to be priests. And it is this truth to which Suarès rivets our attention.[2]

> When communication purports to convey *the* Revelation, ... [it] can only lead to ... religious interpretations which obstruct the immediate perception of the fact that **the very existence of a speck of dust is ... the first and the last mystery.** No mystery is greater than any other: the Qabala has always known [this], and has therefore never raised the question as to whether God exists. For those of the Qabala – for Abraham, Moses or Jesus, **the unknowable unknown is a presence. The knowing of that presence is the un-known. There is no other revelation.**
>
> **It is** therefore and above all **necessary to reject all interpretations, explan-ations, creeds and dogmas, all faiths and moral laws, all traditions, philos-ophies and theologies, so as to allow the unknown to operate directly in our minds.** Then thought is free to observe the interplay of life and death and existence be-cause it moves along with it, **having shattered its fetters.** The Qabala postulates that **knowledge is not a formulation, but a cosmic energy imparted to the mind** by the letter-numbers.
>
> Carlo Suarès.

As with all religions, the religion which Moses creates is for "earthy" mankind; but it surpasses earthy religions, in that it hints at a greater understanding. It beckons to all to shatter their "fetters." Its symbolism is more easily seen than Christianity's, for Moses' symbolism is tied neither to historical time nor to a personality. It is indefinite; therefore, it tells us that there is more than meets the eye in the form, the furnishings, the ritual, and the priestly obligation.

The introduction to the form of worship begins as the LORD lists the objects of the Tabernacle (in the order of their

[2] Suarès, p. 58.

206

importance). The LORD'S requirements for the Tabernacle begin with the specifications for the **Ark,** designed with proportions approximating the trunk of a man. Next comes the "throne of mercy" – the **mercy seat,** the Ark's covering, made of pure gold. The next requirements are for the **table for** *shew bread* and the **seven-branched lamp-stand** *so mounted as to give the light on its front side.*[3] Apparently next in importance are the fabrics for the Tabernacle hangings; and finally we are given instructions for the **veil** which serves *as a partition between the Holy and the Holy of Holies.* Ex. 26:33.

The **Tabernacle**

*The LORD said to Moses, "Speak to the people of Israel, that they **take for me an offering; from every man whose heart makes him willing you shall receive the offering for me.** And this is the offering which you shall receive from them: **gold, silver, and bronze, blue and purple and scarlet stuff and fine twined linen, goats' hair, tanned rams' skins, goatskins, acacia wood, oil for the lamps, spices for the anointing oil and for the fragrant incense, onyx stones, and stones for setting, for the ephod and for the breastpiece.** And let them **make me a sanctuary, that I may dwell in their midst.** According to all that I show you concerning the pattern of the tabernacle, and of all its furniture, **so you shall make it."** Ex.25:1-9*

The symbols for worship in the Tabernacle offer direction for the climb; in fact, many have likened the Tabernacle's proportions to the human body. It is the **righteous** man/woman which we are constructing. The Tabernacle is a symbol, and the righteous person is "constructed" of the choice materials; but regardless of its finery, the Tabernacle is still a *tent.* It is a moveable sanctuary. The intellect accepts *a tent* as appropriate

---

[3] *The Torah,* p. 144.

for a people still on the move, but the intuition acknowledges *a tent* as indicating an understanding that is still changing. We cannot yet construct the "Temple." The Temple can be built only by the fully *developed* King, seven generations away from Moses. For now, a Tabernacle expresses our understanding.

Shittah (*Acacia seyal*)

The "wood" to be used throughout for structural supports as well as furnishings is **acacia.** Interestingly, the **acacia** tree has spines which make it noxious, yet it has great practical value. Some call it "the tree of life," and many see it as representing immortality.[4] This tree of life forms the upright pillars – as well as all other structural supports – of this *tent* of sanctuary; and for the most important features of the sanctuary, the acacia wood will be covered with gold.

It is no easy task to "worship the LORD." It requires exceptional tenacity throughout the climb; most importantly, it requires a "clear" statement from the "worshiper." Remember, the designation for "Tabernacle" requires its **being "clear,"** i.e., visible from a distance, and made with **upright** pieces of wood. We've advanced from Jacob's time when entwined boughs made *booths for the cattle.* (See p. 128.) The Tabernacle is the *tent of meeting* for the righteous man or woman.

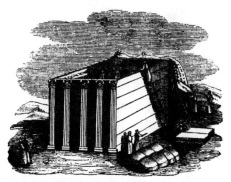

---

[4] Gaskell, p. 21. And Corinne Heline, Vol. 1, p. 248.

Its design symbolizes the process for advancement. Entering the Sanctuary from the East, the celebrant or the priest first encounters the **Brazen Altar**, constructed of acacia wood and covered with *copper* (*brass, bronze* in some translations). It is here that the animal natures must be eliminated with **FIRE**.[5]

```
                    Holy of Holies

                    Mercy Seat
                    and Ark

            --------- The Veil ---------


                        Incense
                         Altar

  7-Branched                         Table of
  Lampstand                          Shewbread
  7 + 4                              2x6=12
                    Holy Place



                      (Laver)


                      oooooo
                      Brazen
                       Altar
                      oooooo


                  Tent of  Meeting

                         E
```

Notice that it is surrounded by **10** bowls for blood (10 being physical *accumulation*). These, too, are made of copper. The "world" is represented by the lesser metals (copper, brass or bronze). Neither brass nor bronze is pure.[6] The celebrant washes his hands and feet with **WATER** (feet representing the understanding; hands representing the activity). It is our angers, our passions, our fears with which we must first deal, then our emotions. Both *fire* and *water* in their primitive states are of an earthy nature. These parts of us must be ***burned out*** (as is the sacrifice on the brazen altar) and then ***washed away*** (as in the laver).

---

[5] Interestingly, *The Jerusalem Bible* calls each altar an Altar of Holocaust. *Holocaust* means *whole burning*.

[6] *The Torah* says the altar for burnt offerings is of acacia wood, covered with **copper**See Ex. 38:1,2. With regard to the laver, *The Torah* again uses copper. Ex. 30:17.

Only he/she who knows that he/she is God's child and "possesses" all that he/she needs has conquered *fire* and *water*. Only such can advance to the Holy Place which holds those symbols required for entry to the Holy of Holies, those symbols which are separated from the profane. **The "Holy Place"** has no recognition of the profane; in fact, the lesser metals have changed to gold. Herein, we are expressing at a different vibration; symbolically, we have advanced to another plane.[7] In this Holy Place we find the lampstand which indicates the physical expression, the table which indicates the spiritual expression, and the altar for worship.

As we enter the Holy Place through the covers for the Tent of Meeting, on our left hand we encounter the **Seven-Branched**

Holy Place Holds Lampstand, Table, &Altar for Incense

Lampstand, projecting light only in front of itself and symbolizing earthly plenty with **six branches on either side** – each branch having **three** cups shaped like almond-blossoms (with calyx and petals all from **one piece**). Completion comes with the seventh "piece," the lampstand itself, which displays **four** cups shaped like almond-blossoms, again with each calyx and petals being of **one piece**, *the whole of it a single hammered piece of pure gold.* Ex. 25:36 Hear the subtle metaphor that likens us to this flowering? We are a single "hammered" piece of pure gold intended to provide light before us.

Opposite our earthly light is the **Table of "Shew" Bread** (lit. "the loaves of the face" [8]), symbolizing the truth about ourselves: that we are spiritual beings. Thereon sit a total of

---

[7] The progression through the Tabernacle is echoed in Isaiah 48:10. (Notice the numbering: 4x12= 48 and 10.) Is. 48:10 *Behold, I have refined you, but not like silver; I have tried you in the furnace of affliction. For my own sake, for my own sake, I do it, for how should my name be profaned? My glory I will not give to another. "Hearken to me, O Jacob, and Israel, whom I called! I am He, I am the first, and I am the last. My hand laid the foundation of the earth, and my right hand spread out the heavens; when I call to them, they stand forth together."* Is. 48:10-13.

[8] *The Jerusalem Bible,* p. 109 fn., see Lv. 24:5-9.

12 loaves, placed in two six-tiered stacks, accompanied by utensils of pure gold. *And you shall make a **table** of acacia wood... You shall overlay it with pure gold, and make a molding of gold around it. ... And you shall make its plates and dishes for incense, and its flagons and bowls with which to pour libations; of pure gold ... And you shall **set the bread of the Presence on the table before me always**.* Ex. 25:23-30.

The **Altar for Incense**

Immediately in front of us – immediately next to the veil and centered between the lampstand and the table – is another altar, this time an **Altar for Incense.** This third item in the Holy Place proves we have arrived at another level, for here is advancement.

*You shall make an **altar to burn incense** upon; of acacia wood shall you make it. ... it shall be [one cubit] square, and two cubits shall be its height; its horns shall be of one piece with it. And you shall **overlay it with pure gold**... And two golden rings... on two opposite sides of it... shall be holders for poles with which to carry it. ... And you shall **put it before the veil that is by the ark of the testimony, before the mercy seat that is over the testimony, where I will meet with you.** And Aaron shall **burn fragrant incense on it**; every **morning** when he dresses the lamps... and... [when he] sets the lamps in the **evening** ... a perpetual incense ... throughout your generations. **You shall offer no unholy incense thereon**, nor burnt offering, nor cereal offering; and you shall pour no libation thereon. **Aaron shall make atonement upon its horns once a year; with the blood of the sin offering** of atonement he shall make atonement for it once in the year throughout your generations; **it is most holy to the LORD.*** Ex. 30:1-10.

The altar for incense is of acacia wood and has four horns, but it is distinct from the altar of burnt offering in that it is **one** cubit wide and long (square) but two cubits high. This altar which is the **measurement of ONE** could not even be mentioned until we had entered into the true **Tabernacle.**

Though the physical and the spiritual are with us always, only as we unite them do we recognize something beyond the physical; but this, too, demands sacrifice. We have reached the third of the four elements, **AIR**. Only with concentration can we can pull ourselves away from the physical expression. Our attention is "concentrated" by its awareness of symbols. But we must take care not to turn the symbols into concrete regulations; we must keep "loose."[9]

> Take pure **spices**...*with pure* **frankincense** *(of each shall there be an equal part), and make an incense blended as by the perfumer, seasoned with* **salt,** *pure and holy; and you shall beat some of it very small, and put part of it before the testimony in the tent of meeting where I shall meet with you;* **it shall be for you most holy.** *And the incense which you shall make, according to its composition, you shall not make for yourselves;* **it shall be for you holy to the LORD.** *Whoever makes any like it to use as perfume shall be cut off from his people.* Ex. 30:34-37.

Notice what has been suggested so far for this "sanctuary" we are building. We are invited to *see* that what "appears" to be a human body is actually the dwelling place of the LORD. It is in this earthly experience that we are to develop to where eventually we experience "one-to-one" communication with the Divine. But the experience must be an individual effort that focuses itself at an altar, an altar made from the tree of life and covered with gold.[10] On this altar the "holy" individual will "perpetually" burn "sanctified" incense – not profane incense and not the animals of the "brazen altar" – for the "holy" individual has been lifted up above the physical and the profane. And on a regular basis (in this case once a year), Aaron (the High Priest when we are at that level) will *"perform the rite of atonement on the horns of the altar with the blood of the sacrifice offered for sin."*

---

[9] Interestingly, in the initial giving of the requirements for an "altar," i.e., Ex. 27:1-8, the description is for the Altar for Burnt Offering. It is five cubits long and five cubits wide and three cubits high and has horns at all four corners. The Altar for Burnt Offering is for the carnal expression. Its focus number is five. On the other hand, the Altar for Incense is for a heightened expression. Again its form makes a square, but this time its measurement is **one** rather than **five** and **its height is twice its breadth.** The altar of incense is **visibly placed on a symbolically higher plane;** and **it is covered with gold** rather than copper. Although both altars are for "burning," they are for cleansing with fire on two different levels of expression.

[10] The Temple's "altar" will be of solid gold, but again that is for a state of greater development. See: I Chronicles 28:18. (*The Altar for Incense is made of refined gold*).

The altar for incense provides a symbolic sacrifice for Moses' celebrants. However, Christians feel no need for even a symbolic *sacrifice*, under the argument that the sacrifice of Jesus Christ negates the need for a sin offering. Logically, once having reached the understanding of the Christ, the individual can no longer sin, because he/she is "at-one" with God. The disagreement stems from our difficulty with esoteric thinking. Until we reach the point of Christhood and oneness with God, it is necessary that we admit our "shortcomings" – the difference between the level of our expression and the perfection of the Christ. It is this that the incense altar invites.

As with the sacrifice of the Christ, in this Tent of Meeting, at this "Holy Place," we can see that man's form replicates that of a "cross." Mystics see the human body – with arms outstretched – as forming a cross. With such an interpretation, the pivotal centers are the heart and throat – back to our LAW – what we **hold in our heart** and what we **say** are what determines our expression. So too with the human-formed Tabernacle. If the Holy of Holies is seen to replicate the higher centers in the head, then the instruments of worship in the "Holy Place" take on an even greater importance, for they occupy the location of man's pivotal centers.

The Veil Even though we now have three of the elements needed for completion, we are restricted by the **veil** – that which separates us at all times except the time appointed – from the Holy of Holies. *And you shall make a veil of blue and purple and scarlet stuff and fine twined linen; in skilled work shall it be made, with cherubim; and you shall hang it upon four pillars of acacia overlaid with gold, with hooks of gold, upon four bases of silver. And you shall hang the veil from the clasps, and bring the ark of the testimony in thither within the veil; and the veil shall separate for you the holy place from the most holy.* Ex. 26:31-34.

The Ark and the Mercy Seat are so special that (for the time being) they are to be veiled from the other elements of worship in the remainder of the Tabernacle and veiled from all but the high priest. The veil keeps us from seeing the Holy of Holies – the "dwelling place" of YHWH – into which only the high priest can enter, and that only once a year on the Day of Atonement. But the veil itself gives us instruction.

It is to be **made with blue, purple, and scarlet** (or crimson) **yarns**. That through which we must pass to reach the Holy of Holies takes the lowest vibration of the primary colors (red) and combines it with the highest vibration of the primary colors (blue), producing something higher than either, i.e., purple. It symbolizes what happens to us as we take within us that which is base and merge it with higher understanding. Eventually, we produce something new which gives us access to the LORD.[11] But again, this is a paradox. This new "something" which we become needs to "see" that it actually has immediate and perpetual access to the LORD.

The veil represents the approach of those who still see themselves as separated from God. While they acknowledge the existence of God – even to the point of granting to God the most special place – they keep themselves from seeing the "residence" of God except on the day chosen for such at-one-ment. The veil will eventually split, but only with the crucifixion of the Christ. At the end of the process, the veil must go; but for now it remains to separate the most-holy place from that which is not yet "complete."

The unenlightened mind may assume that by "moving" through the required "worship," it will become "complete." That might appear to be true from a casual observation of the rules for the Tabernacle, but let's not insult the understanding of Moses. Obviously, the completion does not come just because the individual starts at the East gate and progresses through the "stations." Rather, the "stations" of the Tabernacle (as do the "stations" of the Cross) symbolize the changes and challenges

---

[11] Corinne Heline sees the colors of the Tabernacle this way:"the blue of truth and spiritual devotion; the scarlet of loving works; the purple wherein the red of physical, passionate activity is being uplifted by the spiritual powers of blue. By forces of transmutation operating through the purple ray, power is engendered; therefore, the color is identified with rank and nobility. So it was the color prescribed for the robes of priests who were to serve in the Tabernacle precincts." Heline, *New Age Bible Interpretation: Volume 1*, p. 253.

214

that the individual on the climb will encounter. Our completion can come only as we regularly **"burn" what is unlike God out** of us, only as we regularly **"wash" the sediment away**, only as we **recognize the perfection** of our earthly expression, only as we **acknowledge our spiritual nature**, and only as we **continually "burn" even the remaining portions** of our earthliness in the air.

Edgar Cayce, the 20th Century American clairvoyant, nicely expressed the esoteric view of this phase of worship. He told his Tuesday Night Bible Class: "To have our bodies and minds conform to the same pattern as the temple [Tabernacle] outlined in Exodus, it is necessary to do certain things uniformly and with the proper attention to detail. But not so ritualistic as to forget the spirit or purpose behind the rite. The daily ritual should remind us of the necessity to make our lives in accord with our spiritual purposes. Some part of our day should be dedicated to meditation, to entering into the holy of holies within ourselves. We should prepare ourselves for this communion with the highest forces known. **We need to make a habit of doing those things each day which will keep us in remembrance of the fact that the body is the temple. There He has promised to speak with us.**"[12]

It is as the LORD "speaks" to us that the veil is lifted; only then do we truly "see." This "seeing" takes place in the Holy of Holies. Symbolically it is undertaken by the HIGH PRIEST, the one anointed by the LORD, and it takes place upon the Mercy Seat, that which covers the Ark of Covenant. *They shall make an* ***ark of acacia wood;*** *two cubits and a half shall be its length, a cubit and a half its breadth, and a cubit and a half its height. And you shall **overlay it with pure gold, within and without** ....* Ex. 25:10-11.

The Ark and The Mercy Seat   **The Ark** is that which "holds" the **power** inherent in mankind (Aaron's rod), as well as the **understanding** that God will provide (the bowl of "manna"), and the **disciplined expression** (the Tablets of the Commandments). Like the Tabernacle itself, the Ark's proportions are reminiscent of man's form. Mankind (even mankind which is still changing) is to be overlaid with "gold" – both **within** and **without.** Moses establishes the Ark, and

[12] Robert W. Krajenke, *Edgar Cayce's Story of the Old Testament,* Edgar Cayce Foundation, p. 207.

through the next 264 years, the Hebrews place great importance on it.[13] Without it, they don't thrive. Yet, when Solomon opens it, ***There [is] nothing in the ark except the two tables*** *which Moses put there at Horeb (to parch), where the LORD made a covenant with the people of Israel, when they came out of Egypt.* 2 Chr. 5:10.

What is being said here? Possibly that everything except the "physical Law" is evidence of **internal** "perfection," for (only the manifestation of the LAW can be viewed on the physical level.) Possibly the most important thing to "see" is that **in truth,** our spiritual "covering" is the essence of us, as is the Ark's covering, the **Mercy Seat.**[14] *Then you shall make a **mercy seat** of pure gold;... And you shall make two cherubim of gold ... of one piece with the mercy seat.... The cherubim shall spread out their wings above, overshadowing the mercy seat with their wings, their faces one to another... And you shall put the mercy seat on the top of the ark; and in the ark you shall put the testimony that I shall give you. **There I will meet with you, and from above the mercy seat, from between the two cherubim that are upon the ark of the testimony, I will speak with you of all that I will give you in commandment for the people of Israel.*** Ex. 25:17-22.

The High Priest in the Holy of Holies with Ark, Mercy Seat & Cherubim.

---

[13] Tradition sets Moses' presentation of the Law at Sinai at approximately 1230 B.C.; Solomon's beginning of the Temple is approximately 966 B.C..

[14] The Ark was "a rectangular chest (3 3/4 x 2 1/4 x 2 1/4 feet) " carried on poles; resting on it was the 'throne of mercy' with the cherubs. *The Jerusalem Bible*, p.109, fn.

The Mercy Seat is the most esoteric of all the symbols of the Tabernacle. Formed from gold in **one piece**, its two cherubim (*one grasped, held fast*) represent the **duality** of physical life.[15] Most representations of the cherubim are as winged bestial creatures, having characteristics of both the physical (beast) and the representation of spiritual (wings). And it is in the midst of this symbolism, covering the expression of man, that the *Shechinah* (presence of God) appears in the form of a column of smoke.[16] *Oneness* with the *Shechinah* is something available only to the "high priest" who enters the Holy of Holies at the appropriate time, the time of *atonement*. Ideally, the *appropriate time* will come daily.

He/she who is truly on the climb **will take time** to enter the Holy of Holies daily. One never knows when will be the *appropriate time* for the LORD to speak with us. The *appropriate time* may come after an extended period where we have diligently held to spiritual thoughts and tenaciously held to meditation and worship. It may come, instantaneously, in time of crisis, when we triumph over fear and concern. Possibly it is what the esotericists call the test of EARTH. It is evidence of our having become the "high priest."

The Priesthood   I remember the first time I told a class that we are all "priests." It was a class of very Protestant ladies, and there was an almost audible gasp from the group. But remember, this is what we are told: *and you shall be to me a kingdom of priests and a holy nation.* Ex. 19:6. In fact, requirements for the "office" of "priest" contain almost as many lessons as do the requirements for the Tabernacle.

---

[15] This definition of *cherubim* comes from Young, p. 157. What a lovely concept, that even the physical expression should give us notice that we are "grasped" and "held fast" by the Father. Even in the physical expression we are One with God.

[16] The concept of the *Shechinah* lifts us to an additional dimension. It is an advancement that is uncommunicable, for the intellect will call it imagination. Only the loosely held intuition can "see" the smoke on the Mercy Seat and "know" that it is the presence of God. Only the loosely held intuition can "feel" it as a nurturing, loving – almost feminine – presence. The *Shechinah* "appears" only to the mystical.

It is Aaron – the mental aspect of Moses – which is directed by the provisions for "priesthood." The symbolism lies in the priestly attire, in the priestly duties, and in the priestly responsibilities. Finally, the symbolism heightens with the rules for the Nazirites.

Aaron: Mental Aspect

    Before delineating the requirements for the priesthood, *The Torah* gives us a signpost.[17] תצוה One wonders if we are being told that the rituals and the priesthood, of themselves, do not express at the level of earthly completion (7). They add up to 6 (coming from a third level; but still 6). But as such, they represent two expressions of equilibrium, a balanced *three* – as with the symbol of Judaism.

✡

    On the surface, the only given obligation of the priesthood is to keep the light shining: i.e., physically, to keep the lamp lit; symbolically, to keep the "knowledge" available. *"And you shall command the people of Israel that they bring to you **pure beaten olive oil** for the light, that a lamp may be set up to burn continually. **In the tent of meeting, outside the veil which is before the testimony, Aaron and his sons shall tend it from evening to morning before the LORD. It shall be a statute for ever to be observed throughout their generations by the people of Israel.*** Ex. 27:20. But the esoteric obligation is to "make sacrifice." On the surface that means just burning various animals, or grains, or incense; but in esoteric language it means that the "priest" gives up (sacrifices) the outer world to be able to enter the inner world. *"Then bring near to you Aaron your brother, and his sons with him, from among the people of Israel, to serve me as priests ... And you shall make **holy garments** for Aaron your brother, **for glory and for beauty**. And you shall speak to all who have ability, whom I have endowed with an able mind, that they make Aaron's garments to consecrate him for my priesthood."* Ex. 28:1-3.

    The Torah presents it more meaningfully: *"... instruct all who are **wise of heart**, whom I have filled with a spirit of wisdom to make Aaron's vestments, for consecrating him to serve Me as priest. ... they, therefore, shall receive the gold, the blue, purple, and crimson yarns, and the fine linen."*

    My class of Protestant ladies was partially right to react to my saying all are "priests." It would be better to say that

---

[17] תצוה according to the formula of Suarès would be 5·6·90·400 = 501.

"all shall *become* priests. " My intuition "sees" everyone as eventually coming to a place of wisdom; but, needless to say, at this moment few of us express at this level, constantly. Moreover, there is the esoteric admonition that only that which is "perfect" sees no "imperfection." Only as our worship comes from a "spirit of wisdom" do we reach perfection.

The priest is not "perfect." All "religion" is confined to the outer, like the garments and the trappings which the priest wears. "Religion" simply represents what ideally is found within mankind. So, too, the priesthood only represents what man/woman can find in himself/herself. On the surface it is such: *"These are the garments which they shall make: a breastpiece, an ephod, a robe, a coat of checker work, a turban, and a girdle; they shall make holy garments for Aaron your brother and his sons to serve me as priests."* Ex. 28:3-5.

The attire and trappings represent what is "within" – gold, blue and purple and scarlet, and fine linen. *"They shall receive gold, blue and purple and scarlet stuff, and fine twined linen. And they shall make the ephod ... And you shall take two onyx stones, and engrave on them the names of the sons of Israel, six of their names on the one stone, and the names of the remaining six on the other stone, in the order of their birth. ... you shall enclose them in settings of gold filigree. ...Aaron shall bear their names before the LORD upon his two shoulders for remembrance. ..."* Ex. 28:1-14.

The principal attire is for Aaron, high priest, and symbol of our mental aspects. And notice what Aaron wears **"upon his shoulders"** – two onyx stones engraved with the names of the sons of Israel (six on each stone) in the order of their birth.[18] Look back at page 108 for the names of the sons of Jacob. One onyx stone is engraved with: **sight, hearing, loving, praise, righteous judgment**, and **strength.** The second onyx stone is

---

[18] There are three uses for the word *ephod*. 1. The *ephod bad*, a linen loincloth worn by sacred ministers (1Sam. 2:18). 2.The *ephod*, an instrument of divination, used for consulting Yahweh (1 Sam.2:28). 3. The *ephod* of the high priest as described here in Exodus, but which was not worn with the description given until after the exile. *The Jerusalem Bible*, p. 113, fn.b. After David, the "oracular ephod" is not mentioned. Esoterically, this suggests that when the "priestly candidate" places his head (that which is between his shoulders) at an understanding which brings about all of the characteristics of Israel's sons in himself/herself, **a greater psychic awareness** comes upon him/her. But this psychic awareness comes only as one is celibate (conserving of the life force). Then the psychic awareness energizes the Urim and Thummin, two stones that act as sort of a "yes"/ "no" computer that we all have. The physical "Urim and Thummim" are stored inside the folded breastplate.

"engraved" with: **abundance, happiness, reward, order, perfection, and power.**[19] Notice that the **mental aspect must first achieve perfection within**; only then does it **receive perfection without.** All this symbolism is placed on the ephod, that which supports and carries the "breastplate of decision."

It is time for some hang-loose thinking. We are beyond the Patriarchs. The climber is no longer expressing as did Adam, Noah, Abraham, Isaac, Jacob (Israel) or even Joseph. Now we are talking about the man/woman who is expressing at the level of Moses: he/she who has *been drawn from the water*; he/she who has *turned;* he/she who has *received the Law.* Only this heightened level of consciousness qualifies to be "seen" as the *enlightened high priest.* But to an extent, this level is an ideal rather than a "reality." Certainly the high priest and the entire "priesthood" of Jesus' time was not at this level. By that time, the office of "high priest" was even available to the highest bidder. The priesthood had fallen into corruption and decadence – certainly an expression incapable of experiencing the presence of the *Shechinah.*

The "priesthood" may represent the ideal, but the symbols for an *enlightened priesthood* are possibly best understood with the requirements for the Nazirites, (interestingly) given in the **6th** chapter of Numbers.

*And the LORD said to Moses, "Say to the people of Israel, **When either a man or a woman makes a special vow, the vow of a Nazirite, to separate himself to the LORD,** he shall **separate** himself from wine and strong drink; he shall drink no vinegar ... and shall **not** drink **any juice of grapes or eat grapes, fresh or dried.** All the days of his separation he shall **eat nothing that is produced by the grapevine,** not even the seeds or the skins. ... **no razor** shall come **upon his head;** ... he shall let the locks of hair of his head grow long. All the days that he separates himself to the LORD he **shall not go near a dead body.** **Neither for his father nor for his mother, nor for brother or sister,** ... because his separation to God is upon his head. **All the days of his separation he is holy to the LORD.***

*"And if any man dies very suddenly beside him, and **he defiles his consecrated head,** then **he shall shave his head on the day of his cleansing; on the seventh day** he shall shave it. On the eighth day he shall bring two turtle doves or young*

---

[19] The designation "on his shoulders" is almost a "pun." What do we bear on our "shoulders"? Our head, that which traditionally carries our mind, our mental aspects.

*pigeons ... and the **priest shall offer one for a sin offering** and **the other for a burnt offering, and make atonement** for him, ... **And he shall [reconsecrate] his head** and [rededicate to the LORD his term as nazirite]; and bring a male lamb ...for a **guilt offering; but the former time shall be void, because his separation was defiled.*** Num. 6:1-13. [*The Torah*]

If we are to function as the "high priest," somewhere along the line we must accept the requirements for the Nazirite. Modern interpretation has for the most part ignored these thirteen verses, allocating them to an obscure sect; but look what is being said in hang-loose terms. He/she who would take on the role of ***enlightened high priest*** offers himself/herself as sacrifice to the LORD. There can be ***no blemish*** in that which is offered.[20] Nor shall one's hair be shorn (***no weakening of self***).[21] Moreover, there can be ***no false heightening*** as is related to wine – not even grapes or raisins.[22] But most importantly, there can be ***no contact with the dead*** even if it is your dearest loved one – or even if it happens by accident, just because you are next to someone who dies. This last admonition brings many questions. We may always have wondered about Jesus' comment to his disciple whose father had just died. *Jesus said to him, "Follow me, and leave the dead to bury their own dead."* Mt. 8:22. Both the Nazirite and the follower of Jesus must always remember that **there is no death.** This knowledge **distinguishes** the *living* from the *dead;* **it distinguishes righteous judgment.** Righteous judgment recognizes **no death**; it recognizes **no separation.** Righteous judgment recognizes **no duality. All is ONE. It is this *righteous judgment* which the "high priest" must practice.**

---

[20] *The Torah* says it slightly differently: *If anyone, man or woman, explicitly utters a nazirite's vow, to set himself apart for the LORD...* then refers us to Lev. 22:21, which is followed by: *Anything blind, or injured, or maimed, or with a wen, boil-scar, or scurvy – such you shall not offer to the LORD.*

[21] Esoterically, hair, whether of the beard or the head, stands for strength.

[22] I have a friend who claims that grapes, and any portion of the grape plant, contain an enzyme that the lower vibrational body cannot tolerate. Many years ago, my aunt contacted a "doctor" who said the same thing about the forbidden meats from Leviticus. His explanation was that things such as "shrimp" were the equivalent of "aviation fuel" which will destroy the motor of a regular automobile.

The wording for the requirements for the Nazirite causes problems for our literal mindset. It doesn't mean that we're restricted from touching a body, or having a funeral, or grieving for a time. What we are restricted from is *unrighteous* judgment; we are restricted from thinking that there is any separation from that loved one. We are not to be among the "dead." It is this "dead" understanding that necessitates the crucifixion and resurrection in order to demonstrate that "death" is not separate from "life." Only he/she who has fully incorporated this understanding into his/her mind and body and soul   is "enlightened." Only the ***enlightened* high priest** has this knowledge and this understanding.[23]

*"This is the law for the Nazirite who takes a vow. **His offering to the LORD shall be according to his vow as a Nazirite, apart from what else he can afford; in accordance with the vow** which he takes, **so shall he do** according to the law for his separation as a Nazirite." And the LORD said to Moses, "Say to Aaron and his sons, Thus you shall bless the people of Israel: you shall say to them, 'The LORD bless you and keep you: The LORD make his face to shine upon you, and be gracious to you: The LORD lift up his countenance upon you, and give you peace.'** So shall they put my name upon the people of Israel, and I will bless them."* Num. 6:21-27.

<u>**The Breastpiece of Judgment**</u>   Only the enlightened high priest has right to the rest of his vestments, for they represent characteristics of enlightenment. *"And you shall make a **breastpiece of judgment**, ...gold, blue and purple and scarlet stuff, and fine twined linen shall you make it. It shall be **square and double**, a span its length and a span its breadth. ...[With] **four rows of stones**. A row of **sardius, topaz, and carbuncle...emerald, a sapphire, and a diamond; ...a jacinth, an agate, and an amethyst;** and ...**a beryl, an onyx, and a jasper;** they shall be set in gold filigree .... And they shall bind the breastpiece ... with a lace of blue, that it may lie upon ...the ephod, and **that the breastpiece shall not come loose from the ephod.** So Aaron shall bear the **names** of the sons of Israel... **upon his heart, when he goes into the holy place,** to bring them to **continual remembrance before the LORD.*** Ex. 28:15-29.

---

[23] *"And this is the law for the Nazirite, **when the time of his separation has been completed: he shall be brought to the door of the tent of meeting, and he shall offer his gift to the LORD,** ... for a burnt offering, ... as **a sin offering, and ... a peace offering** ... and their cereal offering and their drink offerings. And the priest shall present [the offerings] before the LORD ... And the Nazirite shall shave his consecrated head at the door of the tent of meeting, and shall take the hair ...** and the priest shall wave them for **a wave offering...** and after that the Nazirite may drink wine."* Num. 6:13-20.

222

The **breastplate** represents what is in the heart: **sight, hearing, loving, praise, right- eous judgment, strength, abundance, happiness, reward, order, per- fection, and power.** These attributes must **continually** be *brought before the LORD.* When they are, we're granted the Urim and Thummim.

*And **in** the breastpiece of judgment you shall put the **Urim** and the **Thummim**, and **they shall be upon Aaron's heart,** ... thus **Aaron shall bear** [the oracle of the sons of Israel] **the judgment of the people of Israel upon his heart before the LORD continually.*** Ex. 28:15-30.

Whatever we continually bear upon our heart is our *judg- ment.* The Urim (lum- inous) and the Thum- mim (emblem of complete

The Breastplate of the High Priest

truth) is the "oracle" of the sons of Israel.[24] *The New Jerusalem Bible* says they are like dice or sticks; I have always thought of them as rocks or precious stones. They are two *things* that are so similar that they cannot be distinguished by "feel," only by sight. They are carried between the two layers of the high priest's *breastplate of judgment.* When the time comes for direction or consultation, the question is posed (likely stipulating

---

[24] The *Urim* and the *Thummim* are two of the most esoteric elements of the religious symbols. Esoterically, our judgment is based on what we "feel," but only the righteous judgment can "see" truth. Whatever our judgment is, comes from our "heart." When judgment and power reside in the heart instead of the head, there is no need for the Urim and Thummim; then there is no need for outer *instruction.*

what each "stone" represents – as with Saul in 1Sam. 14:41), and the hand is drawn out of the pocket of the breastplate, holding one of the items. Whichever "stone" is drawn gives the answer.

Just as our "robe" announces our | **The Robe**
presence, wherever we go, whatever we do
– we announce what is on our heart. *"And you shall make the robe ...all of blue. It shall have in it an **opening for the head, with a woven binding around the opening**, ...that it may not be torn. ... You shall make **pomegranates of blue and purple and scarlet** stuff, ... with bells of gold between them,..., round about on the skirts of the robe. And it shall be upon Aaron when he ministers, **and its sound shall be heard when he goes into the holy place before the LORD, and when he comes out, lest he die.*** Ex. 28:31-35.

If our "head" can wear the "robe" without tearing it, we are expressing at the level of pomegranates (unlimited fruit) made of blue and purple and scarlet; and we loudly proclaim this abundance as we go in and out of the holy place.[25] Our proclamation proves that we are of the "living." But we must hold our "head" to this knowledge, and so there is another item of apparel. *"And you shall make a **plate of pure gold**, engrave[d] ... **'Holy to the LORD.'** Fasten it on the turban by a lace of blue ... **on the front of the turban.** ... **upon Aaron's forehead**, and Aaron shall take **upon himself any guilt** incurred in the **holy offering** which the people of Israel hallow as their holy gifts; **it shall always be upon his forehead**, that they may be accepted before the LORD.* Ex. 28:36-38.

It is our mental self that carries our "guilt." Our mental self, both its conscious expression and that which is hidden in the unconscious, carries the remembrance of our iniquities and our triumphs; and it colors both by what is in our heart. There are even some esotericists who say that we bring about our own "iniquities" in order to exercise being triumphant. Notice, it is the holy "gift" that will be accepted. Maybe this is why the outer covering appears as a "checker work." And

---

[25] *The Jerusalem Bible* states that there is evidence in Babylonian sources of an idea "that the sound of bells would drive off the demons who haunted the threshold of sanctuaries." p. 115, fn.

maybe this is why the "head" is covered with a turban.[26] *"And you shall weave the **coat in checker work of fine linen**, and you shall make **a turban of fine linen**, and ... a **girdle embroidered** with needlework. And for Aaron's sons you shall make coats and girdles and caps; you shall make them for glory and beauty. And you shall **put them upon Aaron** your brother, **and** upon **his sons** with him, and shall **anoint them and ordain them and consecrate them,** that they may serve me as priests. Ex. 28: 38-41.*

 Anointing represents a visible "choosing" – a double *entendre* indicating the participant's being chosen as well as his/her choosing. Although all mankind can reach this point on the climb, only he/she who "chooses" to do so will do so. And it is the spiritual self who anoints the mental self and its offspring, ordaining and consecrating them.[27]

 *And you shall make for them **linen breeches to cover their naked flesh; from the loins to the thighs** ...; and **they shall be upon Aaron, and upon his sons, when they go into the tent of meeting,** or **when they come near the altar to minister in the holy place; lest they bring guilt upon themselves and die.** This shall be a perpetual statute for him and for his descendants after him.* Ex. 28:42,43.

 An easy interpretation of this admonition would be that the "priest's" sexual organs must be covered, i.e. he/she has to be celibate. But "easy answers" belong to the intellect, not the intuition. Celibacy is not a requirement for the "priesthood." In fact, none of our characters on the climb have been celibate; yet, all of our characters have been on the climb. One wonders if celibacy is a question only for the unenlightened. However, my assumption is that he/she who is the "high priest" who

---

[26] Numerous cultures and religions have "turbans" which are wound in a particular fashion (to the left or right, depending on the beliefs), which brings the highest point over the "crown" of the head. The headwear in the Catholic Church and the mitre of the Pope echo the traditions where the crown chakra is either accentuated (if it is opened) or camouflaged (if it has not been opened). But the Hebrew high priest has the gold "frontlet" to declare what his status is.

[27] *The Torah,* p. 151, defines *ordination* as "fill their hands." I have an interesting book, published in 1837, which gives the "official" position regarding "ordination." Those who ascribe to Jesus' having "laid hands" on Peter, and thus (in a linear succession) having "ordained" all Catholic, Orthodox, and Episcopalian priests were somewhat contemptuous of those Lutheran, Presbyterian, etc. priests (or ministers) who were not in the linear succession. Interestingly, the author, who was Episcopalian, apparently forgot that Luther had been duly ordained in his capacity as an Augustinian monk.

communicates with "God" and becomes one with the Shechinah no longer is concerned with the "desire" for sex.

Although the Western intellectual mindset may question my observation, I propose that *celibacy* is either an inborn tendency in an individual or a tendency which comes upon him/her as the climb progresses. All religions have groups which are celibate. Eastern religions even incorporate it into the progression one follows (after procreation) as he/she ages.[28] The Jews at the time of Jesus had both the ***Essenes*** in Judea and the ***Therapeutae*** in Alexandria whose devotees (both men and women) were celibate. (Not all Essenes were celibate.) [29]

It is not a question of celibacy that is the most difficult challenge for the enlightened high priest; it is the question of controlling the "*head.*" Isn't this our chief challenge, too? It is so difficult to control our thinking. In order to reach Moses' Promised Land and Jesus' Kingdom of Heaven, we must *continually* have "righteous judgment" written on both our heart and head.[30]

---

[28] The most lucid explanation for celibacy that I have found comes from the writings of Elisabeth Haich in her book *Initiation.* "The power of reproduction can not only be manifested by the body, but also on another plane as energy. ... In order to set in motion a certain process in various materials (such as gold) a person needs the radiation of his own vital energy. However, if he expends this energy through his sexual organs, he automatically puts into a latent state the very nerve centres he needs to radiate vital energy in its original, basic form. These nerves open and close automatically. A person can either channel this energy into his sexual organs or into other, higher nerve centres, *but he cannot simultaneously channel it into both!"*

Speaking of Indian (Eastern) healers, Haich continues: "You can easily understand that when a father initiates his son into this science, the son, along with his oath of silence, must take a vow of complete continence. That's why the son can only be initiated when he is already married and has several sons of his own, in order that there be no interruption in the chain of knowledge. But just show me a Western physician who would be willing to live a life of complete continence for the sake of this knowledge!" pp.128, 129.

[29] Josephus, the Jewish historian at the time of Christ, wrote that there were some 4000 Essene probationers and initiates. The compound at Qumran, which was the source of the "Dead Sea Scrolls," was a Essene community. Ausubel, *...Knowledge,* p. 144-145. Philo, the philosopher-rabbi of Alexandria, described the Therapeutae in his *On the Contemplative Life.* Ausubel, *...Knowledge,* p. 468-469.

[30] Judah stands for **Praise**; Dan stands for **Righteous Judgment**. *Bezalel [in the protection of God - Judite] and Oholiab [tent of his father- Danite]* build the sanctuary, *and*

(continued...)

The heart seems to do pretty well, but the "head," as represented by Aaron has to be trained! And the sanctuary hasn't even been built, yet. Moses is still up the Mountain, and Aaron – the mental aspect – is about to weaken to the demands of the "people." *When the people saw that Moses delayed to come down from the mountain, **the people gathered themselves together to Aaron,** and said to him, **"Up, make us gods, who shall go before us;** as for this Moses, the man who brought us up out of the land of Egypt, we do not know what has become of him." And Aaron said..., "Take off the rings of gold which are in the ears of your wives, your sons, and your daughters, and bring them to me." So all the people took off the rings of **gold which were in their ears,** and brought them to Aaron. And **he received the gold at their hand, and fashioned it with a graving tool, and made a molten calf;** and **they said,** "These are your gods, O Israel, who brought you up out of the land of Egypt!" When Aaron saw this, he built an altar before it; and **Aaron made proclamation and said, "Tomorrow shall be a feast to the LORD."** And they rose up early on the morrow, and offered burnt offerings and brought peace offerings; and the **people sat down to eat and drink, and rose up to play**.* Ex. 32:1-6

It is possible to see Aaron as Moses' brother who – not having as much understanding as Moses – "goofs," but such "seeing" misses what the story has to teach. It's just like us to "see" inaccurately. We would rather say "sin is to blame" or the "devil was afoot" or give some other such excuse for Aaron's behavior. In fact, it makes us "uncomfortable" to consider Aaron as that part of ourselves that is connected to the conscious mind or to the "ego" that runs it.

The story of Aaron and the molten "calf" comes immediately after the following: *"Say to the people of Israel, 'You shall keep my sabbaths, for this is a sign between me and you throughout your generations, that you may know that I, the LORD, sanctify you.'"* Ex. 31:13.

Keeping the Sabbath is the fourth commandment. It applies to how the individual relates to this LORD which we know to be I Am. The enlightened High Priest must be *sanctified – consecrated* (totally given over to the Lord) – wholly dedicated to righteous expression.

---

[30](...continued)
every able man in whom the LORD has put ability and intelligence to know how to do any work in the construction of the sanctuary shall work in accordance with all that the LORD has commanded. And Moses called Bezalel and Oholiab and every able man in whose mind the LORD had put ability, every one whose heart stirred him up to come to do the work; and they received ... all the freewill offering ... the people ... had brought. Ex. 36.

Aaron, our mental aspect, is not denying the LORD God. In fact, after finishing the calf, he proclaims *"Tomorrow shall be a feast to the LORD."* But Aaron is not yet *consecrated.*[31] Our mental aspect does not understand the LORD; it does not have the I Am understanding that Moses, the spiritual aspect, has. Aaron, our mental self – which we *experience* as the conscious mind – is still tied to earthly expression.

What is the difference between Aaron's expression and that of Moses? It is a subtle difference possibly best explained in two negative statements: it is **not a physical "form"** that brings us out of bondage; and there is **no tomorrow.**

Remember the old song – "There's no tomorrow, there's just today..."? Just as in the song, our problem is that we don't always remember this. Our conscious mind is more comfortable with a "god" that has form; our conscious mind is more comfortable in putting the final *oneness* somewhere in the future. Why? Because the

Mental Aspect Gives In To The Lesser Thoughts

little "i" isn't quite ready to relinquish control to the I Am.

It's the spiritual self that has to bring the mental self around. And finally, after all sides are covered – after fire, water, air, earth have all been completed (4) and multiplied by accumulated equilibrium (10) – on the **40th** day Moses comes down from the Mountain. *And he took the **calf which they had made,** and burnt it with **fire,** and ground it **to powder,** and **scattered** it upon the **water, and made the people of Israel drink it.** Ex. 32:20.*

From the esotericist's point of view, the spiritual self puts into operation those circumstances and experiences necessary for growth and eventual perfection. The intellectual mindset will deny this; it tends to see all physical conditions as coming to us for no apparent reason – unless possibly as a consequence of cause and effect – but, otherwise, as a result of mere happenstance. Moses' absence allowed Aaron's action.

---

[31] *Sanctified* is defined as "to set aside as holy; to consecrate." But it is almost as though *sanctify* means a conscious and "spoken" connection. In this case, it is the LORD "sanctifying" us.

228

The story as presented in Exodus is only too familiar to those on the climb. Here, our spiritual self has been communing with the Divine; nevertheless, upon returning to the conscious mind, we find an earthly expression in operation. It may be an illness or a crisis in our relationships – any sort of distraction

Doubts, Fears, Angers Must Be Eliminated

which threatens to pull our attention away from the spiritual expression. How can we reestablish our previous calm and peace?

We must take the "calf" which our fears and doubts, etc., have made and "burn it with fire," put it in the light, then grind it to powder, i.e., turn it into its smallest possible pieces so that it is totally exposed. Then we scatter its former parts on our emotional side and drink it down. Hopefully, when we're finished, we will find that there is no longer a "golden calf."

It takes great determination and courage to truly look at ourselves. Do we look at the anger that brings about our arthritic pains? Do we look at the fears that bring about our ulcers or our "lack" or shortages? Do we look at the fears and doubts that produce our needs?

Remember, just as the Buddhist achieves enlightenment only when all desire is gone – so is it with the "Promised Land." The *sanctified* mental aspect must be fully consecrated; all desire must be gone. Thus the golden calf is eliminated; and – as with what we drink – we absorb it, take what is needed, and let the rest go!   *And Moses said to Aaron, "**What did this people do to you** that you have brought a great sin upon them?"   And Aaron said, "... **you know the people, that they are set on evil.   For they said... 'Make us gods, who shall go before us**; as for this Moses, the man who brought us up out of the land of Egypt, we do not know what has become of him.'   And I said to them, 'Let **any who have gold** take it off'; so they gave it to me, **and I threw it into the fire, and there came out this calf."**   Ex. 32:21-24.*

Our mental self has all sorts of excuses, as do we – Haven't you heard the following? Mother didn't show that she loved me ... Daddy abused me ... my folks got a divorce ... my folks didn't get a divorce ... the kids at school didn't like me ... my parents over-protected me ... we were always poor ... it's what everyone else was doing ... – there are endless excuses to cover up our ego's reluctance to "let go." Whatever our excuses, they're just like Aaron's. ...

"... I took what I had that was valuable and threw it into the fire, and (surprise, surprise) *out came this calf."* That's why the "calf" has to be pulverized.

We squander our gifts; we refuse to admit that we simply are doing what our little "i" wants to do. We expend our energy on all these "energy sappers," then we're surprised that we get sick or befuddled. Don't we see the truth of being of the "living"? We have the choice of how to live our lives. We can sit and complain about our misfortunes, or we can look at our life and then **microscopically look** at ourselves. What characteristic in our mental self attracts the negativity that we see in our life? Are we willing to **eliminate** that mental belief so that the negativity will find no attraction in us? Remember *"Aaron shall bear their names* (whether good or bad) *before THE LORD upon his two shoulders for remembrance."* Ex.28:12.   At least Aaron is contrite. Despite his excuse-making, he's willing to admit that the "calf" is not the "highest" and "best" expression he could have made, and he goes along with its elimination. Recently I came across something I wrote in the margin of my study Bible many years ago: **"A contrite heart will eliminate the idle thoughts."** If we are truly "contrite" and ready to be healed, we must eliminate the idle thoughts. Moreover, only the contrite heart can clear the idle thoughts. It is the idle thoughts that "do us in." If we are to be healthy and productive and climbing, we must truthfully see what our doubts and fears and angers produce in our lives.

Moses knows that these "rebellious" thoughts, these doubts, fears and angers must be eliminated. *And when Moses saw that* ***the people had broken loose (for Aaron had let them break loose,*** *to their shame among their enemies),* *then* ***Moses stood in the gate*** *of the camp, and said,* ***"Who is on the Lord's side? Come to me."*** *And all the sons of Levi gathered themselves together to him. And he said to them, "Thus says the LORD God of Israel,* ***'Put every man his sword on his side, and go to and fro from gate to gate throughout the camp, and slay every man his brother, and every man his companion, and every man his neighbor.'"*** *And the sons of Levi did according to the word of Moses; and there fell of the people that day about* ***three thousand men.*** *And Moses said,* ***"Today you have ordained yourselves for the service of the LORD, each one at the cost of his son and of his brother,*** *that he may bestow a blessing upon you this day."* Ex. 32:25-29.

This is important enough to repeat: **Today you have ordained yourselves for the service of the LORD.** Do we recognize the importance of this statement? It is not some divine personality coming down and picking us for "his" work. There is no divine "personality." It is I Am, and we have ordained ourselves with our having eliminated these thoughts that were other than of the LORD. It is the house of Levi which follows Moses; it is that which has come from "Levi" (joined to, attached, uniting, loving) which can deal with our doubts, fears and angers. It is this loving approach which ordains itself for service of the LORD.

However, once having identified the source of our discomfort, we must be careful to approach it only with *love.* If we try any other approach – particularly any approach which tries to force the discomfort out – we will get the opposite reaction, thus entrenching the problem even more.[32] Jesus made a similar point to those who accused him of casting out demons by Beelzebul. *But he, **knowing their thoughts,** said to them, **"Every kingdom divided against itself is laid waste, and a divided household falls.** ... if Satan ... is divided against himself, how will his kingdom stand? ... But **if it is by the finger of God that I cast out demons, then the kingdom of God has come upon you.** When a strong man, fully armed, guards his own palace, his goods are in peace; but when one stronger than he assails him and overcomes him, he takes away his armor in which he trusted, and divides his spoil. **He who is not with me is against me, and he who does not gather with me scatters. When the unclean spirit has gone out of a man, he [it] passes through waterless places seeking rest; and finding none he says, 'I will return to my house from which I came.'** And when he [the unclean spirit] comes he finds it [his former house] swept and put in order. Then **he goes and brings seven other spirits more evil than himself, and they enter and dwell there; and the last state of that man becomes worse than the first."* Luke 11: 17-26.

Nature abhors a vacuum; therefore, only a "house" refilled with "love" is then protected. This "house," as well as Aaron,

---

[32] I have never studied Scientology, but I have a friend who has studied it. His explanation is that previous "difficulties" tied to emotional reactions produce what he calls a "charge." It is these "charges" which prompt (almost) a chemical reaction if a similar pattern comes by us again. Therefore, it is these "charges" which must be approached and comforted with *love*, thereby eventually eliminating them. My explanation adds that since the mind operates in a manner similar to the way a hologram works, any situation similar to that which produced the original *charge* can easily convince the psyche that the same scenario is taking place again. Therefore, any *charge* can only be approached with love.

represents our mental aspect– not only our conscious mind, but our subconscious as well. But those elements in our conscious and subconscious minds which require "gods to go before them" must be "blotted out of the book." He/she who is to serve as "high priest" – he/she who is climbing the Mountain – must operate at the suggestion of the spiritual self, not a wayward rabble. Aaron has to learn.

The rabble is within us. We've produced it through our numerous expressions of *woe* and *fear* and *doubt* and *conceit* and *selfishness* and *self-absorption*. And by the Law, such expression brings to us what is in ourselves.[33] Therefore, the rabble must be addressed.

*The LORD said to Moses, "Speak to the people of Israel, and bid them to make tassels on the corners of their garments throughout their generations, and to put upon the tassel of each corner a cord of blue; and it shall be to you a tassel to **look upon and remember all the commandments of the LORD, to do them, not to follow after your own heart and your own eyes, which you are inclined to go after wantonly.** So you shall **remember** and **do** all my **commandments,** and **be holy** to your God. I am the LORD your God, who brought you out of the land of Egypt, to be your God: I am the LORD your God."* Num. 15:37-40.

This is the greatest lesson for the "priest," that which represents the mental aspect. The challenge is ***not to follow after your own heart and your own eyes, which you are inclined to go after wantonly.*** Supposedly, all it takes is for us to ***remember all the commandments*** and **not to do** what our rabble would have us do. The question then is what constitutes "rabble"? Unfortunately, our ***own heart*** and ***own eyes*** are "rabble" **unless they are of the LORD.** And we are reminded **to be holy.** Our expression must be consistent.

But we thought we were so important, didn't we? Here we thought we had arrived at the point of the I Am, and here we thought we were ordained and given all these

---

[33] These destructive thoughts may be a result of incidents from "this life," or (even more complicated) from "another life." Needless to say, the left-overs from other lives are the most complicated of all. This is particularly true since Western thought has successfully blotted out an awareness of what we might call "reincarnation," first through *judging it heretical* under the power of religion and, more recently, through *judging it ridiculous* under the power of science.

responsibilities... **not yet!** The mind is not always consistent. From time to time we overstep our understanding. Aaron's two elder sons do not "remain" as priests, because they overstep their understanding; they offer "unholy fire" before the LORD in comparison to the "holy fire" offered

> **Mental Aspect Cannot Assume**

by Moses/Aaron.[34] *Now Nadab and Abihu, the sons of Aaron, **each took his censer, and put fire in it, and laid incense on it, and offered unholy fire before the LORD,** such as he had not commanded them. And fire came forth from the presence of the LORD and **devoured them, and they died** before the LORD.* Lv. 10:1,2.

Even though we're on the climb, we may not be ready for the "Promised Land" – certainly, not for the Kingdom of Heaven. One of the dangers is a temptation toward arrogance. It seems this is what Aaron's two elder sons were expressing. Their sin was in thinking that their **still "earthly focused minds"** could choose when to light the incense. Nadab (liberal) and Abihu (worshiper of God) should have been okay in approaching the Altar of Incense. They were ordained. But the key line is: ***such as he had not commanded them***. Notice that the discussion at the moment is "who" or "what" can act as "priest," but there is a corollary which asks the question: are we "living" or "dead." Because of their "overstepping," Aaron's two elder sons join the "dead" – thus making way for the two younger sons Eleazar and Ithamar– replacing the older understanding. The answer is: only the *living* can administer to the LORD.

This level of worship is special. *Moses said to Aaron, "This is what the LORD has said, **'I will show myself holy among those who are near me**, and before all the people I will be glorified.'"* ***And Aaron held his peace***. Lv. 10:3.[35]

---

[34] The point of Leviticus 10 can be understood only in comparison to what immediately precedes it: *And Moses and Aaron went into the tent of meeting; and when they came out they blessed the people, and the glory of the LORD appeared to all the people. **And fire came forth from before the LORD and consumed the burnt offering and the fat upon the altar;** and when all the people saw it, they shouted, and fell on their faces.* Lv. 9:23,24.

[35] As a hang-loose observation, compare this statement to Jesus' statement: *Now is the judgment of this world, now shall the ruler of this world be cast out; and **I, when I am lifted up from the earth, will draw all men to myself.*** Jn. 12:31,32.

Our conscious mind in its early expression "sees" with the eyes of the world. It sees itself as having already arrived at the top of the Mountain. But unless we are truly "near" the LORD, this arrogance will backfire on us, as with Aaron's two elder sons.[36] Our worldly expression is relegated to the land of the "dead" – only the *living* can proceed.

These elder sons represent a mistaken view of the LORD and must be eliminated. Our mental aspect (Aaron) accepts the elimination and holds its peace. The younger sons are Eleazar (God is helper) and Ithamar (coast of the palm tree), thoughts closer to the reality of God. The spiritual aspect (Moses) tells the mental aspect (Aaron and his remaining sons) not to sorrow over those lost "thoughts" *lest you die, and lest wrath come upon all the congregation. ... And do not go out from the door of the tent of meeting, lest you die; for the annointing oil of the Lord is upon you.* Lv. 10:6,7.
There, is another difficult point for us to remember. Those who have been "ordained" are no longer "free agents," at least not "free" in the eyes of the world. The remaining sons, i.e., the remaining thoughts, are to keep themselves in the "tent of meeting." They are no longer of the world; they are *living*.
Simple observation will expose those who mistakenly have assumed their own "spirituality" and yet remained of a worldly mind. Newspapers, television and "checkout-stand magazines" overflow with priests who have strayed, ministers who have philandered, "saints" who have fallen. The difficulty may be that, mistakenly, we all expect "enlightenment" to be a "constant." We expect to be able to dictate the time and place for us to light our censers. And we expect to do so regardless of the "enlightenment" of our "sight." Needless to say, our mental self will learn from its mistakes.
Aaron's training seems like an endless process. Now Aaron, our mental aspect, must learn to accept its responsibility.

---

[36] Those esotericists who are of the highest understanding warn against attempting to open the chakras – thus activating great power – before having totally spiritualized the mind. See Alder, *The Finding of the Third Eye.*

Interestingly, the exercise brings us to the namesake of all priests, i.e., Levi (love). To oversimplify we could say that we just have to *love;* but that doesn't say enough. Even "love" must be disciplined. And the disciplining continues.

> Now Korah the son of Izhar, son of Kohath, **son of Levi**, and Dathan and Abiram the sons of Eliab, and On the son of Peleth, **sons of Reuben,** took men; and they rose up before Moses, with a number of the people of Israel, **two hundred and fifty** leaders of the congregation,...and they assembled themselves together against Moses and against Aaron, and said ... "You have gone too far! For **all the congregation are holy**, every one of them, and the LORD is among them; why then do you exalt yourselves above the assembly of the LORD?"
>
> When Moses heard it, ... he said to Korah and all his company, **"In the morning the LORD will show who is his, and who is holy, and will cause him to come near to him; him whom he will choose he will cause to come near to him.** Do this: take censers, Korah and all his company; **put fire in them** and put **incense** upon them before the LORD tomorrow, and **the man whom the LORD chooses shall be the holy one.** You have gone too far, sons of Levi!" And Moses said to Korah, "Hear now, you sons of Levi: **is it too small a thing for you that the God of Israel has separated you from the congregation of Israel, to bring you near to himself, to do service in the Tabernacle of the LORD, and to stand before the congregation to minister to them;** and that he has brought you near him, and all your brethren the sons of Levi with you? And **would you seek the priesthood also?** Therefore it is against the LORD that you and all your company have gathered together; **what is Aaron that you murmur against him?"** Num. 16:1-11.

It sounds like a petty political battle between Aaron and his sons and their cousins, the Korahites; but in hang-loose logic it has great importance. Supposedly, the Korahites represent *love*; but it is an "icy" love, for they come from Korah (ice). Moreover, it is this "love" that gives access to the worship

Even "Love" Is Disciplined

of the LORD. The difficulty is that the Korahites who are so concerned about their role are expressing only on the physical level.[37] Notice that they join forces with that which is related to "sight" (Reuben). Moreover, the protesters number 250 – that which is on a third level, but sees only one-half of what the heightened senses (500) would deal with.

---

[37] The particular duty of the Korahites was care of the vessels for worship; they were in charge of the camp of the LORD, keepers of the tent. See 1 Ch. 9:19. They *were in charge of the work of the service, keepers of the thresholds of the tent, as their fathers had been in charge of the camp of the LORD, keepers of the tent.* 1 Ch. 9:19

Isn't this the way our lives on the physical plane operate? It's hard to look at ourselves objectively. We see ourselves as "loving," never recognizing the true "icy" nature of our attachment. Usually our "love" has something to do with our "desires" – something from which we derive "something." "Love" that centers only on a sexual attraction easily fits in this category. Even our love for our children places our children above others, because we feel an emotional need for them. So it is with practically everyone whom we "love;" there's always something in it for us. Like the Levites, we don't see the full truth.

It is this "undisciplined" nature that thinks it has finished climbing. It is this nature that thinks it deserves to be "priestly" just as much as the mental aspect of ourselves. Yet, no other nature can function as the mind does. It is the mind that observes and "sees." It is the mind that classifies, stipulates and brings order. It is the mind that practices righteous judgment and "speaks." It is the mind that loves. And he/she who will inhabit the "Promised Land" will find "love" to be quite different from that experienced on the physical plane.

And Moses says: "*... tomorrow;... let every one of you take his censer, and put incense upon it, and ... bring before the LORD his censer, two hundred and fifty censers; you also, and Aaron, each his censer." ... and they stood at the entrance of the tent of meeting with Moses and Aaron. Then Korah assembled all the congregation against them at the entrance of the tent of meeting. And the **glory of the LORD appeared to all the congregation**. And the LORD said to Moses and to Aaron, "Separate yourselves from among this congregation, that I may consume them in a moment."*

*And they ... said, "O God, the God of the spirits of all flesh, **shall one man sin, and wilt thou be angry with all the congregation?"** Num. 16:16-21.*

Unfair as it may seem, the whole individual suffers from the "unrighteous judgment" our "sight" conjures up. This is probably the supreme test for our mental side. It makes descisions only on the basis of what is fed into it, and here are these thoughts – which claim to be related to love – but which deny the sole right of the mental to offer the worship to the LORD. Now comes the test. *And the LORD said to Moses, "Say to the congregation, '**Get away from about the dwelling of Korah**, (ice, grandson of Levi (love) Dathan,(?) and Abiram (lofty, grandson of Reuben (sight).'"... And he said* *to the congregation, **"Depart, I pray you, from the tents of these wicked men, and touch nothing of theirs, lest you be swept away with all their sins."***

*... Dathan and Abiram came out and stood at the door of their tents, together with their wives, their sons, and their little ones. And Moses said, ... the LORD has sent me to do all these works;... it has not been of my own accord. If these men die the common death of all men,...then the LORD has not sent me. But **if the** LORD creates something new, and **the ground opens its mouth, and swallows them up, with all that belongs to them, and they go down alive into Sheol, then you shall know that these men have despised the LORD."** And as he finished speaking all these words, the ground under them split asunder; and the earth opened its mouth and swallowed them up, with their households and all the men that belonged to Korah and all their goods. **So they and all that belonged to them went down alive into Sheol; and the earth closed over them, and they perished from the midst of the assembly. ... And fire came forth from the LORD, and consumed the two hundred and fifty men offering the incense.*** Num. 16:16-35

What a gruesome story. It's much more palatable if it is regarded as symbolic.[38] So, what does it symbolize? The key line seems to be ... *Will you put out the eyes of these men?* The whole story seems to deal with how "he/she who is near the LORD" goes about giving the "sacrifice of Incense." As you know, the whole sequence revolves around Korah, a great-grand-son of Levi. But it seems that the more important parts of the puzzle are Dathan and Abiram, the sons of Eliab.[39]

By the definitions of their names, they should have had great understanding. But their comments reveal that they are basing their judgment on what they *see* with their physical eyes. To Moses' (the spiritual self's) call, they answer: *"We will not come up... You have not brought us into a land flowing with milk and honey, nor given us inheritance of fields and vineyards. Will you **put out the eyes** of these men?"* Num. 16:12-14.

How often we do this. Even though we're on the climb and intellectually *know* that the promises will somehow come to be, we still base our judgment on what we "see." It is this "judgment" that prompts Moses' command to Korah and his followers. It is this "judgment" that will bring their destruction.

---

[38] The fact that the Korahites were still performing their duties at the time of Chronicles shows that they were not all consumed.

[39] Dathan (fount [Young]), Abiram (father of elevation), Eliab (God is father).

We will always have to rely on our (5) senses to provide input into the mental aspect of us. The question is the state of the senses. Are they operating at a mere earthly 5, or have they reached the 500 mark? [40] In this case, they are operating at 250 – ½ of 500. Semi-enlightened, they would be symbolized by 500. Obviously, we haven't reached any higher. Then the question becomes what are "semi-enlightened" senses?

Notice, our principal sense is "sight. " These people "see" Moses as having "made himself a prince over them" and as having brought them *out* of a land of milk and honey "to die in the wilderness." In hang-loose thinking we can understand their frustration. Change is always threatening. No matter how bad our former life was, it can always look better when we're undergoing change. Not only that, but this spiritual self keeps intruding into our thoughts

We Must Practice Righteous Judgment

and suggesting things that we're not sure will accomplish our desires – things like *"turn the other cheek"* or *"let it go."* Moreover, this spiritual self even questions what the "ego" sees as truth. And the entire congregation challenges Moses. ... *Will you put out the eyes of these men?* i.e., will the spiritual side reject what the ½ of the semi-enlightened senses see? **Yes! It must.** Finally – if we hold to the spiritual side – these rebellious thoughts and fears and everything that is with them, even their smallest portions, are "swallowed up" by the earth.

I'll give you a personal example. I had a friendship which deteriorated. My conscious mind blessed the friend and let her go; but I kept talking and thinking about the situation – again I would bless her, and let her go – only to again talk about the situation. Needless to say, the situation did not go away. It "died the common death of all men," i.e., it drug on and on – occupying less and less of my thought, but still taking time and energy. Eventually, two of my aunts died; so my attention was totally occupied, and I was no longer "talking"

---

[40] Fully enlightened (having finished the climb), they would be symbolized by 5000.

about the former situation. My concern with the former friendship was gone. It was as if it had been "swallowed up."

Our intellectual mind has difficulty expecting such

> **Mental Aspect Must Accept Its Responsibilities**

happenings. Having been trained to "judge" and "decipher" what comes into it from unenlightened senses and then to dictate on that basis, our mental self finds it difficult to trust "the LORD." But Aaron represents the initiated mental aspect. He has learned "righteous judgment." Aaron knows that if he is aligned with Divine order, anything unlike him will be "swallowed up."

Once, he kept his peace about his elder sons; this time, he stands squarely with Moses. He accepts the role he is given; he accepts Moses' rule that *no one who is not a priest, who is not of the descendants of Aaron, should draw near to burn incense before the LORD.* Num. 16:40.

The intellectual mind rankles at such a statement; it is egalitarian. But remember, we're being taught by symbols. What is actually being said is: only **those who are ready** can approach the Altar for Incense – that which immediately preceeds the Veil and entry into the Holy of Holies.

There are differences in burning "meat," "grain," or "incense." Symbolically, the burning of "meat" implies the elimination of the carnal mind. The different "meats" indicate the distance from the physical – the larger the animal, the closer to the physical. The "grain" implies a more advanced level, a more "holy" offering, but not yet an offering of pure "air" containing only aroma. Finally, the burning of "incense" implies the holiest offering of all; therefore, it can only be undertaken after the grosser elements have been eliminated.

Only a mindset that acknowledges that there is more than just what the physical eyes "see" and the mental ears "hear" is truly ready to worship. But our physical body is often slow to give in to the spiritual self, and all sorts of plagues come upon us – the diseases of mankind. *And Moses said to Aaron, "Take* *your censer, and put **fire therein from off the altar**, and lay incense on it, and carry it quickly to the congregation, and **make atonement for them**; for... the plague has begun."* *So Aaron ... put on the incense, and made atonement for the people.   And **[Aaron] stood between the dead and the living; and the plague was stopped**. Now those who died by the plague were **fourteen thousand seven hundred**, besides those who died in the affair of Korah.   And **Aaron returned to Moses** at the entrance of the tent of meeting, **when the plague was stopped**. Num. 16:46-50.* [41]

The whole question is whether our mental self accepts the responsibility to stand between the "dead" and the "living." Is our mental self willing to declare us to be **of the living**? Aaron accepts the job, and his name is written on the "rod" for the house of Levi.   The mental aspect accepts the

> **Once separated elements are now all working as "ONE": The Mental self becomes responsible; the Feminine side is integrated; then the old Mental aspect is "renewed."**

lead of the house of "love." And when the various "rods" from each tribe – sight, hearing, loving, praise, righteous judgment, strength, abundance, happiness, reward, order, increase, power – are deposited *before the* LORD *in the tent of the testimony,... the rod of Aaron for the house of Levi had sprouted and put forth buds, and produced blossoms, and it bore ripe almonds.* Num. 17:7,8.

The intellectual mind is sceptical of this story, not only in the Bible but in life. On the other hand, the intuitional mind knows that it happens. The story symbolizes what **can** happen in our lives. Only *love* produces as we would have it produce. Only *love* is "win,win." But this is not a love tied to the carnal; this is a love expressed by the enlightened mind. This is a "love" attuned to the spiritual; it is not "of this world." Remember, even though the "budded" rod of Aaron is placed in the Ark of the Covenant with the manna and the commandments, only the commandments can be *seen* when Solomon opens the ark.

Aaron is the fully accepted "high priest." Only Aaron and his sons can approach the Tabernacle vessels; only they can perform the ritual.   Moreover, they will be assisted in the

---

[41] Notice 14,700 +250 = 14,950 = 19 = 10 (new beginning).

240

tent of meeting by the Levites. It's a bonanza. Aaron and his sons keep what is left from what is given to the LORD, and they even have "loving" servants to help them in their duties.

What a tremendous portion those who are "near the LORD" are promised. We will be totally provided for, and our load will be easy; for we will have our whole "house" to help in the service. But being "near the LORD" will bring other changes to our lives. At this point of the climb, our entire self is in the process of change, positive change – whether or not we can "see" it. *And the people of Israel, the* **whole congregation,** *came into the* **wilderness of Zin in the first month**, *and the people stayed in* **Kadesh**; *and* **Miriam** *died there, and was buried there.* Num. 20:1.

Our mental aspect has accepted its responsibility and has "cured the people," i.e., revealed and dealt with those portions of us that bring difficulties; and we – the

> **Feminine Cured Of Rebellion and "Transformed"**

whole congregation – have arrived at Kadesh (sanctuary) in the wilderness of Zin (to prick). It is here that we let go of the feminine side that has been with us. Our feminine aspect (now cured of its "leprosy" and its rebellion) has become so integrated that we have not heard of it for a long time. Now, here without fanfare, Miriam dies and is buried.[42]

Saying that Miriam "dies" is misleading; we always keep our feminine side with us. It would probably be more appropriate to say that our feminine side simply becomes so integrated that it no longer maintains a separate awareness. In fact, it may be that this feminine side – what began as our feminine side – becomes so heightened that it begins to operate as the Christ mind – the I Am – which then directs the conscious mind.

Miriam dies in the first month as we reach a place of "a prick" – something that catches our attention. But, the death

---

[42] We may not give our feminine aspect enough respect. Micah has an interesting line: *For I brought you up from the land of Egypt, and redeemed you from the house of bondage, and* **I sent before you Moses, Aaron, and Miriam.** Mi. 6:4. The feminine side is not just incidental. Miriam dies in the first month after 40 years on the march.

of the feminine side is only one of the important changes that takes place. Notice, we are at the first month, i.e., a new beginning, but we are presented with an old problem.

*Now there was no water for the congregation; and they assembled themselves together against Moses and against Aaron.... and said, "Would that we had died when our brethren died before the LORD! Why have you brought the assembly of the LORD into this wilderness, that we should die here, both **we and our cattle**? And why have you made us come up out of Egypt...? It is no place for grain, or figs, or vines, or pomegranates; and there is no water to drink." Then Moses and Aaron went from the presence of the assembly to the door of the tent of meeting, and fell on their faces. And the glory of the LORD appeared to them, and the LORD said to Moses, **"Take the rod, and assemble the congregation,** you and Aaron your brother, and **tell the rock before their eyes to yield its water;** so you shall bring water out of the rock for them; so you shall give drink to the congregation and their cattle." And Moses took the rod from before the LORD, as he commanded him. And Moses and Aaron gathered the assembly together before the rock, and he said to them, "Hear now, you rebels; **shall we bring forth water for you out of this rock?"** And Moses lifted up his hand and struck the rock with his rod twice; and water came forth abundantly, and the congregation drank, and their cattle.* Num. 2: 2-11

It sounds as though Moses/Aaron did as they were directed; but because of this, Moses won't enter the Promised Land. *And the LORD said to Moses and Aaron, **"Because you did not believe in me, to sanctify me in the eyes of the people of Israel, therefore you shall not bring this assembly into the land which I have given them."** These are the waters of Meribah, where the **people of Israel contended** with the LORD, and he showed himself holy among them.* Num. 20:12 &13.

Notice the numbers of these verses? A definite point is being made here for our hang-loose logic. You may remember a similar

"More" Is Required of Heightened Initiate

scene taking place in Exodus 17:1-7. There are many similarities in the two accounts. As is usually the case, it is the people who are complaining; and when the water is "delivered," Moses names the place *Meribah* (contention) because of the people's faultfinding. However, there are several important differences: First: Aaron is now united to Moses; second: Moses is using the budded rod. These are both positives. But let's repeat the LORD'S wording: *"... you did not believe in me, to sanctify me in the eyes of the people of Israel."*

It is the third difference that causes the problem: by the "words" he says to the people and by "striking" the rock with his *rod*, Moses implies that he, himself, accomplishes the feat. He says: *"shall we bring forth water..."*

He/she who recognizes the I Am is unique. But as a "unique" individual, he/she has "unique" obligations. Where a lesser individual does not have to be so meticulous in his/her expression, the "unique" individual walks a fine line. It is a fine line between accepting the I Am and pronouncing I Am. In this instance, Moses has said I Am "producing this water."

The Promised Land is always unattainable for the Moses mindset. Maybe it is because he still remembers having been *drawn from the waters*. Possibly it is because despite his great advances, Moses remains a *man of war*. Until we get to the place where we have no rememberance or recognition of anything other than the "perfect" – our being a part of the I Am – we are "men/women of war." We are warring within ourselves to determine whether we are a part of the "living" or the "dead." We are warring within ourselves to determine whether we are individuals who have power just in ourselves or whether we are individuals connected to the power that "IS."

Moses will never enter the Promised Land; nevertheless, for the "Promised Land" to be realized, the spiritual self will need a new mental aspect, a mental aspect having no thought of separateness from the divine, Eleazar (God is helper). The

New Nature of Mental Aspect Closer to the Divine

mental aspect that has functioned as Aaron (enlightenment) is heightened to the place where it recognizes that "God is helper" – a mental awareness that knows a beginning of "oneness" with God. It is this new awareness that will wear the "mantle" of Aaron. Moses is told: *"... take Aaron and Eleazar his son, and bring them up to Mount Hor; and strip Aaron of his garments, and put them upon Eleazar his son; and Aaron shall be gathered to his people, and shall die there." Moses did as the LORD commanded;... in **the sight of all the congregation**. ... and Aaron died there on the top of the mountain. Then Moses and Eleazar came down from the mountain. And when all the congregation saw that Aaron was dead, all the house of Israel **wept for Aaron thirty days.** Num. 20:25-29.*

We are given two signposts. The chapter number, Numbers 33 (3x11) and מסעי. [43]

To summarize the lessons of Moses we are given a convenient summary of the entire 40-year journey.

These are the stages of the people of Israel, when they went forth out of the land of Egypt by their hosts **under the leadership of Moses and Aaron.** *Moses wrote* **down their starting places, stage by stage, by command of the LORD;** *and these are their stages according to their starting places.* See Num.33:1-56.

1. ***Rameses*** (name of Egyptian Pharoahs) [44] They left Rameses on the fifteenth day of the first month, i.e., the day after Passover.
2. ***Succoth*** (plural of "booths")
3. ***Etham,*** *which is on the edge of the wilderness.* (7 wells)
4. *and turned back to* **Pihahiroth,** (a cavity or hole - mouth) *east of Baalzephon*
5. (Typhon-the destroyer) *and they encamped* **before Migdol** (tower)
6. **before Hahiroth,** (*mouth*) *and passed through the midst of the sea into the wilderness, and they went a three days' journey in the wilderness of Etham,*
7. *and encamped at* **Marah.** (bitter)
8. ***Elim;*** (erect palm trees)... ***twelve springs*** *of water and* **seventy** *palm trees.*
9. *by the* ***Red Sea.*** (Papyrus - reed sea)
10. *in the* **wilderness of Sin.** (the most easterly edge of Egypt ; a cliff)
11. *and encamped at* **Dophkah.** (a knock)
12. *and encamped at* **Alush.** (wild place)
13. *and encamped at* **Rephidim** . (to spread) *where there was no water*
14. *and encamped in the* **wilderness of Sinai.** (a mountain ; sharp, jagged, cliffs) Where Moses received the Ten Commandments.
15. *and encamped at* **Kibrothhattaavah.** (burying place + pleasant connotation)
16. *and encamped at* **Hazeroth.** (protected ; surrounded by fence or wall)
17. *and encamped at* **Rithmah.** (pole-like stems; Juniper trees)
18. *and encamped at* **Rimmonperez.** (upright growth + breaking forth)
19. *and encamped at* **Libnah.** (whitish tree)
20. *and encamped at* **Rissah.** (to temper ; to moisten with water)
21. *and encamped at* **Kehelathah.** (convoke ; assemble selves together) note 3x7
22. *and encamped at* **Mount Shepher.** (glisten; to make fair)
23. *and encamped at* **Haradah.** ("fearful"; reverential/ trembling)
24. *and encamped at* **Makheloth.** (assembly; same as # 21; convoke) note 2x12
25. *and encamped at* **Tahath.** (to "depress"; to humble)
26. *and encamped at* **Terah.** ("turning"; wandering)

---

[43] According to Suarès' formula, מסעי calculates out as 10·70·60·40 = 180 = 9 at two levels. We are still at the level of the initiate.

[44] Some of the names have not been translated. Those who have a command of Hebrew have an advantage here. Most likely, the verse numbers may also make a suggestion, as does the place in the sequence. The reader can exercise his/her hanging loose with Moses' list of starting places.

244

27. *and encamped at* **Mithkah.** (sweetness)

28. *and encamped at* **Hashmonah.** (fertile)

29. *and encamped at* **Moseroth.** (from "a haltar"; restraint/chastisement)

30. *and encamped at* **Benejaakan.** (sons of " to twist"; tortuous)

31. *and encamped at* **Horhaggidgad.** ("hole of the cleft")

32. *and encamped at* **Jotbathah.** (pleasantness)

33. *and encamped at* **Abronah.** ("to work"; "to husband"; transitional)

34. *and encamped at* **Eziongeber.** ("backbone," as of a man)

35. *and encamped in the wilderness of* **Zin.** ("to prick"; crag; woe) *that is,* **Kadesh** (sanctuary)
It is here that **Miriam dies** in the first month, 40th year of the trek.

36. *and encamped at* **Mount Hor,** (Mount Mountain) *on the edge of the land*   *of Edom* (ruddy). *And* **Aaron the** *priest went up Mount Hor at the command   of the LORD, and* **died there, in the fortieth year** *after the people of Israel had come out of the land of Egypt, on the first day of the* **fifth** *month. And Aaron was a* **hundred and twenty-three** *years old* [6]....
And the **Canaanite,** *the king of Arad, who dwelt in the Negeb ...,* **heard** *of the coming of the people of Israel.* Notice that this occupies the 36th position, 6x6 and 3x9.

37. *and encamped at* **Zalmonah.** (shadiness) [To a desert people a luxury.]

38. *and encamped at* **Punon.** (perplexity)

39. *and encamped at* **Oboth.** (a "necromancer"; mumble)

40. *and encamped at* **Iyeabarim,** (ruins of the passers) *in... Moab.* (mother's father - [Moab son of Lot by his daughter] i.e., sterility)

41. *and encamped at* **Dibon-gad.** (to pine; to sorrow)

42. *and encamped at* **Almondiblathaim.** ("to veil from sight" + fig cakes [press together x 2])

43. *and encamped in the* **mountains of Abarim,** (Mountains of "passages") *before   Nebo.* (Babylonian deity)

44. *and encamped in the* **plains of Moab** (sterility) **by the Jordan** (descending)   *at Jericho;* (fragrant) **by the Jordan from Bethjeshimoth** (house of the deserts) *as far as Abel-shittim in*(grassy plain of the Acacia [thorny]) *the plains of Moab.* (sterility). **[Note: This is verse 49, i.e., 7x7.]**

The symbolism is clearer in light of the line at the beginning: *These are the stages of the people of Israel, when they went forth out of the land of Egypt by their hosts* **under the leadership of Moses and Aaron.**
The "people of Israel" represent our individual lives, and this is the path we will follow to our own "Promised Land." You may have noticed that the path has stopping places both pleasant and unpleasant – as do our lives. Obviously, our lives have "ups" and "downs." More importantly, as with the Israelites, our lives have "numerous miracles." Food, water, and safety are constantly provided for the Israelites – despite their constant straying from righteousness and despite their complaints. And even though we have our moments in the deserts, we also have our moments on the Mountains.

There are many times in our lives when we feel as though we're in a desert with no water to drink; there are other times when we feel that we're on the top of a mountain or in the middle of a oasis – with 12 springs and 70 erect palm trees. And, likely as not, there are numerous times we long for the simplicity of our life of bondage in Egypt – but are locked into the path we're on. Like the Israelites we are under the leadership of our spiritual selves/aided by our mental selves. Hopefully, they are unified. If so, we will get to *fragrance,*ready to enter the Promised Land. But the LORD throws a "curve." He says: *"Ascend this mountain ... and view the land of Canaan, which I give to the people of Israel for a possession; and die on the mountain which you ascend, and be gathered to your people,... because you broke faith with me in the midst of the people of Israel at the waters of Meribathkadesh, in the wilderness of Zin; because you did not revere me as holy in the midst of the people of Israel. For you shall see the land before you; but you shall not go there, into the land which I give to the people of Israel."* Deut. 32:51,52.

We're outraged with the LORD'S pronouncement! How did Moses break faith with the LORD? [45] Check page 241. The key word seems to be **"sanctify."** Can it be that we're expected **to "give back"** to the LORD **to the full measure that we have been given** – whether we "see" it or not. It's the *shall we bring forth water* that causes what we see as the effect. Apparently it is this "crediting" ourselves that is the failure to "sanctify" the LORD in the eyes of the people. The "word" is that we *sanctify – consecrate –* our work. But, if we "see" our accomplishments as our own work, we're not "sanctifying" the LORD; if we "see" our possessions as having anything to do with us, we're not "sanctifying" the LORD. If we fail to "consecrate" all that we are and all that we experience as the

---

[45] Possibly the wording of Numbers makes it easier to understand. *The LORD said to Moses, "Go up into this mountain of Abarim, and see the land which I have given to the people of Israel. And when you have seen it, you also shall be gathered to your people, as your brother Aaron was gathered, because you rebelled against my word in the wilderness of Zin during the strife of the congregation, to sanctify me at the waters before their eyes." (These are the waters of Meribah of Kadesh in the wilderness of Zin.)* Num. 27:12-14. Notice the importance of the verses and chapter numbers. The book of Deuteronomy supposedly was found by Ezra in the ruins of the Temple, as the Jews were beginning to rebuild. Traditionally, it is accepted as a book of Moses as much as the other four earlier books.

gift of the LORD, we are not "sanctifying" the LORD. It is this failure that is Moses' shortcoming; Moses' confinement to this side of the Jordan is not a punishment. Moses knows that a new expression must proceed with the climb. *Moses said to the LORD, "Let the LORD, the God of the spirits of all flesh, **appoint a man** over the congregation, **who shall go out before them and come in before them, who shall lead them out and bring them in; that the congregation of the LORD may not be as sheep which have no shepherd."** And the LORD said to Moses, "Take **Joshua** the son of Nun, **a man in whom is the spirit**, and lay your hand upon him; ... You shall **invest him with some of your authority**, that all the congregation of the people of Israel may obey.... **at his word they shall go out, and at his word they shall come in, both he and all the people of Israel with him, the whole congregation."** And Moses did as the LORD commanded him....* Num. 27:15-23.

All life is as the LORD directs. *The LORD said to him, "This is the land of which I swore to Abraham, to Isaac, and to Jacob, 'I will give it to your descendants.' I have let you see it with your eyes, but you shall not go over there." So Moses the servant of the LORD died there in the land of Moab, according to the word of the LORD, and he buried him in the valley in the land of Moab opposite Bethpeor; **but no man knows the place of his burial to this day.*** Dt. 34:4-6.

We must leave Moses. Since we don't even know where he was buried, we can't worship him. We must bring that which has been **pulled from the water** and been **given the Law** and **found union with its mental self** to an end – otherwise, we can't go to the next level. In fact, I wonder if the next level isn't almost a retrenching of the lessons supposedly learned.

Once in the Promised Land, we'll find more challenges. Like the progression of the Patriarchs, like the progression through the Tabernacle, and like the progression through the wilderness, the land of Caanan will also be a progression. The Promised Land requires "a conquering." In many ways the conquering will repeat what we've already endured. The climber **must be worthy** of the climb. **Anything unlike** the LORD must be **eliminated. And the climber must sanctify the LORD.** But the "conquering" of the Promised Land requires a physical "warring," greater than anything we have experienced. Thus, it requires a **King**, he/she who can conquer and rule.

Moses is never King; but Moses is the ideal man, surpassed only by Jesus, the Christ. He dies at the age of 120 (12 x 10), in Suarès terms 100 (ק - man's perfection) plus 20 (ב [son] x ' [Aleph's projection in temporal continuity.])

Moses was a hundred and twenty years old when he died; his eye was not dim, nor his natural force abated. And the people of Israel wept for Moses in the plains of Moab thirty days; then the days of...mourning ... were ended. And Joshua the son of Nun was full of the spirit of wisdom, for Moses had laid his hands upon him; so the people of Israel obeyed him, and did as the LORD had commanded Moses. And there has not arisen a prophet since in Israel like Moses, whom the LORD knew face to face, [whom the Lord singled out , face to face, - The Torah] none like him for all the signs and the wonders which the LORD sent him to do in the land of Egypt, to Pharaoh ... and to all his land, and for all the mighty power and all the great and terrible deeds which Moses wrought in the sight of all Israel. Dt. 34:7-12.

If you look closely at each picture, you can see what are called the "horns" of Moses. They appear as stylized "horns," but they represent the energy coming from his head as an expressed "light." It is the "light" above his head on page 182.

Moses by Michelangelo.

When they came to Gibeah, behold, a band of prophets met him [Saul]; and the spirit of God came mightily upon him, and he prophesied among them.

1 Sam. 10:10.

Chapter Eleven

Preparing the King: Samuel and Saul

*After the death of Moses the servant of the LORD, the LORD said to Joshua the son of Nun, Moses' minister, "Moses my servant is dead; now therefore **arise, go over this Jordan, you and all this people, into the land which I am giving to them,**.... Every place that the sole of your foot will tread upon I have given to you, as I promised to Moses. From the wilderness and this Lebanon as far as the great river, the river Euphrates, all the land of the Hittites to the Great Sea toward the going down of the sun shall be your territory. No man shall be able to stand before you all the days of your life; as I was with Moses, so I will be with you; I will not fail you or forsake you. Be strong and of good courage; for you shall cause this people to inherit the land.... Only be strong and very courageous, being careful to do according to all the law which Moses my servant commanded you; turn not from it to the right hand or to the left, that you may have good success wherever you go. This book of the law shall not depart out of your mouth, but you shall meditate on it day and night, that you may be careful to do according to all that is written in it; for then you shall make your way prosperous, and then you shall have good success. Have I not commanded you? Be strong and of good courage; be not frightened, neither be dismayed; for the LORD your God is with you wherever you go."* Jsh. 1:1-9.

Is the LAW constantly in "our mouths"? Do we believe this promise is true for us? If not, we'll have to go back to the bottom of the Mountain and start the climb again, for we haven't learned the lessons taught by our various characters.[1] On the other hand, if our answer is "yes" to both questions, we can conquer the "promised land." And we'll notice that we've arrived at another level on the climb. This is the level of the King. Actually, it is the level for the "proving" of the King, he/she who personally directs his/her life and expression to conquer the land.

Until the time of Saul, the people of Israel have no king over them (other than Pharaoh). Central leadership rests first with Moses, then with Joshua; but after Joshua the

---

[1] The scheme for this Bible study shows a progression comprised of four groupings:

Abraham	Moses	Samuel	John the Baptist
Isaac	Aaron	Saul	Mary
Jacob	Miriam	David	Jesus/Judas
Joseph	Joshua	Solomon	Mary Magdalene

Hebrews operate as clans, each tribe (except for the Levites) assigned to a particular portion of the land, each tribe (most likely) having a "judge" over it.[2] Supposedly, Moses had designated certain locations for each tribe, but the designations may have been, principally, for organization. There is a centralizing priesthood (the tribe of Levi), but everything is loosely organized – the book of Judges making it clear with its *... In those days there was no king in Israel; every man did what was right in his own eyes.* Jgs. 21:25.

Using political terms, Israel is a *theocracy*. But it keeps falling under the control of larger, foreign, political entities, and such happenings necessitate military leaders (the 7 Judges) for certain periods.[3] In physical reality there is very little land to be distributed among the eleven tribes, even if they can drive out the current inhabitants.[4] For instance, the allotment of land to Benjamin, the smallest tribe, occupied a territory of about three hundred square miles – what Asimov compares to New York City's five boroughs. Moreover, the land is already occupied, sometimes by superior forces.

Although we think of the conquest of Canaan as being one "swoop" of success, this was not the case. Most likely, the conquest consisted of intermittent victories which allowed the

---

[2] Isaac Asimov calculates the period of time covered by the Book of Judges as between 125 and 150 years. Additionally, he considers the "most likely date for the Exodus at about 1200 B.C. and the death of Joshua at about 1150 B.C. *Asimov's Guide to the Bible,* pp. 230-231.

[3] As Asimov suggests, there were probably judges for each of the 12 tribes, but the Book of Judges highlights 7 out of however many were considered "judges." These are 1. **Othniel** (son of Caleb) defeats Mesopotamia, then 40 yrs of peace. Jgs. 3:7-11; 2. **Ehud** (a left-handed Benjaminite) defeats Moabites; land has peace for 80 yrs. Jgs. 3:12-30; 3. **Shamgar** (against Philistines) Jgs. 3:31; 4. **Deborah** (a prophetess)combines with Barak to destroy the king of Canaan, and the land has rest for 40 years. Jgs. 4:4 - 5:1-31; 5. **Gideon** (found beating out wheat in the wine press) defeats the Midianites and the Amalekites Jgs. 6-8; 6. **Jephthah** (an illegitimate "border ruffian") defeats the Ammonites Jgs. 10:1-12:7; 7. **Samson** (a Nazirite,"*who shall **begin to deliver Israel from the hands of the Philistines.** "*), a judge for 20 years. Jgs. 12:8-16:31.

[4] The tribe of Levi is supported by the entirety of Israel in lieu of land.

Israelites to occupy the higher land (because the inhabitants fled) but which left the larger towns and the valleys to the resident "nations." Asimov describes the Israelites as "clinging precariously to the highlands, disunited, technologically backward." [5]

> *Now these are the nations which the LORD left, to test Israel by them, that is, all in Israel who had no experience of any war in Canaan; it was only that the generations of the people of Israel might know war, that he might teach war to such at least as had not known it before. These are the nations: the five lords of the Philistines, and all the Canaanites, and the Sidonians, and the Hivites who dwelt on Mount Lebanon, from Mount Baalhermon as far as the entrance of Hamath. They were for the testing of Israel, to know whether Israel would obey the commandments of the LORD, which he commanded their fathers by Moses. So the people of Israel dwelt among the Canaanites, the Hittites, the Amorites, the Perizzites, the Hivites, and the Jebusites; and they took their daughters to themselves for wives, and their own daughters they gave to their sons; and they served their gods. And the people of Israel did what was evil in the sight of the LORD, forgetting the LORD their God, and serving the Baals and the Asheroth.* Jgs. 3:1-7.

Let's indulge our intellectual mindset for a minute. At this time in history, the Israelites are a somewhat disconnected movement of semi-nomadic people moving into the most hotly contested "real estate" of the known world. In many ways they are not unlike the wild tribes on the periphery of other times and other "civilizations." In many ways, the Israelites are like the Greeks taking over and destroying the Minoans, like the Romans conquering the Etruscans, and (many centuries later) like the Anglo Saxons threatening the Britons.[6] The difference is that the inhabitants of Canaan at the time of Joshua are themselves recent invaders, not having much greater technology (other than the Hittites and Canaanites having iron and chariots). The Philistines, who eventually become the

---

[5] *Ibid.*, p. 230.

[6] In the last few years, women have begun to rewrite ancient history. Probably, most important for our consideration is the current historical "approach" which sees traditional ancient history as having been masculinized. Under the feminized paradigm, current cultures are all the result of "goddess" cultures being overrun by "god" cultures. One of the few long-lived "goddess" cultures was that of early Crete. See Riane Eisler's *The Chalice & The Blade;* Harper Collins.

principal opponents, may have been portions of "Greek" migrations that had also threatened Egypt. Asimov describes the Philistines as a culture – Greek in origin but Semitic in language and customs.[7] Possibly, the Philistines are never totally defeated by the Hebrews, although the Bible suggests that they are subdued. Regardless of the specifics, their "conquering" takes several generations.

At this time, "conquering" is unlike "conquering" in more recent times. At this time, it is a matter of "limited war." A "conquering" army might succeed in taking over an enclave, eliminating the inhabitants and replacing them; but those areas which are adjacent, likely as not, simply become eventual allies. Thus instead of the Hebrews moving "full bloomed" into Canaan and being able to wipe out any and all opposition and difference, they're continually surrounded by different cultures, cultures geared toward nature.[8]

But questions of religion, history, government and size are for the intellectual mind-set; what information do we have for the intuition? Esoterically, we are simply at another level of expression; we will realize even greater truths at this level of the climb. We have grown from where we began the climb, but we're surrounded by temptations to stray from what we **know** we should *see* and *say*. Although each one of us is an individual which is part of a **ONEness** which is ALL, the "individual-self" of us doesn't always recognize its **oneness** with the whole. It must learn the truth of its existence.

However, at some point, our individual-self began to listen to something inside itself that told it to "move." Then, increasingly, it continued to listen and obey, until it reached the place where it is now – to the place where it "**hears**." But the "whole" of us cannot yet "**see**" nor "**say**."

---

[7] Asimov, *op. cit.*, pp. 200,201.

[8] It is an interesting observation that if the Hebrews had immediately entered Canaan, instead of "wandering" for 40 years, the "religion" of Moses would have been less pure. Most likely it would have picked up even more "pagan" practices than it did.

Nevertheless, as it enters into the "promised land," our individual-self knows that it must follow rules. Unfortunately, it feels itself alone and unguided. We are so unguided that we only get a "glimpse" of what is true, no matter how "spiritual" we think we are. For the "whole" of us, *seeing* and *saying* are still ahead on the climb – higher up the Mountain. At this point, the intuition needs to be remembering some of the last words that Moses said: *"The LORD your God himself will go over before you; he will destroy these nations before you,... you shall dispossess them; and Joshua will go over at your head ...* **Intuition Given** *And the LORD will do to them* **as he did** *to Sihon and Og,* **New Level** *the kings of the Amorites, and to their land...And the* **of Expression** *LORD will give them over to you, and you shall do to them according to all the commandment which I have commanded you. Be strong and of good courage, do not fear or be in dread of them: for it is the LORD your God who goes with you; he will not fail you or forsake you."* Dt. 31:3-6.

Let's stop for just a minute. Did you catch the mention of the Amorites? Do you remember the enigmatic statement given to Abraham? (Gen.15:16) See pages 63 and 78. One wonders if "the iniquity of the Amorites" (related to *to say*) is finally "complete." Are we finally beginning **to say** properly? Are we finally going **to express properly?**

Moses gave explicit instructions: *"When you draw near to a city* **to fight** *against it,* **offer terms of peace** *to it. And if its answer to you is peace and* **it opens to you,** *then all the people who are found* **in it shall** *do forced labor for you and shall* **serve you.** *But if it... makes war against you, then you shall besiege it; and... put all its males to the sword, but the women and the little ones, the cattle, and everything else in the city, all its spoil, you shall take as booty for yourselves; ... Thus you shall do to all the cities ... which are not cities of the nations here. But in the cities of these peoples that the LORD your God gives you for an inheritance, you shall save alive nothing that breathes,... utterly destroy them, the Hittites and the Amorites, the Canaanites and the Perizzites, the Hivites and the Jebusites, ... that they may not teach you to do according to all their abominable practices which they have done in the service of their gods, and so to sin against the LORD your God. "* Dt. 20:10-18.

Symbolically, the "cities" we have been given for an "inheritance" means those portions of us which will serve the righteous man/woman, those portions which must be working totally and perfectly. The difficulty is that we take the

254

statements literally instead of symbolically.[9] Symbolically – in hang-loose thinking – we can see that we must "utterly destroy" those elements in ourselves (more properly in our thinking) which detract from our being able **to "see"** and **"say"** properly. Ever since the chapter on Noah when Ham (the father of Canaan) **"saw"** Noah's "nakedness," we've been dealing with the human tendency to "see" only what the physical "sees." Now we are where we must deal with this frailty. Consequently, any "descendent of Canaan" must be eliminated, regardless of how innocuous.

These innocuous tribes don't sound as though they're a threat to us, do they? Can we be negatively affected by "bending the knee" or "life giving" or "Jah has dipped"? To put it in current terms, can we be affected by "being a wimp" or mistakenly thinking we are involved with the divine aspects of "life giving" or "God has provided," when **we don't even recognize that we are basing our "judgment" only on what we physically "see"** – as did Ham? The answer is "Yes!" We can be negatively affected!

Various "Tribes" Must Be Eliminated

And what about the Amorites? Ever since Abraham we've been dealing with our inability "to say" properly; now we will be given the chance to deal with this, too. Consequently, "the Amorites," too, must be eliminated. In our expression – in "seeing" and "saying" as well as "hearing" – **we must be making righteous judgment**. Needless to say, if we are "seeing" and "saying" correctly, we will simultaneously have eliminated the Hittites, "terror." And in having eliminated all of these "fetters," we will have become "protected," eliminating the final tribe of "unprotected" that can hold us back from possessing the

---

[9] Changing the order, consider the definitions: **Canaanites** - *to bend the knee* [desc. of Ham who "saw" Noah's "nakedness"]; **Hivites** - from *life-giving* [desc. of Canaan]; and **Jebusites** - *Jah has dipped.* [also desc. of Canaan]; **Amorites** - *to say;* **Hittites** - *terror, to prostrate;* **Perizzites** - *inhab. of the open country, unprotected.*

"promised land." The "land" is just a "promise" until it is "conquered" and "ruled."

Like the Israelites at this point, we find ourselves trying to occupy a land that is already occupied by others. In other words, we have habits and activities that keep hampering our holding to the instructions given by the LORD. We make some progress under Joshua (Jehovah saved; **to be opened wide**) and Eleazar (**God is helper**). But finally they die and we are ruled by several "judges" who triumph when the people follow God. However, the judges can bring only temporary periods of peace. For whenever the Israelites stray from the path, they always come under the control of another *warring* nation. The last judge, Sampson (sunlight), is the "strongest" man in the whole Bible; but even he cannot complete the conquering of the Philistines.

The symbology of **Sampson** is too much to ignore. Sampson (coming from a root which means **"Earthy" Sampson** *brilliant* and *east)* is a Nazirite and therefore pledged to the highest expression; he's the seventh judge (earthy **7)**. Moreover, he keeps peace for 20 years, ½ of the normal 40-year reign of kings. His life is brought to an end because of the Philistine Delilah's (to slacken or be feeble) betrayal and the "cutting" of his hair.[10]

Like Sampson, we, too, often fail; and like Sampson, our *conquering* at our "death" is *more than those whom he had slain during his life."* Jgs. 15:30 And Sampson is buried between Zorah (to screech) and Eshtaol (to request, inquire).[11] The logical question is: **Why do we fail when we should be succeeding?** In a very extended hang-loose comment, I wonder if part of the reason

---

[10] Previously, I would have said his time was shortened because of Delilah and the "cutting" of his strength; but if Joshua's term was only 10 years, this might not be the case. Sampson's expression of "lessened strength" led to his downfall.

[11] Notice that the designated chapter and verse for the end of the story of Sampson is 16:31. I propose that the number 16 is one of the most esoteric numbers, for it comprises 4x4. It should show the end of something. Furthermore, 31 is a prime number and the next chapter, Chapter 17, is also a prime number. In my "eyes" we're being told to "look" here.

256

we fail "to say" is because we, too, end up somewhere between "screech" (where we "demand" what we want) and "to request, inquire" (where we "inquire" what the LORD'S will is). Only the *inquiring* state of mind "says" properly. It is going to take an individual greater than Sampson to continue *to climb.*

Apparently, the loose rule of "judges" is not going to be enough to help us progress up the Mountain. We're going to have to have a king. But before we begin the process of *kingship,* two "stories" must be explored.

Two Symbolic Stories One of the stories is probably the saddest story in the whole Bible. It is the story of Jephthah (he will open), a mighty warrior and a son of Gilead (heap of testimony) by a harlot. His legitimate brothers throw him out, but he's invited back to become the sixth judge and leader in the fight against the Ammonites (descendants of Lot [inbred]). "The spirit of the Lord [comes] upon Jephthah" and he easily triumphs in his battles. *And Jephthah made a vow to the LORD, and said, "If thou wilt give the Ammonites into my hand, **then whoever comes forth from the doors of my house to meet me, when I return victorious from the Ammonites, shall be the Lord's, and I will offer him up for a burnt offering."** So Jephthah crossed over to the Ammonites to fight against them; and the LORD gave them into his hand.* Jgs. 11:30-32.

If you know the story, that *"who comes through the doors to meet me"*– that which is destined for a burnt offering – is Jephthah's only child, his young daughter.[12] He refuses to go back on his vow, but he does give her two months to *"go and wander on the mountains, and bewail [her] virginity..."At the end of two months, she returned to her father, who did with her according to his vow which he had made. She had never known a man. And it became a custom in Israel that the **daughters of Israel went year by year to lament the daughter of Jephthah the Gileadite four days in the year.*** Jgs. 11:39,40.

---

[12] See Judges 11: 1- 40.

We've really got to hang loose on this one! We are fighting the Ammonites – that within us (that which we "say") that comes from an "inbreeding" (incestuous) relationship with the lesser parts of us. Remember that "burnt offerings" are for the elimination of our carnal habits (expressions). Aren't we saying here that in "fighting" whatever is left of our lesser parts, even those base thoughts that are "virgins" – pure – must be cleansed from us – even if it is that which we love most in the world. Only he/she who is willing to do so – even to the level of "great sacrifice" becomes he/she who "will open" the way for us.

What isn't said is that the "sacrifice" may not be obvious to us. For instance, there is nothing "wrong" with our "loving" particular individuals – such as our children or our family or those who "love" us; but such a "focused loving" is still carnal. He/she who is climbing the Mountain will eventually come to a place of loving all; there will be no distinction between *loved* and *unloved* – there will be only **loved**.

The second story's importance is even more nebulous. The story is told like a parable, and I will leave the entire evaluation to you; but I see some of the lines as being of particular interest to us. The story begins: *There was a man of the **hill country** of Ephraim, whose name was Micah.* (Who is like Jah?) It continues that Micah takes 1100 sheckles of silver and makes a graven image and a molten image. Not only that, but he makes a shrine and *he made an ephod and teraphim, and installed one of his sons, who became his priest.* Here are three forbidden activities, and here is the explanation: ***In those days there was no king in Israel; every man did what was right in his own eyes.*** Jg.17:6.

The story continues (in verse 7) with a young man from Bethlehem, a Levite, who journeys to this **hill country** and ends up at the house of Micah; and Micah invites him to become "a father and a priest" for him. The story contains several important lines: *"Keep quiet, put your hand upon your mouth, and come with us, and be to us a father and a priest. Is it better for you to be priest to the house of one man, or to be priest to a tribe and family in Israel?"* And the *priest's heart was glad; he took the ephod, and the teraphim, and the graven image, and went in the midst of the people.* Jgs. 17:19,20. But the Danites (tribe of Dan [to judge]) take over what Micah had made and set up their own priest, and such remained *as long as the house of God was at Shiloh.*[13] Jgs. 18:31.

Until we reach the level of King, the maxim of ***"every man did what was right in his own eyes"*** is in operation. So it is with us. It has been my observation of myself, that there is a place on the climb – just as we are beginning to *hear, see, and say* – that we get a little over-impressed with ourselves. It comes at a level where we are just beginning to function properly and express the I Am – but where we are still *seeing* with "our own eyes." At this place, we may be expressing at a higher level than ever before – we may be *hearing, seeing,* and *saying* more perfectly than ever before – but we're still relying on a "self" which has yet to become the King. Likely, we may not recognize that this is true, for we won't even know what it means to **be** the **King** until we finish with Solomon.

Samuel Is Highest Judge Even with an established religion and rules for practically any occurrence in life, we're not going to make it up the Mountain unless we have a "leader." Ultimately, it will be a King who is *a man of war.* The process begins with Samuel (to hear intelligently + God). Only a leader of such qualities can pull us from an individual expression that *"does what is right in its own eyes"* to an expression which unites its wayward parts into being a functioning part of the whole.

---

[13] *Shiloh* means *tranquil*; it is an epithet of the messiah. Hang-loose reasoning says that this *tranquility* allows each individual to pursue his/her spirituality as he/she will. When it is established, the spiritual center will be moved to Jerusalem (founded peaceful), that which is originally peaceful and tranquil.

Samuel's story begins: *There was a*

"Kingship" Lessons
Begin with Samuel

certain man of Ramathaimzophim of the **hill**
country of Ephraim, whose name was **Elkanah** ...
He had two wives... Peninnah had children, but
Hannah had no children. Now this man [would]... worship and... sacrifice to the
LORD ... at Shiloh... On the day when Elkanah sacrificed, he would give portions
to Peninnah his wife and to all her sons and daughters; and, **although he loved**
Hannah, he would give Hannah only one portion, because the LORD had closed
her womb. *And her rival used to provoke her sorely... So it went on year by*
year... 1 Sam 1:1-7.

The story sounds familiar doesn't it? We heard the motif of a "barren woman" with Sarah, with Rachel, and with the mother of Sampson; now, here it is again. But there is a difference with the birth of Samuel. Previously, the birth of the climber has come by the LORD'S promise. For instance, with Sampson's mother, it was the LORD declaring that the son would be a Nazirite. On the other hand, Hannah (from *to bestow; to stoop in kindness to an inferior*) implores the LORD for a son, promising that she *will give him to the Lord all the days of his life, and no razor shall touch his head.* 1 Sam. 1:11.

There is a lesson for us, here. The level of *kingship* is different from what has preceded it. In the previous cases where the exalted feminine has been barren, it has always been the LORD bringing the spiritualized masculine. In other words, our advancement to this point has come because that was the "LORD'S" intent and because we were attentive to what was being "said" to us. But this sequence of *kingship* begins because our feminine side makes the promise. Notice, "Hannah" comes from a softer, more gentle, more giving feminine side than we've experienced before. Not only that, but Hannah has greater understanding than anyone we have yet encountered – male or female.

The child is born. *And when she had weaned him, she took him up with her, along with a* **three-year-old bull**, *an ephah of flour, and a skin of wine; and she brought him to the house of the LORD at Shiloh; and the child was young. Then they slew the bull, and they brought the child to Eli. And she said, "Oh, my lord! As you live, my lord, I am the woman who was standing here in your presence, praying to the LORD. For this child I prayed; and* **the LORD has granted me my petition which I made to him.** *Therefore I have lent him to the LORD; as long as he lives, he is lent to the LORD." And they worshiped the LORD there.* 1 Sam. 1:24-28.

The Prophets, the second book of the new Jewish translation, carefully points out that the Talmud implies that Elkana goes with Hannah to make the sacrifice;[14] but it still says: ***And Hannah prayed.*** It is the feminine side of us relating to the LORD which *allows* things to happen. Only this side can evoke the King. Listen to Hannah's prayer.

> *My heart exults in the LORD;*
> *My strength is exalted in the LORD.*
> *My mouth derides my enemies,*
> *Because I rejoice in thy salvation.*
>
> *There is none holy like the LORD,*
> *There is none besides thee;*
> *There is no rock like our God.*
>
> *Talk no more so very proudly,*
> *Let not arrogance come from your mouth;*
> *For the LORD is a God of knowledge,*
> *And by him actions are weighed.*
>
> *The bows of the mighty are broken,*
> *But the feeble are girded with strength.*
> *Those who were full have hired themselves out for bread,*
> *But those who were hungry have ceased to hunger.*
> *The barren has borne seven,*
> *But she who has many children is forlorn.*
> *The LORD kills and brings to life;*
> *He brings down to Sheol and raises up.*
> *The LORD makes poor and makes rich;*
> *He brings low, he also exalts.*
> *He raises up the poor from the dust;*
> *He lifts the needy from the ash heap,*
> *To make them sit with princes*
> *And inherit a seat of honor.*
> *For the pillars of the earth are the LORD'S,*
> *And on them he has set the world.*
> *He will guard the feet of his faithful ones;*
> *But the wicked shall be cut off in darkness;*
> *For not by might shall a man prevail.*
>
> *The adversaries of the LORD shall be broken to pieces;*
> *Against them he will thunder in heaven.*
> *The LORD will judge the ends of the earth;*
> *He will give strength to his king, and exalt the power of his anointed.*
>
> 1 Sam. 2:1-10.

---

[14] *The Prophets: A new translation of the Holy Scriptures according to the Masoretic text, Second Section;* The Jewish Publication Society of America, 1978; p.105, fn. The *Talmud* is the depository of the doctrines and opinions of the Jews.

That which is the product of this "understanding" begins the process of *kingship*, replacing the sons of Eli (the high priest) who would have received this portion; for *the sons of Eli were worthless men; they had no regard for the LORD.* They were greedy, fearful, arrogant, and impatient; *they treated the offering of the LORD with contempt.* 1 Sam. 2:12,17. On the other hand, he who begins this step of the climb, Samuel, *was ministering before the LORD, a boy girded with a linen ephod.* 1 Sam. 2:18.

The "priesthood" is not deserving of the "crown." The LORD declares: *I promised that your house [Aaron]... should go in and out before me for ever; but now... Far be it [the house of Aaron] from me! For **those who honor me I will honor, and those who [spurn] Me shall be [dishonored.]**... I will raise up for myself a faithful priest, who shall do according to what is in my heart and in my mind; and I will build him a sure house, and **he shall go in and out before my anointed for ever**.* 1 Sam. 2:30-35.

It is the ***faithful priest*** who does ***according to...my heart and ...mind*** who will eventually bring "kingship."[15]

Achieving **seeing** and **saying** is hard with Eli in charge. *The boy Samuel was ministering to the LORD under Eli, and the **word of the LORD was rare** in those days; there was **no frequent vision**.* In fact, Eli's eyes *had begun to grow dim, so that he could not see...* but, we're reassured that *the **lamp of God had not yet gone out**, and Samuel was lying down within the temple of the LORD where the ark of God was.* 1 Sam. 3:1-3.

We certainly can identify with Eli. Like Eli, we've been on this climb so long. We try so hard. We try to hold to the LORD'S commandments. But not all parts of us have the exalted vision. Eventually, we're not even aware of our shortcomings, while we continue in the supposed role of high priest – assisted by a "dedicated" boy in a linen ephod. But we must become aware. As Eli tells his wayward sons: *"If a man sins against a man, God will mediate for him; but if a man sins against the LORD, who can intercede for him?" But they would not listen to the voice of their father; for it was the will of the LORD to slay them.* 1 Sam. 2:25.

---

[15] *To go in and out before me forever* can have two meanings. The literal level refers to the high priest's yearly duty to enter the Holy of Holies and make atonement. The intuitional level is the "daily" and "constant" duty of the climber to commune with the LORD, to "know" the "heart" and "mind" of I Am. And it is this which the "atuned" conveys to the "anointed" (again we have double meaning) – the King and ourselves, the chosen.

262

The LORD declares that the undisciplined, arrogant, greedy, fearful, impatient portions of us will be eliminated – all that is unlike the LORD will be eliminated.

Hang loose, for a minute. This book *Climbing the Mountain* is not written for beginners. This book is not written for those whom the ladies of the 19th Century called "carnal minded." This book is written for those of the 20th Century who **know** they are on the climb. But this **knowing** isn't always enough to progress up the Mountain. Eli **knows**, but he doesn't **hear.** It takes a more "innocent" mindset to continue the climb.

The "Innocent" Mindset Will Be "Called"

Then the LORD called, "Samuel! Samuel!" and he said, "Here I am" and ran to Eli, and said, "Here I am, for you called me." But he said, "I did not call; lie down again." So he went and lay down. And the LORD called again, "Samuel!" And Samuel arose and went to Eli, and said, "Here I am, for you called me." But he said, "I did not call, my son; lie down again." Now Samuel did not yet know the LORD, and the word of the LORD had not yet been revealed to him. And the LORD called Samuel again the third time. And he arose and went to Eli, and said, "Here I am, for you called me." Then Eli perceived that the LORD was calling the boy. Therefore Eli said to Samuel, "Go, lie down; and if he calls you, you shall say, 'Speak, LORD, for thy servant hears.'" So Samuel went and lay down in his place. And the LORD came and stood forth, calling as at other times, "Samuel! Samuel!" And Samuel said, "Speak, for thy servant hears." Then the LORD said to Samuel, "Behold, ... I am about to punish his house [Eli's] for ever, for the iniquity which he knew, because his sons were blaspheming God, and he did not restrain them. ... Samuel lay until morning; then he opened the doors of the house of the LORD. And Samuel was afraid to tell the vision to Eli. But Eli called Samuel and said, "Samuel, my son." And he said, "Here I AM." And Eli said, "What was it that he told you? Do not hide it from me. May God do so to you and more also, if you hide anything from me of all that he told you." So Samuel told him everything and hid nothing from him. And he [Eli] said, "It is the LORD; let him do what seems good to him." And Samuel grew, and the LORD was with him and let none of his words fall to the ground. ... And the LORD appeared again at Shiloh, for the LORD revealed himself to Samuel at Shiloh by the word of the LORD. 1 Sam.3:1-21.

Shiloh comes from a primitive root which means *to be tranquil; to be secure or successful,* but Strong's *Concordance* adds an important comment. It says that **Shiloh is "an epithet of the Messiah."** An epithet is a word or phrase that concisely conveys the essence of something. This is a very important point, for it suggests that *Messiah* is not so much an "individual" as a "state of mind."[16] A similar explanation for the terms "Promised Land" and "Kingdom of Heaven" can be made.[17] It is always our "state of mind" that determines what we are experiencing.

Samuel is at the "state of mind" – the level of consciousness – which is so "one" with the Lord that *none of his words fall to the ground.* And everyone *from Dan* (righteous judgment) *to Beer-sheba* (well of an oath) *knew that Samuel was established as a prophet of the Lord.* 1 Sam. 3:20.

Well, we're getting closer to being able "to say." We're almost at the place where we can "see." But we're still "warring," and the Philistines keep defeating us – to the point of even capturing the Ark of the Covenant. And the official "religion" has no power, for Eli's state of mind is old and worn. He is 98 years old – and his eyes are *set, so that he [can]not see.*[18] His sons have been killed, and the Ark has been captured; and upon hearing the news, Eli falls over and breaks his neck. (Not quite the point of losing the "head" and the "state of mind," but a start!)

We find ourselves in Eli's shoes, don't we? We, too, "see" ourselves as being of a high consciousness. We're *circumcised* (dedicated to the LORD) and careful to follow the Commandments; but like Eli, our vision is *set, so that we*

---

[16] Fillmore makes an interesting point. He sees Shiloh as this "place" of peace, etc., but "centered" in the "head" rather than the heart. Fillmore says the Ark must be settled in Jerusalem rather than Shiloh for it to have its full power. See: Fillmore, *Metaphysical Bible Dictionary,* p. 283.

[17] Somehow, it is this explanation that comes to my intuition in hearing Erico Rocco's translation of the Lord's Prayer. Rocco translates the Aramaic *Malakutha* as *"thy kingdom."*

[18] The number "17" is interesting in itself. Notice, it adds up to 8, that number at which we are to *receive*; however, number 17 is not always as positive as it might be. Possibly the importance of the number 17 is that it makes it apparent that we are receiving in accordance with our **seeing and saying.**

[cannot] see. And what we rely on for our strength gets taken away. We may experience total defeat: to the point of 4000 (absolute defeat on all sides) and 30,000 foot soldiers. How can this be? We go to church, we help the poor, and we try to love our neighbors; we don't cheat on our spouses – we don't even cheat on our income tax. Why aren't we succeeding? Why aren't we happy in the Promised Land?

Why? Because we're fighting the *Philistines* and the problem is that we can't *see*. *See* what? **See** that what our five senses "pick up" isn't the "whole picture." Actually, we've been dealing with these Philistines (to wallow oneself) for a long time; they've been a nuisance from the beginning of this climb. Intermittently we've warred against them, but it is only now that we are ready **to** *war* in earnest.

Just who and what are these *Philistines* that we're at war with? We know that to the intellectual mind they're some Greek-type "sea people" who are somewhat more advanced than we. We know that they're "uncircumcised." But what does all this mean to the intuitional mind? To the intuition, the *Philistines* are those habits and characteristics that keep us from *peacefully* living in the Promised Land. A clue to their identity is that they have **5** lords.

We all know what **5** means, don't we? It means that we **hear** what others say about us and believe it; we **hear** what others "think" about us and believe that. We **look** at a "dead" person as "dead"; we **look** at a "sick" person as "sick." We **feel** on the basis of how others treat us; we often **feel** how we were taught to feel many years ago. Even our **taste** and **smell** are limited. Cheer up! We won't stop hearing, seeing, feeling, tasting and smelling; instead, we'll find our senses being heightened if we continue on the climb. How? *Seek ye the LORD, wait patiently on Him.*

Everything will be taken care of by something other than our conscious mind. For instance, the Ark proves to be a great burden to the Philistines. They place it in the house of their god, Dagon (the fish, representing abundant production on the sense plane), only to find the statue of Dagon is on its face the next morning. So the Philistines again set Dagon upright; but next morning they again find the statue face down, this time its head and hands cut off – only the trunk remains. The

Dagon, "god" of the Philistines.

world of senses cannot function when opposed to the LORD. *The hand of the Lord [is] heavy upon the people of Ashdod (thieving thoughts),* afflicting the people with tumors.[19] In fact, for the next seven months, in every town that the Philistines place the Ark, the men – both young and old – are afflicted with tumors and many die.

Judging with the senses, particularly the unenlightened senses, confines us to the land of the "dead." Finally, the lords of the Philistines instruct that the Ark be returned, *that it*

---

[19] *The Prophets* says the Philistines are afflicted with **hemorrhoids**.

may not slay us and our people. And the Philistinian priests and diviners suggest a *guilt offering* to the LORD.[20] *Then you will be healed, and it will be known to you why his hand does not turn away from you. Now then, take and prepare a new cart and two milch cows upon which there has never come a yoke, and yoke the cows to the cart, but take their calves home, away from them. And take the ark of the LORD and place it on the cart, and put in a box at its side the figures of gold, ... as a guilt offering. Then send it off, and let it go its way. And watch; if it goes up on the way to its own land, to Bethshemesh, then it is he who has done us this great harm; but if not, then we shall know..., it happened to us by chance." The men did so,... And the cows went straight in the direction of Bethshemesh along one highway, lowing as they went; they turned neither to the right nor to the left, ...* 1 Sam. 6:3-12.

> **If the "milch cows" leave their calves and go up the road, it is the LORD's doing.**

One way to "see" if we're beginning to *see*, is to try the "impossible." Certainly, that is the case here. Two cows, heavy with milk, who have never been yoked together, simply will not leave their calves and run up a road, turning neither to the right nor left. It is only as we give up our worldly senses that such "impossibilities" begin to happen in our lives. If we hold to our *oneness* with God, supposed "impossibilities" do take place. This is much more than positive thinking. Test the system. Try looking for a parking place where finding one is unlikely – **expecting that you will find one**. Amazingly, a parking

---

[20] The Ark is returned to Bethshemesh (house of the sun), but not wishing to give pagan religions any publicity, the Bible is subtle. *Now the people of Bethshemesh were reaping their wheat harvest in the valley; and when they lifted up their eyes and saw the ark, they rejoiced to see it. The cart came into the field of* **Joshua** (Jehovah saved) *of Bethshemesh, and stopped there. A great stone was there; and they split up the wood of the cart and offered the cows as a burnt offering to the LORD. And the Levites took down the ark of the LORD and the box that was beside it, in which were* **the golden figures, and set them upon the great stone**; *and the men of Bethshemesh offered burnt offerings and sacrificed sacrifices on that day to the LORD. And when the five lords of the Philistines saw it, they returned that day to Ekron* (rooting out where truth is). 1 Sam. 6:13-16.

The whole question here is whether the Israelites will stick to this **new** mindset Moses gave them, or will they revert to the religions of the surrounding nations? The *Ashtaroth* refers to the "stone" dedicated to the "goddess" Astarte, which represented the morning star. Despite protestations of "goddess" followers to the contrary, "goddess" worship (although acknowledging other planes) was directed at control of the physical plane. Moses' "religion" on the other hand acknowledges other planes and then invites the initiate to become **one** with the whole, never trying to individually *control* the earthly plane.

place will appear just about where you want it. If it is farther away from your destination than you hoped for, you need the exercise. The "system" is no magic formula; the "system" *is* your *seeing.* It is "atunement" with what the Bible calls the will of the LORD. I watch where my parking place is. If it is immediately in front of my destination, I know I'm right where I'm supposed to be; and I give thanks!

The heightening of our senses announces this "atunement," but we must pay attention and keep things in perspective. Only as we begin to see the senses as *helpers* rather than as ultimate reality is it a heightening. My sense of "smell" and my "sight" were heightened for a time. These changes came after several years of regular meditation; but the phenomena were just to be observed, until I needed them. Finally, one New Year's Day as my family and I were recovering from the previous night's late hours, I greatly needed the sense of smell. Everyone was sound asleep, but in my sleep I "smelled" smoke, and this got me up. The furnace had shorted out and the sparks were just beginning to start a fire. I was awake, able to call 911 and get everyone outside because of my heightened sense of smell.

I also needed the enhanced sight; apparently it was just for my own edification. Emotionally, I was at a "place" where I saw and felt nothing but denigration from all of my associates. I felt lowest of the low. This was 1986, the first year that the Harmonic Convergence took place throughout the world, and I went with a friend and her husband to Mount Evans, one of the highest highways in the world. My other-worldly eyes went into operation. I spotted **11** mountain sheep and **3** mountain goats (something I had never seen in the wild). The next weekend, as my husband and I were driving in the lower mountains, my enhanced vision spotted **12** elk, led by a bull elk with a **9**-point rack.

I'm not sure about the *reality* of my experiences; I'm not sure a 9-point rack is possible. But what I *saw* reassured me so that my doubts and fears weren't so controlling. I was reassured. I'm still working on enabling my conscious mind to disregard what it "thinks" it "sees." Some will say that my "vision" conveniently saw what my "self" needed for it to heal itself. They could be right. Regardless of the explanation, my extended vision and enhanced sense of smell eventually faded.

Heightening isn't intended to tie us more completely to the physical plane; it is a help for a need. *Heightening* is an expansion into other planes. With heightening, we "hear" things that to the physical ears make no sound. We "see" things that to the physical eye don't exist. We "feel" vibrations that are generated from a level other than the physical plane. But these "new" senses develop only as we know there is more than the physical hearing, seeing, feeling, tasting and smelling; they develop only as we *accept* them.

Senses Heightened by "Uplifting"

Samuel says it a different way: *Then Samuel said to all the house of Israel, "**If you are returning** to the LORD with all your heart, then **put away the foreign gods and the Ashtaroth from among you**, and **direct your heart to the LORD,** and serve him only, **and he will deliver you out of the hand of the Philistines."** So Israel put away the Baals and the Ashtaroth, and they served the LORD only.* 1 Sam. 7:3,4.

Only as we serve the LORD – *only* – can we be delivered from the Philistines! If we can be delivered from the Philistines, we will begin **to see** and **to say.**[21] Samuel's level of understanding lifts us up; now we see farther than ever before. *Then Samuel took a stone and set it up between Mizpah* (watchtower) *and Jeshanah* (crag), *and called its name Ebenezer* (stone of the help); *for he said, "Hitherto the LORD has helped us."* Samuel set the stone where previously Israel had been defeated in battle.

---

[21] The difference between the religions is very subtle. The existence of a "molten image" or even an "established rock" brings the mind to a physical relationship with a physical God. On the other hand a religion based on no physical form, and culminating in *incense*, which we know has no real physical form, invites a different type of relationship with a different type of "God."

Samuel sets up stone, calling it *stone of help.*

So the Philistines were subdued ... And the hand of the LORD was against the Philistines all the days of Samuel. The cities which the Philistines had taken from Israel were restored to Israel, from *Ekron* (rooting out where truth is) *to Gath* (see all as trials)..*There was peace also between Israel and the Amorites.* Samuel judged Israel all the days of his life. 1 Sam. 7:12-15.

Notice the first part of the last line. Believe it or not, we've finally reached *peace* with the Amorites? Have we learned **to say**? *And Samuel judged Israel all the days of his life. And he went on a circuit year by year to* **Bethel** (house of God), **Gilgal** (to roll together), *and* **Mizpah** (watchtower); *and he judged Israel in all these places ... [returning] to* **Ramah** (heights). 1 Sam. 7:15,16,17.

But peace with the Amorites and returning to the heights (mountain) is not the end of the climb. Even though he makes them judges over Israel, Samuel's sons *did not walk in his ways, but turned aside after gain; they took bribes and perverted justice. Then all the elders of Israel ... came to Samuel ..., and said to him, "Behold, you are old and your sons do not walk in your ways; now* **appoint for us a king to govern us like all the nations."** *... And the LORD said to Samuel, "Hearken to the voice of the people ... for* **they have not rejected you, but they have rejected me from being king over them.** *... only, you shall solemnly warn them, and show them the ways of the king who shall reign over them."* 1 Sam. 8:3-9.

Our desire is for permanent control of the Promised Land, isn't it? But remember the Buddhist's view of *desire?* And remember Jacob's vision of a stairway with white-robed individuals ascending and descending? There is no permanent control for the individual; rather, it is each individual's challenge to "match" the whole. The function of the King is to bring this "matching" about. The King is to bring order to this chaotic expression that we've had for so long. The King is to govern those elements of ourselves that are unruly. But the

King will exact a high cost, as Samuel tells the people.[22] Despite Samuel's warning: *...the people refused to listen to the voice of Samuel; and they said, "No! but we **will have a king over us, that we also may be like all the nations,** and that our **king may govern us and go out before us and fight our battles.**"* 1 Sam. 8:19,20.

We Want a King Like Other Nations

Well, we all have to learn, don't we? We still find ourselves *at war.* Here we thought the Philistines were our problem – certainly, they're still here. We also thought the Amorites were our problem – keeping us from **seeing;** they're still here, too. Maybe **we** are our problem. I guess we'll find out.... Enter, the King that gets chosen...

Saul Is Chosen As King

To the physical eye, Saul (to request) appears fit to be King. He's described as *a handsome young man. There was not a man among the people of Israel more handsome than he; **from his shoulders upward** he was **taller** than any of the people.* 1 Sam. 9:2,3. But the fact that he's a Benjaminite is a drawback.[23] To the Hebrews, *Benjaminite*

---

[22] Samuel warns: *"These will be the ways of the king who will reign over you: he will take your sons and appoint them to his chariots and to be his horsemen, and to run before his chariots; and he will appoint for himself commanders of thousands and commanders of fifties, and some to plow his ground and to reap his harvest, and to make his implements of war and the equipment of his chariots. He will take your daughters to be perfumers and cooks and bakers. He will take the best of your fields and vineyards and olive orchards and give them to his servants. He will take the tenth of your grain and of your vineyards and give it to his officers and to his servants. He will take your menservants and maidservants, and the best of your cattle and your asses, and put them to his work. He will take the tenth of your flocks, and you shall be his slaves. And in that day you will cry out because of your king, whom you have chosen for yourselves; but the LORD will not answer you in that day."* 1 Sam. 8:11-18.

[23] Saul's heritage is important. His father is **Kish** (bent bow), the son of **Abiel** (possessor of God), son of **Zeror** (bound up, related to being in distress), son of **Becorath** (fem. of firstling), son of **Aphiah** (to blow breath). We learn later his clan is **Matri** (to rain upon). But the most important part of his heritage is that he's a Benjaminite, that tribe which became the object of "correction" by the other eleven tribes of Israel. The story is found in Judges 19, 20, and 21; it takes place when *there was no king in Israel; every man did what was right in his own eyes.*

From its elements, the story appears to be an esoteric presentation. *Benjamin* means *son of the right hand,* yet the tribe of Benjamin was the lowest of all. Part of their lowly status came from their having repeatedly raped (thereby "murdering") the "concubine" of a Levite (loving). But, although it's never clearly stated, I suspect that it's not so much the rape and murder that was *an abomination* as the

(continued...)

is a red-flag for "less-than-topnotch." Although having potential because he's handsome, **a head** taller than anyone else and his father is rich, Saul lacks good credentials. Why? Because he's of the tribe of Benjamin. The term *Benjaminite* immediately brings to mind the story in Judges of the Levite and his "concubine," who is raped by an entire town; *Benjaminite* brings to mind the story's symbolic element.[24]

So far, the feminine side of our "kingly" expression isn't thriving. Samuel had a "saintly" mother, but there is no mention of his wife – even though his unrighteous sons are mentioned. Now, we get a king who comes from a heritage

---

[23](...continued)

fact that the man was a "traveler" and therefore their obligation to protect. The rape took place in Gibeah (a height; to be *convex),* and the men of Gibeah more than failed in their obligation to a traveler (more importantly, to a fellow Hebrew).

Consequently, their correction is undertaken by the remaining tribes, and the LORD appoints Judah (praise) to *go up first... against the Benjaminites.* The ensuing **three-day** battle takes a great toll on Israel, resulting in the death of (22,000; 18,000; 30; 30 = 40,060) 40,060 Israelites; it also takes a great toll on Benjamin (25,100; 18,000; 5,000; 2,000=50,100). Literally, the actions of the Benjaminites (representing our lesser expressions) result in a greater loss to themselves than to the other Israelites. But esoterically, the actions of the Benjaminites (resulting in a **6** x 000) raises the Hebrews to a **10** x 000. But the whole activity (unexplainedly) leaves the remaining 600 Benjaminites without women. This question of "women" requires even greater hang-loose logic for any explanation. The first question is with regard to the woman who was repeatedly raped. The translation in *The Prophets* refers to the woman as a "concubine," i.e., a feminine side that is not accepted as legal or equal. The Jewish version does somewhat vindicate the Benjaminites by saying that her leaving her "husband" came about as she "played the harlot." However, this can simply mean that she refused to do as directed by the man. Probably symbolically, as a result of this whole tragedy, there are no women left in Benjamin. The remaining 600 Benjaminite men have to steal wives; all Israel vows to keep their daughters from marrying Benjaminites.

[24] The Levite, upon finding his concubine "murdered," cuts her body into **12** pieces. This would be only a gruesome detail, except for the similarity to world myths. The scheme is repeated with Isis and Osiris (Egyptian) as well as with Demeter and Dionysus (Greek). In both instances, although the gender is reversed, the remaining mate cuts up the murdered partner. Only after the body parts are collected together, can the "god" be restored. A similar scheme exists in astrology. Only as all 12 of the zodiacal challenges are met and conquered does the individual reach the expression that allows restoration of "wholeness." Will the woman be restored to wholeness?

272

that "stole" its women. In other words, the feminine expression was not genuinely a part of Saul. Nevertheless, the remembrance of the "raped concubine" and the story's esoteric elements emphasize an important element in the whole Bible – that the "symbolic" relationship with *women* is crucial to the climb. In fact, it is imperative that the climber treat his/her feminine side with respect. Interestingly, climbing the Mountain exalts the feminine.

Saul starts the rise to kingship as he and his servant search for Saul's father's "donkeys." Finally they come to Zuth (honeycomb).[25] Saul is discouraged and ready to turn back, but the servant suggests that they consult the "seer" who lives in the town. Climbing the hill to the town, they encounter "fair maidens," who tell them that the holy man has just come to town and has gone up the hill for a sacrifice *"for the people will not eat till he comes, since he must bless the sacrifice; afterward those eat who are invited. Now go up, for you will meet him immediately." ... they saw Samuel coming out toward them on his way up to the high place. Now the day before ..., the LORD had revealed to Samuel: "Tomorrow about this time I will send to you a man from the land of Benjamin, and you shall anoint him to be prince over my people Israel. He shall save my people from the hand of the Philistines;..." When Samuel saw Saul, the LORD told him, "Here is the man of whom I spoke to you! He it is who shall rule over my people."* 1Sam. 9:11-17. *Then Saul approached Samuel... and said, "... where is the house of the seer?" Samuel answered Saul, "I am the seer; go up before me to the high place, for today you shall eat with me, and in the morning I will let you go and will tell you all that is on your mind.* 1 Sam. 9:18,19.

Saul Looks for Father's "Donkeys"

Samuel is not King, but he is a man of war. Most importantly, he has recognized the I Am. He knows that whatever is in our minds determines who we are and what we do. Although he knows what is on Saul's mind, he continues with Saul: *"As for your asses that were lost three days ago, do not set your mind on them, for they have been found. And for whom is [is all Israel yearning, if not for you and all your ancestral house?]"*

Saul answered, "Am I not a Benjaminite,... the least of the tribes of Israel? And is not my family the humblest of all the families of the tribe of Benjamin? ..."

---

[25] *Zuthi* (honeycomb) stands for sweetness and orderliness.

*Then Samuel took Saul and his servant and brought them into the hall and **gave them a place at the head of [the guests],** who [numbered **about thirty.]** And Samuel said to the cook, "Bring the portion I gave you, of which I said to you, 'Put it aside.'"* So **the cook [lifted up the thigh and what was on it,]** *and set [it] before Saul; and Samuel said, **"See, what was kept is set before you. Eat; because it was kept for you until the hour appointed, that you might eat with the guests."** So Saul ate with Samuel that day.* 1Sam: 9:18-24.

These few lines tell much. First, Saul had intended only to ask direction from *one who sees*; he was inquiring only about the physical level, his father's asses.[26] But notice, the physical inquiry puts him at a time and place where he finds out much more than he had anticipated. More importantly, **Saul reverses and negates** I **Am,** saying: *Am I not...?* Nevertheless, the *seer* has been waiting for Saul and places him at the head of the table (an extreme honor). Not only that, but the *seer* gives him the choice portion (the portion saved from the time of Jacob when he wrestled with the angel and was injured in the thigh). He/she who is rising to the position of "King" is presented with more "honors" than he/she could possibly ask for. Samuel says: *"Go up before me to the high place, for today you shall eat with me."* [27]

This whole "kingly" process began with the spiritual side (Samuel) weakly answering I Am. Now, in compliance with the "people's" demand, Samuel will place the intellectual side (Saul) in power. *Then Samuel took a vial of oil and poured it on his [Saul's] head, and kissed him and said, "[The LORD herewith anoints you ruler over His own people.] ... and you will save them from the hand of their enemies round about. And this shall be the sign to you that the LORD has anointed you to be prince over his heritage. When you depart from me today you will meet two men ..., and they will say to you, 'The asses which you went to seek are found, and now your father has ceased to care about the asses and is anxious about you . ... Then*

---

[26] Interestingly, both "Saul" and "Eshtaol" (the farthest boundary for Sampson's burial) are defined as *to request.* See p. 255)

[27] This line is very close to one found in the New Testament; it is what Jesus says to Zacchaeus. *And there was a man named Zacchaeus; he was a chief tax collector, and rich. And he sought to see who Jesus was, but could not, on account of the crowd, because he was small of stature. So he ran on ahead and climbed up into a sycamore tree to see him, for he was to pass that way. And when Jesus came to the place, he looked up and said to him, "Zacchaeus, make haste and come down; for I must stay at your house today." So he made haste and came down, and received him joyfully.* Luke 19:2-6.

274

... [at] the oak of Tabor; three men going up to God at Bethel will meet you there, one carrying three kids, another carrying three loaves of bread, and another carrying a skin of wine. **And they will greet you and give you two loaves of bread,** *which you shall accept from their hand.* *After that you shall come to Gibeathelohim, where there is a garrison of the Philistines; and there, as you come to the city, you will meet* **a band of prophets coming down from the high place** *with harp, tambourine, flute, and lyre before them,* **prophesying.** **Then the spirit of the LORD will come mightily upon you, and you shall prophesy with them and be turned into another man.** *Now when these signs meet you, [act when the* **occasion arises]***, for God is with you.* *And you shall go down before me to Gilgal; and [I will come down to you to present] burnt offerings and to sacrifice peace offerings.* **Seven days you shall wait, until I come to you and show you what you shall do."** *[As Saul turned around] to leave Samuel,* **God gave him [Saul] another heart;** *and all these signs came to pass that day.* 1 Sam. 10:1-9

All it takes is a little "oil" – and our spiritual side's announcement to us that we've been "chosen" – to make a new man or woman out of us. ... But if that was all it took, we could climb easily. The difficulty is that the higher the climb, the steeper the grade. And this is Saul, the Benjaminite – he's not quite up to steep grades. Esoterically, we're warned about this. Notice: Saul is to be given only **two loaves**; to Saul there is always duality.

When they came to Gibeah, behold, a band of prophets met him; and **the spirit of God came mightily upon him, and he prophesied** *among them.* *And when* **all who knew him before** *saw how he prophesied with the prophets, the people said to one another, "What has come over* **the son of Kish?** *Is Saul also among the prophets?"* 1 Sam. 10:10,11.[28]

If we have ever reached this place on the climb, this portion of the story should be familiar to us.[29] Precious are the times when "God gives us a new heart" and we feel "the spirit of God come mightily upon us." At these times, we find ourselves filled with such *joy* that we're in awe of it. It produces *an ecstasy* – a real "high." But, as with Saul, our associates can't see that any change has taken place in us, and they ridicule our new expression. Such is the case with Saul as

---

[28] *The Prophets*, fn. p. 120, sees calling anyone *the son of*... as a "put down." Such a comment denies his status as a "man."

[29] The verse and chapter is important. The number 10 is for "new beginning," twice stated, and followed by the number which usually indicates "fruition."

he nears home, and his town's people make fun of him. "Home" is Gibeah, *to be convex.* Saul's usual place of abode is a "little hill," just a little knowledge greater than the norm; but unfortunately, *convex* will absorb nothing. Remember, Gibeah was the town where the men ravaged the concubine. Obviously, such a place won't accept this new wisdom that we've been given. Compare the image of *concave* with *convex*; only the concave image can absorb what is given it.

Upon seeing Saul's ecstasy, the people of Gibeah start making "comments." *And all who **knew him before** do their* "darndest" to pull him down. The comments are subtle, but effective.[30] *.....the people said to one another, "What has come over the **son of Kish?** Is Saul also among the prophets?" And a man of the place answered, "And **who is their father?"** Therefore it became a proverb, "**Is Saul also among the prophets?"** When he had finished prophesying, he came to the high place. Saul's uncle said to him and to his servant, "Where did you go?" And he said, "To seek the asses; and when we saw they were not to be found, we went to Samuel." And Saul's uncle said, "Pray, tell me what Samuel said to you." And Saul said to his uncle, "He told us plainly that the asses had been found." **But about the matter of the kingdom, of which Samuel had spoken, he did not tell him anything.*** 1 Sam. 10:11-16

Despite Saul's reticence, it's time to install the demanded King of Israel; so Samuel calls the people together to draw lots for King. Of the twelve tribes, Benjamin is drawn; among the clans of Benjamin, Matri is drawn; and from the men of Matri, Saul's name is drawn – but Saul is nowhere to be found. Saul is **hidden among** the baggage. But when Saul is out of the baggage, it is obvious – since he towers above everyone else – that *there is none equal to him.* 1 1 Sam. 10:24.

Esoterically, Saul (to request) stands for our intellectual mind. Nothing equals our mind. It allows our whole being to function and express. Without it, we can do nothing; but the

---

[30] *Who is their father?* is pretty close to calling someone a *bastard.* Part of the criticism is of the "prophets," groups of young men who lived together and who, according to *The Jerusalem Bible,* worked themselves in to "ecstatic" conditions with music and "gesticulation"(similar to the dervishes of today), p. 355, fn.. However, a change of one's heart, i.e., a raising of consciousness, results in a similar ecstasy, one which the surrounding people would not be able to recognize.

mind's *expression* depends on what directs it. Is it directed by Self (by the higher mind) or by Desire?[31] There, for a minute, we thought Saul was going to be directed by a Self that recognized its gifts from God; but now he's hiding in the baggage. The only way we get him to stand tall is to pull him out. Some parts of us follow; but not all parts honor someone so cowardly.

Almost immediately, we're confronted with an outer enemy, an Ammonite (inbred) threatening to gouge out our right eye. Oohhh! We just got so we could **see** a little. Well, we don't need to worry; we've got a king to fight for us – don't we? He's just coming in from herding the **cattle. Whoa!** Esoterically, that doesn't speak too well for him. Upon hearing the news of the Ammonite's threats, Saul becomes angry and takes a yoke of oxen, cutting them to pieces and sending the pieces throughout Israel warning: *Thus shall be done to the cattle of anyone who does not follow Saul and Samuel into battle.* 1 Sam. 11:7.

Needless to say, everyone shows up to do battle; and the Israelites wipe out the Ammonites. Some Israelites say to kill those who didn't fully support Saul, but Saul forgives those who had doubted him. And all of Israel goes to Gilgal (a wheel; a dust storm) and proclaims Saul "king," and Samuel bows out, saying: *"And now behold the king whom you have chosen, for whom you have asked; behold the LORD has set a king over you. ... **if both you and the king who reigns over you will follow the LORD your God, it will be well;** but if you ... rebel against the commandment of the LORD, then the hand of the LORD will be against you and your king. ... **Is it not wheat harvest today?** ... you shall **know** and **see** that your wickedness is great... in asking for yourselves a king."* So Samuel called upon the LORD, and the LORD sent thunder and rain ... Samuel said to the people, "Fear not; you have done all this evil, ... **do not turn aside after vain things which cannot profit or save,** ... For the LORD will not cast away his people... **Only fear the LORD, and serve him faithfully with all your heart;**... if you still do wickedly, you shall be swept away, both you and your king." 1 Sam. 12:13-25.

---

[31] This is the distinction Charles Fillmore uses in commenting on Kish (bent-bow). Its value is dependent upon what directs it, whether Self or desire-mind.

It is written: *Saul was . . . years old when he began to reign; and he reigned two years over Israel.* 1 Sam. 13:1.[32] Who knows what the intent of this line was. It would be logical for Saul to become king at the age of forty. But, if that is the case, there is no excuse for his hiding in the "baggage." Saul represents our intellectual mind; but the **Saul Represents Intellectual Mind** omission of his age indicates that this intellectual mind isn't commensurate with its "supposed" physical age. *Forty* indicates having achieved complete control over something. It expresses **4,** but it is raised to a second level. *Forty* is a powerful number; it would be inappropriate to use it to represent something that could be found *hiding in the baggage.* So, Saul's age is blank.

This strictly intellectual mind isn't up to the role of King. Although the intellectual mind surpasses all of our other faculties, it is not far from the carnal mind. In fact Saul keeps his 2000 troops in Michmas (hidden, in the memory). He still is tied to the earthly expression. This intellectual mind has several more levels to climb before it will express as the Christ mind. But at least Saul has a younger portion of himself, his son Jonathan.

Jonathan (Jehovah given) has his 1000 troops in Gibeah (hill), and it is Jonathan who "strikes down" the Philistine prefect (high official) in Gibeah. And Saul has the *ram's horn sounded throughout the land, saying: "Let the Hebrews hear."*[33] At least Jonathan starts the elimination of the Philistines. But striking at their leader brings the Philistines out in full force; and Saul – now at Gilgal (a wheel; from *to roll,*

---

[32] *The Prophets,* fn. p.124, says that this verse is lacking in the Septuagint. Unlike the King James version and the RSV, which read: *and he reigned over Israel ... and two years,* the new Jewish translation suggests a definite period, reading: *reigned over Israel two years.* However, the *Amplified Old Testament,* Zondervan, 1964 reads: *Saul was [forty] years old when he began to reign; and when he had reigned two (2) years over Israel, Saul chose 3,000 men...*

[33] These Philistines will keep bothering us for quite a while, until David (love) finally takes complete charge of our lives. At least we are *hearing* here.

278

wallow) – is challenged by more than ten times his numbers. The Philistines have 30,000 chariots, 6,000 horsemen, and unnumbered troops. Not only is the enemy more than 10 times stronger, it has technological superiority – they have horses, chariots and iron. Israel has only foot soldiers armed with brass or copper.[34]

Well, Samuel told Saul part of what was going to happen, but he left out a few things. "Two years" ago he told Saul that Saul was to *act when the occasion arises,* and Saul has. And he succeeded for a while. At that time Samuel told Saul then to go to Gilgal, saying: *"And I will come down to you to present burnt offerings and offer sacrifices of well being. Wait seven days until I come to you and instruct you what you are to do next."* 1 Sam. 10:7-9. *The Prophets.*

Of course, Samuel forgot to mention that at the time Saul would be faced by unnumbered troops and 36,000 advanced warriors. Nevertheless, as instructed, Saul waits for seven days. That was what Samuel had said – but then the people begin to scatter. Saul is going to get his first dose of "discipline." He finds himself with a huge outer threat, and the people are beginning to run away. Samuel appears to have deserted! So, Saul figures the only thing to do is take things into his own hands – perform the priestly function himself! Just as he finishes the burnt offering, Samuel shows up!

> **Undisciplined Mind Lacks Patience**

Don't you love it when this happens? We keep asking God to fix something, but God really doesn't seem to have a time schedule. Even though we think it should be just the **seven** days that it's supposed to be, things don't get fixed. So the intellectual mind jumps in and decides to fix things itself.

---

[34] We have to hang loose here. A younger portion of our intellectual mind has just "zapped" one of our five senses – Maybe we have dismissed what we "heard" some-one say about us; maybe we did not "buy into" the "doom and gloom" that we heard on the nightly news. This simple act will bring out the sensual judgments in force. The habits of the carnal mind will reveal themselves, full bloomed – maybe to the count of 30,000 chariots – much more skilled and powerful than this young, Jehovah-given experience. All we can do is stand and wait, keeping the "high watch."

Then we find we shouldn't have done that. We should have been **patient!** It certainly shows that we are the "burnt offering." And why do we "jump in" even though we know we're supposed to wait for direction? Because we're afraid; we're afraid the *people* will run. We're afraid that things won't go the way we want, the way we **desire**.

Of course, the intellectual mind has an excuse. *Samuel said, "What have you done?" And Saul said, "When I saw that the people were scattering from me, and that you did not come within the days appointed, and that the Philistines had mustered at Michmash, I said, 'Now the Philistines will come down upon me at Gilgal, and I have not entreated the favor of the LORD'; so I forced myself, and offered the burnt offering." And Samuel said to Saul, "**You have done foolishly; you have not kept the commandment of the LORD your God,...;** for now the LORD would have established your kingdom over Israel for ever. But now your kingdom shall not continue; **the LORD has sought out a man after his own heart; and the LORD has appointed him to be prince over his people, because you have not kept what the LORD commanded you."** And Samuel arose, and went up from Gilgal (wheel) to Gibeah (little hill) of Benjamin. And **Saul numbered the people who were present with him, about six hundred men.** 1 Sam. 13:11-15.*

By itself, the intellectual mind always gets in trouble.[35] According to logic, Saul has done correctly. Feeling that he hadn't asked "*the favor of the LORD,*" he goes ahead and offers the burnt offering. What can be so wrong with that? Can we **"see"** that Saul's "foolishness" lies very close to Moses' "failure to sanctify" – that which kept him out of the Promised Land. (See pp. 244, 245.) Although Saul offers the burnt offering, it is not an offering which is "sanctified" or "consecrated," i.e., dedicated to the LORD out of love and

---

[35] Part of Saul's activity is with the intellectual mind in "concert" with the spiritual. For a time he succeeds. *When Saul had taken the kingship over Israel, he fought against all his enemies on every side, against **Moab**, against the **Ammonites**, against **Edom**, against the kings of **Zobah** (to station), and against the **Philistines**; **wherever he turned he put them to the worse**. And he did valiantly, and smote the **Amalekites**, and delivered Israel out of the hands of those who plundered them. Now the sons of Saul were **Jonathan, Ishvi, and Malchishua**;... his two daughters were these: ... the first-born was **Merab**,... the younger **Michal**; and the name of Saul's **wife was Ahinoam** the daughter of Ahimaaz. ... There was hard fighting against the Philistines all the days of Saul; **and when Saul saw any strong man, or any valiant man, he attached him to himself.** 1 Sam. 14:47-52.*

280

adoration. It is not an offering of the *righteous*. Instead, **Saul's offering is given out of fear**.

In a sense, the story of Saul is actually the story of Samuel – more properly the story of us all. We, like Samuel, once having answered I Am, do our own fighting for a time; then we give everything over to the intellectual mind. And with the intellect in charge, we *reason* and we *count* and often we *act foolishly*, not taking the time to consult our spiritual Selves for direction. We constantly find ourselves at Gilgal, the *wheel*, the *whirlwind*, where repet-itive experiences come round and round to us – as though on a wheel. Have you ever noticed the similarities in the experiences you attract? We are all trying to learn to fully "consecrate" ourselves to the LORD, aren't we?

"Righteous Judgment" Is A Question of "Consecration"

What in the world does that mean? asks the intellectual mind. Possibly, the question is answered more easily with another question. What is our view of the LORD? Do we see the LORD as I Am? Unless we do, we are not "sanctifying" the LORD: we are not "consecrated." If we still fear – if we think the *people* might leave and leave us all by ourselves – we're not sanctifying the LORD. Such a consciousness is going to have to be replaced by another – *a man after his own heart.*

*Now there was **no smith** to be found throughout all the land of Israel...; for the Philistines said, **"Lest the Hebrews make themselves swords or spears"**; but every one of the Israelites went down to the Philistines to sharpen his **plowshare**, his **mattock**, his **axe**, or his **sickle**; ... So **on the day of the battle** there was **neither sword nor spear** found **in the hand of any of the people** with Saul and Jonathan; **but Saul and Jonathan his son had them.** And the garrison of the Philistines went out to the pass of Michmash.* 1 Sam. 13:19-23.

We were told long ago that we were at "war." But here we are disadvantaged. At the moment we can't make our own weapons. Only the king and his son have sword and spear. All we can do is get our "tools" sharpened; the Philistines control the smith (the fire for metal). Our tools can deal only with earth (plowshare), hard ground (mattock), wood (axe) and grain (sickle). Other than that we're helpless. Yet, we're at war with the Philistines. Only a new leader can get us out of this fix. Maybe it is Jonathan.

Saul has always been "among the baggage," but his son, Jonathan, has some real metal/mettle (pun intended). Jonathan, alone except for his servant, attacks the Philistines in their own camp. He accepts that the LORD is with him, and he slaughters twenty men. Of course, this upsets the Philistine camp, and **Maybe Jonathan Can Be the Leader** the Israelites see the unusual activity. But instead of taking the initiative, Saul holds back and inquires of the priest before he moves; and he does succeed. However, he makes an oath that no one should eat until the Philistines are conquered.

Knowing nothing of Saul's oath, when Jonathan finds honey *dropping*, he *puts forth the tip of his staff that was in his hand, and dipped it in the honeycomb, and put his hand to his mouth; and his eyes became bright.* 1 Sam. 14:27,28. In fact, Jonathan *sees* so much that he knows the truth. [36] *Jonathan said, "My father has troubled the land; see how my eyes have become bright, because I tasted a little of this honey. How much better if the people had eaten freely today of the spoil of their enemies which they found; for now the slaughter among the Philistines has not been great."* 1 Sam. 14:29,30.

Although Jonathan may be operating at a high consciousness, the people aren't; they even eat blood as they slaughter the sheep, oxen and calves of the enemy. At least Saul is aware enough to tell them to take a rock (build an altar) and slay the animals there. This is Saul's first altar.
But as Saul prepares to attack the Philistines by night, he gets no answer when he inquires of the LORD. So, in intellectual-mind fashion, he asks if the "sin" is in him (that's atypical) – or ... if it's in Jonathan (that's typical). My, how the

---

[36] We have not talked about "staff" for quite a while. Esoterically, Jonathan is dealing with his Kundalini; and it is sweetness and orderliness. And his "eyes become bright"; he can *see!*

intellectual mind loves to be proven right; the sin is almost always in someone else ... right?[37] The only thing that saves Jonathan is that the people recognize that it is Jonathan who has brought the day's victory.

Jonathan is the more-spiritualized intellectual mind. He's so different from Saul that he works independently of his father; but he won't be able to save his father. Eventually **the intellectual mind which is not joined to the spiritual mind will get in trouble.** Saul seals his fate with regard to the Amalekites (descendants of Esau). Samuel tells him that the Lord has instructed that he is to *smite Amalek, and utterly destroy all that they have; do not spare them, but kill both man and woman, infant and suckling, ox and sheep, camel and ass.* 1 Sam. 15:1-3.

We're again at a place where the esoteric takes over. If you remember, Esau was the twin brother of Jacob; but Esau put greater stock in the earthly expression than the spiritual. Now we're being told that Esau's descendants – this nature – must be absolutely eliminated from us. To be *consecrated,* our attention must be *only* on the spiritual.

The Amalekites were the ones against whom Moses fought. When he held up his arm, the Israelites were triumphant, even if he had to have help holding up his arm. Well, we can do this, can't we? Surely, we have enough "oomph" to keep our intellectual mind on the spiritual. Sure we can! So Saul defeats great numbers of Amalekites; he *utterly destroy[s] all the people with the edge of the sword.* The only trouble is that he takes the king, Agag (flame), alive; and *Saul and the people spared Agag, and **the best of the sheep** and of the **oxen** and of the **fatlings**, and the **lambs,** and **all that was good,...; all that was despised and worthless they utterly destroyed.** 1 Sam. 15:9.*

We're certainly like Saul – we know that Samuel said that YHWH said to destroy absolutely everything; but, obviously, we know better. Why waste all these good animals?

---

[37] If he were truly expressing as the King should be expressing, Saul would get an answer at night. Experiences at night have been taking place on the climb since the "time" of Jacob. Saul should be beyond the understanding of Jacob.

We destroyed whatever was *worthless*; isn't that enough? In fact, we're greatly pleased with ourselves. Saul is so self-righteous that he sets up a **monument for himself** at Carmel (planted field) and then *turns and passes on ...down to Gilgal.* 1 Sam. 15:12. This isn't an altar to God that Saul has set up; it's to himself. No wonder he ends up back at the "wheel" again. Do we see ourselves?

We're so much like Saul. We **know** that we have to eliminate those things of Esau, those things from our mind that would "sell our birthright" for a bowl of soup, those things that deny our kingship. Saul once felt the spirit, but then he heard what the world said and hid in the baggage. Like Saul, we may once have felt the spirit, but now the question is what do we now feel about ourselves in our hearts. Samuel knows what Saul feels. Having heard the bleating of lambs and lowing of oxen, Samuel knows Saul has disobeyed. He says: *"Though you are **little in your own eyes**, are you not the head of the tribes of Israel?"* 1 Sam. 15:17.

But as is the habit of the intellect, Saul blames the people, and he embellishes his answer. He answers: *"I have obeyed... the LORD, ... and I have utterly destroyed the Amalekites. But **the people took** of the spoil, sheep and oxen, **the best of the things** devoted to destruction, **to sacrifice to the LORD your God** in Gilgal."* 1 Sam. 15:20,21.

This last part of the quotation shows Saul's basic problem. Although he has felt the spirit, Saul does not "see" the LORD as *his* God; he sees the LORD as *Samuel's* God. Samuel answers Saul with what may be one of the most important verses in the entire Bible. Samuel says: *"Has the LORD as great delight in burnt offerings and sacrifices, as in obeying the voice of the LORD? **Behold, to obey is better than sacrifice, and to hearken than the fat of rams.** For **rebellion is as the sin of divination, and stubbornness is as iniquity and idolatry.** Because you have rejected the word of the LORD, he has also rejected you from being king."* 1 Sam. 15:22,23.

The intellectual mind doesn't like this verse, but we must repeat it: *To obey ... and to hearken* is better than *[sacrificing and] the fat of rams. ... rebellion* is *[as bad as] divination; stubbornness* is *[like] iniquity and idolatry.*

The story of Saul is a tragedy. Here is a man who ostensibly was destined for greatness, yet because of his weakness he falls into failure. And what is his weakness? That's what is so tragic! His only weakness is that he *is little in his own eyes* and, like Aaron, he *transgresses the commandment of the Lord and (Samuel's) words, **because I feared the people and obeyed their voice.*** He rejects the Spirit which he once felt. Although he listens, because of his **fear** Saul does not obey and is rebellious.

We have to stop here for clarification. Saul's actions didn't break many commandments – "just" the **first:** *you shall have no other gods before me.* Ever wonder why it is the *first commandment?* Because, if we disregard the first commandment, there's no hope of following the remaining nine. Do you see that *have no other gods before me* means that we are to **bow to nothing other than "God"** – not even the people. Not even the lesser habits and fears we have within us are to rule us. By disregarding the **first** commandment, Saul had no way of following the LORD's instructions. A lesser consciousness than that of Saul might never have "heard" the instructions. A lesser consciousness would be given another chance; but Saul has been crowned king, and by his disobedience he proves he is not worthy of being king. He must lose his kingship.

How does this apply to us? It applies as we reach the level of kingship; it applies as we feel the spirit come upon us. It is in that instant that the conscious mind recognizes that it is to do God's bidding. At Saul's level of the climb there may be questioning and challenging and doubting if this is the instruction, for Saul does not have internal strength. The true king, however, will not experience the challenging and doubting; but such an *enlightened* view is properly the expression only of one who accepts *the spirit of the LORD* which comes upon him/her – and continues in it. Only such a person is operating at the level of kingship.

We sort of knew this was true, didn't we? A **King** has to feel good enough about himself/herself that he/she would not be found hiding in the baggage. A **King** would wait as he had been instructed; a **King** would not give the sacrifice until Samuel got there, even if Samuel was late.

Since the time of Saul, there have been other supposed "kings" who have also been impatient. You may remember the story of Napoleon's grabbing the French crown out of the hands of Pope Pius VII (whom he had specially invited to crown him Emperor) and

Napoleon Impatiently Crowned Himself

crowning himself and his queen, Josephine. Certainly, Napoleon's was not the act of the **"Kinged"** conscious-mind; this was the act of the little "I" – the unregenerate ego. And the unregenerate ego is going to be replaced. A **King** would have waited for the crowning by the spiritual representative. A **King** would have followed the LORD'S instructions. Once more Saul exposes the truth about himself; yet, he asks Samuel to *"honor [me] before the elders ... and before Israel, and return with me, that I may worship the Lord your God."* 1 Sam. 15:30.

Since Saul sees the LORD only as Samuel's God, it is left to the spiritual representative to right the "wrong." Samuel hews Agag, the symbol of earthly understanding, to pieces. *And Samuel did not see Saul again until the day of his death, **but Samuel grieved over Saul.*** 1 Sam. 15:35.

As soon as our spiritual self (Samuel) recognizes that we are not quite following the first commandment, we are partially a new person. But the old habits of the conscious mind are hard to break; the conscious mind is reluctant to let go of power. Eventually, the LORD prompts Samuel: *"How long will you grieve over Saul, seeing I have rejected him from being king over Israel? Fill your horn with oil, and go..."* 1 Sam. 16:1.

I don't know about you, but I can easily see that in the past I've grieved over situations and people far too long. Probably, this is a characteristic of the carnal mind. Not only are we tied to habits and ways of thinking, we're also tied to familiar individuals and familiar situations. It takes courage to leave the familiar. It takes courage to see that whatever is taking place is intended for the highest good.

Not quite willing to challenge Saul's authority, Samuel goes to Bethlehem carrying a **heifer for sacrifice**, and he invites the elders of the city, including Jesse, to join him to **be consecrated**. He fears Saul. Even this spiritual self isn't quite brave enough to face the intellectual/conscious mind, so it takes a "virginal, feminine, earthly" expression (heifer) for

| **Samuel Given David as Kingly Substitute** |

sacrifice; and after anointing David, Samuel retires to Ramah (feminine, active participle of *to inundate*).

The Spiritual expression pulls itself back. At this point on the climb, our Spiritual Self isn't quite sure of its power; it holds back. At least Samuel goes to the tribe of Judah (praise YHWH) to get his new king. Bethlehem (house of bread) is in Judah.[38] Jesse (from a root which means *to stand out, to exist*) has eight sons, and he parades them past Samuel, beginning with the eldest.

On seeing the first son, Samuel is impressed; surely the Lord will choose him. *But the LORD said to Samuel, "Do not look on his appearance or on the height of his stature, because I have rejected him; for the* **LORD sees not as man sees; man looks on the outward appearance, but the LORD looks on the heart."** 1Sam.16:7. [Not finding one who seems to be the right one for King, Samuel asks if there are any more sons. Jesse answers:] *"There remains yet the* **youngest,** *but behold, he is* **keeping the sheep."** *And Samuel said to Jesse, "Send and fetch him; for* **we will not sit down till he comes here."** *And he sent, and brought him in. Now he [David] was* **ruddy,** *and had* **beautiful eyes,** *and was* **handsome.** *And the LORD said, "Arise, anoint him; for this is he." Then* **Samuel** *took the horn of oil, and* **anointed him** *in the midst of his brothers;* **and the Spirit of the LORD came mightily upon David from that day forward.** 1 Sam. 16:11-13.

---

[38] Compare the two characters. Saul represents *a request* – that of the "son of the right hand" – but he comes from something that is "convex," which cannot absorb; and its experiences resemble a wheel – continually coming around again. On the other hand, David (*to love*) comes from a "house of bread" – that which sustains physical life – and he is upheld by *praise*.

According to one source, the word *David* is an ancient Semitic word for *commander* or *military leader.*[39] Subtly, it emphasizes that we are still *at war*. Remember Moses' request that the LORD *"appoint a man over the congregation, ... who shall lead them out and bring them in; that the congregation of the LORD may not be as sheep which have no shepherd."* Num. 27:16,17 Is it any wonder that David is a "shepherd"?[40] However, his other characteristics are even more meaningful. He is *ruddy*, i.e., red haired or of rosy complexion. Notice that the word *'admoniy* (ruddy) originates with the word *'adam.* David returns our expression back to the individual consciousness which was originally designed – he/she who is "naked" before the LORD – and unashamed.

"Man of War" Necessary To Return Us to "Naked"

Like Saul, David is "handsome," i.e., of balanced proportions; but David's *handsome* is almost a pun, meaning of *good sight*, for the most important characteristic of David is that he has "beautiful" *eyes*. This David as King may lead us to *seeing*.[41] Saul, on the other hand, cannot *see*; for he *is little in [his] own eyes*.

As much as we would like to see Saul triumph, he cannot; for Saul points out a subtle difference experienced by climbers. It is the difference between the climber who "once" feels the Spirit and then concentrates his/her attention on the psychic, as opposed to the climber who feels the Spirit, notices the psychic, then concentrates his/her attention on the Spirit which comes.

---

[39] *The New Jerusalem Bible,* p. 365, fn. d.

[40] Esotericists see the Hebraic "shepherds" as symbolic. Remember, "sheep" were repulsive to Pharaoh, and according to followers of the Zodiac, the age of the Bull is replaced by the age of the Ram. With the Christ Jesus, the age of the Ram is replaced by the age of the Fish – thus, most of Jesus' followers were "fishermen."

[41] The "handsome" for Saul is *towb* (beautiful) 1 Sam. 9:2; "handsome" for David is *towb ro'iy ro'iy.* 1 Sam. 16:12 Apparently, the *ro'iy ro'iy* (which is not translated) accents *towb* (beautiful) with the double emphasis *ro'iy* (**of good sight**).

*Now **the Spirit of the LORD departed from Saul, and an evil spirit from the LORD tormented him.** And Saul's servants said to him, "... seek out a man who is skillful in playing the lyre; and **when the evil spirit from God is upon you, he will play it, and you will be well."** So Saul [agreed]. ... One of the young men answered, "... I have seen a son of Jesse the Bethlehemite, who is **skillful in playing,** a **man of valor,** a **man of war, prudent in speech,** and a **man of good presence;** and **the LORD is with him."** Therefore Saul sent messengers to Jesse, and said, "Send me **David** your son, **who is with the sheep."** And Jesse took an ass laden with bread, and a skin of wine and a kid, and sent them by David his son to Saul. And David came to Saul, and entered his service. And **Saul loved him greatly, and he became his armor-bearer.*** 1 Sam. 16:14-21.

The old English teacher in me "bristles" at this last line. Here is a perfect example of an "indefinite pronoun"... *he became his armor-bearer.* Given the subject of the sentence, it is saying "Saul" became his (David's) armor-bearer. Of course, we know that the reverse is the literal interpretation; but what about the esoteric? Remember, Saul still represents our conscious mind, our intellect.

Saul is still king. Whether or not our spiritual self is "seeing" the need for a new king, the intellectual mind still rules us. But the intellectual mind recognizes that it is being displaced, and Saul feels himself to be tormented by an *"evil" spirit from the LORD.*[42]

Conscious Mind Which "Sees" Self Separated from God Feels Pressed by "Evil" Spirit.

It is hard to say what the purely intellectual mind knows. The intuitional mind knows that the LORD is I Am, and it knows that "evil" simply means the *opposite* of "live." The intuitional mind can infer that it is Saul's own exterior understanding that produces these periods which appear to be the opposite of "live." Therefore, it is necessary for David – the man **of war, of valor, of prudent speech, of good presence, of the Lord** – to minister to this exterior understanding. In this sense, David is Saul's armor-bearer; but at the same time, Saul, the conscious mind, "bears" the "armor" that protects this

---

[42] In today's terms, we would probably call Saul's problem *depression*, possibly even *schizophrenia* (which Webster defines as *disintegration of personality*).

fledgling man of war in us. For a time, the "David" in us is protected by Saul, but this situation won't last forever. Finally, David must become King; so, change takes place.

Again we're besieged by those pesky Philistinians! Only this time, they've got this "giant" – Goliath (from a primitive root meaning *to denude, to exile, to reveal*).[43]

Now the Philistines gathered their armies...; and they were ... encamped between Socoh (to shut in; to entwine) *and Azekah* (help), *in Ephesdammim* (boundary of blood drops). *And **Saul and the men of Israel** were ... encamped in the valley of Elah,* (fem. of oak, i.e., strong tree) ... *And the Philistines stood on the mountain on the one side, and Israel stood on the mountain on the other side, with a valley between them. And there came out from... the Philistines a champion named Goliath, of Gath* (wine-press; "feeling" them out), *whose height was six cubits and a span. He had a **helmet of bronze** on his head, and he was armed with a **coat of mail**, and the weight of the coat **was five thousand shekels of bronze**. And he had greaves of bronze upon his legs, and a javelin of bronze slung **between his shoulders**. And the shaft of his spear was like a weaver's beam, and his spear's head weighed **six hundred***

> **"Sensual" Judgment Heavily Armed**

*shekels of iron; and his shield-bearer went before him. He stood and shouted to the ranks of Israel, "Why have you come out to draw up for battle? Am I not a Philistine, and are you not servants of Saul? Choose a man for yourselves, and **let him come down to me**. If he is able to fight with me and kill me, then we will be your servants; but **if I prevail against him and kill him, then you shall be our servants and serve us.**" And the Philistine said, "... **give me a man, that we may fight together.**" When Saul and all Israel heard ..., they were dismayed and greatly afraid.* 1 Sam. 17:1-11.

All our old habits and mindsets hear the words coming from that which would "denude" them, and they accept the words as true. It is only this "fledgling" within us – this young "Self" that has recently been anointed, this "Self" upon which the Spirit of the LORD comes mightily – for whom the words have no effect. Even the words of Saul (the conscious mind) don't dissuade us.

David is not like Saul. David came prepared with "parched grain," with "ten" loaves, and with "ten" cheeses, but David left his "gifts" with the keeper of the baggage – and stepped out. David is unafraid. He has had practice fighting the "carnal" world. As a shepherd, whenever a lion or a bear

---

[43] How truly lovely is the English language. Notice: If you are **not denuded**, you are **nude**. David, our "ruddy" champion, is going to accomplish the reversal of what has been going on since the time of Noah.

took a lamb from the flock, he would go after it and strike it and "deliver" the lamb out of its mouth; and if the lion or bear attacked him, *I caught him by his beard, and smote him and killed him.* 1 Sam. 17:34,35.

David has the confidence which Saul lacks. He "listens" to this spirit of the LORD which comes upon him. He is as ready to act in this situation as against the animals which threatened his flocks. He says: *"...this uncircumcised Philistine shall be like one of them, seeing he has defied the armies of the living God."And David said, "The LORD who delivered me from the paw of the lion and from the paw of the bear, will deliver me from the hand of this Philistine." And Saul said to David, "Go, and the LORD be with you!"* 1 Sam. 17:36,37.

The intellect/conscious mind blesses the younger portion in its planned attack upon that which "denudes," but the conscious mind doesn't see that its ways are

We Can't Use the Intellect's Armor

not God's ways.[44] *Then Saul clothed David with his armor; he put a helmet of bronze on his head, and clothed him with a coat of mail. And David ... tried in vain to go, for he was not used to [the armor.] Then David said to Saul, "I cannot go with these; for I am not used to them." And David put them off. Then he took his staff in his hand, and chose five smooth stones from the brook, and put them in his shepherd's bag ... his sling was in his hand, and he drew near to the Philistine.* 1 Sam. 38-40.

If you have any doubt whether you use the armor of the intellect, anticipate doing something out of the norm. Just think about doing anything contrary to your usual habits... maybe changing your career! If you are as I am, just the mental suggestion prompts immediate reactions from the conscious mind. The conscious mind will put all sorts of "fetters" out to protect us. If it's not our conscious mind putting them out, it will be the logical world that will question the wisdom of such an action. ... Likely as not, we'll back down.We're not King, yet; David is ... almost.

---

[44] Obviously, we must utilize those things which we are used to using. But notice, we are stripped to having "nothing on the outer." The **staff** is the Kundalini, activated with the anointing; the **sling** has been ours from youth; the **5 stones** are the senses that have been smoothed by the *waters*. It is **only what is *within* us** that **can challenge that which *denudes.***

And ...the Philistine ... disdained him; for he was but a youth, ruddy and comely in appearance. ... **David** *said to the Philistine, "You come to me with a sword and with a spear and with a javelin; but I come to you in the name of the LORD of hosts,...* **This day the LORD will deliver you into my hand, and I will strike you down, and cut off your head; and I will give the dead bodies of the ...** *Philistines* **this day to the birds of the air and to the wild beasts** *of the earth;* **that all the earth may know that there is a God in Israel, and that all this assembly may know that the LORD saves not with sword and spear; for the battle is the LORD'S and he will give you into our hand."** 1 Sam. 17:41-47.

When the Philistine arose and came and drew near to meet David, David ran quickly toward the battle line to meet the Philistine. And **David** *put his hand in his bag and* **took out a stone, and slung it,** *and struck the Philistine on his forehead;* **the stone sank into his forehead,** *and he fell on his face to the ground. So* **David** *prevailed... with a sling and with a stone, and struck the Philistine, and killed him;* **there was no sword in the hand of David.** 1 Sam. 17:48-50.

Hang loose! We may see more than the literal story if we recognize that *sword* (desolation) **is the opposite of** *Promised Land*.[45] **Both are states of mind,** but we mistakenly think that they

> **"Sword" Indicates Desolation**

are finite conditions. The problem is that we are these "denuded" creatures who "see" only in physical terms. However, we can decide to be this "David," the "warrior" who feels the spirit of the LORD. We, too, can recognize that *desolation* doesn't fit us, and we can approach the threatening *giant* of the "senses," armed with a "stone" for building and a "sling." I wonder if "sling" isn't the most important term here. Strong enigmatically defines *sling* as coming from a root which means *into light forms*. Hang loose! It depends what you put in the sling. If it's a stone, it goes to one place and does its work; if it's a watery substance, it spreads the substance out in ever-decreasing amounts, eventually ending in something blended fully with light. If you don't believe me, "sling" a water balloon at something; as the balloon bursts, see what you get.

The narrative continues: *Then* **David** *ran and stood over the Philistine, and* **took his [Goliath's] sword and drew it out of its sheath, and killed him, and cut off his head with it.** *When the Philistines saw that their champion*

---

[45] Strong relates "sword" to a root implying *desolation*. "Stone" relates to *building*, and "sling" relates to the *action of "slinging."*

was dead, they fled. And the men of Israel and Judah rose with a shout and pursued the Philistines as far as Gath and the gates of Ekron,... *(54)And David took the **head of the Philistine and brought it to Jerusalem***; but he put his [Goliath's]* **armor** *in his [David's] tent.* 1 Sam. 17:51-54.

The Philistines in us are eliminated by their own "desolation." And the head of the ex-champion is brought to Jerusalem ([Salem] from a primitive root *to be safe* or *to be completed* added to dual [two hills] but *a true pointing; founded peaceful*). We have heard little of Jerusalem other than its being the city of the Jebusites, but from now on it will be quite important. It was the old Salem; it is the city which David will choose as his own, and it will become the capital of Israel. Eventually, it will house the Temple, and it will have symbolic meaning for the remainder of the Bible.[46]

We have met Saul's successor, but Saul is still king. Nevertheless, his fate has been sealed, and he knows it. He tries to delay his passing. He, himself tries to kill David, twice

Saul's Decline – the explanation being that *Saul was afraid of David, because the LORD was with him but had departed from Saul.* 1 Sam. 18:12. Saul hopes David will be killed battling the Philistines, but David always survives. And when David brings Saul 200 Philistine foreskins he has to make him son-in-law as he had promised. *Saul was still more afraid of David. So Saul was David's enemy continually.* 1 Sam. 18:29.

On the surface we have a case of jealousy, complicated by paranoia. Saul is unsure of himself and so anyone who *is*

---

[46] *The New Jerusalem Bible* points out that verse *54 was added, since Jerusalem was not captured until later (2 Sam. 5:6-9) and since David had no tent of his own. *The Prophets*'s version makes it even more confusing, adding a footnote that says that David ... *brought it to Jerusalem* after he conquered it. (*The Prophets*, p. 138.) Our intellectual mind can add that the sword and armor have a monetary value; the head has no value, but my assessment is that the verse was added for symbolic reasons. The Philistine giant's *head*, i.e., that which directs (the conscious mind) is deposited "at that place which will eventually lead to completion." But the *sword* and *armor* are kept for a later date, and placed in David's *tent*, i.e., that which is susceptible to change. That way, David has access to the sword and armor.

Esoterically, verse *54 may be making a definite statement regarding the climber's achievement at this point. Notice, David is **not** king, but he has "control" over **"5"** (the senses) to the point of having all **"4"** directions covered. It is *completion*. Combining the two numbers, David is at the level of the initiate, **"9,"** but he is not the Christed man.

sure of himself is perceived as an enemy. This happens, doesn't it? The esoteric is even more revealing. If Saul represents the intellect/conscious-mind portion of us, what does David represent? David represents the portion of us called the Christ-mind. This innocent, super, loyal, perfect part of us that communes directly with the LORD and continually battles the Philistines for the conscious mind, to the point of recognizing (and consecrating) the duality x 100 nature of the senses. This innocent Self does not "buy into" the paranoia produced by the subconscious; it knows the **truth** of itself, that **it is the child of God**.

The "game" continues for at least "two" years, with Saul continually inviting others to slay David. David escapes because Michal (Saul's daughter) saves him. Finally, it comes to the place where (with Jonathan's help) David admits that Saul intends to kill him. In the esoteric, the Christ-mind of us has to hold to its knowledge of who it is, regardless of what the outer picture is.

Therefore, David leaves the house of the king, stopping by Nob (to germinate) where Ahimelech (similar to the king) is priest ... *and Ahimelech came to meet David trembling, and said to him, "Why are you alone, and no one with you?" And David said to Ahimelech the priest, "The king has charged me with a matter, and said to me, 'Let no one know anything of the matter about which I send you, and with which I have charged you.' I have made an appointment with the young men for such and such a place. Now then, what have you at hand? Give me five loaves of bread, or whatever is here." And the priest answered David, "I have no common bread at hand, but there is holy bread; if only the young men have kept themselves from women." And David answered the priest, "Of a truth ...the vessels of the young men are holy, even when it is a common journey; how much more today will their vessels be holy?" So the priest gave him the holy bread; for there was no bread there but the bread of the Presence, which is removed from before the LORD, to be replaced by hot bread on the day it is taken away.* 1 Sam. 21:1-6.

On the surface, David seems to be lying **David Is On King's Business** to this priest who is somewhat allied with Saul, doesn't he? But esoterically, David isn't lying. The Christ-mind *is* on the "King's" business, and the business must be undertaken in secret. The climb cannot be made with the climber talking about what is going on. The "business" of the climber must be kept to himself/herself. Interestingly, David asks for only ½ the number of loaves of bread which he originally brought to Saul (see page 289). Only **holy bread – that which is set aside and new each day** – is available; but it is available only if the "young men" have been celibate.[47] *... And* **David said** *to Ahimelech,* **"And have you not here a spear or a sword at hand?** *For I have brought neither my sword nor my weapons with me, because the* **king's business required haste."** *And the priest said,* **"The sword of Goliath the Philistine, whom you killed in the valley of Elah, behold, it is here wrapped in a cloth behind the ephod;** *if you will take that, take it, for there is none but that here." And David said,* **"There is none like that; give it to me."** *And David rose and fled that day from Saul, and went to Achish* (serpent-charmer) *the king of Gath* (wine press, fortune). 1 Sam. 21:7-10.

The King's business does require "haste." When it is appropriate, we must become King, but we must stay prepared. Jesus used the image of the faithful virgins who keep their lamps trimmed and their oil near at hand. It is not that David has neglected his *wick and his oil*; it is that David has "had no sword." He has had no "desolation" in him, but now it's time to accept "desolation." And without doubt, there is no sword like Goliath's; it is like Excalibur. When David defeated Goliath, he conquered that *which would denude*. Now he's armed with the "desolation" which such understanding brings. Two *negatives* make a *positive,* and David progresses on the "King's business." He has half the number of "loaves" owed to him; he has in his grasp the *"desolation"* of *that which would denude;* and he has 600 chaste "young men" waiting for him.[48]

---

[47] It is interesting that in the *Grail* literature, celibacy is necessary for the seeker of the Grail. The requirement for *celibacy* is not because *sex* is considered a "sin," but because *sex* is so closely tied to an earthly expression. The *holy bread* is available only for those who have risen above the earthly expression. We probably should also see this occurrence as relating to Jesus' five loaves.

[48] Six hundred men of Benjamin had to steal women; now there are 600 young men who have no need of women. We are dealing with **6,** that which precedes earthly completion (**2 x 3**). It is ✡, the star of David multiplied by two levels, i.e., 100.

From this simple beginning, David will eventually become King; but first he flees to a place that represents a wine press, ruled by a "serpent-charmer."

Our lives are like grapes, aren't they? Ever see what a "wine-press" does to a grape? It is much like what the "threshing floor" does to wheat. But the "serpent charmer" is most esoteric. The esoteric sees the "power" of man as a "serpent," possibly one which has to be "charmed" into operation. *David was much afraid of A'chish,* and to escape, he feigns madness. David's pretended madness could mean something else. It might be saying that David had acquired greater psychic power. Nevertheless, David runs to the cave of Adullam (resting place), where his brothers and all his father's house come to join him, as does *every one who was in distress, and every one who was in debt, and every one who was discontented, gathered to him; and he became captain over them. And there were with him about four hundred men.* 1 Sam. 22:2.

If we were completely happy with our lives, there would be no reason to read this book. If we were completely happy with the rule of the intellect/conscious mind, we would not follow after the Christ-mind. If Saul was not pursuing us, we wouldn't run to the cave of Adullam – where the Christ-mind aligns us to the "perfect" expression.

What more do we have to learn from our association with the intellect/conscious mind? We have to learn infinite patience. We cannot replace the intellect/conscious mind until the appropriate time. David has two chances to kill Saul, but he works no evil toward Saul. *... David is in the wilderness of Engedi* (fountain of a kid). *Then Saul took three thousand chosen men ... and went to seek David and his men ... And... there was a cave; and Saul went in to relieve himself.... David and his men were sitting in the innermost parts of the cave. And the men of David said to him, "... the LORD said to you, 'Behold, I will give your enemy into your hand, and you shall do to him as it shall seem good to you.'" Then David arose and stealthily cut off the skirt of Saul's robe. And afterward David's heart smote him, because he had cut off Saul's skirt. He said to his men, "The LORD forbid that I should do this thing to my lord, the LORD'S anointed, to put forth my hand against him, seeing he is the LORD'S anointed." So David...did not permit them to attack Saul. And Saul rose up and left the cave, and went upon his way.*

296

Afterward David .. went out of the cave, and called after Saul, "My lord the king!" And when Saul looked behind him, **David bowed with his face to the earth, and did obeisance**. And David said to Saul, "Why do you listen to the words of men who say, 'Behold, David seeks your hurt'? **Lo, this day your eyes have seen how the LORD gave you today into my hand in the cave; and some bade me kill you, but I spared you. I said, 'I will not put forth my hand against my lord; for he is the LORD'S anointed.'** See, my father, see the skirt of your robe in my hand; for by the fact that I cut off the skirt of your robe, and did not kill you, you may know and see that there is no wrong or treason in my hands. I have not sinned against you, though you hunt my life to take it. May the LORD judge between me and you, **may the LORD avenge me upon you; but my hand shall not be against you.** As the proverb of the ancients says, 'Out of the wicked comes forth wickedness'; but my hand shall not be against you. [You chase something that is meaningless.]... **May the LORD therefore be judge,.... and deliver me from your hand."** ...

Saul said, "Is this your voice, my son David?" And Saul lifted up his voice and wept. He said to David, **"You are more righteous than I; for you have repaid me good, whereas I have repaid you evil. And you have declared this day how you have dealt well with me, in that you did not kill me when the LORD put me into your hands.** For if a man finds his enemy, will he let him go away safe? So may the LORD reward you with good for what you have done to me this day. And now, behold, **I know that** you shall surely be king, and that **the kingdom of Israel shall be established in your hand.** Swear to me therefore by the LORD that you will not cut off my descendants after me, and that you will not destroy my name out of my father's house." And David swore this to Saul. Then Saul went home; but David and his men went up to the stronghold. 1 Sam. 24

The process whereby our carnal mind is replaced by our spiritual mind is lengthy. It may involve numerous opportunities for the spiritual-self to fail; for the challenge is for the spiritual-self to be unlike the carnal. Here David has the chance to kill that enemy which pursues him. The carnal expression (Saul) would have had no qualms about killing David, but David has a higher understanding. He **will not put forth [his] hand against ... the LORD'S anointed.** David hasn't escaped the carnal mind. He doesn't bless Saul, and he hopes that the LORD will punish Saul. David is not the Christ. But David allows the Christ-mind – that which "sees" that Saul is the LORD'S anointed – to determine his action.

This story is useless unless we relate it to ourselves. Maybe the question to be asked is "Who is the LORD'S anointed?" Have we ever met people in whose eyes we can do no *right*? In most cases, we just avoid such people; but if we are on the climb, I'll bet that we keep running into them. Jesus, eventually will tell us to bless them and then wipe the dust from our feet, but David isn't at the level of the Christ; the David consciousness must address them first.

Esotericists would tell us that only that which is within us comes to us. Therefore, these people or challenges echo something within ourselves. But they cannot be "chopped out" as the carnal mind would try to do; they must be approached with deference. According to psychology and myth, most often our challenges come from our subconscious minds; they are related to things far distant and likely forgotten. David encounters Saul in a cave, and David "snips away" a portion of his challenge – just enough to prove to Saul that David has spared him.

If we are on the climb, we will finally recognize that **all challenges** (be they individuals, illness, or conditions) **come to us for our betterment**. Only if we are willing to let Saul go, without harming him – even promising that we will not harm his descendants – are we worthy of advancement. For the second time, David refuses to kill Saul, and he says: *"Do not destroy him; for who can put forth his hand against the LORD'S anointed, and be guiltless? As the LORD lives, the LORD will smite him; or his day shall come to die; or he shall go down into battle and perish. The LORD forbid that I should put forth my hand against the LORD'S anointed; but take now the spear that is at his head, and the jar of water, and let us go."* 1 Sam. 26:9-11.

> **All That Comes to Us Is for Our Betterment**

David goes to the other side of the valley, standing *"afar off on the top of the Mountain, with a great space between them,"* and David calls to Abner and holds up the jar of water and the spear, chiding:*"... Why ... have you not kept watch over your lord the king? ... As the LORD lives, you deserve to die, because you have not kept watch over your lord, the LORD'S anointed.And now see where the king's spear is, and the jar of water that was at his head."* 1 Sam. 26:15,16.

Then Saul said, "I have done wrong; return, my son David, for I will no more do you harm, because my life was precious in your eyes this day; behold, I have played the fool, and have erred exceedingly."

298

*And David made answer, "**Here is the spear, O king!** Let one of the young men come over and fetch it. **The LORD rewards every man for his righteousness and his faithfulness; for the LORD gave you into my hand today, and I would not put forth my hand against the LORD'S anointed.** Behold, as your life was precious this day in my sight, so may my life be precious in the sight of the LORD, and **may he deliver me out of all tribulation."* [49]

Then Saul said to David, "Blessed be you, my son David! You will do many things and will succeed in them." So David went his way, and Saul returned to his place. 1 Sam. 26: 21-25.

There is a great difference between the expression of David and the expression of Saul. David's fear is of Saul; his hope is in the LORD. David's "way" is to

Saul and David Are Far Apart In Expression

return to the "serpent-charmer," where, ostensibly, he serves the Philistines. But while there, David totally "eliminates" *the inhabitants of the land from of old* – even as far as Egypt. And David stays with the Philistines for 16 months. (4x4) Although he thinks he's still going to "perish" at the hands of Saul, David still keeps "cleansing the land."

Saul's fear is of the LORD. He wants the strength he used to get from Samuel; but Samuel is dead. Saul's "place" is so nebulous that he doesn't recognize that he, himself is also among the "dead"? He sees threats in those who expose truth. He eliminates all of the mediums and wizards from the land; but, nevertheless, *he [is] afraid, and his heart tremble[s] greatly.* And when he inquires of the Lord, the Lord does not answer – *either by dreams, or by Urim, or by prophets.* Imagine his wondering what's so different now than from his youth when the spirit came upon him? No wonder he visits the witch of Endor.

Isn't it just like us to think we can recapture our triumphs by returning to the *old*? Saul, disguised so that the witch won't

Samuel's Ghost Warns Saul of Coming Death

---

[49] In a very "hang-loose" statement, might we agree that if we do not *keep watch* over the *LORD's anointed*, we are *of the "dead."* What goes unsaid is that **we, too, are the LORD's anointed.** In an equally hang-loose exposition – Gaskell defines *a spear* as "a symbol of the Divine Ray of Life through all nature, which puts an end to illusion." Therefore, the Christ-mind destroys the illusion of the conscious mind – its "delusion" that the physical is "reality." The "spear" makes obvious to the conscious mind the truth of the divinity of all life.

recognize him, asks to speak to Samuel; and as Samuel rises from the earth, *Saul knew that it was Samuel, and he bowed with his face to the ground, and did obeisance. Then Samuel said to Saul, "Why have you disturbed me by bringing me up?" Saul answered, "I am in great distress; for the Philistines are warring against me, and God has turned away from me and answers me no more, either by prophets or by dreams; therefore I have summoned you to tell me what I shall do." And Samuel said, "Why then do you ask me, since the LORD has turned from you and become your enemy? The LORD has done to you as he spoke by me; for the LORD has torn the kingdom out of your hand, and given it to your neighbor, David. Because you did not obey the voice of the LORD, and did not carry out his fierce wrath against Amalek, therefore the LORD has done this thing to you this day. Moreover the LORD will give Israel also with you into the hand of the Philistines; and tomorrow you and your sons shall be with me; the LORD will give the army of Israel also into the hand of the Philistines." Then Saul fell at once full length upon the ground, filled with fear because of the words of Samuel; and there was no strength in him, for he had eaten nothing all day and all night.* 1 Sam. 28:14-20.

Isn't it interesting how the same old "sins" plague us – whether or not we've had triumphs in between. It isn't the "sins" that are the problem. It's that the "sins" reveal who we are; they reveal what we are "seeing" and "saying." Saul has yet to eliminate the habits of Esau's descendants; therefore, Saul still places no value on his birthright. Since Saul has not eliminated them, they continue to plague the area; and while David and his men are out, the Amalekites overcome Ziklag (a town which David and his men have been given) and burn it with fire, taking *their wives and sons and daughters... captive.... David's two wives also had been taken captive, ...And David was greatly distressed; for the people spoke of stoning him, ... But David strengthened himself in the LORD his God. And David said to Abiathar the priest, the son of Ahimelech, "Bring me the ephod." ... And David inquired of the LORD, "Shall I pursue after this band? Shall I overtake them?" He answered him, "Pursue; for you shall surely overtake and shall surely rescue." So David and the six hundred men who were with him [set out] and they came to the brook Besor... David... [pursued with] four hundred men; two hundred stayed behind, who were too exhausted to cross the brook Besor.* 1 Sam. 30 2-10.

Conveniently, David's men find an Egyptian who had been enslaved by the Amalekites, and he leads David to the enemy camp. *And when he had taken him down, behold, they were spread abroad over all the land, eating and drinking and dancing, because of all the great spoil they had taken from the land of the Philistines and from the land of Judah. And David smote them from twilight until the evening of the next day; and not a man of them escaped, except four hundred young men, who mounted camels and fled.*

300

David recovered all that the Amalekites had taken; and David rescued his two wives. Nothing was missing, whether small or great, sons or daughters, spoil or anything that had been taken; David brought back all. David also captured all the flocks and herds; and the people drove those cattle before him, and said, "This is David's spoil." 1 Sam. 30: 16-20.

*Then David came to the two hundred men, who had been too exhausted to follow David, and who had been left at the brook Besor; and they went out to meet David ... and when **David** drew near ... he **saluted them**. Then all the wicked and base fellows among the men who had gone with David said, "Because they did not go with us, we will not give them any of the spoil which we have recovered, except that each man may lead away his wife and children, and depart." But David said, "**You shall not do so**, my brothers, **with what the LORD has given us; he has preserved us and given into our hand the band that came against us....For as his share is who goes down into the battle, so shall his share be who stays by the baggage; they shall share alike.**"* 1 Sam. 30:21-25.

My intuition tells me there is some hang-loose lesson here. On the surface, the disagreement comes from those who actively participated in the rout of the Amalekites; they contend that those who were too tired to proceed, should not share in the spoils. The disagreement is not as important as David's conclusion. Milton says it nicely: *They also serve who only stand and wait.*[50]

It is up to David to eliminate the Amalekites; it is up to the David-like portion of us to eliminate that within us which "does not accept its birthright." It is up to the "loving" King within us **to be righteous.** This is the climb; but we must know that part of the climb is to stand quietly and wait – like those who wait at the brook Besor. [51] And to these portions which stay at Besor, an equal portion will be given. Only the 400 fight; 200 stay back; together they are 600 – the star of David.

*Now the Philistines fought against Israel; and the **men of Israel fled before the Philistines**, and fell slain on Mount Gilboa (*gushing fountain). *And the*

---

[50] John Milton, *On the late Massacre in Piedmont;* Bartlett, *Familiar Quotations.*

[51] One concordance defines *Besor* as *fresh;* but Young's concordance points out that the brook (a small body of running water) runs directly into the sea (the full expression).

*Philistines overtook Saul and his sons; and **the Philistines*** ┌─────────┐
slew Jonathan and Abinadab and Malchishua, the sons of │ **Saul and** │
Saul. *The battle pressed hard upon Saul, and the archers* │ **Three Sons** │
found him; and he was badly wounded ... Then Saul said to │ **Die at Gilboa** │
*his armor-bearer, "**Draw your sword, and thrust me through*** └─────────┘
**with it, lest these uncircumcised come and thrust me through, and make sport of
me."** *But **his armor-bearer would not;** for he feared greatly. Therefore **Saul took
his own sword, and fell upon it.** And when his armor-bearer saw that Saul was
dead, **he also fell upon his sword**, and died with him. **Thus Saul died, and his
three sons, and his armor-bearer, and all his men, on the same day together.** And
when the men of Israel who were on the other side of the valley and those beyond
the Jordan saw that the men of Israel had fled and that Saul and his sons were
dead, they forsook their cities and fled; and the Philistines came and dwelt in them.
On the morrow, when the **Philistines** came to strip the slain, they **found Saul and
his three sons** fallen on Mount Gilboa. And **they cut off his head, and stripped off
his armor**, and sent messengers throughout the land of the Philistines, to carry the
good news to their idols and to the people. They put his **armor in the temple of
Ashtaroth**; and they fastened his body to the wall of Beth-shan* (house of security).
*But when the **inhabitants of Jabeshgilead** heard what the Philistines had done to
Saul, all **the valiant men** arose, and went all night, and **took the body of Saul and
the bodies of his sons from the wall of Beth-shan; and they came to Jabesh and
burnt them there.** And they took their **bones** and **buried them under the tamarisk
tree** in Jabesh* (dry, dried away), *and fasted seven days.* 1 Sam. 31.

Saul doesn't rate an *oak*; his expression, except for one brief moment, has been "dry," certainly not the expression that represents an environment for a strong, productive tree.[52] And his death is less than honorable. [53] His only accomplishment is to produce sons: Ishbaal (man of shame), who survives him, and three warrior sons, Jonathan (*Jehovah* [self existent or eternal] *given* [bring forth]), Abinadab (father of generosity) and Malchishua

---

[52] Trees symbolize the expression of he/she associated with it. The more water a tree requires, the more advanced is the structure. If you remember, the supports for the Tabernacle were acacia wood. The *acacia* (or sycamore) is a tree, capable of surviving drought. The *tamarisk* is more like a bush. The *palm* is erect, but requires water and has few branches and little shade. The *oak*, obviously requires much water, it is strong, and it provides great shade.

[53] There are two versions of Saul's death. The first has Saul falling on his own sword, (1 Sam. 31:4) but the second version has a young Amalekite assisting Saul in his death. (2 Sam. 1:1-16.) The numbers involved in the latter suggest esoteric importance. The dishonor is greater than just Saul's suicide (from *cowardice* as opposed to ritual suicide). His body is beheaded and then hung up for all to see. *Beheading* indicates that "a certain nature" has to be eliminated from us; it is accomplished by beheading – a determined effort of the conscious mind to reverse the sub-conscious. Goliath (that which *denudes*) was beheaded; John the Baptist will be beheaded.

302

(to take counsel/to shout [halloo]; king of riches); but they are all killed at Gilboa.[54]

> *After the death of Saul,...* **on the third day**... *a man came from Saul's camp, with his clothes rent and earth upon his head. And when he came to David, he fell to the ground and did obeisance. David said to him, ..."How did it go? Tell me."*
>
> *And he answered, "The people have fled from the battle, and many of the people also have fallen and are dead; and* **Saul and his son Jonathan are also dead.**"
>
> *Then David said to the young man who told him, "How do you know that Saul and his son Jonathan are dead?" And the young man who told him said, "By chance I happened to be on Mount Gilboa; and* **there was Saul leaning upon his spear**; *and lo, the chariots and the horsemen were close upon him. And when he looked behind him, he saw me, and called to me. And I answered, 'Here I am.' And he said to me, 'Who are you?' I answered him, 'I am an Amalekite.' And he said to me, 'Stand beside me and slay me; for anguish has seized me, and yet my life still lingers.' So I stood beside him, and slew him, because I was sure that he could not live after he had fallen;* **and I took the crown which was on his head and the armlet which was on his arm, and I have brought them here to my lord.**" 2 Sam. 1:1-10.

When David is informed of the battle's outcome by an Amalekite (descendant of Esau) "messenger" who anticipates reward, David is heartsick. He had just gained Saul's attention, and now Saul and his sons are no more. Saul had just ceased to war against David; David never enjoyed the peace. He had never stopped loving Saul, and he greatly loved Jonathan. So it is with us; we never "abandon" our intellect/conscious-mind expression.

> *David said to him (the Amalekite), "How is it you were not afraid to put forth your hand to destroy the LORD'S anointed?" Then David called one of the young men and said, "Go, fall upon him." And he smote him so that he died. And David said to him,* **"Your blood be upon your head; for your own mouth has testified against you, saying, 'I have slain the LORD'S anointed.'"**2 Sam 1-16.

David has no qualms about killing *the messenger*. Like his ancestor Esau, the *messenger* had no regard for his "birthright;" he slew the LORD'S anointed. And David laments for Saul and Jonathan.

---

[54] Notice the difference with the first listing of Saul's sons: *Now the sons of Saul were Jonathan, Ishvi (to adjust), and Malchishua; and the names of his two daughters were these: the name of the first-born was Merab (increase, esp. in number) and the name of the younger Michal(rivulet).* 1 Sam. 14:49. Apparently Saul did *adjust* during his lifetime.

David's Lamentation

Thy glory, O Israel, is slain upon thy high places! How are the mighty fallen!
Tell it not in Gath, ... lest the daughters of the Philistines rejoice,
lest the daughters of the uncircumcised exult.
Ye mountains of Gilboa, let there be no dew or rain upon you, ...
For there the shield of the mighty was defiled, the shield of Saul,
not anointed with oil.
From the blood of the slain, from the fat of the mighty, **the bow of Jonathan**
turned not back, and the sword of Saul returned not empty.
Saul and Jonathan, beloved and lovely! In life and in death they were not
divided; they were swifter than eagles, they were stronger than lions.
Ye daughters of Israel, weep over Saul, who clothed you daintily in scarlet,
who put ornaments of gold upon your apparel.
How are the mighty fallen in the midst of the battle!

Jonathan lies slain upon thy high places.
I am distressed for you, my brother Jonathan; very pleasant have you been to me;
your love to me was wonderful, passing the love of women.
How are the mighty fallen, and the weapons of war perished!

2 Sam. 1:19-27.

David always says things for us, doesn't he? Notice that the last line has an exclamation point, not a question mark. Isn't this the truth of our lives? Those things that we once considered *so* important become unimportant! The "mighty" fall! Those "weapons" within us which were constantly warring finally perish. Saul was never David's enemy; **Jonathan** was "ever" David's friend. We and David lose/loose both in this war which takes place as we climb.

DAVID by Michelangelo.

And David danced before the LORD with all his might; and David was girded with a linen ephod. So David and all the house of Israel brought up the ark of the LORD with shouting, and with the sound of the horn. 2 Sam. 6:14,15.

Chapter Twelve

The Kings: David and Solomon

The LORD is my shepherd, I shall not want; he makes me lie down in green pastures. He leads me beside still waters; he restores my soul. He leads me in paths of righteousness for his name's sake. Even though I walk through the valley of the shadow of death, I fear no evil; for thou art with me; thy rod and thy staff, they comfort me. Thou preparest a table before me in the presence of my enemies; thou anointest my head with oil, my cup overflows. Surely goodness and mercy shall follow me all the days of my life; and I shall dwell in the house of the LORD for ever. Psalm 23: *A Psalm of David.*

This is the Psalm (song) of the "righteous person." The *righteous* one **sees** and **says** his oneness with the Lord. The *righteous* one recognizes the blessings, the protection, the exaltation, and the selection of himself/herself. In addition, the *righteous* one recognizes the "consecration" necessary on his/her part.[1]

As I was teaching a Bible study class several years ago, I asked the members of the group which of the Biblical characters was their favorite. I was somewhat surprised that the greater portion of them (particularly the men) replied that it was David. Their reason was that he was most like how they saw themselves – having received the spirit of the LORD, but "failing" because of human weakness.

Are We Like David?

In some ways, the description nicely summarizes David. As do we, David has to contend with the intellectual/conscious mind and its offshoots. Like us, David has to ally himself with the senses (Philistines) to keep from being destroyed by the intellectual/conscious mind. Yet, David repeatedly holds his hand from destroying the intellectual/conscious mind, allowing growth to take place at

---

[1] Notice: *though I walk through the valley of death... thy rod and thy staff they comfort me.* The "righteous one" is **not** "of the dead." He/she recognizes that death is a shadow, an appearance, not a "reality."

306

its own pace. And while at Hebron (a spell) – where he is chosen as King by the tribe of Judah – David grows, produces sons and triumphs. Finally, he is chosen King by all

Evaluating the David Level of Expression
of Israel; and after conquering Jerusalem, he establishes the Ark there. Jerusalem becomes the center of Israel.

David has a personal relationship with YHWH, and he "talks" to YHWH constantly. But, as are we, David is sabotaged by his physical desires.[2] Although he functions at the level of King, he's cursed in that the "sword" (desolation) will never leave his hands. Although David conquers and stabilizes the "Promised Land," he won't be allowed to build the Temple.

Let's return to the scheme established in Genesis. To evaluate David, we can look at his wives, at his sons, at his relationships, and at his ages. First, let's examine his wives.

David's Wives
David's first wife is Michal (brook, rivulet), younger daughter of Saul. Initially, she loves David and is instrumental in his escaping Saul; but when David leaves Saul's association, Michal is given to another. However, as soon as Abner and David make peace, Michal is returned to David's house.2 Sam. 3:13 But the former feminine expression is not happy in the forced reinstatement. The feminine expression of the intellect cannot tolerate the exuberance of the psychic energy of the advanced soul.

We must let go of the former feminine expression. The former feminine expression forces the issue as David brings the Ark into Jerusalem, an obviously joyous intellectual as well as esoteric occurrence. The feminine of the conscious mind cannot abide the energy level, and

---

[2] Don't be misled by this statement. "Physical desires" does not only refer to sexual lust. It also refers to our attachment to the physical, this includes our attachment to other individuals. And in this respect David is challenged more than any other character we have met.

Michal criticizes David for dancing in the streets clad only in his ephod, i.e., almost naked.[3] *And David returned to bless his household. But Michal the daughter of Saul came out to meet David, and said, "How the king of Israel honored himself today, **uncovering himself today before the eyes of his servants' maids,** as one of the vulgar fellows shamelessly uncovers himself!"* 2 Sam. 6:16-20.

Despite the lesser feminine reaction, the advanced soul knows that its "nakedness" is appropriate. David is too strong to be undone by the psychic energy; he can control it and himself, but at the cost of no longer associating with the lesser feminine.[4] David has an answer to her criticism. *And David said to Michal, "**It [dancing in the ephod] was before the LORD, who chose me above your father, and above all his house, to appoint me as prince over Israel,** the people of the LORD -- and **I will make merry before the LORD.** I will make myself yet more contemptible than this, and I will be abased in your eyes; but by the maids of whom you have spoken, by them I shall be held in honor." And Michal **the daughter of Saul had no child to the day of her death.*** 2 Sam. 6:21-23.

The other wives of David are more "friendly" to the advanced soul. Seven "positive" wives are mentioned.[5] The first six are acquired while David is still at Hebron, but David only finds his feminine expression in Jerusalem. She is Bathsheba, the fruition of David's feminine expression. It is she who provides the heir, and it is she who ensures Solomon's succession to the throne. Appropriately, she does not surface until David (loving) is firmly entrenched as King.

---

[3] David's "performance" at this time (2 Sam. 6:16-23) reflects that which comes upon the advancing soul, a euphoria produced by a psychic energy unexperienced before.

[4] Esotericists warn that aspirants must be well grounded, i.e., spiritually sound, before undertaking exercises which raise the psychic vibrational level. Supposedly, in India there are people called "Musts," former monks who simply roam the countryside because their conscious minds have been inundated by the psychic energy to the point of "burnout." The psychic phenomenon is not an area for experimentation any more than is the physical mind an area for experimenting with drugs.

[5] Although there apparently are other wives and concubines, only eight wives are mentioned. David's "**positive**" wives are: 1. Abigail (**joy evidenced**), who also saves David's life; 2. Ahin'oam of Jezreel (my brother is delight, **activity without discord**); 3. Ma'acah (**thought habits of sense reasoning**) mother of Absalom and Tamar; 4. Haggith (festive, joyous, **rejoicing**); 5. Abi'tal (**seeing God as source of all**); 6. Eglah (**productive feminine**); and 7. Bathsheba (**daughter of an oath**).

If we use the names of David's sons to assess his spiritual growth, David is in pretty good shape. Six sons are born at Hebron, and the whole family moves to Jerusalem.[6] And there, eleven more sons are born to him.[7] Isn't it interesting how the sons add up to **17**; but, remember, "17" is either positive or negative. Its status reflects how well we are doing with our "seeing" and "saying." See p. 263, fn.

David's Sons Evidence His Kingly Level

Even before Jerusalem, David is doing well, better than has anyone previously. He doesn't yet live in Jerusalem; he's centered at Hebron (a society; a spell), where he rules only Judah (praise). If you remember, Hebron was the site of Abraham's purchased burying grounds, and it contains numerous **oak trees,** but it still speaks of a spell. Only after being crowned King of all Israel does David leave Hebron and march on Jerusalem.

> Then all the tribes of Israel came to David at Hebron, and said, "Behold, we are your bone and flesh. In times past, **when Saul was king over us, it was you that led out and brought in Israel;** and the LORD said to you, '**You shall be shepherd of my people Israel, and you shall be prince over Israel.**'" So all the **elders of Israel** came to the king at Hebron; and King David made a covenant with them at Hebron before the LORD, and they **anointed David king over Israel.** David was **thirty years old when he began to reign, and he reigned forty** years. At Hebron he reigned **over Judah seven years and six months;** and at Jerusalem he reigned **over all Israel and Judah thirty-three years.**

---

[6] And sons were born to David at Hebron: his first-born was Amnon (**faithfulness**), of Ahinoam of Jezreel; and his second, Chileab (**totality of the father**), of Abigail the widow of Nabal of Carmel; and the third, Absalom (**father of peace**), the son of Maacah the daughter of Talmai king of Geshur; and the fourth, Adonijah (**Jehovah is** LORD), the son of Haggith; and the fifth, Shephatiah (**Jehovah sets upright**), the son of Abital; and the sixth, Ithream (**abundance of the people**), of Eglah... These were born to David in Hebron. 2 Sam. 3:2-5.

[7] And David took more concubines and wives from Jerusalem, after he came from Hebron; and more sons and daughters were born to David. And these are the names of those who were born to him **in Jerusalem:** Shammua (**renowned**), Shobab (**rebellious**), Nathan (**to give**), Solomon (**peaceful**), Ibhar (**choice; to select**), Elishua (**God of riches**), Nepheg (**to spring forth**), Japhia (**to be light; shine**), Elishama (**God of hearing**), Eliada (**God is knowing**), and Eliphelet (**God of deliverance**). 2 Sam. 5:13-16. One person not mentioned is Tamar (**erect palm tree**), David's daughter by Maacah and full sister to Absalom.

*And the king and his men went to Jerusalem against the **Jebusites**, the inhabitants of the land, who **said to David, "You will not come in here, but the blind and the lame will ward you off"** -- thinking, "David cannot come in here." Nevertheless **David took the stronghold of Zion, that is, the city of David.** And David said on that day, "Whoever would smite the Jebusites, let him **get up the water shaft to attack the lame and the blind, who are hated by David's soul."** Therefore it is said, "The blind and the lame shall not come into the house." And David dwelt in the stronghold, and called it the city of David. **And David built the city round about from the Millo inward.** And David became greater and greater, for the LORD, the God of hosts, was with him.* 2 Sam. 5:1-10.

The city which David conquers is still called Jebus; it has yet to be called Jerusalem *(founded peaceful)*. Nevertheless,

Jerusalem

David's choice of city is significant. "Jerusalem" was first mentioned in Genesis 14:18 under the name of "Salem" (from a root which means *to be safe in body or mind;* fig. *to be completed.*) Salem was the home of Melchizedek, to whom Abraham gave obeisance. From this center of peace, the city becomes "Jebus," which means *threshing floor, Jebus* coming from a root meaning *trodden.*

Everything regarding Jerusalem is both literal and esoteric. The change of names, in some ways, reflects the process which the individual soul undergoes.[8] Beginning with "peace," the individual soul is then *trodden* on a *threshing floor* until he/she is again ready to be *founded in peace.* For this reason, the Temple is built on the *threshing floor,* for there is the "dwelling place" of the Holy Spirit. Similarly, the conquering of Jerusalem is from the mount of Zion, and it is "up the water shaft."

Several years ago I read an archeological account that showed pictures of newly discovered "cisterns" dug out of

---

[8] The basic esoteric premise lies in Jerusalem's belonging to the Jebusites (*to retreat; to advance again*); hence, it is the nature of the city. Jerusalem's history follows such a pattern. It is repeatedly destroyed and again rebuilt, again destroyed, and finally restored to everlasting glory in Revelation. However, the most esoteric statement is "***attack the lame and the blind, who are hated by David's soul.*** " In fact, the statement makes me question my sequence of accomplishments. I have been assuming that we have **to say** before we walk; but in rethinking the sequence, it is more logical that we **hear, walk, see,** and *say* – in that order.

solid rock that had held water for Jerusalem and, according to this speculation, had provided David access to the walled city. Whether or not the speculation is correct, symbolism makes the assumption important. Access to the "founded peace" is from "the Mountain" and is made possible through "water," the ever-present intuitional substance.[9] David, the King, can make use of both. And the city itself is "built" inward from the Millo (rampart) which gives access to it.

David is established in Jerusalem, even contemplating building YHWH a house; but YHWH tells Nathan (Samuel's successor) to tell him: *"Thus says the LORD of hosts, I took you from the pasture, from following the sheep, that you should be prince over my people Israel; and I have been with you wherever you went, and have cut off all your enemies from before you; and I will make for you a great name,.... And I will appoint a place for my people Israel,...and [they will] be disturbed no more; and violent men shall afflict them no more, as formerly, ... and I will give you rest from all your enemies. Moreover the LORD declares to you that the LORD will make you a house."* 2 Sam. 7:8-12. Nathan tells him that the LORD has said: *'I will raise up your offspring after you, who shall come forth from your body, and I will establish his kingdom.. He shall build a house for my name, and I will establish the throne of his kingdom for ever. I will be his father, and he shall be my son. When he commits iniquity, I will chasten him with the rod of men, with the [affliction of mortals]; but I will [never withdraw My favor from him] as I took it from Saul, whom I [removed to make room for you.] And your house and your kingdom shall be made sure for ever before me; your throne shall be established for ever."* 2 Sam. 7:8-16.

Well, that's a pretty good guarantee. We can just see David thinking that one of the kids, probably Amnon or Chileab – maybe even the "beautiful" Absalom – is going to follow and prosper. That means we can relax. Right? Wrong! At least we can rest a little bit, but even kings – those who reach this part of the climb – have to maintain their postion. So: *In the spring of the year, the time when kings go forth to battle, David sent Joab, and his servants with him, and all Israel; and they ravaged the*

---

[9] Gregory the Great considered David's use of "water" to symbolize "knowledge." Gaskell, p. 805. But the phrase *get up the water shaft* has even more meaning, esoterically. It indicates a rise in consciousness. It is similar to *come up hither* (Rev. 4:1.) which Swedenborg saw as signifying "divine influx, and thence an elevation of the mind followed by manifest perception."*Ibid*. p. 167.

*Ammonites, and besieged Rabbah. But **David remained at Jerusalem.*** 2 Sam.11:1.

David (loving) is in such a sure position that he can allow the maintenance to be done by others, even to besiege Rabbah (abundance of quantity).

Here we are, King of Israel, we are even designated to be "loving," and we are on a high plateau (roof) when we see something "beautiful," Bathsheba.[10] Ooh, ooh! Now comes the challenge.

It happened, late one afternoon, when David arose from his couch and was **walking upon the roof of the king's house,** *that he saw from the roof a woman bathing; and the **woman was very beautiful.** And David sent and inquired about the woman. And one said, "Is not this Bathsheba, the **daughter of Eliam** (God of the people), the **wife of Uriah** (flame of Ja) the Hittite (terror)?" So David sent messengers, and took her; and she came to him, and he lay with her. (Now she [had just purified] herself from her uncleanness.) Then she returned to her house. And the woman conceived; and she sent and told David, "**I am with child.**"* 2 Sam.11:1-6.

David's Sin

Do we see ourselves? We're full of praise of YHWH; we have a constant relationship with the LORD. But we *see* this *beautiful* thing, and we "take" it.[11] David, this "loving" Self, just broke commandments number *seven* and *ten.* Oooh! According to Levitical law: *If a man commits adultery with the wife of his neighbor, both the adulterer and the adulteress shall be put to death.* Lev. 20:10. No wonder David tries every way imaginable to get Uriah to come home and "lie" with Bathsheba, but Uriah is such a conscientious warrior that he does not.

Where is YHWH? YHWH promised that "He" would not "withdraw His favor" away as it was taken from Saul. Does that mean David won't be punished?[12] The problem word here is ***punished.*** *Punishment* means *to inflict a penalty for the commission of an offense.* Implied is *...in retribution or* retaliation.

---

[10] According to Young, p. 72, Jewish tradition holds that Bathsheba composed Proverbs 31 (it is called The Sayings of Lemuel [symbolic name of Solomon]) and recited it as an admonition to Solomon as he married Pharaoh's daughter. Bathsheba is not **just** a "pretty face."

[11] Women were considered "unclean" during their periods. See Lev. 20:18.

[12] Webster's adds: **chasten** *suggests any affliction or trial that leaves one humbled or subdued;* **discipline** *implies a punishing or chastening in order to bring under control;* **correct** *implies punishing aimed at reforming an offender.*

What is difficult to recognize is that **none of our characters have been** *punished*. More accurately stated, **each of our characters has** *reaped* **as he/she** *has sown*. Each character has been *given the measure* with which he/she *meted*. Although we haven't mentioned the LAW for a long time, the LAW always applies. (See page 58.)

And with *what judgment* has David "spoken"? He has "pronounced" that he desires the "beautiful." At the same time, he has "pronounced" that he desires the beautiful "act of seeing."[13] The only problem is that this "judgment" is wed to "flame of Ja", i.e., "the light of the LORD" even though he is a Hittite (terror). But by his actions, David has also "said" that he (David) disregards the law of Moses. And David "takes" Bathsheba. Then, upon finding that she has conceived, David tries to cover up by inviting Uriah to go home for the night. But Uriah is the noblest of warriors and rejects the opportunity to sleep with his wife.

We are ashamed of David. He has disobeyed two of the Commandments: he has committed adultery, and he has "coveted" his neighbor's wife. To that he adds "murder" by placing Uriah in the front lines of a "suicide squad." To the intellectual mind, David's "sin" is far greater than that of Saul; yet David won't get defeated in battle and beheaded. Remember, *God's ways are not our ways.*

There have been *sins*. Adam/Eve "ate" from the tree of the knowledge of good and evil. Cain was upset that the LORD didn't like his offering. Ham "saw" his father *naked*. Lot's wife *looked back*. Esau *disregarded* his birth-right. Moses didn't *believe* enough *to sanctify* his action. Saul "was little in his own eyes" and was disobedient. What about David? Certainly, David's sin surpasses the others.

"Sins" Of Other "Climbers"

---

[13] The line which is simply translated...*the woman was very beautiful* in English, in Hebrew is *'ishshah* (woman) *me'od:* (exceedingly) *towb*(beautiful). *mar'eh:*(the act of seeing; countenance). Again we're given a pun.

In fact, my worldly judgment "sees" David's sin as greater than any to date. And as Nathan tricks him into making a judgment,[14] David agrees: *"As the LORD lives, the man who has done this deserves to die; and he shall restore the lamb fourfold, because he did this thing, and because he had no pity."* 2 Sam. 12:5,6 *Nathan said to David, "You are the man.* **Thus says the LORD, the God of Israel,** *'I anointed you king over Israel, and I delivered you out of the hand of Saul; and I gave you your master's house, and your master's wives into your bosom, and gave you the house of Israel and of Judah; and if this were too little, I would add to you as much more.* **Why have you despised the word of the LORD, to do what is evil in his sight?** *You have smitten Uriah the Hittite with the sword, and have taken his wife to be your wife, and have slain him with the sword of the Ammonites. Now* **therefore the sword shall never depart from your house, because you have despised me, and have taken the wife of Uriah the Hittite to be your wife.'** *Thus says the LORD, 'Behold,* **I will raise up evil against you out of your own house;** *and I will take your wives before your eyes, and give them to your neighbor, and he shall lie with your wives in the sight of this sun.* **For you did it secretly; but I will do this thing before all Israel, and before the sun.'''**

David said to Nathan, **"I have sinned against the LORD."** *And Nathan said to David,* **"The LORD also has put away your sin; you shall not die.** *Nevertheless, because by this deed you have utterly scorned the LORD, the child that is born to you shall die."* *Then Nathan went to his house. And the LORD struck the child that Uriah's wife bore to David, and it became sick.* 2 Sam. 12:7-15.

But David confesses his sin and is forgiven.

Eastern religions use the word *karma* to explain those things in our lives which have no clear explanation. We mistakenly think of *Karma* as "destiny." But more correctly, it is a series of events set into motion by a previous action. Essentially, it is simply the LAW. By his actions, David has set into motion events that will bring him great sorrow. It begins with the death of this newborn son.

David therefore besought God for the child; and David fasted, and went in and lay all night upon the ground. And the elders of his house stood beside him, to raise him from the ground; but he would not, nor did he eat food with them.

---

[14] Nathan tells David the following story: *There were two men in a certain city, the one rich and the other poor. The rich man had very many flocks and herds; but the poor man had nothing but one little ewe lamb, which he had bought. And he brought it up, and it grew up with him and with his children; it used to eat of his morsel, and drink from his cup, and lie in his bosom, and it was like a daughter to him. Now there came a traveler to the rich man, and he was unwilling to take one of his own flock or herd to prepare for the wayfarer who had come to him, but he took the poor man's lamb, and prepared it for the man who had come to him.* 2 Sam. 12:1-4.

314

On the seventh day the child died. And the servants of David feared to tell him that the child was dead; for they said, "Behold, while the child was yet alive, we spoke to him, and he did not listen to us; how then can we say to him the child is dead? He may do himself some harm." But when David saw that his servants were whispering together, David perceived that the child was dead; and David said to his servants, "Is the child dead?" They said, "He is dead."

Then David arose from the earth, and washed, and anointed himself, and changed his clothes; and he went into the house of the LORD, and worshiped; he then went to his own house; and when he asked, they set food before him, and he ate. Then his servants said to him, "What is this thing that you have done? You fasted and wept for the child while it was alive; but when the child died, you arose and ate food." He said, "While the child was still alive, I fasted and wept; for I said, 'Who knows whether the LORD will be gracious to me, that the child may live?' But now he is dead; why should I fast? Can I bring him back again? I shall go to him, but he will not return to me."

Then David comforted his wife, Bathsheba, and went in to her, and lay with her; and she bore a son, and he called his name Solomon (to be safe; to make completed). And the LORD loved him, and sent a message by Nathan the prophet; so he called his name Jedidiah (beloved of the LORD) at the instance of the LORD. 2 Sam. 12:16-25.

Again there is almost an indefinite pronoun. Is it Solomon who is "beloved of the Lord" or David? It makes no difference to the intuitional mind. David has confessed his sin! He has repented! He is forgiven! And at the "instance" of the LORD "he" is declared *beloved of the Lord.*[15]

The climber must take care **not** to separate that which is not separated. The climb is not a matter of an advanced "Self" supplanting a more primitive "self." More correctly, it is an evolutionary process; the more primitive self eventually sees and understands more and more. It is "precept upon precept" that produces the more advanced "Self." The intellect and spiritual are finally reunited; all is working together, under the leadership of a "loving" King.

Supposedly, except for Jesus, none is more loving than David. This must be considered in our assessment of

---

[15] *Instance* means *request.* Interestingly, the only other use of this *beloved of the Lord* term *is: Of Benjamin he said, "The beloved of the LORD, he dwells in safety by him; he encompasses him all the day long, and makes his dwelling between his shoulders."* Dt. 33:12. Can it be that the *karma* of Benjamin has been forgiven in the kingly heritage?

David. First to consider is David's relationship with Saul and Saul's house. David's services to Saul were many and varied: soother, healer, armor bearer, warrior, protector, avenger. David's music soothed and healed Saul for a time. David eliminated Saul's greatest threat, Goliath, and afterwards continued to battle for Saul despite Saul's ingratitude. David refused to kill Saul in the two chances he had

David's Connection To Saul

to do so; for David knows there can be only one king. David is given the *crown* that had been on Saul's head and the *armlet* which had been on his arm, but David slays the *messenger.* 2 Sam. 1:10-16.

Are you confused? I just said that David was so "loving," and here he kills the messenger that tells him about Saul. Is there something wrong, here? No, it's just that we haven't reached the level of the Christed King. Although David has greater understanding than anyone we have met before, he still is expressing at the level where *love* is conditional; he *loves* only that which meets with his desires.[16]

There is only one character in the entire Bible who even begins to approach the love of Jesus Christ: **that is Jonathan.** Jonathan begins that which will be furthered by Jesus Christ; he begins the move toward "unconditional love." Paradoxically, although he never becomes King, Jonathan surpasses David in his expression. Although he had been the heir apparent, Jonathan seems to have had no desires. His loyalty to David surpasses his desire for his legacy. And David honors Jonathan with the enigmatic*: How have the mighty fallen in the thick of battle – Jonathan, slain on your heights! I grieve for you, my brother Jonathan. You were most dear to me. Your love was wonderful to me, more than the love of women.* 2 Sam. 1:25,26 *The Prophets.*

---

[16] Again, you may want to challenge me. How can we say that Saul "loved" David? Esoterically, the opposite of "love" is not "hate"; it is "indifference." "Hate" is simply negative "love," probably turned negative by fear. Such was Saul's feeling for David. The messenger, on the other hand, was indifferent; he had no feeling for either Saul or David.

In the last fifty years, the common American culture has almost totally changed the meaning of the word *love*. Most destructive has been the culture's pervasive replacement of "love" with "sex."[17] Even on the physical level, "sex" is not a synonym for *love*.

The climber is likely to notice different intensities of *love* as he/she climbs. Subconsciously, one senses the differences. I've always liked the comparison of the Greek words for *love*,[18] but I think David's comment is even more meaningful. Obviously, physical "attachment" produces a particular vibratory experience, but the attachment between David and Jonathan is not physical; it is mental and spiritual.

And as David returned from the slaughter of the Philistine, Abner ... brought him before Saul with the head of the Philistine in his hand. ...When he had finished speaking to Saul, the soul of Jonathan was knit to the soul of David, and Jonathan loved him as his own soul. And Saul ... would not let him return to his father's house. Then Jonathan made a covenant with David, because he loved him as his own soul. And Jonathan stripped himself of the robe that was upon him, and gave it to David, and his armor, and even his sword and his bow and his girdle. And David went out and was successful wherever Saul sent him; so that Saul set him over the men of war. And this was good in the sight of all the people

---

[17] Some members of the "gay" community say that David's comment regarding Jonathan, i.e., *Your love was wonderful to me, more than the love of women,* exposes a homosexual relationship between the two. Such comments reveal the great distance between the understanding of the individual tied to the carnal world as opposed to the individual who has risen above it.

Homosexuality is condemned as an *abomination* by the Old Testament. Lev.18:22-26 reads: *You shall not lie with a male as with a woman; it is an abomination. And you shall not lie with any beast and defile yourself with it, neither shall any woman give herself to a beast to lie with it: it is perversion. Do not defile yourselves by any of these things, for by all these the nations I am casting out before you defiled themselves; and the land became defiled,* so that I punished its iniquity, and the land vomited out its inhabitants.

Recognizing that science has found some observable differences in the physical genetics of "homosexuals," I would suggest that at least some of those who feel this inclination are experiencing a higher level of consciousness than the carnal world experiences. As such they have no "desire" for "carnal pleasures" with members of the opposite sex. It is not the social and psychological "connection" which the Bible condemns; but the physical "waste" of the life force. By equating "sex" with *love*, they revert to the carnal expression even more than if their relationship was with one of the opposite sex.

[18] There are three Greek words for **love**: *eros* (sexual), *philĕō* (denoting personal attachment), and *agapaō* (in a social or moral sense); and the New Testament often uses the word *agapē* (affection or benevolence; *a love feast*).

and also in the sight of Saul's servants. 1 Sam. 17:57,58; 18:1-5.

From the physical viewpoint, David is an historical character – the King who brings about Israel's "Golden Age." By the time of Jesus, the age of David is more dearly longed for than the time of Solomon, for Solomon so heavily taxed Israel that the decline began. Not so with David. David extends Israel's borders to their greatest extent; David brings valor, wealth, prosperity, honor, quiet and "peace" to Israel. From the esoteric viewpoint, this level of *King* nears the top of the Mountain. Only Christ's level remains. But ascent to the **King** level cannot be accomplished without this *"more than the love of women"* being recognized by the climber.[19]

The love of women is a double-*entendre*. The one meaning is almost a "sexist" remark: it is *a love* that is weak and underdeveloped. The second meaning is the love that a man has for a woman. This too has two meanings: one meaning refers to sexual "desire," but the other refers to a *love* based on an exchange relationship. The man *loves* the woman in exchange for sexual favors and for the children which the "sex" produces.

But the *love* which Jonathan "bestows" upon David is different. Jonathan's *love* is totally unselfish; it is totally undemanding. It is a *love* in which *his soul is "knit,"* i.e., cannot be separated without destroying the whole, *to the soul of David.* Jonathan loves David as he does himself. Note:...*thou shalt love thy neighbor as thyself.* [20]

---

[19] It has been my observation and experience that we all are given "loves" in our lives. There are those with whom only the noun *eros* applies, usually in our youth. There are those with whom *philĕō* applies, and these last throughout our lives. David ex-presses at both of these levels. However, continuing the climb, we must extend our *love* beyond the *philĕō* expression. We must reach the level of *agapē.*

[20] In my life, I ascribe such an immediate "bonding" to relationships in previous lives. Don't be shocked at my admission; I can clearly "feel" previous association with certain individuals that have absolutely no relation to today. The strongest "bonds" have been with those whom I totally *loved* in another lifetime. Particularly strong are the feelings toward those who have been parents or children in previous

(continued...)

David has been given *agape,* this unselfish level of love. He recognizes it, but it is not really a part of him. Once, David dealt with *eros.* He admitted his sin; he repented (he will never again commit the sin of adultery), and he is forgiven (by evidence of son Solomon.) But David's challenge is with *phileō.* Nathan says:[21] *"'...You have smitten Uriah the Hittite with the sword, and have taken his wife to be your wife, and have slain him with the sword of the Ammonites. Now therefore the sword shall never depart from your house, because you have despised me, and have taken the wife of Uriah the Hittite to be your wife.' Thus says the LORD, 'Behold, I will raise up evil against you out of your own house; and I will take your wives before your eyes, and give them to your neighbor, and he shall lie with your wives in the sight of this sun. For you did it secretly; but I will do this thing before all Israel, and before the sun '"* 2 Sam.12:9-12.

The "challenge" begins almost immediately, with the "beautiful" Absalom's beautiful sister, Tamar (erect, palm trees).

| **Eldest Son Rapes Tamar** | David's first born, Amnon, becomes lustful toward his half-sister, Tamar. His cousin Jon'adab suggests that he trick Tamar into |

coming into his quarters to "nurse" his pretended illness.[22] When she does so because of her love for him, he rapes her. But – once he has indulged his lust – he hates her and refuses to marry her. See 2 Sam. 13:1-20.

Seeing his sister's distress, "beautiful" Absalom guesses what has happened, but he tells Tamar to be quiet

| **David Does Nothing!** | about it; so Tamar remains in Absalom's house, a "desolate woman." David hears of the tragedy, but neither *does* nor *says* anything! *But* |

*Absalom spoke to Amnon neither good nor bad; for **Absalom hated Amnon, because he had forced his sister Tamar.*** 2 Sam. 13:22.

---

[20](...continued)
lifetimes. Although I have seldom encountered strong antipathies, I assume that these immediate reactions were enlarged by memories of which I was unaware.

[21] Check out the numbers: 12:9-12. Pretty powerful, and though the pronouncement is dismal, it is simply the LAW. As with all of our life, we have the *opportunity* to view this "challenge" as *half-empty, half-full,* or *full-full.* By his "seeing" and "saying" David can set into motion new *karma.* The LAW works constantly.

[22] Jon'adab comes from the roots for YHWH and "to know" (prop. to ascertain by "seeing.") It is this that is being "tested," and David's first born (maybe lowest parts) fails the test.

Two years of silence go by, and a sheepshearing gives excuse for a party. Absalom invites David, probably knowing that David will decline, and then presses David until he agrees that Amnon and all the King's sons be allowed to come to the shearing. The party proceeds and Absalom tells his servants: *"Mark **when Amnon's heart is merry with wine, and when I say to you, 'Strike Amnon,' then kill him**. Fear not; have I not commanded you? Be courageous and be valiant."* 2 Sam. 13:28.

We're not too distressed, are we? Only the *feminine* has been injured. Amnon gets what he deserves! The LAW is operating. However, the LAW has another multiple, this time Absalom! Of course, confusion takes place with the murder, and rumor has it that all the king's sons are dead; but Jon'adab assures David that only Amnon is dead.[23] And Absalom (father of peace) flees. *So Absalom fled, and went to Geshur,* (bridge) *and was there three years. And the **spirit of the king longed to go forth to Absalom; for he was comforted about Amnon, seeing he was dead.*** 2 Sam. 13:38,39.

> **But... David Does Nothing!**

Joab intervenes, finding an old lady who, like Nathan before, gets David to make pronouncement against his own actions. And David agrees to deal with Absalom. The old lady blesses David: *"... And your handmaid thought, 'The word of my lord the king will set me at rest'; **for my lord the king is like the angel of God to discern good and evil**. The LORD your God be with you!"* 2 Sam. 14:17.

Joab's trick catches David's attention, and David instructs that Absalom be called back; **but**... David says: *"**Let him dwell apart in his own house; he is not to come into my presence.**" So Absalom dwelt apart in his own house, and did not come into the king's presence. ... So Absalom dwelt **two full years** in Jerusalem, without coming into the king's presence.* 2 Sam. 14:24; 28.

... and, again, David does nothing! Oh, how like David we are! How often our "doing" is "doing nothing." How often we say nothing; how seldom we are willing to be the first to speak. An old Beatles' song has a line in it that is so profound: ... *silence, like a cancer, grows...* And so it is

---

[23] Remember that Amnon means "faithfulness." Needless to say, he did not live up to his name. Or are we saying that David's faithfulness is lacking?

with David. Absalom repeatedly tries to get Joab to arrange for him to see the King, but to no avail. Finally, after two years in Jerusalem without seeing David, Absalom sets Joab's field on fire, telling Joab: *"Behold, I sent word to you, 'Come here, that I may send you to the king, to ask, "Why have I come from Geshur? It would be better for me to be there still." Now **therefore let me go into the presence of the king; and if there is guilt in me, let him kill me.'"** Then Joab went to the king, and told him; and he summoned Absalom. So he came to the king, and bowed himself on his face to the ground before the king; and the king kissed Absalom.* 2 Sam. 14:32,33.

Shame on David! This is no *loving* father/son relationship. Absolom is driven to desperate acts by David's indifference. We, like David, are wooed by Absolom's beauty ... or maybe it's the mother in me that feels for him. But David holds back from the beauty for too long, and Absalom becomes a "cancer" in David's nation. Predictably,

Absalom Promotes Rebellion

he takes advantage of any dissatisfaction he finds in the kingdom,...and *so Absalom stole the hearts of the men of Israel.* Four years go by and still the breach has not been healed, and Absalom asks to go to Hebron, ostensibly to offer a sacrifice to the LORD. *But Absalom sent secret messengers throughout all the tribes of Israel, saying, "As soon as you hear the sound of the trumpet, then say, 'Absalom is king at Hebron!'"* 2 Sam. 15:5-10.

It has been seven years since Amnon raped Tamar. The earthly completion has taken place. Absalom acquires David's "counselor" and other supporters, and he grows stronger. Finally *a messenger came to David, saying, **"The hearts of the men of Israel have gone after Absalom." Then David said to all his servants** who were with him at Jerusalem, **"Arise, and let us flee; or else there will be no escape for us from Absalom**; go in haste, lest he overtake us ... and smite the city with the edge of the sword." And the **king's servants said to the king, "Behold, your servants are ready to do whatever my lord the king decides."** So the king went forth, and all his household after him. And the king **left ten concubines to keep the house**.* 2 Sam. 15:12-16.

Let's hang loose for a minute. Do we see what has happened to David, the King? First, he **became angry**; but he **did nothing** about it. Then he became **indifferent.** Now he has become **fearful**, and all he can do is "run." And he leaves all of his affairs with ten "illegitimate" feminine expressions. Somehow, he is reverting to Saul's view of himself as "little." Does this happen to us, too? Even though we're climbing the Mountain, even though we feel ourselves advancing – even to the level of being "crowned" – we likely will be given some tests. More than likely, the tests will come from those whom we "love" the "most." Only those we love have the "clout" to hurt us; only those we love can be the "test."

David takes those things that are truly his, leaving the "concubines" with the outer trappings, and passes toward the wilderness. He even sends the Ark back when the priests try to follow him with it. (The Ark must remain in Jerusalem while we "gather" ourselves together.) Now David (as will the Son of David twenty-eight generations hence [4x7]) climbs the Mount of Olives, *weeping as he went, barefoot and with his head covered; and all the people who were with him covered their heads, and they went up, weeping as they went.* 2 Sam. 15:30. [24]

We've noticed before that this climb is not all "sweetness and light." Much of it is sorrow and weeping. But remember what the climb is all about! We must learn to *see* and to *say!* ... And that does not mean just sitting back and *doing NOTHING* about whatever needs to be dealt with – as has David in the last few pages. But as David passes the summit of the mountain, the servant of Mephibosheth (dispeller of shame) meets David with asses laden with **200** loaves of bread, **100** bunches of raisins, **100** summer fruits, and **1** skin of wine.[25] Mephibosheth is the "lame" son of

---

[24] This is the ritual for official "mourning." Notice its esoteric significance. The feet are bare so that nothing comes between the mourner and the earth. Remember, the feet represent understanding, so the understanding of the mourner is increased. Moreover, the head is covered so that the energy which is absorbed by the feet does not leave the body through the crown chakra. The energy is then there to invigorate.

[25] Note: 200 + 100 + 100 + 1 = 401. The number 401 is a prime number.

Jonathan whom David saved after Saul's death, and to whom he granted privileges and wealth.

Again let's hang loose! Remember the term *karma?* By his "sin" with Bathsheba, David set in motion all of this disaster with Amnon and Absalom. By his "sins of omission" he furthers the rebellion of Absalom. But by an even earlier action, he "caused" Mephibosheth's allegiance. And Mephibosheth is giving him things he needs. *Karma* is neither good nor bad. It depends on what we *see* and *say.*

Everyone establishes his/her own *karma.* By rejecting Tamar, Amnon brought his own death. Absalom could have peacefully dealt with Amnon, but he stayed silent; and silence only furthered his hatred, resulting in his having Amnon killed. Even at that point he could have changed his *karma* by asking for David's mercy, but instead he flees. Once more, if he had repented, he might have changed his *karma*, but he does not. Instead, he rebels against his father,

leading the dissident elements of Israel in open rebellion. He even flaunts his position by "taking" David's concubines in full view of all of Jerusalem, thereby declaring his takeover of David's throne. Absalom is self-destructive. Finally, he's in a massive battle with David's forces. In the battle, **20,000** men are slaughtered. Fleeing the carnage, Absalom's *karma* comes full circle. He "sees"

Absalom's Tomb

the truth of life: *Absalom CHANCED to meet the servants of David. Absalom was riding upon his mule, and the mule went under the thick branches of a **great oak**, and **his head caught fast in the oak, and he was left hanging between heaven and earth**, while the mule that was under him went on.* 2 Sam. 18:9.

We all get "caught" by the strongest things of life; we all hang between heaven and earth. But, it is not by **chance**. There is no **chance**! There is only *cause* and *effect.* There is only the LAW.

Absalom Is Killed

Too bad Absalom didn't mend his *karmic* obligations when he had a chance! Joab comes upon him and thrusts **three darts** in his **heart** while he is alive, *and ten young men, Joab's armorbearers, surround [Absalom]... and kill him.* 2 Sam. 18:14,15. David keeps his throne; Solomon inherits. Everything is as it is intended to be, but Absalom was David's favorite son – David's heart is "broken," and it never mends. And *... the sword ... never [departs] from [David's] house...* The LAW is in operation; **it always is.**

As with Absalom's death, it is Joab who **makes all possible.** Joab is he who has done David's "Kingly warring" ever since Hebron. Joab's activity has insured David's throne. He is David's nephew; but he represents "the individual *will.*"[26] More importantly, Joab gives us clear evidence of how the LAW works. Each action he takes prompts another of similar quality.

Let's review Joab's *karma* for a moment. The *karma* began long ago, when Abner (Saul and Ishbosheth's military chief) killed Asahel (Joab's brother). Next, Joab kills Abner, even though David had made peace with him. Joab stays with David when Absalom rebels, and Joab tries to bring Absalom and David back together. Yet Joab is instrumental in killing Absalom, despite David's instructions that he should not be harmed. Still, only Joab can rouse David. Joab kills David's rebellious nephew, Amasa; and arranges for the beheading of Sheba, thus purging Israel of rebels.[27]

---

[26] Fillmore, *Metaphysical Bible Dictionary*, p. 353.

[27] David warns Solomon against Joab. *"... you know also what Joab the son of Zeruiah did to me, how he dealt with ... **Abner** the son of Ner, and **Amasa** the son of Jether, **whom he murdered, avenging in time of peace blood which had been shed in war, and putting**

(continued...)

324

David and Joab have conquered most of the alien enemies. But David wants reassurance of his strength. So, Joab's last service to David is to take a census; but taking the census brings on a plague.[28] *So David said to Joab and the commanders of the army, "Go, number Israel,* **from Beer-sheba to Dan....**" *But Joab said, "...***Are they not, my lord the king, all of them my lord's servants? ...**" *But the king's word prevailed against Joab. So Joab departed and went throughout all Israel...,In all Israel there were* **one million one hundred thousand men who drew the sword, and in Judah four hundred and seventy thousand...** *he did not include Levi and Benjamin ..., for the king's command was abhorrent to Joab. But God was displeased with this thing, and he smote Israel. And* **David said to God, "I have sinned greatly in that I have done this thing. But now, I pray thee, take away the iniquity of thy servant; for I have done very foolishly."** *And the LORD spoke to Gad, David's seer, saying,... 'Thus says the LORD, Three things I offer you; choose one of them... either* **three years of famine**; *or* **three months of devastation by your foes**, *...or else* **three days of the sword of the LORD, pestilence upon the land, and the angel of the LORD destroying throughout all the territory of Israel.'** *... Then David said to Gad, "...* **let me fall into the hand of the LORD, for his mercy is very great; but let me not fall into the hand of man.**" *So the LORD sent a pestilence upon Israel; and there fell* **seventy thousand men** *of Israel. And God sent the angel to Jerusalem to destroy it; but when he was about to destroy it, the LORD ... said ..."It is enough; now stay your hand." And the angel of the LORD was standing by the threshing floor of Ornan the Jebusite.* **And David lifted his eyes and saw the angel of the LORD standing between earth and heaven, and in his hand a drawn sword stretched out over Jerusalem.**

Then David and the elders, clothed in sackcloth, fell upon their faces. And David said to God,... It is I who have sinned and done very wickedly. ... Let thy hand,... be against me and against my father's house; but let not the plague be upon thy people." *Then the angel of the LORD commanded Gad to say to David that* **David should go up and rear an altar to the LORD on the threshing floor of Ornan the Jebusite.** *Now Ornan was threshing wheat; he* **turned and saw** *the angel... Ornan looked and saw David and went forth from the threshing floor, and did obeisance to David with his face to the ground. And David said ...,* **"Give me the site of the threshing floor that I may build on it an altar to the LORD -- give it to me at its full price -- that the plague may be averted from the people."** *Then Ornan said...,* "Take it; and let the lord my king do what seems good to him; see, I give **the oxen for burnt offerings**, and the **threshing sledges for the wood**, and the **wheat for a cereal offering**. ...." *But King David said...,* "No, but I will buy it for the full price; I will not take for the LORD what is yours, nor offer burnt offerings which cost me nothing." *So David paid Ornan* **six hundred shekels of gold**...*And David built there an altar to the LORD and presented burnt offerings and peace offerings, and called upon the LORD, and he answered him with fire from heaven upon the altar of burnt offering. Then* **the LORD commanded the angel; and he put his sword back into its sheath.** *...*

When David saw that the LORD had answered him at the threshing floor ..., he made his sacrifices there....[and] said, **"Here shall be the house of the LORD God and here the altar of burnt offering for Israel."** 1 Chron. 21:1-30.

---

[27](...continued)

innocent blood upon ...[me.] *Act therefore according to your wisdom...* 1 Kings 2:5,6.

[28] A census means to "count" the people of Israel, but it has an esoteric meaning in that its purpose is to calculate whether or not one has the "power" to fight the enemy. To one who knows that there is no *duality*, there is no need to "count" the people. Therefore, the plague is the acceptance of *duality*, and it can be eliminated only by man/woman being "threshed" upon the "threshing floor."

You most likely saw the similarities between this last story and that of Abraham's purchase of the burying field. (See pages 85, 86.) Remember, the Bible not only tells the "history" of Israel, it also instructs for righteous "speech."

Both Abraham and David had to make a purchase. Abraham was at the level of trusting only slightly. His "purchase" required *four hundred shekels of silver,* and the land was required to *bury the dead...out of my sight.* David's "purchase" requires *six hundred shekels of gold,* and the "threshing floor" is required *that the plague may be averted from the people.* It is more costly to be King; it is more costly to be "of the living."[29]   And notice what David is purchasing; David's purchase is a "threshing floor," a place where cattle pull a "sled" across wheat and its chaff. The purpose is to separate the kernel – that which can be ground into flour for bread – from the debris that surrounds it. Once it has been "threshed," it must be "winnowed." Winnowing is done with a "light forked-broom" which lifts the lighter chaff into the air and takes it out of the way – leaving only the kernel.

Cattle threshing grain; men winnowing.

Although he has disobeyed David in some things, Joab takes the census, even though he does not want to. Our

---

[29] The Kingly level of the climb requires our total triumph over all of our challenges. Where Abraham only had to control fire, water, air, and earth (■), David has to control body, mind and spirit, conscious mind, sub-conscious mind and super-conscious (✡).

Kingly self – that which speaks righteously of its relationship with God, that which confesses its mistakes, that which *lifts up its eyes and sees* – must direct our will. But the will is to be eliminated as we progress to the height of the Kingly expression; for we are no longer to have a "will" separate from that of the LORD.

And as David is about to die, Joab allies himself with Adonijah. Therefore, upon Solomon's selection as King, Joab runs to the Tabernacle and catches hold of the horns of the altar, to no avail.[30] He is killed by Solomon's man and buried in his own house in the wilderness. 1 Kgs 2:34.

Representing the "individual will," Joab is necessary for the positive actions which David takes while King. But at the same time, each action that the "will" takes is tied to other happenings. Symbolically, the "will" is forced to "accept" the "threshing floor." And ultimately, the "individual will" has to be eliminated, to be replaced by the Divine Will. Only when we accept the "Divine Will" is *karma* and the whole process complete.

It is the purpose of the King to further the whole process toward completion, i.e., to learn *discernment.* Isn't this what Cain was told? *"If you do well, will you not be accepted? And if you do not do well, **sin is couching at the door; its desire is for you, but you must master it.**"* Gen. 4:7. The *sin* that is waiting at the door is the *original sin*. It's the *sin* of *internalizing* anything from the "tree of *the knowledge of good and evil.* "It's in accepting *duality.* Mastery requires that we *discern* that **there is no duality**. David finally discerns that the *individual will* must be eliminated. And Solomon, he who always knew he would be King, accepts the charge. This is Solomon (safe, **at peace**), whom Nathan calls Jedidiah (**beloved of the LORD**) and whom his mother calls Lemuel (**for God**). Finally, **YHWH** and **El** are combined in one expression, the KING.

---

[30] The carnal will of the individual man cannot survive if we are to finish the climb.

By man's law, Adonijah should have been acclaimed king, but David had done no better with Adonijah than with Amnon and Absalom. We are told that *His father had never at any time displeased him by asking, "Why have you done thus and so?" He was also a very handsome man; and he was born next after Absalom.* 1 Kgs. 1:6.

Interestingly, this time there is no mention of the LORD'S deciding Solomon's kingship; it is human activity which places Solomon in power. Some call it a "court intrigue." Its participants are those whom Adonijah leaves out of his plans for the crown. Nathan starts the process: *Then Nathan said to Bathsheba ..., "Have you not heard that Adonijah the son of Haggith has become king and David our lord does not know it? Now ..., let me give you **counsel, that you may save your own life and the life of your son Solomon**. Go in at once to King David, and say to him, 'Did you not, my lord the king, swear to your maidservant, saying, "Solomon your son shall reign after me, and he shall sit upon my throne"? Why then is Adonijah king?' Then while you are still speaking with the king, I also will come in after you and confirm your words." So Bathsheba went to the king into his chamber.* 1 Kgs. 1:11-15.

Once more the feminine makes the difference. Even though the masculine side is ailing – *Now King David was old and advanced in years; and although they covered him with clothes, he could not get warm.* 1 Kngs. 1:1. – the feminine side functions and is strong enough to rouse the ailing masculine to accomplish what is proper and intended. *King David said, "Call to me Zadok the priest, Nathan the prophet, and Benaiah the son of Jehoiada." ... And the king said to them, "Take [my] servants.... and **cause Solomon my son to ride on my own mule, and bring him down to Gihon;** and let **Zadok the priest** and **Nathan the prophet** there **anoint him king over Israel**; then blow the trumpet, and say, 'Long live King Solomon!' You shall then come up after him, and he shall come and sit upon my throne; for he shall be king in my stead; and **I have appointed him to be ruler over Israel and over Judah."** 1 Kgs. 1:32-35.* [31]

Solomon has discernment. He discerns those who "speak righteously." He discerns Adonijah's true intent in his request to marry Abishag (a woman of David's harem), and so he

---

[31] It is mentioned in verse 10 that Adonijah invited all of his brothers except Solomon. Nor did he invite Nathan or Benaiah **or the mighty men (of David).** As we later learn with Julius Caesar, "he who rules the army, rules Rome." So it is here. On the physical level, it can be argued that without the support of the *mighty men of David*, Solomon would not have ruled Israel.

328

denies the request.[32] Furthermore, he discerns the threat Adonijah is to his keeping the throne, so he sends Benaiah (Jah has built) to eliminate him. For having followed Adonijah, Abiathar (Eli's last son) is stripped of the priesthood. (This had been Samuel's prophecy.) Benaiah is also instructed to execute both Joab (to eliminate *the guilt for the blood which Joab shed without cause*) and Shimel (who kept not his oath).

Solomon Has Wisdom, Understanding, Prosperity, Rest and Supply

But most importantly, Solomon discerns "true" *desire*. *At Gibeon the LORD appeared to Solomon in a dream by night; and God said, "Ask what I shall give you." And Solomon said, "Thou hast shown great and steadfast love to thy servant David my father,* **because he walked before thee in faithfulness, in righteousness, and in uprightness of heart toward thee;**... *And now, O LORD my God, thou hast made [me] king in place of David my father, although I am but a little child;* **I do not know how to go out or come in.** *And [I am] in the midst of thy people ..., a great people, that cannot be numbered or counted for multitude.* **Give thy servant therefore an understanding mind to govern thy people, that I may discern between good and evil;...** " *It pleased the Lord that Solomon had asked this. And God said to him,* **"Because you have asked this, and have not asked for yourself long life or riches or the life of your enemies, but have asked for yourself understanding to discern what is right, (12) BEHOLD, I NOW DO ACCORDING TO YOUR WORD. Behold, I give you a wise and discerning mind, so that none like you has been before you and none like you shall arise after you.** *I give you also what you have not asked, both riches and honor, so that no other king shall compare with you, all your days. And* **if you will walk in my ways, keeping my statutes and my commandments**, *as your father David walked,* **then I will lengthen your days."** 1 Kgs. 3:5-14.

Solomon can discern *truth*. When two women claim the same baby, he calls for a sword to divide the child. Discerning the difference in the women's reactions, he recognizes the true mother. *And all Israel heard of the judgment which the king had rendered; and they stood in awe of the king, because they perceived that the wisdom of God was in him, to render justice.* 1 Kgs. 3:28. **And Judah and Israel dwelt in safety, from Dan even to Beer-sheba, every man under his vine and under his fig tree, all the days of Solomon.** *Solomon also had forty thousand stalls of horses for his chariots, and twelve thousand horsemen. And those officers supplied provisions for King Solomon, and for all who came to King Solomon's table, each one in his month; they let nothing be lacking. Barley also and straw for the horses and swift steeds they brought to the place ... And God gave Solomon wisdom and understanding beyond measure, and largeness of mind like the sand on the seashore, so that Solomon's wisdom surpassed the wisdom of all the people of the east, and all the wisdom of Egypt.*

---

[32] Adonijah is asking to marry a concubine of David. Such an occurrence would be an official declaration of Adonijah as heir.

*... He also uttered **three thousand proverbs; and his songs** were a **thousand and
five.** He spoke of trees, from the **cedar that is in Lebanon** to the **hyssop that
grows out of the wall;** he spoke also **of beasts,** and **of birds,** and **of reptiles,** and
of fish. And men came from all peoples to hear the wisdom of Solomon, and
from all the kings of the earth...* 1 Kgs.4:25-34.

It is time to hang loose again. We must evaluate
David and Solomon together. David is thirty (30) when he
begins to reign; he reigns for forty (40) years. Solomon, too,
reigns for forty (40) years.[33]   But most important is God's
comment to him *I now do according to* YOUR WORD.

Solomon symbolizes the highest level of the earthly
plane. From this point on, only the Christ expression is on
the climb. Life has always been delivering *according to our
word*; previously, we just weren't aware of it. Now we are
aware. Now we "see." Now we are "naked" and ashamed
not. Now we "say" *righteously*.

And Solomon discerns that it is
time to build the LORD a house. *Now Hiram,
king of Tyre,...always loved David. And Solomon sent*

The **"King"**
**hears, walks,
sees and says
righteously.**

*word to Hiram, "You know that **David** my father **could
not build a house for the name of the LORD his God because of the warfare
with which his enemies surrounded him, until the LORD put them under the
soles of his feet.** But now the **LORD my God has given me rest on every side;
there is neither adversary nor misfortune.** And so **I purpose to build a house
for the name of the LORD my God,** as the LORD said to David my father, **'Your
son,** whom I will set upon your throne in your place, **shall build the house for my
name.'*** 1 Kgs. 5: 1-5.

David had always wanted to build the Temple; but he
knew it was not to be. He had told Solomon: *"My son, I had it in
my heart to build a house to the name of the LORD my God. But the word of the
LORD came to me, saying, '**You have shed much blood and have waged great
wars; you shall not build a house to my name, because you have shed so much***

---

[33] If the intellectual mind insists on knowing when Solomon began to reign, we can
guess that Solomon was born somewhere between 11½ years after David's Hebron
reign began, which would make him somewhere between 28½ down to a young
child. Logic suggests that a young child would not have been able to defeat
Adonijah's claim to the throne, and Solomon's comment that he is *but a little child*
is overstatement, intended for emphasis and effect. So we can assume that he was
somewhere near 70 when he died. Traditional numbering probably would be such.

blood before me upon the earth.' ... Only, may the LORD grant you discretion and understanding, that when he gives you charge over Israel you may keep the law of the LORD your God. Then you will prosper if you are careful to observe the statutes and the ordinances which the LORD commanded Moses for Israel. Be strong, and of good courage. Fear not; be not dismayed. With great pains I have provided for the house of the LORD a hundred thousand talents of gold, a million talents of silver, and bronze and iron beyond weighing, for there is so much of it; timber and stone too I have provided. To these you must add. You have an abundance of workmen: stonecutters, masons, carpenters, and all kinds of craftsmen without number, skilled in working gold, silver, bronze, and iron. Arise and be doing! The LORD be with you!" 1 Chron. 22:12-16.

David Prepares What's Required for the Building of the Temple

Esoterically, this *loving, warrior King* of our Self has prepared most of our needs for building the Temple, the "permanent" structure for worship of the Lord. No longer will our "site" of worship be "temporary." And similarly, no longer must we be a "warrior." Everything is finally provided for us, and there are no "threatening" evils.

And notice what is provided for us: **100,000** – 10x10 to a cosmic level of **gold; 1,000,000** – cosmic level upon cosmic level of **silver**; uncountable amounts of bronze and iron; and timber and stone (building stone and precious stones). But we are admonished: ***To these you must add.*** Climbing the Mountain is never finished.

Like the Tabernacle, the Temple is a physical form designed to remind man/woman of the process through which he/she must pass.[34] Built on Mount Moriah, it is at a high place with outer court, inner court, and inner sanctuary.

---

[34] Solomon's Temple was dedicated approximately 955 B.C. after 20 years in the building. It lasted nearly four centuries until it was destroyed in 586 B.C. by Nebuchadnezzar, king of Babylonia. It was restored, in the same form – with most of the returned ceremonial objects – beginning in 519 B.C.. But neither the Ark of the Covenant nor the Urim and Thummin were to be found, according to the Talmud. Reconstruction took three years. The Temple was again rebuilt by Herod, king of Judea, in 20-19 B.C.; but it was destroyed again with its burning during the sack of Jerusalem by the Romans in 70 A.D. The only remnant of Herod's Temple is the "wailing wall." See Ausubel, *Jewish Knowledge,* pp. 460-465.

And its entry is between two massive pillars, [south] Jachin (he will establish) and [north] Boaz (strength). Like the Tabernacle, the Temple, in its dimensions and design, symbolizes the form of man; and it provides an earthly focus for the physical expression. Paul clearly expresses the esoteric: *For we are the temple of the living God; as God said, "I will live in them and move among them, and I will be their God, and they shall be my people...."* 2 Cor. 6:16.

Esoterically, Solomon is almost mythical; but like the Temple, he is of the physical. His expression represents the height of physical expression. He even builds a "house" for the daughter of Pharoah. (He rules symbolic "Egypt.") And even the Queen of Sheba comes to hear his profound wisdom. But he does not live forever, and his descendents are not able to keep the throne; eventually Israel is split and declines. The "priestly" explanation is that Solomon married foreign women and followed after their gods. But intuition wonders: can the physical expression ever retain the "glimpse" of the Divine which it is given? Physical mankind must be transformed. *For as by a man came death, by a man has come also the resurrection of the dead.* 1 Cor. 15:21.

Almost five hundred years after Solomon, Malachi, the last prophet, writes of the coming of the Day of the LORD, and he says: *For behold, the day comes, burning like an oven, when all the arrogant and all evildoers will be stubble; the day that comes shall burn them up, says the LORD of hosts, so that it will leave them neither root nor branch. But for you who fear my name the sun of righteousness shall rise, with healing in its wings. You shall go forth leaping like calves from the stall.... Behold, I will send you Elijah the prophet before the great and terrible day of the LORD comes. And he will turn the hearts of fathers to their children and the hearts of children to their fathers...* Mal .4:1-6.

The Old Testament lessons are complete.

The Holy Family (Mary and Jesus; Elizabeth and John) by Bartolomé Estéban Murillo.

Chapter Thirteen
The "Christ"

Truly, truly, I say to you, **the hour is coming,** *and now is,* **when the dead will hear the voice of the Son of God, and those who hear will live.** *For as the Father has life in himself, so he has granted the Son also to have life in himself,* **and has given him authority to execute judgment, because he is the Son of man.** *Do not marvel at this; for the hour is coming when all who are in the tombs will hear his voice and come forth, those who have done good, to the resurrection of life, and those who have done evil, to the resurrection of judgment. I can do nothing on my own authority;* **as I hear, I judge; and my judgment is just, because I seek not my own will but the will of him who sent me.** Jn. 5:25-30.

From the viewpoint of David, the *loving* King, and all those who preceded him, the climb has been completed; the Promised Land has been fully conquered. Then, why aren't we at rest? Because the climb is not finished. Now we must enter the Kingdom of Heaven, the lesson of the Messiah – the Christ.[1] But what we seldom realize is that to enter the Kingdom of Heaven, we must let go of the Promised Land! A deeper understanding is required for the Kingdom of Heaven than was required in the Promised Land. In some ways the Promised Land is still the land of the intellect; in the Kingdom of Heaven, the intuition takes precedence. Our intellect understands *Sabbath* as one day of the week dedicated to God; only the intuition can understand

---

[1] *Messiah* literally means "anointed," a *consecrated* person, but it implies a "Redeemer" or a "Savior." The term is only used in Daniel and in John. But John uses it only twice; usually (as do the rest of the New Testament writers) he uses *Christ,* the Greek term, again coming from a verb meaning to "smear" or "rub with oil." It comes from a root which implies *to furnish what is needed.*

Ausubel (*Knowledge),* p. 281, says: "Its [the Messiah's] early origins lie half-concealed, due to the fact that no unitary or fully developed conception of the Messiah was ever rendered in ancient Jewish writings." Yet, he writes: "The predetermined mission of the Messiah was definitive and clear: the establishment of God's Kingdom *on earth* ... when brotherhood, peace, and justice would usher in the eternal Sabbath for Israel, and for the rest of mankind as well, provided it accepted the belief in One God and his Torah."

the *eternal Sabbath*, for it is on a different plane.[2] It means the difference between the "living" and the "dead." Only those who "hear" are among the living.

By the time of the Roman Empire, much of the Jewish expression was no longer of the "living." Nearly 1000 years of challenges had taken their toll. The kingdom became an empire, but after Solomon's death **it split in two,** with Judah (the tribes of Judah and Benjamin) centered in Jerusalem and Israel (the other ten tribes) centered in Samaria. Warfare between the two – with only short periods of peace – continued for the next 108 years, until in 722 B.C. **Samaria was overrun** by Sargon II of Assyria.[3] Judah survived for a time, but eventually it fell to **Babylonia** (Assyria's successor c. 604 B.C.) and **Nebuchadnezzar** carried the first set of Jewish elite (including Daniel and his friends) to Babylonia. Systematically the Babylonians took the cream **70-Year Babylonian Captivity** of Jewish society to Babylonia, until the **Persians** under Cyrus conquered Babylonia and incorporated its many peoples into the Persian Empire. Most likely anticipating an ally in a Jewish state, Cyrus sent some Jews back to Jerusalem (537-536 B.C.). Those returning began to rebuild the Temple; and with additional returnees and the support of Darius (Cyrus' successor), they completed the Second Temple in twenty years (516 B.C.). Under the Persians, the Jews were again autonomous, at least on the surface, and the priests ruled the area from Jerusalem.

---

[2] Remember the requirements for the Sabbath? *You shall keep the sabbath, because it is holy for you... whoever does any work on it, that soul shall be cut off from among his people. Six days shall work be done, but the seventh day is a sabbath of solemn rest, holy to the LORD;* **whoever does any work on the sabbath day shall be put to death.** *... It is a sign for ever between me and the people of Israel that in six days the LORD made heaven and earth, and on the seventh day he rested, and was refreshed.'"* Ex. 31:14-17.

[3] The Bible predictably gives us a symbolic number for the "life-time" of "Samaria;" it is the product of 9x12. According to Biblical accounts, 28,290 persons were carried into captivity, and foreigners were imported into the partially vacant land. Consequently, by the time of Jesus, all **Samaritans** were considered half-breeds practicing a "contaminated" religion.

Alexander the Great and the Greeks put an end to the Persian Empire (334-332 B.C.), and even though Alexander's death split the political empire in three parts, the **Hellenistic** culture was imposed on much of the world, including Judea and Palestine. However, the Greek Hellenistic culture tolerated religious differences, and some

Alexander dies at 33.

Jews were even taken away to populate Alexandria in Egypt. Alexandria became a literary center with a library housing the greatest collection of world knowledge ever accumulated.[4] It was this colony which undertook the translation of the Hebrew Scriptures into Greek. The Septuagint – so called for the 72 members of the Sanhedrin or for the 70 who did the translation (depending on your authority) – was begun in the 3rd Century B.C. with the Pentateuch (five books of Moses); and completed in 2nd Century B.C., just as the Hellenistic world was about to fall.

The Hellenistic world was not so much conquered by the Romans as absorbed by them. The left-over Greek governmental entities disappeared, and many Greeks became

slaves; but almost everything else of substance remained Greek. Greek gods were simply given different names, and the Greek alphabet simply converted to Roman letter forms. Romans fully accepted Greek learning. But Jewish customs did not fit Roman control as well as they had fit the Persian

Caesar Augustus

---

[4] It was this library (housed in a temple of Jupiter) which fanatical Christians destroyed in 391 A.D.– thus destroying irreplaceable knowledge of the ancient world.

and Greek hegemonies. **The Roman Empire** was a unit, and Roman law was unaccepting of diffferences. The central government closely watched potentially rebellious regions, such as Judea.

We may not regard the Romans as highly as we do the Greeks; but the relative peace brought by the threat of, or the actual presence of, Roman soldiers furthered an enviable distribution system aided by well-designed and well-built Roman roads and a universal Latin language. This "unity" lasted more than 500 years; without it Christianity would not have thrived.

Compared to the duration of the Roman Empire, the 80-some years of the Hebrew Empire pales. By the time of Jesus, 900-some years after its end, the splendor of its Golden Age is remembered only in the Scriptures. Moreover, by the time of Jesus, the Hebrew Empire has been reduced to the Jewish state, the vassal of an empire, ruled by Caesar Augustus in far-off Rome. At home they are ruled by the despotic Herod the Great, who mounts a great building effort and even rebuilds the 500-year-old Second Temple. (Between the death of Solomon (930 B.C.) and Herod's rebuilding of the Temple (20-19 B.C.) is 910 years.) Jewish sentiment longed for a return to the Golden Age of David and his son Solomon.

Through the Bible's account and from the writings of Josephus, we have a fairly good picture of Jewish society at the time of Jesus. We know that there were at least four major philosophical divisions among the Jews: the Sadducees, the Pharisees, the Zealots and the Essenes. Of these, the Sadducees (the priestly aristocrats) were the purists, those who held only to the written law, denying the validity of those beliefs which had crept into Jewish life during and since the Exile.[5] But paradoxically, the Sadducees had embraced some of the characteristics of

---

[5] According to Ausubel, Persian ideas such as beliefs in "angels, spirits, and demons" and "doctrines of resurrection and an afterlife of reward and punishment" had been accepted by the Jews living in Babylon. *Knowledge...* p. 337-339.

Hellenism. They enjoyed the more worldly expression of the Greeks, as well as the private wealth which had been relatively unknown before Hellenism.

The Pharisees, on the other hand, originated as those who "utterly rejected Hellenism" and declared themselves to be the "holy ones." The Pharisees accepted the written Law and "also the oral traditions that had grown up about it." They anticipated the Messiah's coming, and they declared "Unto all are given the Kingdom, the Priesthood, and the Heritage."[6] During the First Century B.C. they had succeeded in outnumbering the Sadducees on the Sanhedrin (the Jewish ruling body). Interestingly, both the Zealots and the Essenes were offshoots of the Pharisees.

The Zealots were more political than religious advocates. They demanded action against Rome.[7] And we know that at least one of the apostles was a Zealot (Simon);[8] and it is possible that *Iscariot*, which heretofore has been presumed to be Judas' city, has been poorly transcribed from "Sicariot," a party of "assassins."[9]

But the Essenes are not mentioned in the Bible. Our knowledge of them comes from three secular sources.[10] However, since the discovery of the Dead Sea Scrolls in 1947,

---

[6] *Asimov's Guide to the Bible,* pp. 806, 807. Asimov points out that "Pharisaic teaching at its best very much resembles that of the New Testament. The Jewish teacher Hillel, who died about A.D. 10, taught a kindly religion of love and represents a kind of Jewish parallel to the doctrines of Jesus. Hillel was even, purportedly, of the line of David. However, no miracles are associated with [his] name, nor did he (or anyone else on his behalf) ever claim Messiah-hood."

[7] *Ibid.,* p. 840.

[8] *Apostles* comes from the Greek *apostolos* meaning *he that is sent.* The *apostles* were those sent to spread the "good news." *Disciples* refers to the follower of a public teacher. Most of the Prophets, Moses, as well as John, had *disciples.* (As did Pythagoras, Socrates, Plato, etc.) Supposedly Jesus had either 70 or 72 disciples.

[9] Asimov (p. 841) does not give his source, but calls it a "recent" interpretation. He says that members of this *Sicariot* party were so called because of a Greek word for "assassins" referring to men carrying little knives, "sicae," under their robes.

[10] The Essenes are mentioned by Josephus (Jewish scholar and historian), Philo (Alexandrian Jewish philosopher), and Pliny (Roman author and scholar who fought in the Jewish wars and was made procurator of Syria).

the Essenes have been the subject of great research; and now many are convinced that Jesus (and probably at least John) was connected to this ascetic sect. To my thinking, it is likely that Jesus and John were part of a group substantially more spiritual than the standard level of Jewish society.

Our intellect calculates time by years, but the Bible sees the period in terms of generations; and Matthew immediately begins with the generations from Abraham to Jesus, *who is called Christ*. And concludes the list with: *So **all the generations** from Abraham to David were **fourteen** generations, and from David to the deportation to Babylon **fourteen** generations, and from the deportation to Babylon to the Christ **fourteen generations**.* Mt. 1:17.

Matthew is continuing the Old Testament. Fourteen generations have passed since the deportation to Babylon. It is time for the Christ![11] Abraham is considered the father of the Jewish people; and since Matthew is writing for Jews, he points out that Jesus is the 42nd generation from Abraham – 42 being three sets of 14.[12] The intellect might wonder if these generational numbers are accurate, but the intuition accepts their esoteric message. All of this tells us that the New Testament will continue the symbolism and the hang-loose approach found in the Old Testament.[13]

---

[11] The number given to the summarizing verse is #17, which symbolizes "receiving," dependent on how we "see" and "say." (See page 16.)

[12] In hang-loose logic, we have passed three levels of duality. It would appear as such: **Abraham** (7+7), **David** (7+7), **Babylon** (7+7), **the Christ**. Therefore, the Christ level will bring **completion**, but logic also insists that this Christ-level will also have to complete the 7+7 sequence of duality, cf. Elizabeth/John; Jesus/Judas; Mary/ Mary Magdalene; therefore, the risen Christ would be number 7.

[13] The difference between the generational lists of Matthew and Luke usually is explained with the answer that Matthew is listing the heritage of Mary. Certainly, the intuition notices Matthew's inclusion of (5) of Jesus' female ancestors. They are **Tamar**, daughter-in-law of Judah, who produced Perez and his twin by **deceiving Judah; Rahab**, the **former harlot;** and **Ruth**, the **former widow**. The fourth woman is Bathsheba, but she is mentioned only by the name of her first husband, Urias **(flame of God.)** All except Mary appear in the first 14 generations, and only Mary is mentioned as herself rather than just as the wife of a man. In fact, Joseph is mentioned as Mary's husband, thereby Mary reverses the patterns used for the previous four women ancestors.

On the other hand, Luke's presentation of the generations is not for the Jews; he is writing for Greeks and Romans. Interestingly, in Luke's list there are no women listed, even though Ruth, the great-grandmother of David was a gentile. And Luke ties Jesus to all *climbing* mankind by placing him **77** generations from Adam. See Luke 3:23-38.

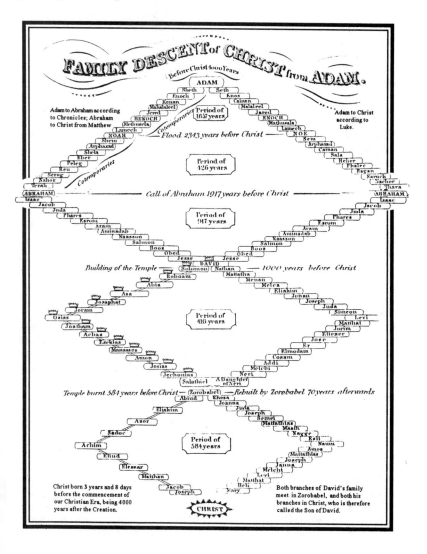

340

Will you hang loose? The New Testament requires even more "flexibility" than the Old![14] The story of the Christ is not just the story of Jesus. Rather, it is the story of that which Jesus "meets" in the process of "being" the Christ. It is the story of what we meet as we approach the Kingdom of Heaven. And we were already given the first step with the last line of the Old Testament: *"Behold, I will send you Elijah the prophet before the great and terrible day of the LORD comes...."*

Matthew has Jesus ask his hearers: *"Why then did you [follow John]? To see a prophet? Yes, I tell you, and more than a prophet. This is he of whom it is written, 'Behold, I send my messenger before thy face, who shall prepare thy way before thee.' Truly, I say to you, among those born of women there has risen no one greater than John the Baptist; yet he who is least in the kingdom of heaven is greater than he. From the days of John the Baptist until now the kingdom of heaven has suffered violence [a watchtower of besiegers], and men of violence take it by force. For all the prophets and the law prophesied until John; [14] and if you are willing to accept it, he is Elijah who is to come. He who has ears to hear, let him hear."* Mt. 11:9-15

Do we "hear" what Jesus is saying? He may or may not be saying that the Baptist is the "reincarnated" Elijah. More important is the second part of his statement. Let me paraphrase "... if you perfected the *hearing* that you worked on through the Old Testament ... then **hear** what I (Jesus) say!"[15]

The gospel of Mark lets Jesus make the point even more strongly: *"... there is nothing hid, except to be made manifest; nor is anything secret, except to come to light. If any man has ears to hear, let him hear." And he said to them, "Take heed what you hear; the measure you give will be the measure you get, and still more will be given you. For to him who has will more be given; and from him who has not, even what he has will be taken away."* Mk. 4:22-25

---

[14] To the Greeks and Romans, as to the Jews, *numbers* were significant. Remember, Pythagoras taught the ancient "symbolism" of numbers, and Rome simply accepted the philosophy of Greece as her own. As a case in point, in The Old Testament much development takes place at the level of 11. Now at the number 77, earthly completion (7) has come to #11 with the birth of Jesus.

[15] Matthew uses "ecumenical enumeration" for Greeks as well as the Jews. Notice the Chapter is 11; the major verse is 14.The most difficult part of the quote is "violence." Actually, Jesus is saying that those who have come before have been of a different mindset, those who had to "war" to attain the kingdom of heaven. Notice, prior to John all have been just a **"lookout."** And remember the number of the summarizing verse is 17. Our "receiving" is dependent on how we "see" and "say."

This is beginning to sound even more intense than the Old Testament, isn't it? We thought we learned *to hear, to walk, to see,* and we were just beginning *to say.* Now, to emphasize that the lessons must be retained, the passage reads: *to him who has, more will be given.* The New Testament will offer the lessons again; but at the Christ level it is imperative that we understand what we have learned, because it also reads: *from him who has not, [all] will be taken away.* The LAW hasn't changed, it has intensified.

John: The Baptist

In the New Testament, we will address similar trials to those in the Old, but we will address them more intensely. And it begins with a new prophet.[16] *In those days came John the Baptist, preaching in the wilderness of Judea, "Repent, for the kingdom of heaven is at hand. For [I am] he who was spoken of by the prophet Isaiah when he said, 'The voice of one crying in the wilderness: Prepare the way of the Lord, make his paths straight.'"* Mt. 3:2.

It is nearly 500 years since the last accepted prophet. But the Baptist is like the previous prophets, "holy men, surrendered to God's service,... who lived in communion with God ... who composed their minds and gave themselves up to quiet contemplation, in order to wait for revelation."[17] And he baptizes and he is accepted; and his disciples follow him.

Now John wore a garment of camel's hair, and a leather girdle around his waist; and his food was locusts and wild honey. Then went out to him Jerusalem and all Judea and all the region about the Jordan, and they were baptized by him in the river Jordan, confessing their sins. But when he saw many of the Pharisees and Sadducees coming for baptism, he said to them, "You brood of vipers! Who warned you to flee from the wrath to come? Bear fruit that befits repentance, and do not presume to say to yourselves, 'We have Abraham as our father'; for I tell you, God is able from these stones to raise up children to Abraham. Even now the axe is laid to the root of the trees; every tree therefore that does not bear good fruit is cut down and thrown into the fire." Mt. 3:1-10.

---

[16] After Solomon, the prophets of Judah and Israel became the focus for the LORD'S communication with the Jewish people. Possibly, chief among the prophets was **Elijah** (c.870 B.C.) who announces that while God is in the whirlwind, he *is found in the still small voice.* Elijah is followed by **Elisha**, who is given a double portion of Elijah's powers, sufficient to *his bones* raising the dead. In the next century, **Hosea** announces that God *desires steadfast love,* not sacrifice and *the knowledge of God,* rather than burnt offerings. His contemporary, **Amos,** adds: *let justice roll down like waters, and righteousness like an ever-flowing stream.* **Micah,** years later adds: *do justice,... love kindness and ... walk humbly with our God.*

[17] Thus, *The Westminster Dictionary of the Bible,* Davis and Gehman, p. 494, describes prophets.

St. John, the Baptist, by Leonardo da Vinci.

Anything in our nature which does not bear "good fruit" will be eliminated; anything less than the finest gold will be burned up. And that portion of our nature which says "Repent" will be "beheaded." The "Christed" man/woman is a new creature, but "repentance" comes first.[18]

The Baptist says: *"I baptize you with water for repentance, but he who is coming after me is mightier than I, whose sandals I am not worthy to carry; he will baptize you with the Holy Spirit and with fire. His winnowing fork is in his hand, and he will clear his threshing floor and gather his wheat into the granary, but the chaff he will burn with unquenchable fire."* Mt. 3:11-12.

---

[18] *Repent* means to *rethink.* Remember that *anything* that makes an *unrighteous* statement **must** be eliminated. Therefore, any thinking that must be *rethought* is unrighteous. Just as the mental-mindset of Saul was cut-off, the mental understanding which requires *rethinking* must be removed.

Like Isaac, Jacob, Joseph, Sampson, and Samuel, the Baptist is the child of a mother who was previously barren.[19] His father, Zachariah, is a priest, not the high priest, but one truly consecrated to God; and he is told that his son is to be a Nazirite, fully dedicated to the LORD and *filled with the Holy Spirit,* one who will go before the LORD *to make ready ... a people prepared.* This portion of us which prepares the "people" is produced by a consciousness that is already consecrated to the LORD; but upon hearing the news, it becomes dumb – speaking again only as it affirms the LORD'S will.

Those of you on the climb will recognize what takes place with Zachariah. As we listen more closely to the Holy Spirit within us, for a time we're tempted to share what we're told with anyone who will let us speak, even with those who cannot "hear." But finally, we find ourselves unable to speak. We find that our understanding cannot be expressed with the spoken word, and so we keep silent.

Unlike the intellectual mind, the intuitional mind can keep silent; but sometimes it must speak. The Baptist is not concerned with the politics of the day; he is not concerned with whether or not the doctrines of Babylon should be accepted in Israel's beliefs. John the Baptist is saying: ***Rethink where your attention is!*** Like 20th-century civilization, 1st-century Judaism's attention is worldly. Judaism had lost the wisdom of David and Solomon.

Having completed this much of the climb, we might think we now possess greater understanding than the 1st-century Jews, but *pride* is never warranted. We will have to work even harder in the New Testament than we did in the Old, for the Old Testament is easier for our *intuition* than is the New, mostly because we are not so close in time to the Old Testament. This temporal proximity lets us approach the New Testament literally; and yet, it is not a literal text. Its presentation is as symbolic as was the Old Testament's.

---

[19] See Luke 1:5-80 for John's birth.

Interestingly, the four gospels give us a choice for our degree of symbolism.[20] Of the four writers, John is clearly the most mystical. He presents Jesus as embodiment of the *logos* of Greek mysticism, and he concludes the entire New Testament with the most mystical of all presentations, *Revelation*. On the other hand, Luke's presentation appeals to the literal mind, but his "physical embellishments" offer greatest opportunity for symbolism. Luke begins with the Baptist's heritage. For from barrenness comes that which comes before the Christ. But, it is a barrenness that is consecrated and dedicated to the LORD. Finally this barrenness is promised a son who will be filled with the Holy Spirit; and the child is conceived. Lk.1:5-24. And Elizabeth says: *Thus the Lord has done to me ... to take away my reproach among men.* Lk. 1:25

---

[20] Usually we think the term *gospel* alludes to a book, written by a particular individual; but it actually means *good news* or *good tidings*. We cannot be entirely sure of the history of the gospels; the commonly held scholastic view is that the three *synoptic* (presenting the same view) gospels – Matthew, Mark, and Luke – are the records put down by those named. Whether Matthew or Mark was the first gospel to be written or whether composition was in Aramaic or Greek is not the subject of this study. The reader is directed to the introductory notes to the New Testament found in *The Jerusalem Bible*, pp. 5 - 14.

By tradition the author of Matthew was he who is named in Mt. 9:9, *Jesus... saw a man, named Matthew, sitting at the receipt of custom:...* a tax collector. The presently accepted view is that Mark was the son of one of the Marys. He is mentioned in Acts 12:12 as *John, whose surname was Mark.* Traditionally, he was associated with Simon Peter, whom he used as his source. He may have been near at hand when Jesus was arrested (see Mark 14:51,52). Luke, according to Asimov (p. 914), was a gentile (other than Jewish) and probably a Roman (since Luke was a Roman name). Reputedly, the author of Luke was also the author of Acts of the Apostles, which chronicles the activities of Paul, and Paul writes to the Colossians 4:14: *Luke, the beloved physician, ... greets you.*

The most mystical of the gospels is that of John. John was the son of Zebedee, a master fisherman on the Sea of Galilee; his elder brother was that James who was martyred by Herod Agrippa – the first of the apostles to be killed. (Acts 12:1,2.) Their mother was Salome, the sister of the mother of Jesus. James was in partnership with Peter and Andrew (Lk. 5:10) and was apparently older than John. John had listened to the Baptist, and had heard him call Jesus "the *Lamb of God.* John is often called the "beloved" disciple. He accompanied Jesus at the raising of Jairus' daughter (Mk. 5:37), at the transfiguration (Mt. 17:1; Mk. 9:2; Lk. 9:28), and in the Garden (Mt. 26:37; Mk. 14:33). During the Last Supper, John sat next to Jesus (Jn. 13:23), and John was apparently the only disciple to follow Jesus to the high priest's palace and to Golgotha. At the crucifixion, Jesus gave his mother into John's keeping. (Jn. 18:15; 19:27.)

Six months later, the literal mind is told that a virgin, by the name of Mary, is visited by the angel Gabriel. And the angel tells her: *"Behold, you will conceive in your womb and bear a son, and you shall call his name Jesus. He will be great, and will be called the Son of the Most High; and the Lord God will give to him the throne of his father David, and he will reign over the house of Jacob for ever; and of his kingdom there will be no end."* Lk.1:31-33.

But generations earlier Isaiah had spoken similarly to the intuitional mind: *Therefore the Lord himself will give you a sign. Behold, **a young woman shall conceive and bear a son, and shall call his name Immanuel.** He shall eat curds and honey when he knows how to refuse the evil and choose the good.* Is. 7:14,15. *The people who [walk] in darkness [will see] a great light; those who [dwell] in a land of deep darkness, on them [will] light [shine].* Is. 9:2. *For **to us a child is born,** to us a son is given; **and the government will be upon his shoulder, and his name will be called "Wonderful Counselor, Mighty God, Everlasting Father, Prince of Peace."*** Is. 9:6,7.

This is a new covenant; this is the second promise. The first promise related to the *promised land*; this promise relates to the *kingdom of heaven.* The

The Annunciation by Burne-Jones.

346

promised land presented almost a transition; we had to address the physical expression first. Now, we must give it up. We're ready to rivet our attention on the spiritual, for the *kingdom of heaven* is the level of the Christ. Henceforth we will always have a *counselor, Immanuel (God with us)*, in us; and it will only *increase...with justice and with righteousness from this time forth and forevermore*. We've finally reached the point of "righteous judgment." We've become the "righteous man/woman."

The Nativity by Sandro Botticelli.

*"The **shepherds said**...let us go over to Bethlehem and see this thing that has happened, which the Lord has made known to us." And they went with haste, and found Mary and Joseph, and the **babe lying in a manger.** And when they saw it they made known the saying which had been told them concerning this child; and **all who heard it wondered at what the shepherds told them.** Lk. 2:15-19.*

But, remember what the shepherds are told? *"Be not afraid; for behold, I bring you good news of a great joy which will come to all the people; for to you is born this day in the city of David a Savior, who is Christ the Lord. And this will be a sign for you: you will find a babe wrapped in swaddling cloths and lying in a manger."* Lk. 2:10-12.

The activity of the Christ in us always begins as a "babe" – all wrapped up and lying in what holds food for our carnal nature. To my intuition, it appears that each of us comes into this life *exactly* where, when and how it is necessary for us to receive what we need either to finish the climb or continue on it. However, whether we *finish* or *continue* or – and we trust it is not the case – *lose ground*, depends on our ability to deal with this carnal nature.[21]

Jesus says as much in answer to the questions of the disciples regarding the man who was "born blind," but it is only the mystical gospel that reveals this understanding.

*As he passed by, he saw a man blind from his birth. And his disciples asked him, "Rabbi, who sinned, this man or his parents, that he was born blind?" Jesus answered, "It was not that this man sinned, or his parents, **but that the works of God might be made manifest in him. We must work the works of him who sent me, while it is day; night comes, when no one can work. As long as I am in the world, I am the light of the world."** As he said this, he spat on the ground and made clay of the spittle and anointed the man's eyes with the clay, saying to him, **"Go, wash in the pool of** Siloam" (which means **Sent**). So he went and washed and came back seeing. The neighbors and those who had seen him before as a beggar, said, "Is not this the man who used to sit and beg?" Some said, "It is he"; others said, "No, but he is like him." He said, "**I am the man.**"* Jn. 9:1-9.

We are each placed so *that the works of God might be made manifest in* us.[22] Notice the lives of Jesus and of John the Baptist. They are probably second or third cousins; they are

---

[21] Even the esoteric "believer" in reincarnation would not anticipate the newly reborn soul to reenter "full-bloomed." Rather, the new incarnation has a "proclivity," a tendency, toward his/her path.

[22] The term *manifest* in itself is esoteric. *Manifest* means *readily perceived by the senses, especially the sight.* We could say that it means that which comes into physical existence. Therefore *in order that the works of God be manifest in him* means that "such and such" condition is put in place *in order* that the *truth* can be readily perceived by him. There is an added inferrence: not only *by him*, but *through him*. Each of us produces more than we are ever aware of.

both children of the Essene community.[23] But they each have a different ministry. John is the son of the older feminine expression; John admonishes *repentance*. John will be beheaded. Jesus is the son of the virginal, prepared feminine expression; Jesus *is* the *Christ*, the *anointed*. Jesus is *crucified* on the *cross;* Jesus is *resurrected*.

Unless I'm mistaken, the world sees the existence of each of us as accidental, simply the result of a sperm fertilizing an egg and growing until it is born. The world sees each of us as simply the product of our physical heritage, sometimes with a glitch or two, but replicating the human form of animal life. In such a mindset, it is only this human-form animal which is *manifest*. Animal-life isn't terribly redeeming. Even with limited "sight" we can see that sometimes we're born incapacitated in one way or another; sometimes we're born into surroundings that incapacitate us. Likely as not, we're born *blind*: all we see is a man or woman going from birth to death.[24]

How different is the viewpoint of he/she who advances to the level of John the Baptist. When his disciples bring Jesus' recent activities to his attention, John answers: *You yourselves bear me witness, that I said, "I am not the Christ, but I have been sent before him." He who has the bride is the bridegroom; the friend of the bridegroom, who stands and hears him, rejoices greatly at the bridegroom's voice; therefore **this joy of mine is now full**. **He must increase, but I must decrease**.* Jn. 3:28-30.

At this stage, there is that within us which has been baptized, which has repented. It is that *within* which is related to the Christ and recognizes the Christ – but it knows that it is not yet operating at the level of the Christ. It is this which must baptize the Christ. So we need to look at *baptism* for a

---

[23] The non-celibate members of the Essene community anticipated procreation, but Elizabeth and Zechariah were barren. Mary, on the other hand, would have been among *twelve maidens who were to be channels that might know truth so thoroughly that they could be moved by the Holy Spirit. Edgar Cayce's Story of Jesus,* ed. Furst, p.126.

[24] Notice the word *incapacitate*. It carries the basic Latin term *cap* meaning *head*. Just as Saul and John the Baptist are *decapitated*, we are *incapacitated* by the worldly view.

moment. Remember, we're in a dusty land where water is precious. The Tabernacle (See page 206) and the Temple provided the *laver*, a basin containing water for the washing of feet and hands, placed in between the altar for burnt offering and the "tent of meeting." In less esoteric terms – between the "burning" lessons of our **Baptism** lives and our entry into a conscious submission and relationship with God, we must be *cleansed,* we must be made ready to receive.[25]

The New Testament adds additional elements to the symbolism. The washing clean, the baptism, takes place in the Jordan River, that which *descends* from the Sea of Galilee to the Dead Sea. How descriptive of our lives when we are still *of the world.* And often it is only as our lives *descend* that we are willing to be *baptized.* Moreover, the baptism is of the "whole" body, not just the hands and feet as in the Tabernacle.

The gospels tell us: *In those days **Jesus** came from Nazareth of Galilee and **was baptized by John in the Jordan**.   And **when he came up out of the water, immediately he saw the heavens opened and the Spirit descending upon him** like a dove;   and a voice came from heaven, "**Thou art my beloved Son; with thee I am well pleased**."   The Spirit immediately drove him out into the wilderness.   And **he was in the wilderness forty days**, tempted by Satan; and **he was with the wild beasts; and the angels ministered to him**.* Mk. 1:9-13.[26]

Baptism and the descent of the Holy Spirit are only symbols of the change that takes place in us as we are totally cleansed. **40 Days In the Wilderness** But this change is not fully internalized until it has been tested and found strong enough to survive. Consequently, Jesus immediately is *placed* into the

---

[25] Don't think that we can keep the habits of the carnal world and be *cleansed.* We are talking about *thinking* habits, *seeing* habits, *speaking* habits, action habits, food habits, drinking habits, sexual habits, and *attachment* habits. B*aptism* is not a casual agreement with God. It is a pledge, a covenant, saying that henceforth all within (and without) us will be of the nature of the *divine.* It will be pure; it will be perfect.

[26] Notice the numbers which Mark uses. The chapter is the whole (1); then the account begins with the number of the initiate (9) and ends with the number of the Christ (13).

wilderness and *temptation*. It is as it was with Jacob and Moses, but we can tell from the duration of the experience that Jesus is an advancement over both Jacob and Moses. Instead of 40 years, Jesus spends only 40 days in the wilderness. But what do *wilderness* and *temptation* mean?

Again, let's hang loose! The *wilderness* means an experience where we no longer have physical control over the "creature" comforts that we think we have to have. Remember the people of Israel complaining that they should have stayed in Egypt where they had "meat" to eat? Most likely, the experience is both physical and psychological. Moreover, it is an aloneness where even though we're surrounded by others, no physical person can lend support. As

Jesus' Temptations

difficult as the "wilderness" is, "Satan's" temptations are even more difficult. Let's look at "Satan" as those "human" tendencies that get us in trouble. These are *spiritual* challenges. *And **Jesus, full of the Holy Spirit**, returned from the Jordan, and was **led by the Spirit** for forty days in the **wilderness, tempted by the devil**. And **he ate nothing** in those days; and when they were ended, **he was hungry**. The devil said to him, "If you are the Son of God, command this stone to become bread." And Jesus answered him, "It is written, **'Man shall not live by bread alone.'"** And the devil took him up, and showed him all the kingdoms of the world in a moment of time, and said to him, **"To you I will give all this authority and their glory;** for it has been delivered to me, and I give it to whom I will. If you, then, will worship me, it shall all be yours." And Jesus answered him, "It is written, **'You shall worship the Lord your God, and him only shall you serve.'"** And he took him to Jerusalem, and set him on the pinnacle of the temple, and said to him, "If you are the Son of God, **throw yourself down** from here; for it is written, 'He will give his angels charge of you, to guard you,' and 'On their hands they will bear you up, lest you strike your foot against a stone.'" And Jesus answered him, "It is said, **'You shall not tempt the Lord your God.'"** And when the devil had ended every temptation, he departed from him until an opportune time.* Lk. 4:1-13.*

Mankind really didn't have to invent a "devil." Just the carnal life itself is "devil" enough. Notice *devil* is "lived" spelled backward. It is the mindset of the "dead." And it says to Jesus, "You're hungry. Your physical body is the important part of you, satisfy it!" But Jesus refrains. It says to Jesus,

"Your psychological self-image can be improved with the glory of the world!" But Jesus knows that the *outer* does not determine the *inner*. He denies it. And it says, "If you're the son of God, you can disregard the physical laws!" Jesus knows this also to be untrue! He resists.

Just as Abram had to leave the mindset that ignored the spiritual expression and tried to control the physical expression through magic – Abram left Ur of the Chaldees – Jesus has to hold to the knowledge that **the spiritual expression is all there is.** Jesus knows that the physical and mental expressions are simply evidence of the "health" of the spiritual. Can you believe it? Try as hard as we can, we can't get away from it. It's our old *friend* or *nemesis* (depending on how we **hear, see** and **say**) – the LAW.

It's interesting that the account of Jesus' wilderness experience is found only in the synoptic gospels. The mystical gospel (John) has no need for the lessons of earth. They have **Water Into Wine** already been learned. John puts the statement in higher terms: Jesus turns the water into wine! Consequently, the account of the miracle at the wedding at Cana is found only in the gospel of John. *On the third day there was a marriage at Cana in Galilee, and the mother of Jesus was there; Jesus also was invited to the marriage, with his disciples. When the wine failed, the mother of Jesus said to him, "They have no wine." And Jesus said to her, "O woman, what have you to do with me? My hour has not yet come." His mother said to the servants, "Do whatever he tells you."*

Now six stone jars were standing there, for the Jewish rites of purification, each holding twenty or thirty gallons. Jesus said to them, "Fill the jars with water." And they filled them up to the brim. He said to them, "Now draw some out, and take it to the steward of the feast." So they took it. When the steward of the feast tasted the water now become wine, and did not know where it came from (though the servants who had drawn the water knew), the steward of the feast called the bridegroom and said to him, "Every man serves the good wine first; and when men have drunk freely, then the poor wine; but you have kept the good wine until now." This, the first of his signs, Jesus did at Cana in Galilee, and manifested his glory; and his disciples believed in him. Jn. 2:1-11.

We are no longer at the level of John the Baptist. Now the Christ in us is beginning to demonstrate its understanding of the LAW. Significantly, the wedding takes place at Cana in Galilee. *Cana* is related to a word that refers to a "reed" that is a rod for measurement. In accord with the LAW, the Christ is producing as it measures; and it measures "full-full."

Whether the literal story of the wedding at Cana takes place or not is of no importance; more important are the hints toward understanding that we are given. Just prior to this, John has told of Jesus' acquiring the most important of his disciples. Apparently, John, along with Andrew, had been following John the Baptist when they heard the Baptist refer to Jesus as "the Lamb of God." So they followed Jesus. Next, Andrew finds his brother Simon and tells him that they have found the Messiah. When Jesus meets Simon, he calls him Peter (the rock). The next day, in Galilee, Jesus comes across Philip, and says, "Follow me." And Philip, from the same location as Andrew and Peter, the town of Beth-sa'ida (fishing house), invites Nathaniel to join them.

These disciples are seekers, they certainly are not at the level of understanding of either the Baptist or Jesus, and Nathaniel is awed by the thought that Jesus had clairvoyantly "seen" him under a fig tree. But Jesus says even more: *And he said to him, "Truly, truly, I say to you, you will see heaven opened, and the angels of God ascending and descending upon the Son of man."* Jn. 1:51. Nathaniel is told that he eventually is going to be operating at the level that Jacob was operating at so long ago.

Then John tells us that **the third day**... there was a marriage at Cana in Galilee. Nothing ever "really" happens until we reach the *third* day. (See page 16) *Three* represents that which is happening. Mystically, it is the action taking place as the #2 (B) moves upon #1(A). If you like, it is the Holy Spirit becoming activated. And, you will note that the whole miracle takes place because *the mother of Jesus was there.* It is Mary who calls Jesus' attention to the fact that *They have no wine.* It is Mary who says to the servants: *Do whatever he tells you.* See Jn. 2:1-11.

From the beginning there has been "water." *...the Spirit of God was moving over the face of the waters.* Gen. 1:2. But "wine" has been with us (symbolically) only since the time of Noah. And we know that with Noah, mankind more stringently establishes its mistaken paradigm. With Noah, mankind "sees" the physical and judges it to be all that there is. Only with the Christ is the misjudgment corrected. Here with the Christ, the water (that which *is*, that which is divine) is shown to be the wine (that which enlivens, that which intoxicates). There is no difference; and it is accomplished at the dictate of the enlightened feminine.

The enlightened feminine is no longer wife or sister; now it is *mother*. Let's hang loose for a moment! Obviously, without *mother* we cannot reach the Christ. Yet, after the narrative of the birth of the Christ, she is only mentioned five more times: after Jesus is found at the Temple as a youth, at the wedding at Cana (in John), as an "insistent" mother at the door, at the foot of the cross and, lastly, in the *upper room* after the resurrection with Jesus' followers. Acts 1:14

Although Roman Catholic tradition has a rich tradition about Mary, Protestant Christianity makes little mention of her. In neither case does the Church address the requirement of the feminine for the expression of the Christ. Even esotericists pay little attention to what we might call the feminine expression of the Christ; but, for now, let's approach this feminine expression only as Jesus' mother.

We know little about Mary. Luke mentions that Elizabeth is of *the daughters of Aaron* (1:5); but this may be an honorary title, although Zachariah might have been of the house of Aaron. According to the 20th-century clairvoyant, Edgar Cayce, both Mary and Elizabeth were members of the Essene community at Carmel. It may be these *daughters* that Cayce says "were chosen (in their early youth) to dedicate and consecrate their bodies, their minds, and their service to become a

354

channel."[27] If we are dedicated and consecrated, we are all channels for the divine to use – and as such we have a *particular* lesson to learn.[28]

What I see as the lesson of Mary is Luke's enigmatic comment: *But Mary kept all these things, pondering them in her heart.* Lk. 2:19. Again it is mentioned after the incident in Jerusalem when Jesus was 12 and he answered the worry of his parents with *"How is it that you sought me? Did you not know that I must be in my Father's house?" And he went down with them and came to Nazareth, and was obedient to them: **and his mother kept all these things in her heart.** And Jesus increased in wisdom and in the Spirit, and in favor with God and man.* Lk. 2:49-52.

Two Lessons

So far we've learned two lessons at the level of *the Christ.* The first comes from the Baptist, that nature which not only says **repent**, but that **which recognizes** the Christ. The Baptist says: *"I baptize with water; but among you stands one whom you do not know,...the thong of whose sandal I am not worthy to untie." The next day he saw Jesus coming toward him, and said, "Behold, the Lamb of God, who takes away the sin of the world! This is he of whom I said, 'After me comes a man who ranks before me, for he was before me.' I myself did not know him; but **for this I came baptizing with water, that he might be revealed to Israel.** "* Jn. 1:26-31.

---

[27] In trance, Cayce said: "...the group we refer to here as the Essenes,... was the outgrowth of the periods of preparations from the teachings of Melchizedek, as propagated by Elijah and Elisha and Samuel."*Edgar Cayce's Story of Jesus,* p. 131. Cayce says that both Mary and Joseph were dedicated to the Essenes by their parents, and that Mary was among 12 girls chosen (apparently perpetually on-going) for special training and preparation, in anticipation of the manifestation of the Christ. Cayce explains that Mary's selection came as she was leading the 12 girls up the stairs to participate in worship (it being her turn that day)when unusual thunder and light (which produced the shadow of an angel) announced her selection as the chosen vessel. *Ibid.*

[28] The term *channel* has always meant where the physical being is used by the divine to accomplish its purposes. In this sense, we are all *channels*, whether or not we are *cooperating* with the action. It is in this sense that Cayce uses *channel*. But since the early 20th Century, *channel* has also taken on the tinge of the occult, where it refers to an individual's being "used" by an *incarnate* being – by a soul that pres-ently has no body. Cayce is **not** using this meaning of the word with regard to Mary.

John the Baptist reveals the nature which comes to all who climb the Mountain. *"He who comes from above is above all; **he who is of the earth belongs to the earth, and of the earth he speaks; he who comes from heaven is above all.** He bears witness to what he has seen and heard, yet no one receives his testimony; **he who receives his testimony sets his seal to this, that God is true.** For he whom God has sent utters the words of God, for **it is not by measure that he gives the Spirit;** the Father loves the Son, and has given all things into his hand. **He who believes in the Son has eternal life; he who does not obey the Son shall not see life, but the wrath of God** rests upon him."* Jn. 3:30-36.

It would be easier to understand if the passage read: *That which comes from above is above all...* Are we willing to let go of our hardened notion that John the Baptist refers *only* to Jesus as the *son*? To the intuition, John refers to the Holy Spirit, the understanding of the Christ that has come upon Jesus. The understanding that can come upon us all, including the Baptist. And John recognizes that *as it comes* upon us, our earthly self *decreases;* for this new understanding is of *heaven above*. It comes not in "measured" spurts, but in complete understanding that we, too, are sons of God. If we accept this understanding which sees itself as the "son," we have eternal life; if we don't, we can't even see "life" – only the wrath of God.[29]

The other lesson comes from *the mother*, that she *kept all these things in her heart*. Likely, at some point, the Baptist's perception echos Mary's, for the Baptist is near the Christ. It is at the Christ level of the climb that the quietude and the internal growth are so vital, for only then do we truly "see" what before were only appearances. The *prepared* and *chosen* feminine expression recognizes the Christ in itself – first from a declaration of the divine, then from the perception of those who have always been dedicated (Simeon and Anna). But

---

[29] At Sunday School, recently, we have had a young Jewish man as a visitor. Last Sunday, he surprised us all when he told us that he had been taught that John had been killed because Jesus wanted to be the only person who was being followed. The Jewish misunderstanding isn't any worse than the fact that medieval Christians believed that Jews sacrificed and ate children. It behooves us all to look at what we have been taught and "see" if it complies with the understanding that both John and Jesus had, i.e., that the Lord God was their father, for they and we are *sons of man*.

recognition isn't enough, we must then *release* the Christ within to "do its thing." What an apt description of motherhood. *Motherhood* is the "supreme" *release* training. The seemingly endless months of pregnancy produce an eternal bonding. Then at the end of 9 months, this precious thing is "painfully" expelled by the body. The relationship changes only slightly: but by the time the child is mobile, it is a separate entity. Then come years of letting go – until the thing most precious is totally its own master.

Christ Taking Leave of His Mother by Dürer.

Only the Christed one is "its own master." The writer of Deutero-Isaiah addresses what comes with the nature of the Christ: *"Seek the LORD while he may be found, call upon him while he is near; let the wicked forsake his way, and the unrighteous man his thoughts; let him return to the LORD, that he may have mercy on him, and to our God, for he will abundantly pardon. For my thoughts are not your thoughts, neither are your ways my ways, says the LORD. For as the heavens are higher than the earth, so are my ways higher than your ways and my thoughts than your thoughts.* Is. 55:6-9.*

"For as the rain and the snow come down from heaven, and return not thither but water the earth, making it bring forth and sprout, giving seed to the sower and bread to the eater, so shall my word be that goes forth from my mouth; it shall not return to me empty, but it shall accomplish that which I purpose, and prosper in the thing for which I sent it. For you shall go out in joy, and be led forth in peace; the mountains and the hills before you shall break forth into singing, and all the trees of the field shall clap their hands. Instead of the thorn shall come up the cypress; instead of the brier shall come up the myrtle; and it shall be to the LORD for a memorial, for an everlasting sign which shall not be cut off." Is. 55:10-13.*

Thus says the LORD: "Keep justice, and do righteousness, for soon my salvation will come, and my deliverance be revealed. Blessed is the man who does this, and the son of man who holds it fast, who keeps the sabbath, not profaning it, and keeps his hand from doing any evil. Let not the foreigner who has joined himself to the LORD say, 'The LORD will surely separate me from his people'; and let not the eunuch say, 'Behold, I am a dry tree.'" For thus says the LORD: "To the eunuchs who keep my sabbaths, who choose the things that please me and hold fast my covenant, I will give in my house and within my walls a monument and a name better than sons and daughters; I will give them an everlasting name which shall not be cut off. And the foreigners who join themselves to the LORD, to minister to him, to love the name of the LORD, and to be his servants, every one who keeps the sabbath, and does not profane it, and holds fast my covenant-- these I will bring to my holy mountain, and make them joyful in my house of prayer; their burnt offerings and their sacrifices will be accepted on my altar; for my house shall be called a house of prayer for all peoples." Isaiah 56:1-7.[30]

It is the Christed one who reaches the *holy Mountain*; it is the Christed one who keeps the *sabbath* and understands its intent. What is difficult to understand – and what the Sadducees and Pharisees of Jesus' time never do understand

---

[30] Compared to the eunuch, the world's production is one of physical production, and one's "name" being perpetuated has been due to sons and daughters who perpetuate one's name. The statement says that this blessing which is to come upon us is beyond physical expression; and our name shall be an "everlasting name which shall not be cut off." The *foreigner* is slightly different. Remember, the rules for the sabbath applied to anyone associated with the household; this included foreigners. *Foreigner* on one level applies to gentiles, i.e., those not of Jewish blood; but on another level it means those (of whatever blood) who are *short* of understanding. All must understand and accept the observation of and participation in the *sabbath*.

358

– is the truth of the *sabbath*. Remember what Jesus told them? *"The sabbath was made for man, not man for the sabbath; so **the Son of man is lord even of the sabbath."** Mk. 2:27,28.

In other words, the *son of man*, he/she who recognizes being the child of God, determines when, and where, and how comes this day of rest. The whole interpretation

The Sabbath Is Made for Mankind

hinges on our definition of two words: first, *sabbath*. *Sabbath* is used 137 times in the Bible, and it is the major emphasis of Moses' rules; but it means more than just a weekly religious observance. It suggests a particular attitude toward *all* and one's relationship to the *all*. Its observance requires an attitude of trust, of respect, of deference, of quietude, of preparation, of rest.

The second word is *lord*, which comes from Middle English and means "loaf keeper"– in today's English, one having **power** and **authority!** Keep loose! The son of man "has" the "power" and "authority" to bring (in himself) this attitude of respect, deference, quietude, preparation, and rest! The son of man has the power and authority to enter the Kingdom of Heaven! And if we don't enter it, the penalty is "death" – we declare ourselves to be "dead," not "living." This has been our challenge all along, hasn't it? As soon as we decided that our manifestation included **both *good*** and ***evil***, we accepted that we were of the "dead." We accepted death. That's why Jesus had to come and be crucified – to correct our *measurement*.

According to one calculator, the Baptist began his ministry in the year 26. Luke lists it as the fifteenth year of the reign of Tiberius.[31] *As the people were in expectation, and all men questioned in their hearts concerning John, whether perhaps he were the Christ, John answered them all, **"I baptize you with water; but he who is mightier than I***

---

[31] At the death of Herod the Great (who had rebuilt the Temple), the "state" was split among three of his sons. Herod Antipas became Tetrarch of Galilee. He had married his sister-in-law; the trouble was that his half-brother was still alive. Therefore, John was condemning bigamy. Tradition lays the blame on Herodias (the wife), saying that she was ambitious. It is she who requests the "head" of John the Baptist.

is coming, the thong of whose sandals I am not worthy to untie; he will baptize you with the Holy Spirit and with fire. His winnowing fork is in his hand, to clear his threshing floor, and to gather the wheat into his granary, but the chaff he will burn with unquenchable fire." So, with many other exhortations, he preached good news to the people. But Herod the tetrarch, who had been reproved by him for Herodias, his brother's wife, and for all the evil things that Herod had done, added this to them all, that he shut up John in prison. Lk. 3:15-20.

John the Baptist's public ministry supposedly lasted almost two years; then he was imprisoned another year before he was executed. But his ministry lasted long enough to gain followers and, apparently, to make such disruption, that officials were fearful that Jesus would cause "trouble" as had John. No longer was the secular world tolerant of prophets, even if they had "signs" accompanying them. The Baptist dressed and behaved as had Elijah, but Herod still imprisoned and then beheaded John.

In previous times, a prophet's "credentials" had been the number of "signs" he produced, and the traditions of **Elijah** were strong. Elijah was the facilitator for a penniless widow's having an endless supply of "meal" and oil. 1 Kngs. 17:14 Then Elijah "revived" this woman's son.[32] Elijah supposedly could disappear at will, **Previous Signs** and reputedly he could "make a path" to walk across the Jordan. Eventually, Elijah was taken up in a "whirlwind" to heaven, and **his protégé, Elisha,** who had asked for a double portion, began to do "signs."[33] Elisha could "see" more than just the physical expression, and Elisha produced even more signs than had his mentor.

Elisha, too (using the mantle of Elijah) could *part the water*; moreover, he turned bad water to good. And his

---

[32] The account is full of symbols. Elijah takes the boy to the ***upper chamber,*** *where he lodged, and laid him upon his own bed.* Then he "complained" to God and *stretched himself upon the child three times, and cried to the LORD, "O LORD my God, let this child's soul come into him again."* The boy revived, and the woman then accepted Elijah as a *man of God.* 1 Kngs. 17:19-24

[33] Remember, Elisha asked for a "double portion." The story of Elijah's "translation" into heaven is important in that Elijah tells Elisha ***if you see me as I am being taken from you, it shall be so for you****; but if you do not see me, it shall not be so.* 2 Kgs 2:10

"curses" were as powerful as his blessings; his curse of some boys resulted in **42** of the boys being mauled by two bears. He facilitated a penniless widow's accumulation of "oil" which she was later able to sell to support herself and her children 2 Kgs .4:1-7. Elisha, too, revived a dead boy 2 Kgs. 4:8-37, and he made a poisonous stew safe. 2 Kgs. 4:38-41 He even fed **100 men** with **20** loaves of barley and fresh ears of grain; and there was food left over. 2 Kngs. 4:42-44

Once, Elisha "healed" a "general" from Syria of his leprosy by having him wash in the Jordan seven times, but he took no recompense for the healing. However, his servant thought he could accept the payment for himself. Elisha knew what had happened and declared that the servant would be leprous; and he became so. 2 Kgs. 5

Another story is that Elisha and his followers were cutting trees, and an axe head fell into the water; but Elisha cut off a stick and threw it in the water and *made the iron float.* 2 Kgs. 6:1-7 Elisha's "signs" extended even into politics, as he accomplished the surrender of a Syrian force, delivering them to the king of Israel, but insisting that they be treated well. *And the Syrians came no more on raids into the land of Israel.* 2 Kgs. 6:8-23

Finally, Elisha died and was buried. But his power did not decay. Years later (during a time when outlaw bands would make raids on settlements) as a man was being buried, Moabite marauders came into view. The people were frightened, and so the mourners threw the body into Elisha's grave. Reputedly, *as soon as the man touched the bones of Elisha, he revived, and stood on his feet.* 2 Kgs. 13:21

The signs of Elijah and Elisha repeat some of the signs of Moses. Any "holy one" will have to repeat the same signs, in one way or another. But by the time of Jesus, the culture has become so worldly – so distant from God – that Jesus' "signs" are regarded as "miracles." If we can believe the accounts which we are given, Jesus' ministry begins when he is 30 years old, and it ends with crucifixion when he is 33, interestingly, the same age as Alexander at death.

Whether *signs* or *miracles* or *numbers*, the activity of Jesus should be viewed with an esoteric understanding.[34] Esoterically, we're saying the following:

1. Jesus is old enough that he is to be "regarded."
2. Jesus surpasses the signs of Elijah, Elisha, and Moses.
3. Therefore, even if just from a physical viewpoint, **we must "hear" what Jesus tells us.**[35]

Isaiah's writer says it nicely: *Incline your ear, and come to me; hear, that your soul may live; and I will make with you an everlasting covenant, my steadfast, sure love for David. Behold, I made him a witness to the peoples, a leader and commander for the peoples. Behold, you shall call nations that you know not, and nations that knew you not shall run to you, because of the LORD your God, and of the Holy One of Israel, for he has glorified you. Is. 55:3-5.*

Each of the four gospels has Jesus' ministry begin with his being **baptized** by John. All of us must be cleansed and dedicated – and pronounced worthy as the Holy Spirit descends on us. Then Jesus'

> **Jesus' Signs: Miracles of Water**

actions prove his acceptance of the pronouncement with the miracle of **water into wine** at the wedding at Cana. With *water into wine*, Jesus surpasses the "signs" of earth; but only the mystical gospel – that of John – mentions the wedding at Cana.[36] Jesus measures his world by his view of what is necessary to celebrate God. This means that the measurement of the world comes in question. So, too, only the mystical gospel mentions Jesus' first effort at healing the sins of the nation as he drives the money-changers from the Temple,

---

[34] We might wonder that the numbers always come up to support an esoteric statement. Apparently, Jewish tradition dictates that a man is not mature until he is 30 years old. Therefore, neither John nor Jesus would have been listened to until they reached 30. But we must acknowledge that the numbers may be contrived to convey the message; we are not reading an historical account for the literal mind.

[35] The standard definition of *miracle* (and probably of *sign*) infers something which defies natural laws. It is based on the premise that the physical laws are supreme. Christian Science offers a more esoteric definition of *miracle;* according to Webster's, it is *a divinely natural occurrence that must be learned humanly.*

[36] See John 2:1-11, and notice the numbers used. See pages 350 - 351. Remember, Cana is related to a "reed" used for measurement.

362

which John places early in Jesus' ministry.[37] John makes an interesting statement: *Now when he was in Jerusalem at the Passover feast, many **believed in his name** when they saw the signs which he did; but Jesus did not trust himself to them, because **he knew all men** and needed no one to bear witness of man; for he himself knew what was in man. Jn. 2:23-25.*

Believed in his name in more modern language would be *accepted his nature*, i.e., "many listened to what he said." But Jesus didn't "buy into" their acceptance, because he could tell what was in their hearts. For a minute, let's put ourselves in Jesus' place. Here is a young man, just old enough to be "listened to," observing his first Passover as an "accepted" adult male – one who feels total *oneness* with the divine. Jesus is operating on a level where he not only knows and follows the divine will, but he can tell at what level others are operating. He's *tuned in* both to the divine and to the earthly, and because of his actions and his demeanor (and his *vibration*), many begin to "listen" to what he says – but *listening* is not "**hearing.**"[38]

As you continue on this climb, you will find many who will "listen" to you – but few who will **"hear"** you. Certainly,

---

[37] See John 2:13-25. If the Temple refers to the body of the individual, then mystically after *cleansing* and *pronouncement*, there must be a concerted effort to *purge* the self of worldly devices. John writes: *The Passover of the Jews was at hand, and Jesus went up to Jerusalem. In the temple he found those who were selling **oxen** and **sheep** and **pigeons**, and the **money-changers** at their business. And making a whip of cords, **he drove them all, with the sheep and oxen, out of the temple;** and he **poured out the coins of the money-changers and overturned their tables.** And he told those who sold the **pigeons, "Take these things away;** you shall not make my Father's house a house of trade." Jn. 2:13-16.*

[38] Whether we're aware of it or not, either consciously or subconsciously we are affected by the *vibration* of everything with which we come in contact. For an easy experiment, choose some selections of music to play in a sequence. Choose one from each: 1. acid rock; 2. rock & roll; 3. gospel-rock; 4. Shostakovich; 5.Tchaikovsky; 6. Satie or Debussy; 7. Wagner, Grieg, or Mahler. Now, take seven items – something red, orange, yellow, green, blue, violet, purple – and match each color to the particular type of music that it echoes. There is no real "right" or "wrong" to the experiment, but recognize that both music and color have levels of vibration. Similarly, individuals exude different levels of vibration, and we are either drawn to individuals or repelled by them, dependent upon the similarity or dissimilarity to our own *vibes.* Some esotericists say that we are particularly attracted to *higher vibrations.* Consequently, since no one's vibration would have been higher than that of Jesus, many would have been drawn to him – as they had been drawn to the Baptist.

such is true for Jesus. At least one person listens. One of the Sanhedrin, Nicodemus, admits that Jesus has produced signs, but his visit is at *night*. He's not willing to publicly declare that Jesus is producing "signs," even though he says: *"Rabbi, we know that you are a teacher come from God; for no one can do these signs that you do, unless God is with him."* Nicodemus listens, but he doesn't *hear*.

*Jesus answered him, "Truly, truly, I say to you, **unless one is born anew, he cannot see the kingdom of God.**" Nicodemus said to him, "How can a man be born when he is old? Can he enter a second time into his mother's womb and be born?" Jesus answered, "Truly, truly, I say to you, **unless one is born of water and the Spirit, he cannot enter the kingdom of God.** That which is born of the flesh is flesh, and that which is born of the Spirit is spirit.*

*"Do not marvel that I said to you, 'You must be born anew.' The wind blows where it wills, and **you hear the sound of it,** but you do not know whence it comes or whither it goes; **so it is with every one who is born of the Spirit.**" Nicodemus said to him, "How can this be?" Jesus answered, "Are you a teacher of Israel, and yet you do not understand this? Truly, truly, I say to you, [I] speak of what [I] know, and bear witness to what [I] have seen; but you do not receive [my] testimony. If I have told you earthly things and you do not believe, how can you believe if I tell you heavenly things? No one has ascended into heaven but he who descended from heaven, the Son of man. And as **Moses lifted up the serpent in the wilderness, so must the Son of man be lifted up, that whoever believes... him may have eternal life."** Jn. 3:3-15.* [39]

---

[39] If you've been listening as we've proceeded, you heard several repetitive motifs in the Old Testament. This third chapter of John repeats them, only now we're given double *entendre* with the several motifs. It's a tongue-in-cheek presentation.

1. Water: Judaic **tradition** says that we are **born of blood and water**; Jesus is saying we must go up a step beyond physical existence – to water and spirit. At Cana, Jesus already has proved that water is not what it appears to be. But this is an "unearthly" understanding; therefore we must be born "anew"or "from above."

2. Kingdom of God: The term is only in the New Testament, and it is the central theme. John only uses the term in the above quote (3:5) because it is assumed for understanding John that one is in this state. Matthew's first use of the term indicates much. *But if it is by the Spirit of God that I cast out demons, **then the kingdom of God has come upon you.*** (Mat 12:28 RSV) The Kingdom of God is much like Elisha's double portion: only **if** you see it, do you have it. Only those who *hear* are near the *kingdom*.

3. Earthly things/heavenly things: *spirit and the Kingdom of Heaven are not earthly.*

4. Son of Man: Throughout the Old Testament, *Son of Man* refers to "enlightened" mankind, that which was first "created." Moses says: *God is not man, that he should lie, or a **son of man**, that he should repent. Has he said, and will he not do it? Or has he spoken, and will he not fulfil it? Behold, **I received a command to bless: he has blessed, and I cannot revoke it.*** Num. 23:19,20. The *son of man* is he/she who *hears* and *does*. It is the *son of man* whose "serpent" is lifted up, producing *eternal life.*

5. Darkness: Again, the term has threaded through the entire Old Testament, and we were told by Isaiah: *The people who walked in darkness have seen a great light; those who dwelt in a land of deep darkness, **on them has light shined.*** Is. 9:2.

6. Light: The *light* shows that our deeds are brought about by God. The *light* is the representative of God.

Can we see the relationship between the last line and that previously mentioned, i.e., *that the works of God might be manifest (made evident; easily understood) in him?*[40] (See page 346.) What Nicodemus can't understand is the term *born again*. Lamsa says that Northern Aramaics understand it to mean "to change one's thoughts and habits."[41] But esoterically, I think it means much more than this. It seems to mean that unless we are *born anew*, i.e., manifesting at a different level of understanding, we can not *perceive the kingdom of God.*

If we are not thinking on the level of the "spirit," we are still seeing only the earthly. Jesus' expression is much more than having changed his habits and thoughts; he expresses at a totally different level – a different dimension – than does the rest of the world, even the Baptist. Following Jesus is a mystical journey; changing habits and thinking is only part of the preparations.

In a way, the "miracles" of water embody the lessons to be learned in the mystical journey. They are almost always connected to "healing" of some sort. We must be healed of our mistaken paradigm. We are not *beings* of earth who should be "ashamed" of our "nakedness." Our "healing" takes place in us as we climb. The disciples of both Jesus and the Baptist are still climbing. After the "water" has been turned to "wine," it is ready to go to work to finish the climb. The first challenge comes as both John and Jesus' disciples are baptizing in the same area of Judea. We are told it is because there was *much water there*; both sets of followers are of the world.

---

[40] Remember, we have no independently "recorded" record of Jesus' words. We have only the canon of the Church, which at the time of canonization of scripture felt threatened by the Gnostics. Gnosticism was most easily identified by acceptance of reincarnation. But the question of *born again* in the name *Nicodemus* reveals the same quandary. *Nicodemus* stems from two roots: one implies *being bound*; the other implies *triumph*. Our challenge is to triumph over the bindings that the world has placed on our understanding for so long.

[41] Lamsa, *Holy Bible*, p. 1054 fn.

Even though John the Baptist is not of this world (his understanding lets him *hear* and *see*), his followers complain that many people are going to Jesus. But he responds: *"No one can receive anything except what is given him from heaven ... **He must increase, but I must decrease.**"* Jn. 3:27, 30.

Either because he does not want to detract from the Baptist's ministry or for some other reason, Jesus and his disciples leave Judea for Galilee. On the way they

Woman At the Well pass near the location of Jacob's well – near Sychar, in Samaria.[42] The disciples go for food, and Jesus sits down beside the well. It is near the sixth hour,

and a Samaritan woman approaches to draw water.[43] After asking her for a drink, Jesus says: *"Every one who drinks of this water will thirst again, but whoever drinks of the water that I shall give him will never thirst; the water that I shall give him will become in him a spring of water welling up to eternal life."* Jn. 4:13,14.

The woman [said], "Sir, give me this water, that I may not thirst, nor come here to draw." Jesus said to her, "Go, call your husband, and come here." The woman answered him, "I have no husband." Jesus said to her, "You are right in saying, 'I have no husband'; for you have had five husbands, and he whom you now have is not your husband; this you said truly." ...Jesus said..., "... the hour is coming when neither on this mountain nor in Jerusalem will you worship the Father. ... the hour is coming, and now is, when the true worshipers will worship the Father in spirit and truth, for such the Father seeks to worship him. God is spirit, and those who worship him must worship in spirit and truth." Jn. 4:15-24.

This wine that Jesus produces gives access to a different level of reality. In it mankind worships in "spirit." Although the Samaritans "listen" and agree that Jesus is the Savior, they are symbolic that even those whom the Jews consider the lesser "vessels" are, too, given the message. This doesn't mean that all will "hear" what he says.

Water is the vehicle through which Jesus comes into

---

[42] The city mentioned, Sychar, means to become *tipsy* from an *intoxicating* drink. Esoterically we're saying that *water* (i.e., the world's drink) makes us "intoxicated," not having full control of our faculties. We see ourselves as *naked*. Moreover, Jesus is talking to a **woman**; something not accepted by the orthodox Jew, because she might be having her period and thereby be *unclean*. Esoterically, **the sixth hour** means it is *almost the seventh hour*, when earthly things will be finished; it may or may not refer to the time of day.

[43] Few passages contain so many esoteric elements. First, Samaria is the portion of Israel that had contained the capital city of the Northern Kingdom. When the Assyrians destroyed it (722 B.C.), they imported varied races into the area and dispersed the Hebrews to other parts of their empire. However, the new inhabitants enthusiastically embraced the Hebrew religion. In the view of "good" Jews of Jesus' time, Samaritans were half-breeds and their form of worship was "tainted." One of the Jewish contentions was that the only true worship took place in the Jerusalem Temple, and Samaritans worshiped on their high hill, Mount Gerizim. See Ausubel, *Knowledge,* pp. 386-388.

contact with the Samaritans, and *water* is the central motif for other revelations. The Sea of Galilee remains central to Jesus' activities. It is the *sea* from which Jesus and his disciples draw substantial fish – even the fish with a gold coin in its mouth; it is the *sea* which Jesus calms, and it is the *sea* upon which Jesus walks. But it is also the *sea* into which Peter sinks because of his disbelief.

Yet *water* is not all important, as is proved by the healing of the man at the pool of Bethesda. Again, the account is only in the gospel of John, and it occurs near the second Passover during Jesus' ministry.[44]

> *After this there was a feast of the Jews, and Jesus went up to Jerusalem. Now there is in Jerusalem **by the Sheep Gate** a pool, in Hebrew called Bethzatha, which has **five porticoes**. In these lay a **multitude of invalids,** blind, lame, paralyzed. One man was there, who had been ill for **thirty-eight years**. When Jesus saw him and knew that he had been lying there a long time, he said to him, **"Do you want to be healed?"** The sick man answered him, "Sir, I have no man to put me into the pool when the water is troubled, and while I am going another steps down before me." Jesus said to him, **"Rise, take up your pallet, and walk."** And at once the man was healed, and he took up his pallet and walked. Now that day was the sabbath.* Jn. 5:1-9.

It is not *water* (unstable emotions, feelings, **The Pool of Bethesda** passions) that is so important; it is the *healing* of these difficulties that we must undergo. Unfortunately, our attitude is like that of those lying in the five porticoes (gateways) at Bethesda. Notice that the pool is by the Sheep Gate. It can be said that mankind has a sheep-like mindset – gentle and placid, but easily led. As a result, we are most like the **impotent man**. We think we can be cured only when "the water moves," and we think we have to have someone else to "put us in the water." Even more dismally, we see ourselves in competition with others. (Remember the **LAW**. We get "as" we measure.) But this man's "excuses" are not the TRUTH. This man is "impotent" in life because his measurement is "impotent." It is only as he approaches the Christ conscious- ness that he *desires* healing; it is only at this "eleventh" level

---

[44] I am indebted to Davis' *The Westminster Dictionary of the Bible*, 1898, rev. ed. 1944, pp. 211-215, for establishing a logical chronology of Jesus' ministry.

(3+8) that he **declares** his **willingness to be healed.** The Christ-mind says *take up your bed and walk.* [45]

We in the late 20th Century think of *impotence* as a man's incapacity to function sexually, but its true meaning is "lacking in power, strength and vigor." It's an apt discription of one who is *ill.* But the most important part of

Jesus' Signs: Miracles of Healing

the whole story comes a few lines later when Jesus encounters the same man in the Temple. Jesus says: *See! You are well! Sin no more, that nothing worse befall you.* Jn .5:14. We don't like to think of illness as "sin," do we? But, remember what *sin* means? It means to *miss the mark.* This man has been *missing the mark*; his "measure" has been inaccurate. But notice, Jesus doesn't say this man is healed forever! Whether the healing remains or not is dependent upon the man himself. From now on, he has to *hit the mark;* he has to "measure" accurately. To truly *walk*, we have to *see* and *say.*

Therefore, it may be that the most important *miracles* are those performed on the **blind** and **dumb**. We already observed the blind man at the Temple. (See

Heal the *blind*

page 346.) Jesus' "cure" on the physical level was *water* (spittle) and *earth* (clay). To *see* we must come to terms with our emotions, feelings, passions; and we must recognize that the earthly existence is just a part of the whole. It is our recognition of the temporality of the physical that is imperative.

*And as Jesus passed on from there [Capernaum], **two blind men** followed him, crying aloud, "Have mercy on us, Son of David." When he entered*

---

[45] Our lives can be endless trips to doctors and psychiatrists, healers of all sorts, and unlimited costs – until we reach this point. This is why the "healers" of the late 19th Century were so successful. People recognized that nothing outside of themselves could heal them. Unfortunately, the understanding of the late 19th Century has been replaced by a 20th Century "know it all" attitude. One wonders if our technology makes this understanding more difficult to reach. Jesus is contending with those who adhere to the physical view. The impotent man can be "healed" because he has reached this #11 place; those who adhere to the physical sabbath won't be healed – they're still looking to the outside.

*the house, the blind men came to him; and **Jesus said to them, "Do you believe that I am able to do this?"** They said to him, "Yes, Lord." Then he touched their eyes, saying, **"According to your faith be it done to you."** And their eyes were opened. And Jesus sternly charged them, "See that no one knows it." But they went away and spread his fame through all that district. As they were going away, behold, a **dumb demoniac** was brought to him. And **when the demon had been cast out, the dumb man spoke**; and the crowds marveled, saying, "Never was anything like this seen in Israel." But the Pharisees said, "He casts out demons by the prince of demons." And **Jesus went about** all the cities and villages, **teaching** in their synagogues **and preaching the gospel of the kingdom, and healing every disease and every infirmity.** When he saw the crowds, **he had compassion for them**, because **they were harassed and helpless, like sheep without a shepherd.** Then he said to his disciples, "The harvest is plentiful, but the laborers are few; pray therefore the Lord of the harvest to send out laborers into his harvest."* Mt. 9:27-37

> **Heal the dumb**

Remember that while resident in Babylon, the Jews had absorbed some of the beliefs of the Persians. Two of these beliefs were the "existence" of demons (or devils) and angels. Esoterically, they are the same phenomenon – just on opposite ends of the *knowledge of good and evil.*

Some of the "demons" speak *unrighteously.* They say "I'm a terrible person, I'm evil, I'm sick, I'm poor!" Demons are those things in our thinking that take charge of us and deny our rightful status. In the above case, the "demon" had become so powerful that the man could no longer speak.

Jesus could drive them all out, but again the scribes and Pharisees, the leaders of the intellectual mindset, want *a sign.* But he warns the challenging scribes and Pharisees: *"When the unclean spirit has gone out of a man, he passes through waterless places seeking rest, but he finds none. Then he says, 'I will return to my house from which I came.' And when he comes he finds it empty, swept, and put in order. Then he goes and brings with him seven other spirits more evil than himself, and they enter and dwell there; and the last state of that man becomes worse than the first. So shall it be also with this evil generation."* Mt. 12:43-45.

> **Heal the demons**

To be "fully" healed, we must maintain the "high watch." We must keep our attention on the *kingdom.* How does Jesus heal? By *preaching the gospel (good news) of the kingdom.* As with the impotent man, it is the individual's responsibility to "refill" the house with the understanding of the *kingdom of heaven.* The next question is "What is the **kingdom?**" The major focus of Jesus' ministry is to reveal the **kingdom of heaven.** Isn't it interesting how we progress from the revelation of the "promised land" to that of the "kingdom of Israel" to that of the "kingdom of heaven"?[46]

*That same day Jesus went out of the house and **sat beside the sea.** And great crowds gathered about him, so that **he got into a boat and sat there;** and the whole crowd stood on the beach. And he told them many things in parables, saying: "**A sower went out to sow.** And as he sowed, **some seeds fell along the path, and the birds** came and **devoured them.** Other seeds fell on rocky ground, where they had not much soil, and immediately they sprang up, **since they had no depth of soil, but when the sun rose they were scorched; and since they had no root they withered away.** Other seeds fell upon thorns,* and the thorns grew up and **choked them.** *Other seeds fell on good soil and brought forth grain, some a hundredfold, some sixty, some thirty. He who has ears, let him hear."* Mt. 13:1-9.

Then the disciples came and said to him, "Why do you

| Heal the deaf |

*speak to them in parables?" And he answered them, "**To you it has been given to know the secrets of the kingdom of heaven, but to them it has not been given.** For to him who has will more be given,* and he will have abundance; but *from him who has not, even what he has will be taken away.* This is why I speak to them in parables, because **seeing they do not see,** and **hearing they do not hear,** nor *do they* **understand.**...For this *people's* **heart has grown dull,** and **their ears are heavy of hearing, and their eyes they have closed, lest they should perceive with their eyes, and hear with their ears, and understand with their heart, and turn for me to heal them.'** But blessed *are your eyes, for they see, and your ears, for they hear. Truly, I say to you, many prophets and righteous men longed to see what you see, and did not see it, and to hear what you hear, and did not hear it.*

"Hear then the parable of the sower. **When any one hears the word of the kingdom and does not understand it,...evil ...comes and snatches away what is sown in his heart; this is what was sown along the path.** *As for what was sown* on **rocky ground,** this is **he who hears the word and immediately receives it with joy;** *yet he has no root in himself,* but endures for a while, and when tribulation or persecution arises on account of the word, immediately he falls away. As for **what was sown among thorns,** this is he who hears the word, but **the cares of the world and the delight in riches choke the word,** and it proves unfruitful. **As for what was sown on good soil, this is he who hears the word and understands it; he indeed bears fruit, and yields, in one case a hundredfold, in another sixty, and in another thirty."** Mt. 13:10-23.

Blessed are [our] eyes if we *see.* Earlier, Jesus had emphasized the *blessings* of living in the understanding of the

---

[46] There will be one more revelation: the *city of the New Jerusalem.*

kingdom. There were some among his followers (disciples) who understood at least part of what he was saying. So from these, he chose twelve to be sent out to spread the *gospel*; these he called *apostles.*[47]

> *And he came down with them and stood on **a level place**, with **a great crowd of** his **disciples** and **a great multitude of people** from all Judea and Jerusalem and the seacoast of Tyre and Sidon, **who came to hear him and to be healed of their diseases; and those who were troubled with unclean spirits** were cured. And **all the crowd sought to touch him, for power came forth from him and healed them all.** And he **lifted up his eyes on his disciples**, and said:*

>> *"Blessed are you poor, for yours is the kingdom of God.*
>> *Blessed are you that hunger now, for you shall be satisfied.*
>> *Blessed are you that weep now, for you shall laugh.*
>> *Blessed are you when men hate you, and when they exclude you and revile you, and cast out your name as evil, on account of the Son of man!* Rejoice in that day, and leap for joy, for behold, your reward is great in heaven; for so their fathers did to the prophets. Lk.6:17-23.*

>> *"But woe to you that are rich, for you have received your consolation.*
>> *Woe to you that are full now, for you shall hunger.*
>> *Woe to you that laugh now, for you shall mourn and weep.*
>> *Woe to you, when all men speak well of you, for so their fathers did to the false prophets.*

>> *"But **I say** to you that hear, **Love your enemies, do good to those who hate you, bless those who curse you, pray for those who abuse you. To him who strikes you on the cheek, offer the other also; and from him who takes away your coat do not withhold even your shirt. Give to every one who begs from you; and of him who takes away your goods do not ask them again. And as you wish that men would do to you, do so to them.** Lk. 6:24-31.*

>> *"If you love those who love you, what credit is that to you? For even sinners love those who love them. And if you do good to those who do good to you, what credit is that to you? For even sinners do the same. And if you lend to those from whom you hope to receive, what credit is that to you? Even sinners lend to sinners, to receive as much again.*

>> *"But love your enemies, and do good, and lend, expecting nothing in return; and your reward will be great, and you will be sons of the Most High; for he is kind to the ungrateful and the selfish.*

---

[47] *Apostle* comes from the Greek *apostolos* fr. *apostellein* (to send away). Those selected were Simon Peter, his brother Andrew, James and John (sons of Zebedee), and Philip, Bartholomew, Matthew, Thomas, James (son of Alphaeus), Simon (the Zealot), Judas (son of James), and Judas Iscariot. Lk. 6:14-16.

Be merciful, even as your Father is merciful.
Judge not, and you will not be judged;
condemn not, and you will not be condemned;
forgive, and you will be forgiven;
 give, and it will be given to you;
  good measure, pressed down, shaken together,
  running over, will be put into your lap.
For the measure you give will be the measure you get back. " Lk. 6:32-38.

Let's repeat it again. *...the measure you give will be the measure you get back!* It's the LAW.

Jesus is using the "measurement" of the Kingdom. Jesus is "measuring" at a level that disregards physical appearances. Not only can he walk on water and heal the sick, he – like Elijah and Elisha – can restore the "dead." [48]

In one sense, Jesus' miracles simply reproduce the miracles of former prophets. But as with

Heal the "dead"

everything else, Jesus' expression is on a higher level. He heals the **nobleman's son** who is on the brink of death. Jn. 4:46-54. And after the second Passover, he, too, *raises* a **widow's son**. Lk. 7:11-17. But, unlike Elijah and Elisha, Jesus' dealings with "death" are not dependent on physical contact. He (accompanied by Peter, John, and James and the girl's parents) simply speaks to Jarius' daughter, who is presumed dead, and she arises.[49]

Some people explain both the prophets' and Jesus' *raisings* as the ancient world's inability to tell the difference between a coma and death. But the *raising* of Lazarus far suppasses such a possibility; Lazarus' *raising* goes beyond the

---

[48] Remember, both Elijah and Elisha had brought "life" back to children, both "boys." See pages 359-360.

[49] Notice that those whom Jesus raises from the dead are of a higher level of society than those "raised" by the prophets. Subtly, we're being notified of a different level of thought. The *raising* of the 12-year-old girl, interestingly, is combined with the story of the woman who had an issue of blood for **twelve** years. In both cases, the criteria for "healing" was "faith." The woman touched the hem of Jesus' robe; and Jesus says to the ruler, Jairus, "Do not fear; only **believe**, and she shall be well." See: Luke 8: 40-56.

accepted 3-day waiting period (which confirmed "death"). The *raising* of Lazarus was such a ***powerful sign*** that the Sanhedrin either had to accept Jesus as the Messiah or it had to silence him.[50]

Jesus "measures" full-full.[51] Jesus is the embodiment of he/she who lives in the kingdom of heaven. There is a nice metaphor in Luke, even though it is expressed in the negative: *no one who puts his hand to the plow and looks back is fit for the kingdom of heaven.* Lk. 9:62. Unless you are somehow related to a farmer, you may not see the allusion. The master farmer takes the plow and goes "straight" forward. If he looks back, the plowed row will not be "straight." The King James version turns it into a pun as Jesus says: *Enter ye in at the **strait** gate: for wide is the gate, and broad is the way, that leadeth to destruction, and many there be which go in there at: Because **strait** is the gate, **and narrow is the way, which leadeth unto life,** and few there be that find it.* Mt. 7:13,14. [52]

The late Manly Hall wrote: "It was general knowledge that the Essenes practiced mystical rites and kept sacraments peculiarly their own.... More specifically, **the release of man's higher self was not a departure from the corporeal part, but was a refining and purifying of the body, thus permitting the light within to flow forth into more perfect expression. ...** the body became the servant of the spirit and not its master."[53]

---

[50] One of the current explanations for Lazarus' *raising* is that Lazarus was possibly being *initiated* and had passed the three-day confinement in the "tomb." Under this reasoning, Jesus was put to death because he revealed the secrets of the *mysteries*. Socrates was condemned to death for a similar reason.

[51] Remember, Luke says that Mary is told that she shall call her son ***Jesus***. Lk. 1:31. *Jesus* is the English rendering of *Iēsosus*, the Greek version of the Hebrew *Yehoshua*. *Joshua* means *Jehovah saved*; but the importance is the root meanings. Strong directs us to *Jehovah,* from a primitve root which means ***to exist, be***, or ***become*** combined with another primitive root which means ***to be open, to be free*** ... by implication, ***to be safe.***

[52] Strong defines *strait* as *narrow*, and he relates it to a root refering to *covenant*. Young adds the word *restrained.* See the paradox when related to the name *Jesus.*

[53] Manly Hall, *The Mystical Christ,* The Philosophical Research Society, Inc., fourth ed., 1975. p. 37.

Detail of the *Pietà* by Giovanni Bellini.

Chapter Fourteen
Revelation of the "Christ"

*Behold, he cometh with clouds; and **every eye shall see him,** and they also which pierced him: and all kindreds of the earth shall wail because of him. Even so, **Amen.** I **Am Alpha and Omega, the beginning and the ending, saith the Lord, which is, and which was, and which is to come, the Almighty.** Rev. 1:7,8.*

O f the sixty-six books in the Bible, two stand out as the most mystical: *Revelation* and *The Song of Solomon.*[1] The difficulty with both books is that they appear to be something that they are not. *The Song of Solomon* appears to be an erotic poem depicting the passions of physical love. *Revelation,* on the other hand, appears to be apocalyptic, predicting the tremendous suffering that is to come upon unredeemed mankind as the last days come upon us, prior to the return of the Christ.

These two books might be considered as the final test. Do we **hear**; do we **walk**; do we **see**; do we **say?** Do we understand the paradox? Do we "ride the seesaw"? Do we "hang loose"? Can we cut an apple in half, horizontally, and see and comprehend the perfect and symbolic symmetry, therein? Have we climbed the Mountain?

Of all of our characters in the Old Testament, Solomon is the most developed. Solomon is the most earthly wise; he is about to step to the next level of understanding. But as Jesus said of John the Baptist, *he that is least in the kingdom of heaven is greater than he.* Mt. 11:9.

---

[1] Some will say that Jonah and Daniel also fit in this category. *Jonah* is such a book, and it may even rival *Revelation.* I categorize *Daniel* as *mystical, but apocalyptic. Apocalyptic* refers to that which expects *the end times. Webster's* says: "One of the Jewish and Christian writings of 200 B.C. to A.D.150 marked by pseudonymity, symbolic imagery, and the expectation of an imminent cosmic cataclysm in which God destroys the ruling powers of evil and raises the righteous to life in a messianic kingdom."

Prerequisite to entry into the *kingdom of heaven* is Solomon's understanding. Mysticism offers the key. Manly Hall writes: Mysticism affirms that **truth cannot be possessed even by the mind.** By virtues peculiar to itself, **however, the heart can be possessed by truth.** We grow, not by demanding, but by accepting. This gradual trans-formation of attitudes is beautifully revealed in the Song of Songs. ... The king first sings: **"My beloved is mine."** Later he broadens his understanding, saying: **"My beloved is mine, and I am my beloved's."** Then, at the end of the Song, he speaks the heart doctrine: **"I am my beloved's."** The motion from the consciousness of possession **to the realization of perfect renunciation** is the path of mysticism. [2]

It is not *love* that is the end of all. It is not *eros*; it is not *philĕō;* it is not *agapē.* It is *being* as was "Christ" Jesus. We must *be* as was Jesus! All other activity – loving, cleansing, repenting, believing, healing, transforming, resurrecting – is prerequisite to our *being.* And our *being* will express as did Jesus, the Christ. We will express *love* in our entire being. Then, as was Jesus, we must be *transformed;* more properly, **we will be *transfigured*.** [3]

Transfiguration Of the "Christ" *And **after six days** Jesus took with him Peter and James and John his brother, and **led them up a high mountain apart. And he was transfigured before them, and his face shone like the sun, and his garments became white as light.** And behold, there appeared to them Moses and Elijah, talking with him. And Peter said to Jesus, "Lord, it is well that we are here; if you wish, I will make three booths here, one for you and one for Moses and one for Elijah." **He was still speaking, when lo, a bright cloud overshadowed them, and a voice from the cloud said, "This is my beloved Son, with whom I am well pleased; listen to him."** When the disciples heard this, they fell on their faces, and were filled with awe. But Jesus came and touched them, saying, **"Rise, and have no fear."** And when they lifted up their eyes, they saw no one but Jesus only. And **as they were coming down the mountain,** Jesus commanded them, "Tell no one the vision, until the Son of man is raised from the dead."* Mt. 17:1-9.

...when they lifted up their eyes, they saw no one but Jesus only. How difficult it is for us to pull away from the world of appearances. Our minds are visually tuned; what we expect to *see*, we **see.** Even Peter, James and John – even those so

---

[2] Hall, *Mystical Christ*, p. 7.

[3] *Transform* implies a major change in form, nature or function; *transfigure* implies a change that exalts or glorifies.

advanced that they can observe Jesus' transfiguration – fall back to the Old Testament expression of hiding their faces. But what Jesus has been trying to teach them (and us) is to *rise*, lift ourselves "up" and have no fear. This has been the whole focus of Jesus' ministry. He has been teaching the *gospel* – that mankind is the "beloved" child of the divine – to all who would listen. He has been teaching that realization of the "Shema"– *Hear, O Israel, the Lord our God is ONE!* – is all there IS.

Jesus' Teachings

Jesus teaches us at our own level. *Seeing the crowds, he* **went up on the mountain,** *and when he sat down his disciples came to him. And he opened his mouth and taught them, saying:* [4]

*"Blessed are the **poor in spirit,** for theirs is the **kingdom of heaven.***

*"Blessed are those who **mourn,** for they shall be **comforted.***

*"Blessed are the **meek,** for they shall **inherit the earth.***

*"Blessed are those who **hunger and thirst for righteousness,** for they shall be **satisfied.***

*"Blessed are the **merciful,** for they shall **obtain mercy.***

*"Blessed are the **pure in heart,** for they shall **see God.***

*"Blessed are the **peacemakers,** for they shall be **called sons of God.***

*"Blessed are those who are **persecuted for righteousness' sake,** for **theirs is the kingdom of heaven.***

*"Blessed are you **when men revile you and persecute you and utter all kinds of evil against you falsely on my account. Rejoice and be glad,** for your **reward is great in heaven,** for so men persecuted the prophets who were before you.* Mt. 5:1-12.

*"**You are the salt of the earth;** but if salt has lost its taste, how shall its saltness be restored? It is no longer good for anything except to be thrown out and trodden under foot by men.* Mt. 5:13.

*"**You are the light of the world.** A city set on a hill cannot be hid. Nor do men light a lamp and put it under a bushel, but on a stand, and it gives light to all in the house. **Let your light so shine before men, that they may see your good works and give glory to your Father who is in heaven.*** Mt. 5:14.

*"Think not that I have come to abolish **the law and the prophets; I have come** not b abolish them but **to fulfil them.** For truly, I say to you, till heaven and earth pass away, **not an iota, not a dot, will pass from the law until all is accomplished.** Whoever then relaxes one of the least of these commandments and teaches men ŋ shall be called least in the kingdom of heaven; but he who does them and teaches them shall be called great in the kingdom of heaven. For I tell you, unless your righteousness exceeds that of the scribes and Pharisees, you will never enter the kingdom of heaven.* Mt. 5:17-20.

---

[4] The Sermon on the Mount is this version of Jesus's teachings here in Matthew 5. Luke's presentation is slightly different (see pages 371-372). Interestingly, Luke specifies the lessons taking place on "level ground." Matthew puts Jesus up the "mountain."

Let's stop to hang loose for a minute. Do we see what Jesus is teaching us? Jesus says we are "blessed." Even if we're not quite at the place of understanding that truly we are children of God, he says it's okay for now, but we have to change. All these "less than perfect expressions" are okay, but eventually we must enter the kingdom of heaven. There **we will know** that **we're "the salt of the earth."** We are important to the earth; but if we have no strength, we're of no value. We'll know **we're "the light of the world,"** but we have to let others see our light. Our true purpose in "being" is to "be righteous," to assess ourselves and our relation to the whole, accurately – and such assessment far exceeds the pinched piety of the scribes and Pharisees. Only in *righteousness* (seeing ourselves as children of God) do we enter the kingdom of heaven.

Righteous Understanding

Anyone who is at the level of the kingdom of heaven will express differently than does typical mankind. Jesus continues with the difference in the understanding of the one "living" in the kingdom of heaven: *"You have heard that it was said to the men of old, 'You shall not kill; and whoever kills shall be liable to judgment.' But I say to you that every one who is angry with his brother shall be liable to judgment; whoever insults his brother shall be liable to the council, and whoever says, 'You fool!' shall be liable to the hell of fire.*[5] *So if you are offering your gift at the altar, and there remember that your brother has something against you, leave your gift there before the altar and go; first be reconciled to your brother, and then come and offer your gift.* Mt. 5:21-24.

"Make friends quickly with your accuser,... lest... you be put in prison;... you will never get out till you have paid the last penny. Mt. 5:25,26.

---

[5] The wording of this passage is one of the supports for the medieval Christian Church's exploitation of the fear of being condemned to "hell." The *Sheol* of the Hebrews is an "underworld" where the deceased has a "shadowy" existence. But the "hell" of (particularly medieval) Christians takes on the dimensions of Danté's *Inferno*. Yet "hell" refers to *GeHinnom (gehenna)*, a "valley of fires" outside of Jerusalem, i.e., the city dump. It was here that the outcasts and the lepers lived. As opposed to the kingdom of heaven where the individual is in harmony, peace, joy... with the whole, *gehenna* is a state of *burning*, a state of having been thrown out. It's a feeling of abandonment, of separation, a feeling of torture.

"You have heard that it was said, 'You shall not commit adultery.' But I say to you that every one who looks at a woman lustfully has already committed adultery with her in his heart. If your right eye causes you to sin, pluck it out and throw it away; it is better that you lose one of your members than that your whole body be thrown into hell. And if your right hand causes you to sin, cut it off and throw it away; it is better that you lose one of your members than that your whole body go into hell.

"It was also said, 'Whoever divorces his wife, let him give her a certificate of divorce.' But I say to you that every one who divorces his wife, except on the ground of unchastity, makes her an adulteress; and whoever marries a divor-ced woman commits adultery.[6]

"Again you have heard that it was said to the men of old, 'You shall not swear falsely, but shall perform to the Lord what you have sworn.' But I say ... Do not swear at all, either by heaven, for it is the throne of God, or by the earth, for it is his footstool, or by Jerusalem, for it is the city of the great King. And do not swear by your head, for you cannot make one hair white or black. Let what you say be simply 'Yes' or 'No'; anything more ...comes from evil. Mt. 5:33-37

Don't be surprised if you're not sure how this fits in modern times. Holding to these admonitions requires the most stringent attention to one's life. Living in the *kingdom of heaven* requires nothing of us more than *everything.* We are simply to say "yes" or "no." Again, let's hang loose. Living in the kingdom of heaven under the LAW is more demanding than living under the law of Moses. But in truth, we always live under the LAW. It is just that he/she who lives in the kingdom of heaven recognizes that the individual always must pay close attention to each thought and action. It is recognition of the LAW; and the LAW's basis for judgment is one's *measurement.*

And the *measurement* is quite different from that of earthly measure. Why? Because all earthly "measure" is based on fear and shortage. Jesus is basing his "measurement" on the premise that "all that the Father has is available to him" and it is the Father's "good pleasure" to provide. In such a mindset, we

---

[6] In our day and age, many people are uncomfortable with this statement. I have heard recent "marriage" ceremonies that have the bride and groom vow *as long as love shall live* instead of *as long as we both shall live.* But that's an easy out, not fit for one who inhabits the Kingdom of Heaven. The difficulty lies in the Kingdom of Heaven's not being of this world. Admittedly, I see any vow as everlasting; I'm not sure this is right, either. Most likely, the point Jesus is trying to make is best shown by his admonition: "Do not swear at all!"

have no adversaries, we have no shortage; we have only love. Jesus continues: *"You have heard that it was said, 'An eye for an eye and a tooth for a tooth.' But I say to you, Do not resist one who is evil. But if any one strikes you on the right cheek, turn to him the other also; and if any one would sue you and take your coat, let him have your cloak as well; and if any one forces you to go one mile, go with him two miles. Give to him who begs from you, and do not refuse him who would borrow from you.*

"You have heard that it was said, 'You shall love your neighbor and hate your enemy.' But I say to you, Love your enemies and pray for those who persecute you, so that you may be sons of your Father who is in heaven; for he makes his sun rise on the evil and on the good, and sends rain on the just and on the unjust. For if you love those who love you, what reward have you? Do not even the tax collectors do the same? And if you salute only your brethren, what more are you doing than others? Do not even the Gentiles do the same? You, therefore, must be perfect, as your heavenly Father is perfect. Mt. 5:43-48. [4 x 12] i.e., perfect!

We are back to בראשית (Bereshyt) – only now we recognize the ***ongoing creation.*** It's no wonder that *carnal* man could not understand Jesus; it's no wonder that carnal man could not abide to let him live. ***Righteous*** man is not of this world. So the world proceeds to eliminate this thorn in its side. Esoterically, that's the world's function – to place the created creature on the cross of life.

✝

The "Cross" is a symbol. It is a symbol of man's struggle to recognize his total oneness with God. It is man's effort to climb the Mountain. Interestingly, it is a universal symbol. It is found in Egypt, in Asia, in India, in South America and with the American Indians. Traditionally, numerous "saviours" have been crucified upon one.[7]

---

[7] The most informative presentation regarding crosses is found in Manly P. Hall's *The Secret Teachings of All Ages,* The Philosophical Research Society, Inc., 3rd Ed., 1979. Hall says that the "martyrdom of the God-Man and the redemption of the world through His blood has been an essential tenent of many great religions." He continues: "The list of the deathless mortals who *suffered* for man that he might receive the boon of eternal life is an imposing one. Among those connected historically or allegorically with a crucifixion are Prometheus, Adonis, Apollo, Atys, Bacchus, Buddha, Christna [Krishna], Horus, Indra, Ixion, Mithras, Osiris, Pythagoras, Quetzalcoatl, Semiramis, and Jupiter." (p. CLXXXIII)

Symbols are used to convey something beyond the physical. The *icons* of the Byzantine Church purposefully were not photographic representations. And the argument between the Eastern Church and Rome over liturgical art was more likely a power-play by Rome than a philosophical and theological matter of principle.[8] In fact, I debated over adding art to this work for the very reason that our minds remember pictures better than words; and pictures place ideas on the level of the "world" rather than the "spiritual," which produces no pictures.

But – just as "pictures" solidify our mental concepts – for this reason, Scriptures utilize symbols to allow expansion of understanding. We have already looked at some of the symbols found in **The Symbology** the Scriptures. There were the symbols **of Jesus' Ministry** inherited from Moses; Moses found water and parted the sea. There were the symbols of the Tabernacle and of the Temple; there were the symbols or "signs" of the prophets. But with Jesus, the symbols take on a greater dimension. Their physical nature is increased.

With Jesus, the water is turned into wine; and a path in the water becomes "walking on **Feeding the** top of it." The "miracles" of food also take on **Multitudes** cosmic proportions. Where Elisha fed 100 men with 20 loaves of barley and wheat (see p. 360), Jesus feeds 5000 at the Sea of Galilee[9] and feeds 4000 in the desert.

---

[8] The final split between the Eastern Church and the Western Church took place in 1054 when Pope Leo IX excommunicated the whole Eastern Church. *The Encyclopedia Americana.*

[9] One of the few times that John corresponds with the synoptic gospels is the feeding of the 5000. When Jesus heard about the murder of the Baptist, *he withdrew from there in a boat to a lonely place apart. But when the crowds heard it, they followed him on foot from the towns. As he went ashore he saw a great throng; and he had compassion on them, and healed their sick. When it was evening, the disciples came to him and said, "This is a **lonely place, and the day is now over; send the crowds away to go into the villages and buy food for themselves."** Jesus said, "They need not go away; **you give them something to eat."** They said to him, "We have only **five loaves** here and **two fish."** And he said, "Bring them here to me." Then he ordered the crowds to sit down on the*

(continued...)

382

If we use our intellects, we come up with Elisha's ratio of 20/100, i.e., a multiple of five (5). Elisha is still dealing with the physical world. Jesus, too, still has to deal with the physical world, but his dealings with it are at the ratio of 5/5000, a multiple of 1000. The two fish seem to remain a constant, reacting upon what number of loaves are presented. Remember: two of *like mind* – as he said *Again I say to you, if two of you agree on earth about anything they ask, it will be done for them by my Father in heaven. For where two or three are gathered in my name, there am I in the midst of them."* Mt. 18:19,20

The symbols provide more information than the surface narration. We're told that if we rise to the level of Jesus, we can deal with the senses (the world) at a cosmic level (5000) and still have (12) divine completion left over. Moreover, if we rise to the level of Jesus, we reach cosmic equilibrium (4000) and have (7) earthly abundance and perfection left over. As with all else in the Bible, the narration intends to teach *above* the intellectual perception. In these two *feeding* instances, the principal recipients are the disciples and us. Of course we wouldn't know this if there were not some other symbols in the Bible that in hang-loose fashion relate to *feeding*.

Bread Is Not Essential   We learned with Moses that our *bread* didn't have to be exactly as we might like it. It was expeditious to leave the leavening out as we pulled ourselves away from the world; but then we were told more. Moses explained what the Israelites were to be learning from God's insistence that they do without their leavening. And

---

[9](...continued)

grass; and taking the five loaves and the two fish he looked up to heaven, and blessed, and broke and gave the loaves to the disciples, and the disciples gave them to the crowds. And they all ate and were satisfied. And they took up twelve baskets full of the broken pieces left over. And those who ate were about five thousand men, besides women and children. Mt. 14:13-21.

Moses said: *And he humbled you and let you hunger and fed you with manna, which you did not know, nor did your fathers know; **that he might make you know that man does not live by bread alone, but that man lives by everything that proceeds out of the mouth of the LORD.*** Dt. 8:3.

Jesus reminds us of this understanding, for he knows that he lives through the expression of the LORD. You well may wonder what this means.[10] I wonder if it is what we see in the understanding of the Aborigines? – people who by our standard of *measurement* should die of hunger or thirst in their desert. As with the Aborigines, Jesus' *measurement* is not ours. He says: ***Consider the lilies,*** *how they grow;* ***they neither toil nor spin;*** *yet ...* ***even Solomon in all his glory was not arrayed like one of these.*** *But if God so clothes the grass which is alive in the field today and tomorrow is thrown into the oven,* ***how much more will he clothe you, O men of little faith! ... do not seek what you are to eat and what you are to drink, nor be of anxious mind.*** *... your Father knows that you need them.* ***Instead, seek his kingdom, and these things shall be yours as well.*** Lk. 12:27-31.

Despite the assurances of Jesus and Moses and all the others whose *measurement* has been greater than ours, we continue to fear; we continue to be anxious about ourselves.

Can we *hear* what Jesus says: *Fear not, little flock, for* ***it is your Father's good pleasure to give you the kingdom.*** *Sell your possessions, and give alms;* ***provide yourselves with*** *purses that do not grow old, with a* ***treasure in the heavens that does not fail,*** *where no thief approaches and no moth destroys.* ***For where your treasure is, there will your heart be also.***

Let your loins be girded and your lamps burning, and ***be like men*** *who are* ***waiting for their master to come home*** *from the marriage feast, so that they may open to him at once* ***when he comes and knocks.*** ***Blessed are those servants whom the master finds awake when he comes;*** *truly, I say to you,* ***he will*** *gird himself and* ***have them sit at table, and he will come and serve them.*** *If he comes in the second watch, or in the third, and finds them so, blessed are those servants! But know this, that if the householder had known at what hour the thief was coming, he would not have left his house to be broken into.* ***You*** *also* ***must be ready; for the Son of man is coming at an unexpected hour.*** Lk. 12:32-40.

---

[10] Even as we're approaching the top of the Mountain, don't we still see ourselves as physical bodies run by a mind and having a spirit which "clicks" in when we "check out"? But the **good news** is something else. For just a minute, think of yourself as part of a divine expression, hooked to this divine expression by the spirit within you, and presently operating on a physical plane with a body and mind that are serviceable. Under such a scheme, that which is LORD provides all that is needed; and you operate as YHWH, for you make the *all* manifest when and how you say I Am....

This passage, along with the story of the rich young man who is told to get rid of his possessions to follow Jesus, (see Luke 18:18-25.) often causes consternation among climbers; but, remember, such consternation comes on the intellectual level.[11] On the intuitional level, the passage refers to our *attention*. If our attention is on the possessions – or if we are *withholding* for any reason, i.e., **not** giving alms – or, even more likely, if we are *fearful* and not paying attention when the knock comes, we will miss the opportunity to receive the Son of man. If our *measurement* is at the level of *bread*, we won't *hear* the knock.

Explanation of hearing the knock comes later as Jesus is preparing for the finish to his earthly assignment. *And when he drew near and saw the city he wept over it, saying, "Would that even today you knew the things that make for peace! But now they are hid from your eyes. For the days shall come upon you, when your enemies will cast up a bank about you and surround you, and hem you in on every side, and dash you to the ground, you and your children within you, and they will not leave one stone upon another in you; because you did not know the time of your visitation."* Lk. 19:41-44.

Why is this included with bread? Because *bread* implies all those *feeding* opportunities that come to us.[12] Jerusalem will have one of these "feeding" opportunities in A.D. 70 with the atrocities of the Romans in Jerusalem.[13]

---

[11] Admittedly, it is difficult to not find the "vow of poverty" requirement in the above passage; however, there is a substantial difference between being *willing to give up one's possessions* (my thinking is that it is anything we're fully attached to) and a vow of poverty.

[12] Clarification is needed, here! We are all the Son of man; but only he/she who recognizes this truth is going to "hear the knock." That does not mean there will not be other "knocks." We are constantly provided choices and "opportunities" to answer the "knock." Look back at the end of David's life. He had so many opportunities to change the outcome with his sons, but he did nothing. Was it lack of attention or lack of caring that made him do nothing? (See pages 318-321.) Isn't this what we must learn? We are to be both attentive and caring at all times. The Kingdom of Heaven is a constant and permanent change in us.

[13] Unhappy with constant sedition on the part of the Jewish malcontents, Rome eventually clamped down. The "final solution" was to lay siege to Jerusalem in the year A.D. 70. The atrocities of the Romans were easily equal to those of Hitler.

We all endure similar episodes in our private lives. They may not make the history books, but they are just as devastating. However, if we know the "things of peace," these episodes will add to our growth. But we're not talking about worldly "peace." We're talking about the "peace" of the soul (and the "peace" of the body and mind that goes with it). According to Solomon: *The righteous eateth to the satisfying of his soul; but the belly of the wicked shall want.* Prov. 13:25

But it is that from which bread is made that gives us the most esoteric understanding. It is *wheat* that **Wheat Teaches Many Lessons** has the greatest meaning. *Wheat* is the symbol for ourselves. It is wheat that is placed on the threshing floor and *threshed*; it is wheat that is *winnowed*. It is wheat that is sown and either thrives and multiplies – or doesn't; and it is wheat that simply must suffer the *tares* until the harvest. [14]

The Revised Standard version uses the word *weeds,* but

(Lolium temulentum)

weeds doesn't convey the whole point. The King James version uses *tares.* We are told that the *tare* is the *bearded darnel (Lolium temulentum),* "**a poisonous grass**, almost indistinguishable from wheat while the two are in the blade, but which can be separated from the wheat without difficulty when ripe." Isn't this true with our lives? Isn't this what Jesus is trying to teach us? Isn't Jesus trying

---

[14] *Another parable he put before them, saying, "The **kingdom of heaven may be compared to a man who sowed good seed in his field**; but while men were sleeping, his enemy came and sowed weeds [tares] among the wheat, and went away. So **when the plants came up and bore grain, then the weeds [tares] appeared also**. And the servants of the householder came and said to him, 'Sir, did you not sow good seed in your field? How then has it weeds?' He said to them, 'An enemy has done this.' The servants said to him, 'Then **do you want us to go and gather them**?' But he said, 'No; lest in gathering the [tares] you root up the wheat along with them. Let both grow together until the harvest; and at harvest time I will tell the reapers, Gather the [tares] first and bind them in bundles to be burned, but gather the wheat into my barn.'"* Mt. 13:25-30

to teach us that we really can't tell what is "good" and what is "bad" in our lives?[15]

It is our **unrighteous judgment** which tries to distinguish between what we need and what we don't need. Just as we would tear the "tares" out, we **judge** our circumstances, never seeing that they represent our **measurement.** But, finally, we will be able to see truly – to separate the tares from the wheat – to separate in our minds those happenings that are for a purpose, and what that purpose is.

Wheat is symbolized in the mystical gospel. John places this pronouncement during the last week of Jesus' life. It is Sunday in the week of Passover; it is the **fourth** Passover of Jesus' ministry. He has come into Jerusalem, riding on the colt of an ass, a significant statement to those familiar with Isaiah (Is. 62:11); and people have come to see him. They have heard of him. They have heard of his "healings," and about the "raising" of Lazarus from the dead. But this frightens the Sanhedrin; it might entice the

Egyptian wheat.

Romans to take action. Caiaphas, who is high priest this year, feels that one death might lessen the Roman threat.[16]

---

[15] Davis and Gehman, p. 591. According to this source, mature *tares* have purple-blue or red colors which make them easy to spot.

[16] The Sanhedrin was fearful; some said: " *If we let him go on thus, every one will believe in him, and the Romans will come and destroy both our holy place and our nation.*" But ...Caiaphas ... said ... "*It is expedient for you that one man should die for the people, and that the whole nation should not perish.*" *He did not say this of his own accord, but being high priest that year he prophesied that Jesus should die for the nation, and not for the nation only, but to gather into one the children of God who are scattered abroad.* Jn. 11:48-52.

Some Greeks (prob. Greek Jews) come to see Jesus, and Philip and Andrew come to tell him. According to John, he responds with this last teaching. He answers: *"The hour has come for the Son of man to be glorified. Truly, truly, I say to you, unless a grain of wheat falls into the earth and dies, it remains alone; but if it dies, it bears much fruit.* He who loves his life loses it, and he who hates his life in this world will keep it for eternal life. If any one serves me, he must follow me; and where I am, there shall my servant be also; if any one serves me, the Father will honor him. **Now is my soul troubled.** And what shall I say? 'Father, save me from this hour'? No, **for this purpose I have come to this hour.** Father, glorify thy name."* Jn. 12:23-28.

" *Now is the judgment of this world,* now shall the ruler of this world be **cast out; and I, when I am lifted up from the earth, will draw all men to myself."** ... *The crowd answered him, "We have heard from the law that the Christ remains for ever. How can you say that the Son of man must be lifted up? Who is this Son of man?" Jesus said to them, "The light is with you for a little longer. Walk while you have the light, lest the darkness overtake you; he who walks in the darkness does not know where he goes. While you have the light, believe in the light, that you may become sons of light."* When Jesus had said this, he departed and hid himself from them. Though he had done so many signs before them, yet they did not believe ... him... Jn. 12:31-36.

Our difficulty is with the word *believe*. The Church early on confined *believe* to meaning that we accept as truth the designation of Jesus as the "only begotten son." The intuition understands *believe* as "understanding." The intuition "understands" the significance of the *wheat* and *tares.* But the intellect turns the teaching into a value judgment. Matthew uses the symbology of goats and sheep.

Jesus says: *"When the Son of man comes in his glory, and all the angels with him, then he will sit on his glorious throne. Before him will be gathered all the nations, and he will separate them one from another as a shepherd separates the sheep from the goats, and he will place the sheep at his right hand, but the goats at the left. Then the King will say to those at his right hand, 'Come, O blessed of my Father, inherit the kingdom prepared for you from the foundation of the world; for I was hungry and you gave me food, I was thirsty and you gave me drink, I was a stranger and you welcomed me, I was naked and you clothed me, I was sick and you visited me, I was in prison and you came to me.'* Mt. 25:32-36.
" *Then the righteous will answer him, 'Lord, when did we see thee hungry and feed thee, or thirsty and give thee drink? And when did we see thee a stranger and welcome thee, or naked and clothe thee? And when did we see thee sick or in prison and visit thee?'*

And the King will answer them, 'Truly...as you did it to one of the least of these my brethren, you did it to me.' Then he will say to those at his left hand, 'Depart from me, you cursed... for I was hungry and you gave me no food, I was thirsty and you gave me no drink, I was a stranger and you did not welcome me, naked and you did not clothe me, sick and in prison and you did not visit me.' Then they also will answer, 'Lord, when did we see thee hungry or thirsty or a stranger or naked or sick or in prison, and did not minister to thee?' Then he will answer them, 'Truly, I say to you, as you did it not to one of the least of these, you did it not to me.' And they will go away into eternal punishment, but the righteous into eternal life." When Jesus had finished all these sayings, he said to his disciples, "You know that after two days the Passover is coming, and the Son of man will be delivered up to be crucified." Mt. 25:32-40; 26:1,2.

According to Ausubel, Judaism's most significant holy day is Yom Kippur, the Day of Atonement, a traditional ceremonial fast-day which concludes the 10-day period of the Jewish New Year. *Atonement* was intended to start the new year *aright*. The idea of a sacrifice providing the atonement goes back to primitive times, and it symbolizes the individual mindset seeing itself as again pure. Logically, a *perfect lamb* might placate an angry god.

It is the intellectual approach that requires the crucifixion. Goats and sheep are wide-spread symbols. Caiaphas' expectation for one death satisfying Rome is obvious allusion to the yearly two "scape-goats" provided in the Old Testament to carry the sins of Israel. Lv. 16:8-10 At Yom Kippur, one goat was *presented alive before the* LORD *to make atonement over it, that it [might] be sent away into the wilderness to Azazel.*[17] The other goat was killed as a *sin offering ... for the people.* And its blood was sprinkled in front of the mercy seat, on top of the sacrificial bull's blood. But the time of year is Passover, not Yom Kippur, and the sacrifice is of a lamb, perfect and unblemished. Caiaphas has a candidate.

From our viewpoint, Jesus' execution is an *outrage!* But then, so are the executions of Prometheus, Osiris,

---

[17] Ausubel, *Jewish Knowledge,* pp. 519-523. According to Ausubel, from primeval times, Yom Kippur was "ceremonially presented as the expression of collective contrition and atonement for transgressions and misdoing by the sacrificial offering of bullocks and goats to the intonation of magical incantations and the shrill blare of music."

Pythagoras, Socrates, Quetzalcoatl, John Huss, Joan of Arc, Anne Frank – all the martyrs of endless time. We are **outraged** at the **bad** that **good** people suffer. Have we learned to *see* yet?

Christ bearing the Cross by Albrecht Dürer.

God's ways are not man's ways. Yet, if there had been no *crucifixion*, there could have been no *resurrection*, and Jesus' teaching would have faded as have the teachings of countless others. Western mankind does not seem to seek the spiritual as does Eastern mankind. Yet, the mindset of generations of Christians seems to have changed a *fully materialistic* Western culture into at least a slightly gentler world. The East's spirituality has had no such effect.

Then how does the enlightened intuition explain the crucifixion? It may **The Symbology of the Crucifixion** be that the greatest message to the intuition lies in the pattern of the crucifixion itself. Popularly, the symbolism is presented as the enactment of the *Stations of the Cross,* fourteen (14) images or pictures representing 14 incidents in the life of Jesus on the day of his crucifixion. Traditionally, the Stations of the Cross are the following: **1.** Sentence of death by Pilate; **2.** Christ receiving the cross; **3.** His first fall; **4.** Meeting with his mother; **5.** Cross borne by Simon of Cyrene; **6.** Veronica, wiping his face with a handkerchief; **7.** His second fall; **8.** Words to the women of Jerusalem; **9.** His third fall; **10.** Stripping him of his garments; **11.** The crucifixion; **12.** His death; **13.** Taking the body down; and **14.** His burial. Certainly, the Stations of the Cross depict the agony suffered by Jesus; and the inclusion of three falls has significance to a sinful mankind.

But to the intuition, the drama is a **triumph** which involves much more than just the crucifixion. It begins when **1. Jesus enters Jerusalem,** the city of Melchizedek, the city of David, the city of the Christ, **riding an ass** (traditional for kings) **in purity** (the colt of the ass has never been ridden) and **humility**, even though some are honoring him with palms waving, greeting him as they would greet a triumphant conqueror.

East

PLAN OF THE CITY OF JERUSALEM

BY THO[S] STARLING.

REFERENCE.
1 Joseph's House
2 Bellona Palace
3 Antiochus House
4 Herod's Palace
5 The Second Gate
6 Lower Fish Pool
7 Fish Market
8 Jeremiah's Prison
9 Wood Market
10 Sheep Market
11 Pool of Bethesda
12 Pilate's House
13 Fort Antonia
14 Solomon's House
15 Elizabeth House
16 Anariah House
17 The Prison
18 The Queen's House
19 The Palace
20 Zion or Sion Gate
21 House of Lebanon W.
22 The Armoury
23 Pool of Bethabeba
24 Kinon Bab Pools
25 House of David
26 Agrippa's House
27 Caiphas House
28 David's Tomb
29 David's Tomb
30 Aaron's House
31 The Strong House
32 The Tower

SCALES
Sacred Cubits
English Yards
100 200 300 400

Leaving Bethany, **1.** Jesus enters Jerusalem on Sunday.(East Gate) **E 2.** During the week he cleanses the Temple. **3.** Sups on Thursday night **4.** Goes to Gethsemane. ✿ **5.** Arrested. ●
6. To Annas at the High Priest's Palace ✪   **7.**   To Pilate at Governor's residence. ✩ (12)
8. To Herod's residence. ✦(4)   **9.**   Jesus scourged at Governor's residence. ✩
10. The Crucifixion ✝ **ll.** Burial ❑ **12.** Resurrection **13.** Ascension on road to Bethany. ✿

2. Jesus again cleanses the Temple. *And Jesus entered the temple of God and drove out all who sold and bought in the temple, and* **he overturned the tables of the money-changers and the seats of those who sold pigeons.** *He said to them, "It is written, 'My house shall be called a house of prayer'; but you make it a den of robbers."*

And **the blind and the lame came to him in the temple, and he healed them.** Mt. 21:12-14.

Interestingly, while John places the cleansing of the Temple early in Jesus' ministry, the synoptic presentation is during the last week. Notice the number of the chapter and verse. The compiler is placing this "cleansing" at 3 x 7. It takes place as we are at the third time round "earthly completion" at verses 12 and 13. We might argue that the climb is a constant round of cleansings, and only after they are accomplished can we heal the "blind" and the "lame." Even the pigeon sellers – even those slightest improprieties must be "cleansed" out of us.

3. Jesus adds to the traditions of Passover,[18] hosting the *Qadosh*, the Feast of Brotherhood (called the Last Supper and celebrated by Christians as *Maundy Thursday),* even washing his guests' feet. Here come the symbolic bread and wine and the total humility of the host, washing the feet of his guests.[19] It may have been customary to wash the feet of guests, but likely it would have been done by servants. It would have been unusual for the host to humble himself to that point.[20] Passover represents Israel's having escaped slavery

---

[18] See Exodus 12. It is the 10th day of the first month when the *lamb* is selected. It is kept until the 14th day, when the blood is placed on the door posts; and the flesh shall be eaten that night, *roasted,* with unleavened bread and bitter herbs, and none of it shall remain. Whatever remains shall be burned. You shall eat it with *loins girded, sandals on your feet, staff in hand, and in haste* in a house that is totally free of leavening; for you have **searched** for any remaining leavening. Ex. 12: 3-11.

[19] One school of thought sees the bread as representing the Old Covenant (with the LORD God, i.e., the Christ) and the grail (wine) symbolizing the New Covenant (with mankind). Peter Dawkins, *The Great Vision*, p. 60.

[20] John writes: *Jesus,* **knowing that the Father had given all things into his hands, and that he had come from God and was going to God,** *rose from supper, laid aside his garments, and girded himself with a towel. Then he poured water into a basin, and began to wash the disciples' feet, and to wipe them with the towel with which he was girded.* He came to Simon Peter; and Peter said to him, "Lord, do you wash my feet?" Jesus answered him, "What I am doing you do not know now, but afterward you will understand." Peter said to him, "You shall never wash my feet." Jesus answered him, **"If I do not wash you, you have no part in me."** Simon Peter said to him, "Lord, not my feet only but also my hands and my head!" Jesus said to him, **"He who has bathed does not need to wash, except for his feet,** but he is clean all over; and you are clean, but not every one of you." Jn. 13:3-11.

(continued...)

and having been *saved* by the "blood." But the most important Passover ceremony may be the "searching" the "house" for any leavening that might have been overlooked.

4. Jesus leaves the city and **goes to Gethsemane**, taking with him his most highly developed disciples. He has known what is coming for quite awhile; but he gives some last instructions to those who have the greatest possibility of understanding. He lifts his eyes and prays that all of the disciples will understand as he has taught them that *"this is eternal life, that they know thee the only true God...I have manifested thy name (nature) to the men whom thou gavest me out of the world... I do not pray for these only, but also for those who believe in me through their word, that they may all be one; even as thou, Father, art in me, and I in thee, that they also may be in us, so that the world may believe that thou hast sent me. ... O, righteous Father, the world has not known thee, but I have known thee; and these know that thou hast sent me. I made known to them thy name (nature), and I will make it known, that the love with which thou hast loved me may be in them, and I in them."* See John 17.

With Peter, James and John, he crosses the Cedron (Kidron) valley. He says: *"Do you now believe? The hour is coming...when you will be scattered... and you will leave me alone; yet I am not alone, for the Father is with me. I have said this to you, that... you may have peace. In the world you have tribulation; but be of good cheer, I have overcome the world."* Jn.16:31-33. Asking the three to stay awake, he goes further into the garden. Luke says: *And he came out, and went, as was his custom, to the Mount of Olives; and the disciples followed him. And when he came to the place, he said to them, "Pray that you may not enter into temptation." And he withdrew from them about a stone's throw, and knelt down and prayed, "Father, if thou art willing, remove this cup from me; nevertheless not my will, but thine, be done."* Lk. 22:39-42.

During this phase of our climb, it's easy for us to falter.[21] We, too, must be reminded to *rise*, in order that we *may not enter into temptation.* Possibly the most difficult time is when we're watching the challenge of one we love; then it's hard to stay "up" with our righteous knowledge.

---

[20](...continued)

    Esoterically, the *feet* represent *understanding.* If we do not accept the understanding of Jesus, we have *no part in him.* We assume that by this point on the climb, we have no need for cleaning our *hands* (actions) and *head* (mind and focus). It is our understanding that must constantly be dealt with – washed by the Christ.

[21] During the *Qadosh*, Jesus had hinted at Judas' betrayal; and on the way to the Garden of Gethsemane, Jesus tells Peter that he will deny him three times.

*And when he rose..., he came to the disciples and found them sleeping for sorrow, and he said to them, "Why do you sleep? **Rise and pray that you may not enter into temptation."** Lk. 22:45, 46.*

Jesus is able to hold himself to what he knows to be truth. Even when Peter cuts off the ear of the high priest's slave, Jesus has the concentration and power to heal the ear.

The Agony in the Garden by Albrecht Dürer.

But the disciples are not up to Jesus' level. They aren't able to stay awake. They offer no support to the one facing such tribulation. They wake up when Jesus speaks to them, but their awareness is so shallow that they have no idea what is happening. Moreover, as soon as Jesus is arrested, they all scatter. As Jesus had predicted, Peter – his most devoted follower – denies having known him three times as different people question him; even John keeps himself in the background. Jesus has no earthly support.

The Night of Agony by Doré.

5. Jesus' arrest. Judas' betrayal simply allows the soldiers of the Sanhedrin to find Jesus. The "play" which Jesus knows to be taking place commences. John writes: *Then Jesus, knowing all that was to befall him, came forward and said to them, "Whom do you seek?" They answered him, "Jesus of Nazareth." Jesus said to them, "I am he." Judas, who betrayed him, was standing with them. When he said to them, "I Am he," they drew back and fell to the ground.* Jn.18:4-6.

6. Jesus is judged by the Sanhedrin. Jesus is first taken to Annas (father-in-law of Caiaphas and the most influential priest). Annas asks him about his disciples and his teaching: *Jesus answered him, "I have spoken openly to the world; I have always taught in synagogues and in the temple, where all Jews come together; **I have said nothing secretly. Why do you ask me? Ask those who have heard me, what I said to them; they know what I said."** When he had said this, one of the officers standing by struck Jesus with his hand, saying, "Is that how you answer the high priest?" Jesus answered him, "**If I have spoken wrongly, bear witness to the wrong; but if I have spoken rightly, why do you strike me?"** Annas then sent him bound to Caiaphas the high priest.*

Annas, Caiaphas and the Sanhedrin represent the "religious" establishment. They can't "hear" Jesus; they have no intention of pulling away from the world's noise. But in some ways they represent the spiritual part of us; it is the spiritual part that determines the course of the whole. And Caiaphas passes Jesus to Pilate. [22]

7. Jesus is judged by Pilate. Pilate seems to represent the mental aspect of us. It is heightened enough to know that Jesus has done no wrong, but it cannot get the physical aspects of us to agree. Finally, it just gives in to the "spiritual" and accedes to its demand for crucifixion.

8. Jesus is judged by Herod. Herod represents the physical aspect of us.[23] The physical has no great power. It accedes to the demands of the mental. Herod treats the Christ with

---

[22] The synoptic gospels place the decision by the "religious" leaders as early Friday morning. Davis and Gehman say the date is April 7, A.D. 30.

[23] It is interesting that only Luke – the gospel for the gentiles – includes Herod as one of those who judges Jesus.

contempt and mocks him: *then, arraying him in gorgeous apparel, he sent him back to Pilate.* Lk.23:11. Most of our struggle during this climb has been with the physical world's opinion. Why think the physical world will change? It is we who must change.

Roman Scourges

9. Jesus is scourged.[24] *Then Pilate took Jesus and scourged him. And the soldiers plaited a crown of thorns, and put it on his head, and arrayed him in a purple robe; they came up to him, saying, "Hail, King of the Jews!" and struck him with their hands. Pilate went out again, and said to them, "See, I am bringing him out to you, that you may know that I find no crime in him." So Jesus came out, wearing the crown of thorns and the purple robe. Pilate said to them, "Behold the man!" When the chief priests and the officers saw him, they cried out, "Crucify him, crucify him!" Pilate said to them, "Take him yourselves and crucify him, for I find no crime in him." The Jews answered him, "We have a law, and by that law he ought to die, because he has made himself the Son of God." When Pilate heard these words, he was the more afraid; he entered the praetorium again and said to Jesus, "Where are you from?" But Jesus gave no answer. Pilate therefore said to him, "You will not speak to me? Do you not know that I have power to release you, and power to crucify you?"* Jn. 19:1-10. [25]

Esoterically, the "mental" has the power to *release* us or *crucify* us. It is our "mental" aspect that decides which we will choose, whether we will be like Joshua ("as for me and my house, we will serve the LORD" Jsh. 24:15) or not. Some say Pilate had Jesus "scourged" thinking that would satisfy the priests. But the priests, as representatives of the world, are not satisfied

---

[24] The scourging weakened the victim and assured a shorter time of crucifixion.

[25] According to the *Encyclopedia Americana*, Pilate was appointed governor of Judea, Samaria and Idumea in A.D. 26. He was removed from office in A.D. 36 for setting his troops on peaceful Samaritan worshipers assembled on Mount Gerizim. Eusebius writes he was banished to Vienna (Vienne) in Gaul and died by suicide. Tradition and myth treat Pilate more kindly. Tradition tells of the dream of Pilate's wife, Claudia Procula, and the Greek Church venerates her as a saint. Tertullian even considers Pilate a Christian (at least of heart); and Pilate has a place in the Abyssinian Church calendar.

with just a bloody whipping. The priests consider themselves to be the final authority. Unfortunately, organized religion often succumbs to the temptation to *make judgment*. The law to which they refer is: *He who blasphemes the name of the LORD shall be put to death; all the congregation shall stone him; the sojourner as well as the native, when he blasphemes the Name, shall be put to death. Lv. 24:16.* The judgment they make is with the words *blaspheme* and *name*. The word for *blaspheme* comes from a root which means *to puncture*. In hang-loose logic, we might say it is destroying *by perforating with violence*. On the other hand, *name* refers to *nature*.

We might wonder if the priests and the Sanhedrin honestly believed that anyone could *perforate* the *nature* of God. Obviously, the proclamation of the priests is contrived. There is a long history of the Hebrews considering themselves "sons of God." Moses said: *"Give ear, O heavens, and I will speak; and let the earth hear the words of my mouth. May my teaching drop as the rain, my speech distil as the dew,... For I will proclaim the name of the LORD. Ascribe greatness to our God! The Rock, his work is perfect; for all his ways are justice. A God of faithfulness and without iniquity, just and right is he. **They have dealt corruptly with him, they are no longer his children because of their blemish; they are a perverse and crooked generation.** Do you thus requite the LORD, you foolish and senseless people? **Is not he your father, who created you, who made you and established you?** Remember the days of old, consider the years of many generations; **ask your father, and he will show you; your elders, and they will tell you.** When the Most High gave to the nations their inheritance, when he separated the sons of men, he fixed the bounds of the peoples according to the number of the sons of God. For the Lord's portion is his people, Jacob his allotted heritage." Dt. 32:1-9.*

But the elders have forgotten the truth, and the "mental" power cannot reverse their decision on its own. Ever wonder if we go along with the Sanhedrin and Pilate? How dare this fellow Jesus tell us that we are the sons of God, and therefore, perfect, whole and complete? We *judge,* right along with the *blind* elders. We proclaim ourselves *ill*; we proclaim ourselves *poor;* we proclaim ourselves less than the sons of God. We crucify Jesus just as much as do Pilate and the Sanhedrin. Don't we recognize the truth of what Jesus has said? Don't we recognize that there can be **no** leavening left – we searched through the whole house and found none.

*Jesus answered him, "**You would have no power over me unless it had been given you from above;** therefore he who delivered me to you has the greater sin." Upon this Pilate sought to release him, but the Jews cried out, "If you release this man, you are not Caesar's friend; every one who makes himself a king sets himself against Caesar." When Pilate heard these words, he brought Jesus out and **sat down on the judgment seat** at a place called The Pavement, and in Hebrew, **Gabbatha.*** (High place) Jn. 19:11-13.

This section often gets lost in the passion of the Good Friday pageants, but Jesus is affirming his acceptance of what is going on in his wordly life. His answer to Pilate, *You would have no power over me unless it had been given you from above...* states the truth of this world. He says that Pilate's power over him is because it is necessary in order *that God's will be manifest on earth.* It is necessary that Jesus be crucified.

Hang loose for a minute. Do not mistake what I am saying! Do you see that **the unfortunate happenstances of our lives are** *not* mistakes! Dismal and horrendous as they may be, they

> It is **distrust of God** to be troubled about **what is to come; impatience against God** to be troubled by **the present;** and **anger against God** to be troubled by **what is past.** *Patrick*

are necessary to get us to the place where we are either writing this (in my case) or reading this (in your case). This outrages us, doesn't it? How could a *loving God* allow us to suffer as we do? How could a *loving Father* allow his *son* to be crucified? But, this loving Father which we call God, makes no distinction between good and bad. It is mankind – who has eaten of the *tree of the knowledge of good and evil* – who makes the distinction. It is mankind which holds itself to the earthly viewpoint – that of there being *good* and *evil*. It is mankind which has no king but Caesar. *Now it was the day of Preparation of the Passover; it was about the sixth hour. He said to the Jews, "Behold your King!" They cried out, "Away with him, away with him, crucify him!" Pilate said to them, "Shall I crucify your King?" The chief priests answered, "**We have no king but Caesar.**"* Jn. 19:14,15.

From appearances, only a few of those living in the 20th Century accept Jesus' view of earthly existence. I once heard a representative of the *Moonies*, followers of Mr. Moon

400

from Korea, state that Jesus did not accomplish his mission. To this man, Jesus had failed. His reasoning was, therefore, there had to be another *saviour,* another *messiah.*

I disagree! Jesus accomplished his mission! Jesus held to the original paradigm. Mankind is the son of the living God. Mankind receives as he/she *judges.* Knowing this, Jesus could rise above his suffering. With the attention on other than the pain, the soul soars to greater understanding; and in this greater understanding there is no death or pain. Death and pain are of the earthly mindset.

Various thinkers through the ages have posed the argument that as a cosmic being, Jesus did not suffer, but produced sort of an explosion that made it so all mankind, henceforth, could evolve to a higher plane. Others have even suggested that the whole story of Jesus' crucifixion is only symbolic and is a representation of what has to happen to us all to get us to a greater expression. But any of these arguments are of the intellect! The intuition makes no judgment! It knows in itself the truth of Jesus the Christ. In *truth,* there is no poverty, there is no leprosy, there is no blindness, deafness, dumbness – there is no illness, there is no pain, there is no death – there is only God! But mankind must learn this truth. So the body is "crucified."

10. Jesus is crucified. *Then he [Pilate] handed him over to them to be crucified. So **they took Jesus,** and he went out, **bearing his own cross, to the** place called the **place of a skull,** which is called in Hebrew Golgotha. There they crucified him, and **with** him **two others,** one on either side, and **Jesus between them. Pilate also wrote a title** and put it on the cross; it read, "Jesus of Nazareth, the **King of the Jews."** Many of the Jews read this title, for the place where Jesus was crucified was near the city; and it was **written in Hebrew, in Latin, and in Greek.** The chief priests of the Jews then said to Pilate, "Do not write, 'The King of the Jews,' but, 'This man said, I am King of the Jews.'" **Pilate answered, "What I have written I have written."** Jn. 19:16-22.*

The mental still controls the scene. "Pilate" puts the whole process into operation, and the process takes place at the ***place of a skull.*** The mental must decide which paradigm to accept. Is the creation *perfect?* Or is the creation *sinful?*

The "mental" *sees* and declares Jesus KING, and upon the protest of the world says: ***That's it!*** The Crucifixion will still happen, but the mental accepts *the truth.*

*When the soldiers had crucified Jesus they **took his garments** and made **four parts,**one for each soldier; also his tunic. **But the tunic was without seam, woven from top to bottom;** so they said to one another, **"Let us not tear it,** but cast lots for it to see whose it shall be." This was to fulfil the scripture. "They parted my garments among them, and for my clothing they cast lots."* Jn. 19:23,24.

It would be possible to consider these two verses simply as part of the narration; but the numbers of the verses indicate more. David, too, once felt that all that is taking place with Jesus, now, was happening to him.[26] But David's attention went to the LORD. He had the knowledge that he was God's vessel on earth.

It is likely, that sometime in our lives we, too, will be pierced in our hands and feet by others or by circumstance. We will not be able to ***do*** or to ***go.*** Our ***outer coverings*** will number ***four*** (covering all four sides, i.e. perfection). However, it is our ***inner covering*** that tells the truth of us, in that it is ***woven from top to bottom, without seam.*** It is ***ONE.*** What happens to this earthly body is of no importance. WE ARE NO LONGER *OF* THE WORLD. And Jesus cries out *"Eli, Eli, lemana shabakthani?"* ***"My God, my God, for this I was spared!"*** [27]

---

[26] The scripture mentioned is Psalms 22:16-24. *Yea, dogs are round about me; a company of evildoers encircle me; **they have pierced my hands and feet--** I can count all my bones -- they stare and gloat over me; **they divide my garments among them, and for my raiment they cast lots.** But thou, O LORD, be not far off! O thou my help, hasten to my aid! **Deliver my soul from the sword,** my life from the power of the dog! Save me from the mouth of the lion, my afflicted soul from the horns of the wild oxen! I will tell of thy name to my brethren; **in the midst of the congregation I will praise thee:** You who fear the LORD, praise him! **all you sons of Jacob, glorify him, and stand in awe of him,** all you sons of Israel! **For he has not despised or abhorred the affliction of the afflicted; and he has not hid his face from him, but has heard, when he cried to him.***

[27] The traditional translation is *My God, my God, why hast thou forsaken me?* This improved translation which is given above comes from Lamsa, p. 1010, Mk. 15:34, and p. 986, Mt. 27:46. In Matthew, Lamsa adds a footnote: ***This was my destiny.***

Lamsa's translation is better than the old translation that saw Jesus as feeling abandoned by God. But my intuition favors another translation for Jesus' outcry: *"My God, my God, how thou hast glorified me!"* I don't know where I found it or where I read it or where I "heard" it, but to my intuition it is the correct translation. Having seen slight glimpses, I can imagine the glory of Jesus' experience. He is no longer *of* or *in* the world. Nevertheless, Jesus still cares for the earth and gives his mother into John's care. All is accomplished. *When Jesus had received the vinegar, he said, "It is finished"; and he bowed his head and gave up his spirit. Jn. 19:30.*

Jesus has been on the cross from about noon to three o'clock.[28] According to Jewish time, the new day will begin at 6 p.m., and the new day is Passover – and it is a special Passover. If the men are still hanging on the crosses by that time, it is defilement. The Sanhedrin is insistent; so the Romans come to hasten the deaths. They break the legs of the first thief; but seeing that Jesus appears to be dead, the soldier just uses his spear to make sure.[29]

We can endlessly search for confirmation of whether or not Jesus is the *messiah*. We can employ theology that insists that we must believe that Jesus was the son of God who was crucified to *save our souls.* But such activity can cause us to forget the message that Jesus brought – something far different from the intellect's desire to deify him. The important part of the story is yet to come, that is the "proof" that he told us what really *is* in this world and beyond. He told us the TRUTH.

---

[28] For a informative view of the day of crucifixion, see *The Day Christ Died* by Jim Bishop, Harper, 1957. Bishop sees Jesus as having been placed on the cross around noon and "dying" around 3 p.m.. In fact, Bishop makes an interesting comment: *Jesus willed himself to die* (p. 309). Such is the mind-set of the Aborigine, to "die" at the appropriate time. "Death" is not what it seems; it is not an end. This is the triumph over "death," to understand its "true" nature – its unreality!

[29] Bishop writes: "The dead do not bleed, ordinarily, but the right auricle of the human heart holds liquid blood after death, and the outer sac holds a serum called hydropericardium. When the soldier withdrew the spear, blood and water were seen to emerge and drop down the side of the body." *Ibid.,* p. 309.

11. Jesus is buried.
Every Passover is a high holy day, but this Passover (A.D. 30) is the seventh in a series of seven. Jews from all over the world will be coming to Jerusalem to worship in the Temple. It would defile the holy day to have bodies out where they could be seen – even if they are outside the wall. Pilate feels the pressure from the Sanhedrin, so he agrees when a member of the council asks for the body of Jesus. *After this **Joseph of Arimathea**, who was a disciple of Jesus, but secretly, for fear of the Jews, asked Pilate that he might take away the body of Jesus, and Pilate gave him leave. So he **came and took away his body**. **Nicodemus also**, who had at first come to him by night, **came bringing a mixture of myrrh and***

The Descent From the Cross by Albrecht Dürer.

*aloes, about a hundred pounds' weight. **They took the body of Jesus, and bound it in linen cloths with the spices, as is the burial custom of the Jews.** Now in the place where he was crucified there was a garden, and **in the garden a new tomb where no one had ever been laid.** So because of the Jewish day of Preparation, as the tomb was close at hand, **they laid Jesus there**.* Jn. 19:38 - 42.

As in the initiatory process of the *mysteries*, "burial" is the hardest test. Can we hold to our knowledge when it seems we are dead – when there is a blackness not of the earth. Yet we can look toward the light. Interestingly, we in this last decade of the 20th Century are now hearing testimonies from

404

those who by clinical standards have "died" – that "at death" there is such a light, accompanied by a feeling of peace, unknown before.

This is not to say that Jesus did not "die" a physical "death." Rather, it says that "death" itself is not what we think. "Death" is a part of the tree of the *knowledge of good and evil*; it is a part of the mistaken paradigm. Remember, in truth, **we are *spiritual beings* having a *physical experience.*** Possibly this is the reason for John's saying: *Now in the place where he was crucified there was a garden, and in the garden a new tomb where no one had ever been laid.* Jn. 19:41. John's statement makes it clear: **we have come full circle.** We are again at the *garden*.[30] And what is a garden? A place for growth.

12. The Christ Rises from the grave. *And when the sabbath was past,* ***Mary Magdalene,*** *and* ***Mary*** *the mother of James, and* ***Salome,*** *bought spices, so that they might go and anoint him.   And **very early on the first day of the week** they went to the tomb when the **sun had risen**.   And they were saying to one another, "Who will roll away the stone for us from the door of the tomb?"   And **looking up, they saw that the stone was rolled back;** -- it was very large.   And entering the tomb, they saw a young man sitting on the right side, dressed in a white robe; and they were amazed.   And he said to them, "Do not be amazed; you seek Jesus of Nazareth, who was crucified.* ***He has risen, he is not here;*** *see the place where they laid him.   But* ***go, tell his disciples and Peter that he is going before you to Galilee; there you will see him, as he told you."*** *And they went out and fled from the tomb; for trembling and astonishment had come upon them;* ***and they said nothing to any one, for they were afraid.*** *Mk. 16:1-8*

If I told you that since the resurrection there has been no *death* on earth, we would both know that it was incorrect. It's easy to answer that Jesus could escape the grave because

---

[30] For those needing such understanding, the physical is even relegated to the reaches of the *underworld*. Explicitly, the Apostles Creed as currently recited and as found in the Book of Common Prayer, includes the following line: ... *Was crucified, dead, and buried, He descended into hell...*   Apparently, this wording did not exist in the creed up to A.D. 600. That means it was added somewhere during the Dark Ages. See *The Lost Books of the Bible;* Bell Publishing Company, NY,1979 Ed.; pp.91-93.   Included in the same collection is an apocryphal book *Nicodemus,* which explicitly accounts the visit of Jesus to "hell," pp. 78 - 88, as supposedly written down by sons of Simeon who rose from the grave during the crucifixion and were allowed to "stay" on earth three days to write the material. Supposedly, they delivered the manuscripts to Pilate, and he circulated them. *Ibid.,* p. 88.

he was the "son of God." The Church then goes on to say that "if we believe" all of its doctrine, then we will join Jesus in heaven either in the "end times" or when we die (depending on the Church). Such an answer is fine for those whom it satisfies. I certainly would not take this assurance from them. But there seems to be another answer for those who are not comfortable with the literal approach of the Church's answer. It fits the intuition's viewpoint more easily. It is that the "resurrection" proves that what Jesus had been saying all along was Truth. It also demonstrates what we've been calling THE LAW; for as with the presentations of the four gospels, **what we "hear" in the resurrection depends on us.**[31]

The mystical gospel's version (John) of the resurrection is slightly different from that of Mark.[32] Instead of three women, it is only Mary Magdalene who comes to the tomb. Finding the stone rolled away, she runs to tell Peter and John that the agents of the Sanhedrin – or someone – has taken the body, *and we do not know where they have laid him.*

---

[31] There is a higher mystical interpretation, apparently inheriting the understanding of the *mysteries.* According to a current writer: "The lower self or personality of Jesus of Nazareth suffered and died on the cross in the culmination of [the] 3rd Initiation, and was buried in a tomb. For three nights he "descended" into Hell, the bosom of the Divine Mother, the pristine state of Chaos or Formlessness. His first, natural form was dissolved and on the third day he arose, reborn in his new spiritual form, as *Jesus,* the Christed soul.

From then on, Jesus demonstrated the higher initiations to his disciples, and hence to the world.... The demonstration of the 4th Initiation took place in the garden of Joseph of Arimathea's house, outside the tomb. As a 'child,' Jesus was too 'young' or delicate to be 'touched' by Mary Magdalene, since he had not reached his maturity (*Ascension*) when he would be sent out into the outer world.... (When he was touched) by doubting Thomas, it marked the start of his demonstration. From then on he carefully instructed his disciples, revealing to them the Higher Mysteries and empowering them with spiritual authority to carry out their subsequent work in the world. ...

The Ascension from the Mount of Olives ... took the Master Jesus into the sphere of Unification with the Christ Light, his individual form of light dissolving into a more universal form of light, disappearing as such from the sight of his disciples..." *The Francis Bacon Research Trust Journal,* Series I, Vol.4., p. 47.

[32] As you saw above, Mark properly ends with 16:8. Apparently, verses 9 through 19 were added. With Matthew and Luke, the resurrection results in a physically restored Jesus, walking, talking, and even eating on earth for a short time longer. (See Lk. 24:43.) With John we have a more mystical conclusion for the story.

406

Peter and John run to the tomb, but John doesn't go in. Only Peter enters the tomb, and he finds *the napkin, which had been on his head,* not lying with the linen cloths but *rolled up in a place by itself. Then the other disciple [John], who reached the tomb first, also went in, and he saw and believed; for as yet they did not know the scripture, that he must rise from the dead. Then the disciples went back to their homes.* Jn. 20:7-10.

Again, Mary Magdalene begins the action. *Mary stood weeping outside the tomb, and as she wept she stooped to look into the tomb; and* **she saw two angels in white, sitting where the body of Jesus had lain, one at the head and one at the feet.** *They said to her, "Woman, why are you weeping?" She said to them, "Because they have taken away my Lord, and I do not know where they have laid him."* **Saying this, she turned round and saw Jesus standing, but she did not know that it was Jesus.**

Christ as the Gardener by Albrecht Dürer.

Jesus said to her, "Woman, why are you weeping? Whom do you seek?"
Supposing him to be the gardener, she said to him, "Sir, if you have carried him
away, tell me where you have laid him, and I will take him away."

*Jesus said to her, "Mary." She **turned** and said to him in Hebrew, "Rabboni!"*
*(which means Teacher). Jesus said to her, "**Do not hold me, for I have not yet***
ascended to the Father**; but **go** to my brethren and **say to them, I am ascending to my
***Father and your Father, to my God and your God.**"* Jn. 20:14-17.

13. Jesus Ascends.

As with the *Resurrection,* Jesus' Ascension depends on *our measurement.* Jesus' previous critics and executioners repeat what the Church eventually says. The apocryphal *Nicodemus* has the Jews admit to Pilate their "mistake" in condemning Jesus.[33] In the "supposed" Jewish account, the Jews "report" what becomes the doctrine of the Church, placing the resurrection on the physical level. Matthew, on the the other hand, is writing for those Jews who "heard," and his terms can be taken either physically or spiritually. Although Matthew takes care to ensure that all of the scriptural prophecies have been fulfilled, he concludes his account of Jesus with: *Now **the eleven disciples** went to Galilee, **to the** **mountain** to which Jesus had directed them. And **when they saw him they** **worshiped him**; but **some doubted.** And Jesus came and said to them, "All authority in heaven and on earth has been given to me. **Go therefore and make** **disciples of all nations, baptizing them** in the name of the Father and of the Son and of the Holy Spirit, **teaching them to observe all that I have commanded you;** **and lo, I am with you always,** to the close of the age."* Mt. 28:16-20.

Luke's account chides the short "measurement" of the disciples. They know that the women told them what had happened, but as they walk with one who appears to be a stranger, they admit: *"... Some of those who were with us went to the tomb, and found it just as the women had said; but him they did not see."*

---

[33] *Nicodemus* is not a part of the canon. (Supposedly, the manuscript was found by the Emperor Theodosius at Jerusalem in the hall of Pontius Pilate among the public records.) I would question its authenticity; it has too many doctrinal statements. For instance, the Jews say: "After we had crucified Jesus, not knowing that he was the Son of God, but supposing he wrought his miracles by some magical arts, we summoned a large assembly in this temple. And when we were deliberating among one another about the miracles which Jesus had wrought, **we found many witnesses of our own country,** **who declared that they had seen him alive after his death, and that they heard him** **discoursing with his disciples, and saw him ascending unto the height of the heavens,** **and entering into them..**" *Lost Books of the Bible,* p. 90.

408

And he said to them, "O foolish men, and slow of heart to believe all that the prophets have spoken! Was it not necessary that the Christ should suffer these things and enter into his glory?" Lk. 24:24 But the disciples do not "see" until the "stranger" takes the bread, blesses it, and breaks it. *And their eyes were opened and they recognized him; **and he vanished out of their sight.*** Lk. 24:31. When they see him the second time, he *opened their minds to understand the scriptures, and said to them, "Thus it is written, that **the Christ should suffer and on the third day rise from the dead,** and that **repentance and forgiveness of sins should be preached in his name to all nations,** beginning from Jerusalem. You are witnesses of these things. And behold, I send the promise of my Father upon you; **but stay in the city, until you are clothed with power from on high."*** Lk. 24:45-49.

Luke concludes his narration with: *Then he led them out as far as Bethany, and lifting up his hands he blessed them. **While he blessed them, he parted from them, and was carried up into heaven.** And they returned to Jerusalem with great joy, and were continually in the temple blessing God* Lk.24:45-53.

We are given three choices for the presentation of the Ascension. The accounts of Matthew and Luke are very similar. Jesus appears **twice**, and commissions the disciples to go forth to other nations. Mark, on the other hand, concludes with the women keeping quiet because *they were afraid,* and – if we can believe the scholars' assessment that the last ten verses were added – he makes no mention of a physical appearance by Jesus.[34] But the full appreciation of Christ's mission, resurrection and ascension is in John.

If you can remember back several hundred pages, there was a somewhat enigmatic statement that *there are two separate paths which lead to enlightenment* (page 34). I think this is what we're seeing here. One path is **the way of the intellect**; it calls for a physical resurrection and ascension witnessed by the world. If we are ***not afraid***, concentration on

---

[34] Bibles differ. As does the standard King James version, Lamsa makes no distinction between verses 9-20 of Mark 16 and the preceeding verses. J.B. Phillips, in *The New Testament in Modern English,* headlines the verses as *An ancient appendix.* Similarly, *The Revised Standard Version* places verses Mark 16:9-20 in small type, with the explanation that *Other texts and versions add ... the following passage.* My "judgment" is that the passage (verses 9 through 20) was an addition to Mark, by other than Mark.

this can raise our consciousness and take us into the Holy City of Jerusalem, the place of realization of the Kingdom of Heaven. The second path is **the way of the intuition,** the way of the mystic; its *resurrection* and *ascension* depend on the perception of the one "perceiving."

No doubt, John's perception is unique. Immediately – with the beginning of his gospel – **John's** he forces our attention to a higher plane. *In the* **Perception** *beginning was the Word, and the Word was with God, and the* **of the** *Word was God. He was in the beginning with God; all things* **Christ** *were made through him, and without him was not anything made that was made.* ***In him was life, and the life was the light of men. The light shines in the darkness, and the darkness has not overcome it.*** Jn. 1:1-5.

John says: *The true light that enlightens every man was coming into the world. He* ***was in the world***, *and the world was made through him,* ***yet the world knew him not.*** *He came to his own home, and his own people received him not. But* ***to all who received him***, *who believed in his name,* ***he gave power*** *to become* ***children of God; who were born***, *not of blood nor of the will of the flesh nor of the will of man, but* ***of God.*** *And the Word became flesh and dwelt among us, full of grace and truth; we have beheld his glory, glory as of the only Son from the Father.* Jn. 1:9-14.

Let's hang loose. Let's step back from ourselves and observe the climb that we've been on. At the beginning of the whole experience, we were connected to this power that created everything; but then we "ate from the tree of the knowledge of good and evil" and decided that we were "naked and ashamed" and separated from this power. Consequently, we perceive this "power" as a LORD separate from us, which we designate YHWH. Finally, we find out that this YHWH is I Am; nevertheless, we still see ourselves as separate, but we keep climbing. From this point we could just keep climbing until we reach the top of the Mountain (where we would see that we are not separate), ***but*** into the physical plane comes one who knows the TRUTH. And it is said "He on whom [we] see the Spirit descend and remain, ... baptizes with the Holy Spirit." And the life of this "one" offers an example for us to follow. Jesus is so confident that he is **not separated** that he lets go of the personal ego to embrace the Christhood.[35] In so doing, he is filled with the Holy Spirit and is truly one with the universal power.[36] This is mysticism. Throughout the ages, mysticism has explained mankind's existence as other than physical.[37]

While mysticism might understand all that has taken place, it is illogical to think that the contemptuous and unseeing members at the Temple can observe the ascension.[38] Remember, Elisha was told that only if he "had" the double portion would he see Elijah ascend. And Jesus once told the three disciples that the only reason they could see Moses and Elijah on the mount was because of what was *inside them.* John has Mary Magdalene first "see" the risen Christ,[39] and she sees the Christ as the "gardener."[40]

---

[35] Remember how Suarès said that the rabbis cried when the Pentateuch was published. So it is with mention of the Christ, for things of the spirit do not lend themselves to words.

[36] It's easier for our "earthly" minds if we go to the intellect. One viewpoint is that the climb is such that it cannot be accomplished in one life-time. Edgar Cayce, the clairvoyant, saw **Jesus** as the same entity which had "begun" the whole activity of mankind, i.e., **Adam**. He also saw Jesus as having been **Enoch, Melchizedek, Joseph** (in Egypt), **Joshua, Asaph** (the recorder mentioned in 2 Kgs. 18:18.), and **Jeshua** (whose name led those who came with Zerubbabel [Ez. 2:2] to revive the religion of the Hebrews and to rebuild the Temple). After **33** incarnations, this entity "evolved" to the recognition of *being* the child of God. See Krajenke's *Edgar Cayce's Story of the Old Testament,* vol. 3, p. 167.

[37] Manly Hall relates that "Christian mystics have taught that at the time of the crucifixion a divine power flowed into the material universe. This was symbolized by the blood which dropped from the wounds of Christ into the earth at the foot of the cross. A dimension of consciousness, previously part of the divine nature, entered into the material state so that it could operate from within living creatures as an element in the compound of counsciousness. By this intensification of spiritual resources, humanity will be able to take the next great step in its journey toward the Infinite. Because the step is exceptional, the help is likewise extraordinary." Hall, *The Mystical Christ;* The Philosophical Research Society, Inc., 175; p. 195.

[38] Somehow the idea (as expressed in *Nicodemus)* that "many witnesses of our own country" observed Jesus' ascension negates the need for advancement to "see."

[39] Mark 16:9, too, has Mary Magdalene seeing Christ first; however, it is this portion of Mark (Mk. 9-19) which is questionable as to origin.

[40] In *mystical* tradition, "the Gardener" is a soul such as St. George, which cares for the world, fulfilling God's plan for mankind. *The Francis Bacon Research...,* p. 56.

Unlike standard theology, mysticism suggests an elevated importance of the feminine side of us. Have we "heard" the subtleties? There are **five** women listed in the ancestry for Jesus.[41] First is **Tamar,** the daughter-in-law of Judah, who **tricks him into sleeping with her** (because he did not keep his word) and produces Perez and his twin. Next is **Rahab, the harlot,**who helped the Israelites scout out Jericho. In return for her help, she said: *"Swear to me by the LORD that as I have dealt kindly with you, you also will deal kindly with my father's house,...And the men said to her, "Our life for yours! If you do not tell this business of ours, then we will deal kindly and faithfully with you when the LORD gives us the land." Then she let them down by a rope through the window, for her house was built into the city wall,... "You shall bind this scarlet cord in the window through which you let us down; and you shall gather into your house your father and mother, your brothers, and all your father's household. "...And she said, "According to your words, so be it."* Jsh. 2:12-21.

The Higher Feminine Produces the Christ

Somewhere along the line, Rahab marries Salmon; and the union produces Boaz, the second husband of Ruth. If you know the story of Ruth, a man from Bethlehem, his wife Naomi, and sons Mahlon (sickness) and Chilion (wasting), move to Moab because of famine.[42] The man dies, but the sons marry Moabite girls. *The name of one was Orpah, and the name of the other Ruth.* However, after about ten years– in keeping with their names – the sons die; so Naomi (having heard that Judah no longer has famine) decides to return to Judah.

Both girls intend to stay with Naomi, but Naomi insists that they should return to their families. Orpah relents and leaves, but **Ruth (friend)** says: *"Entreat me not to leave you or to return from following you; for where you go I will go, and where you lodge I will lodge; your people shall be my people, and your God my God; where you die I will die, and there will I be buried. May the LORD do so to me and more also if even death parts me from you."* And when Naomi saw that **she was determined** to go with her, she said no more. So the two of them went on until they came to Bethlehem. And when they

---

[41] See Matthew 1:1-16 and check out page 338, particularly footnote 14.

[42] *Asimov's Guide to the Bible* makes an interesting point. Prior to Ruth, all incidents concerning Bethlehem have been negative. Rachel died near Bethlehem; the concubine who was brutalized at Gibeah was from Bethlehem-judah. (The *judah* part simply clarifies which Bethlehem we're talking about.)

412

*came to Bethlehem, the whole town was stirred because of them; and the women said, "Is this Naomi?" She said to them, "Do not call me Naomi, **call me Mara**, for the Almighty has dealt very **bitterly** with me. I went away full, and the LORD has brought me back empty. ..." So Naomi returned, and Ruth the Moabitess ... with her, ... from the country of Moab. And they came to Bethlehem at the beginning of barley harvest.*
Ruth 1:16-22.

Although the older portion of the feminine is bitter, the younger portion is willing to pluck even the smallest fruits from the harvest. You know the rest of the story. Ruth is out "gleaning" in the fields (picking up the left-overs after harvest) when Boaz, the owner of the field and a kinsman of Naomi's late husband, sees her. *Then Boaz said to his servant who was in charge of the reapers, "Whose maiden is this?" And the servant who was in charge of the reapers answered, "It is the Moabite maiden, who came back with Naomi from the country of Moab. She said, 'Pray, let me glean and gather among the sheaves after the reapers.' So **she came, and she has continued from early morning until now, without resting even for a moment."** Then Boaz said to Ruth, "... do not go to glean in another field or leave this one, but **keep close to my maidens. Let your eyes be upon the field which they are reaping, and go after them.** Have I not charged the young men not to molest you? **And when you are thirsty, go to the vessels and drink what the young men have drawn."** Then she fell on her face, bowing to the ground, and said to him, "Why have I found favor in your eyes, that you should take notice of me, when I am a foreigner?"* Ruth 2:5-10.

The Gleaners by Millet.

*But Boaz answered her, "**All that you have done for your mother-in-law since the death of your husband has been fully told me, and how you left your father and mother and your native land and came to a people that you did not know before.***

The LORD recompense you for what you have done, and a full reward be given you by the LORD, the God of Israel, under whose wings you have come to take refuge!" Ruth 2:11,12.

To make the story short, Boaz is so impressed with Ruth's loyalty and her dedication and determination that he marries her; and she conceives and bears a son. And the village women say to Naomi: *He shall be to you a restorer of life and a nourisher of your old age; for your daughter-in-law **who loves you**, who is **more to you than seven sons**, has borne him.* Ruth 4:15. And they name him Obed (serving); he is the father of Jesse, grandfather of David.

Most likely, we all admire Ruth. Even though she is a Moabite (Moab was a son of Lot from incest with his daughter) and should still be as fearful and untrusting as Lot's daughters were, Ruth has risen above her heritage. She has advanced to the place where she trusts the LORD. The expression by the feminine side is improving; it is growing in understanding to the place where it will soon be on the same level as the masculine.

Although the feminine's level of expression rises to equality, the feminine is not intended to rule. It is a paradox. Ironically, the feminine rises in a way we might not expect; it becomes stronger with **Bathsheba**, the fourth mentioned ancestress of Jesus. In fact, Bathsheba is so strong that to her description as **wife of David and mother of Solomon,** we can add **adulteress.** But, make no judgment! God's ways are not our ways. Bathsheba is able to stand up to opposition and ensure that Solomon can become King. Bathsheba is the **fourth** ancestress; she represents *equilibrium.* Through her association with YHWH's chosen, David, she reaches a level of understanding which "sees" the truth of the feminine. Her truth of the feminine is presented as Chapter 31, the last chapter of Proverbs. Supposedly, it is for Solomon as he marries the daughter of Pharoah; esoterically it is for the earthly wise, the *enlightened king,* as he/she is combined with the feminine of that which rules the earthly expression.

414

The words of Lemuel,* king of Massa, which his mother taught him: What, my son? What, son of my womb? What, son of my vows? Give not your strength to women, your ways to those who destroy kings. It is not for kings, O Lemuel, it is not for kings to drink wine, or for rulers to desire strong drink; lest they drink and forget what has been decreed, and pervert the rights of all the afflicted. Give strong drink to him who is perishing, and wine to those in bitter distress; let them drink and forget their poverty, and remember their misery no more.

Open your mouth for the dumb, for the rights of all who are left desolate.

Open your mouth, judge righteously, maintain the rights of the poor and needy.

A good wife who can find? **She is far more precious than jewels.**

The heart of her husband trusts in her, and he will have no lack of gain.

She does him good, and not harm, all the days of her life.

She seeks wool and flax, and **works with willing hands.**

She is like the ships of the merchant, **she brings her food from afar.**

She rises while it is yet night and provides food for her household and tasks for her maidens.

She considers a field **and buys it**; with the fruit of her hands **she plants a vineyard.**

She girds her loins with strength and makes her arms strong.

She perceives that her merchandise is profitable. **Her lamp does not go out at night.**

She puts her hands to the distaff, and her hands hold the spindle.

She opens her hand to the poor, **and reaches out her hands** to the needy.

She is not afraid of snow for her household, for **all her household are clothed in scarlet.**

She makes herself coverings; her clothing is **fine linen and purple.**

Her husband is known in the gates, when he sits among the elders of the land.

She makes linen garments and sells them; she delivers girdles to the merchant.

Strength and dignity are her clothing, and she laughs at the time to come.

She opens her mouth with wisdom, and **the teaching of kindness is on her tongue.**

She **looks well to the ways of her household,** and does **not** eat the bread of **idleness.**

Her children rise up and call her blessed; her husband also, and he praises her:

"Many women have done excellently, but **you surpass them all."**

Charm is deceitful, and beauty is vain, but **a woman who fears the LORD is to be praised.**

Give her of the fruit of her hands, and let her works praise her in the gates.

Proverbs 31**

---

* Lemuel (*Godward, God is bright!*). See page 311. *Lemuel* is a symbolic name for Solomon. Massa *(burden).* Solomon is not in the Kingdom of Heaven.

** This is Proverbs 31, and the last verse is #31. We are told of the importance with **two** prime numbers, each of which adds to **4.**

Having reached equilibrium, we come to the mother of Jesus, **Mary**. We can identify her easily, because we call her *the virgin Mary*. There's just one difficulty; there are so many Marys in the four gospels, we sometimes get confused. Isn't it interesting? If we compare the two Testaments, we do find some repetition of certain names in the Old Testament – but never at one time. Yet, in the New Testament we have two Johns, three Judases, four Jameses; and, while Jesus is living, we have *five Marys.*[43]

| Equilibrium |
| of "4" Brings |
| Advancement |

Madonna and Child by Michelangelo.

---

[43] Interestingly, the name *Mary* in Hebrew is ***Miriam*** (bitterness and rebellion).

Coronation of the Virgin by Botticelli.

Adoration of the Virgin, along with medieval art and liturgical concentration, has kept us from seeing the other Marys. While the "Virgin" is claimed as **Queen of Heaven** as in the Botticelli above, the other Marys become obscure. The **Virgin Mary** "hears," and her purity produces the Christ. She "lets go," and she "is given" to the keeping of the beloved disciple. But she is more than appears in the story. She is #5 in the list of Jesus' ancestresses, so she will have to elevate the nature of her modified bitterness and rebellion. But in hang-loose logic, we are being told that the "Mary" which produces the Christ is actually composed of four characteristics. Consequently, she's given **four** other Marys to create the equilibrium.

Let's look at the four other Marys. Of least importance to us is **Mary, the mother of Mark.** She is related to Barnabas (Col. 4:10), but her chief contribution seems to be that her wealth allows her to offer a place in Jerusalem for the disciples to gather. She contributes by what she provides physically.

A second woman is **Mary, the wife of Cleophas, mother of the apostle, James (the lesser).** This Mary is listed as the "sister" of the virgin, but is probably her sister-in-law. She is present at the cross and follows the body of Jesus to the tomb (Mt. 27:61); and, along with Salome (the Virgin's sister) she takes spices that Sunday morning to the sepulcher. This "Mary" is moving beyond the physical into the spiritual, but she does not see the risen Christ.

The third woman is **Mary of Bethany.** She lives "just east of Jerusalem," and she is dedicated to the spiritual. She is the sister of Lazarus and Martha.[44] This latter fact determines this Mary's prime importance; for observation of her, in comparison with Martha, establishes some characteristics of the spiritual quest. Contrary to the applause "Mary of Bethany" usually gets, I see her as the potentially spiritual person in his/her spiritual infancy.[45]

I still remember the first time I heard my grandfather preach about Martha and Mary. I was probably nine or ten, and I remember being outraged that Martha was doing all of the work and Mary was just sitting there.... Even though she's listening to Jesus talk, she is just sitting there! Probably, I have always resented that the role of all women is "to serve." (Bet I got a rise on that one!) Martha is the adult presence, serving those around her; the only problem with Martha is that

---

[44] Bethany is approximately a mile east of the summit of the Mount of Olives (Davis & Gehman, p. 381). See the map on page 390.

[45] An interesting variance is given by Peter Dawkins. He sees this "Mary" as well as Martha and Lazarus as the younger sisters and brother of Jesus. He says that "Mary and Martha represented and acted out the contemplative and active natures respectively of the natural soul, whilst their younger brother Lazarus ('he whom God assists') represented the personal ego itself." *Francis Bacon Research*, p. 60.

her attention is on the world. And like us, she deserves the Christly admonition: *"Martha, Martha, you are anxious and troubled about many things; [only] one thing is needful. Mary has chosen **the good portion, which shall not be taken away from her.** "* Lk. 10:41,42.

It's easy to spot the Marthas of the world; I wouldn't place them lower than the Marys, maybe just tied more closely to the world. Certainly, we are to be "spiritually" inclined; but the spiritual infant is not consistent. When the world becomes too much – when Lazarus is in his tomb – Mary sits pouting in her room (Jn. 11:20) until the adult presence insists that she come out. Even then, Mary places blame, even on Jesus. After Lazarus' resurrection, at Jesus' last visit to Bethany, only then does she lavish "ointment" on the hair and feet of the Christ.[46]

I'm sure we've all seen people like this. When everything is going well, they're quite spiritual, but they have not internalized the full understanding that *there is only God.* They are still making worldly judgments, and when unpleasantness occurs, the spirituality doesn't shine forth. They may "revive" after the spiritual "miracle" has taken place, even to the point of lavishing great praise on the spiritual; but they are not at the cross nor at the tomb.[47] They will see neither the *resurrection* nor the *ascension.*

Only that which knows itself to be crucified, resurrected and ascended can truly "see;" this brings us to the fourth Mary, again bringing equilibrium – **Mary Magdalene.**

---

[46] We know the "feet" to represent the "understanding," but the "hair" is almost more esoteric. Remember it was the "hair" when cut that weakened Sampson. The hair represents the "highest qualities of the lower mind." Gaskell, p. 334. Interestingly, according to Gaskell, "The most common and comprehensive word for *deity* in the Japanese language is *Kami no ke. Kami* is the hair of the head. *Kami* is applied not only to Gods, but to Mikados and nobles." W.C. Aston, *Shinto*, p. 7.

[47] Many would disagree with my view of Mary of Bethany. Usually she is presented as having her attention riveted to the Christ in lieu of the world; then her "great faith" in Jesus' abilities helps the resurrection of Lazarus, and she heaps homage upon Jesus with the ointment. But notice, she places the Christ outside of herself. She still sees herself separated from God; and for this reason, she cannot attend either the resurrection or the ascension.

We meet her in Luke 7:36.[48] She first comes to Jesus as he is eating in a Pharisee's house. [49] *And behold, **a woman of the city, who was a sinner,** when she learned that he was at table in the Pharisee's house, brought an alabaster flask of ointment, and standing behind him at his feet, weeping, she began to wet his feet with her tears, and wiped them with the hair of her head, and kissed his feet, and anointed them with the ointment. Now when the Pharisee who had invited him saw it, he said to himself, "If this man were a prophet, **he would have known who and what sort of woman this is who is touching him, for she is a sinner."** Lk. 8:37-39.*

As a child, I was kept in the dark about "sin." Nobody would tell me what Mary Magdalene's **sin** was. Of course, nowadays we suspect that she was a prostitute, a harlot – someone abhorent to the pious Jew.[50] Judging from the fact that she had an alabaster flask of ointment and that she helped support Jesus and the twelve, we can surmise that she had wealthy clientele. You notice that the Pharisee host knew her so well, that she could even intrude on a private party.

---

[48] Hang loose to notice the symbolism we're being given here. We have reached #10, earthly accumulation and new beginning. We have **five** women ancestors – Tamar, Rehab, Ruth, Bathsheba, Mary. Then we have **five** Marys – the **virgin**, the **mother** of Mark, the **wife** of Cleophas, she of **Bethany**, and the Magdalene.

I find it interesting that Strong's *Concordance* lists Mary Magdalene simply as *a female acquaintance of Jesus.* But Strong lived in the 19th Century when only men were considered the major disciples of Jesus. Only as our vision has changed can we reconsider such a conclusion.

[49] Although the intellect is not sure that the "sinful" woman is Mary Magdalene, the intuition has no doubt. Notice the importance of the chapter and verse beginning the story of the supposedly unidentified "sinful" woman. It is Chapter **7** (earthly completion), and the narration begins with verse 36 (4 x **12**). The chapter ends with Jesus saying to the woman, *Your faith has saved you; go in peace.* Lk. 7:50.

But then immediately with Chapter 8 (surplus, added unto), we are told: *Soon afterward he went on through cities and villages, preaching and bringing the good news of the kingdom of God. And **the twelve were with him, and also some women who had been healed of evil spirits and infirmities: Mary, called Magdalene, from whom seven demons had gone out,** and Joanna, the wife of Chuza, Herod's steward, and Susanna, and many others, **who provided for them** out of their means.* Lk. 8:1-3.

[50] A *harlot* is a **whore,** and *whore* is the greatest contempt that can be heaped on a woman. Nothing is lower. Men can never reach the depth implied by the word *whore*; only women can reach the depth. *Harlot* is not so demeaning. The Hebrew word for *harlot* comes from a root implying *greatly fed and wanton.* It implies voluntary fornication on a regular basis. It is she (usually she) which profoundly commits **adultery,** since the Hebrew people are considered the "spouse" of YHWH.

There are several things that we should notice about Mary Magdalene. She comes from Magdala (a tower), a small town north of Tiberius; and she first meets Jesus in the city of Nain (to be at home). We know for sure that it is she *from whom seven (7) demons had gone out.* Lk. 8:2 & Mk. 16:9. And we know that she was at the cross and observed the burial.[51] Moreover, according to Matthew and Luke, she was with Mary (the wife of Cleopas) and Salome when the three found the stone rolled away; it is she who informs Peter and John. She alone follows the men to the garden, and it is she alone who first "sees" the risen Christ.

Anyone who has been following this study can sense that Mary Magdalene is not just an *acquaintance* of Jesus.[52] Rather, the esoteric evidence indicates to me that Mary may have been the most highly developed of all of Jesus' disciples. She was not an apostle; the apostles had to be on a level somewhat close to that of the people to whom they were ministering. Rather, I would propose that Mary Magdalene was at a level of understanding that no one else attained, except possibly John many years later.[53] There is no intellectual evidence to support this; no great scholar has determined it. But to my intuition, it is fitting. Whether the **harlot, Mary Magdalene,** was the most advanced of Jesus' disciples or not, she presents a motif for the culmination of the teachings – what John uses in *Revelation* – the two women who enable full revelation of the New Jerusalem.

---

[51] For the last 2,000 years Mary Magdalene has prompted speculation. British tradition has her accompanying Joseph of Arimathea to the misty isles after the Ascension. Although it is purely speculative, we might suggest that the teachings of Mary Magdalene and Joseph of Arimathea became the basis of the British *mysteries*, which retained what knowledge we have of the *mysteries* for our time.

[52] Don't get me wrong, I would not degrade their relationship by implying it to be a sexual liason. Such a conclusion can come only from those totally immersed in the carnal world.

[53] You might wonder if I am hanging "too loose," but look at the numbers for the accounts by both Luke and Mark. Luke is **8:2** (*added unto + the feminine*); Mark is even more meaningful – **16:9** both (**2x8**) *surplus and* (**4x4**) *equilibrium* + **9**(initiate).

Hang loose with me one last time. *Revelation* teaches what happens in the "last days" – but this can mean the changes that will come upon the one who "hears" and follows, i.e., the one who returns to the original paradigm.[54]

John explains: *I was **in the Spirit on the Lord's day**, and I heard behind me a loud voice like a trumpet saying, "Write what you see in a book and **send it to the seven churches, to Ephesus and to Smyrna and to Pergamum and to Thyatira and to Sardis and to Philadelphia and to Laodicea."** Then I turned to see the voice that was speaking to me, and on turning I saw seven golden lampstands* [ultimate light], *and in the midst of the lampstands one like a son of man, clothed with a long robe* [priestly]*and with a golden girdle round his breast* [royalty]; *his head and his hair were white as white wool, white as snow* [his eternity]; *his eyes were like a flame of fire* [to see into the hearts of man], *his feet were like burnished bronze* [understanding produced by fire and blending of elements], *refined as in a furnace, and his voice was like the sound of many waters* [encompassing all emotions]; *in his right hand he held seven stars, **from his mouth issued a sharp two-edged sword*** [**paradoxically reveals the duality of the physical**], *and his face was like the sun shining in full strength....But he laid his right hand upon me, saying, "**Fear not, I am the first and the last, and the living one; I died, and behold I am alive for evermore, and I have the keys of Death and Hades.*** Rev. 1:12-18.

As with all mysticism, *Revelation* can be read on several different levels. I choose to see it as speaking to those close to finishing the climb. On the literal level, small groups of Jesus' followers, called followers of *the Nazarene*, are scattered throughout the Mediterrenean world and, according to tradition, reach as far as from Britain to India. Like the Jews, their religious practices often challenge Roman law, particularly after Rome begins to insist on Emperor worship. Eventually these "Christians" will become a focus for Roman stringency; and on a literal level, John is bolstering up those who will soon face Rome's anger. But, when viewed esoterically, John's vision has just as much meaning for us as for those in the 1st Century.

The admonitions to the seven churches are admonitions to those who have "heard" the word, but need a little *push* to

---

[54] Numerous scholars refute the "beloved" John's being the author of *Revelation*. But to the esoteric, it is fitting that John lived long enough and grew in his understanding enough to be its author.

finish the climb. This is the end of the climb; and at this part of the Mountain, we need reassurance. [55]

---

[55] 1. Jesus praises Ephesus for its "patient endurance" and its discernment of what is true from what is false; but he chastises them in that they have "abandoned the love you had at first." He admonishes them to **"repent and do the works you did at first."** He finishes: *"Yet this you have, you hate the works of the Nicolaitans,* * *which I also hate.* *He who has an ear, let him hear what the Spirit says to the churches. To him who conquers I will grant to eat of the tree of life* which is in the paradise of God."* Rev. 2:6,7.

2. To those in Smyrna he begins: *"The words of the first and the last, **who died and came to life.** Do not fear* what you are about to suffer. Behold, ... for ten days you will have tribulation. ... **He who has an ear, let him hear ...He who conquers shall not be hurt by the 'second death.'"** Rev. 2:8-11.

3. To those in Pergamum, the message is from the "sharp two-edged sword." Some in Pergamum are like those in Ephesus and are *Nicolaitans, while others diminish the admonition against having anything to do with what is offered to idols. Jesus tells them to **"repent. He who has an ear... To him who conquers I will give some of the hidden manna, and I will give him a white stone, with a new name written on the stone which no one knows except him who receives it."** Rev. 2:17.

4. To those in Thyatira, the message is from "the Son of God," and the objection is against a woman in the church who is tempting "my servants" to practice immorality and to eat food sacrificed to idols. Throughout history, in all sorts of cultures, there have been those who ascribe the "sensations" of sex to the spiritual. In Greece and Rome some of the temples had prostitutes connected to them (both male and female). Jesus says that her children (her fruits) will be struck dead, and all will know *"that **I am he who searches mind and heart, and I will give to each of you as your works deserve."** But Jesus tells the rest in Thyatira to *"hold fast what you have until I come. **He who conquers and who keeps my works until the end, I will give him power over the nations,** (all aspects of himself) *and he shall **rule them with a rod of iron,**... even as I myself have received power from my Father; **and I will give him the morning star. He who has an ear, let him hear."*** Rev. 2:25-29.

5. To the church in Sardis, he says: *"You have the name of being alive, and **you are dead. Awake, and strengthen** what remains and **is on the point of death,** for I have not found your works perfect in the sight of my God. **Remember then what you received and heard;** keep that, and repent.... **He who conquers shall be clad thus in white garments,** ... and I will confess his name before my Father and before the angels. **He who has an ear, let him hear."*** Rev. 3:1-6.

6. To Philadelphia, he says: *"The words of the holy one, the true one, **who has the key of David, who opens and no one shall shut, who shuts and no one opens.** I know your works. **Behold, I have set before you an open door, which no one is able to shut;** I know that you have but little power, and yet you have kept my word and have not denied my name. ...Because **you have kept my word of patient endurance, I will keep you from the hour of trial which is coming on the whole world, to try those who dwell upon the earth.** I am coming soon; **hold fast what you have, so that no one may seize your crown.** He who conquers, I will make him a pillar in the temple of my God; never shall he go out of it, and **I will write on him the name of my God, and the name of the city of my God, the new Jerusalem which comes down from my God out of heaven, and my own new name.** He who has an ear, let him hear what the Spirit says to the churches."* Rev. 3:7-13.

(continued...)

Whether the challenges at this part of the Mountain are actually greater, or whether they just "seem" greater because of our greater perception, those things

Seven Centers Must Develop that come upon us may appear more threatening. The rituals of the *mysteries* were designed to imitate the challenges that people go through in life. Consider what challenges you have gone through in life. I would bet that your major problems have been like mine. They have been challenges of relationships, of health, of enough money. The greatest challenges have been when our loved ones died. And we are given the same challenges over and over again. Finally we hope that we've learned enough. It is all of this that John is addressing as he writes down what he is hearing. We're cautioned against having our attention on the physical rather than the spiritual.[56] So we are told that we must *have patient endurance,* that we must *be alive,* and that we **must be decisive** (not lukewarm!) We are assured that the door will be opened; all we have to do is "knock" – *all we have to do is*

---

[55](...continued)

7. Lastly, *"And to the angel of the church in Laodicea write: 'The words of **the Amen,** the **faithful** and **true witness, the beginning of God's creation.'** I know your works: you are **neither cold nor hot.** Would that you were cold or hot! So, **because you are lukewarm,** and neither cold nor hot, **I will spew you out of my mouth.** For **you say, I am rich,** I have prospered, and **I need nothing**; not knowing that you are wretched, pitiable, poor, blind, and naked. Therefore I counsel you to **buy from me gold refined by fire,** that you may be rich, **and white garments to clothe you** and to keep the shame of your nakedness from being seen, **and salve to anoint your eyes, that you may see.** Those whom I love, I reprove and chasten; so be zealous and repent. **Behold, I stand at the door and knock; if any one hears my voice and opens the door, I will come in to him and eat with him, and he with me.** He who conquers, I will grant him to sit with me on my throne, as I myself conquered and sat down with my Father on his throne. **He who has an ear, let him hear what the Spirit says to the churches.'"** Rev. 3:14-22.*

[56] *Apparently the Nicolaitans were a sect similar to the Greek Hedonists. While saying they were spiritual, they concentrated on the "joys of the flesh." The hedonism of Epicurus (c. 341-270 B.C.) had as its intent the tranquility and benefit of the whole life; but the focus was on the physical rather than the spiritual. Symbolically, as they increase their understanding, the Church of Ephesus will **eat** of the tree of life.

ask, having no fear. We are assured that the second death is "nothing" for he who is able to conquer.[57]   Do you see? **We have come full circle!** We began at the garden aeons ago; now we have arrived at the New Jerusalem – the fully developed Garden. John expresses as does Ezekiel. Much of what he sees is unpleasant; it is frightening; it is threatening. It threatens to *conquer* us; it threatens to *slay* us. It threatens to *destroy* us; it threatens to *balance* us. This New Jerusalem is not of the earth. But at least we will be compensated for the turmoil; for they who "appear" are clothed in white robes. *"These are **they who have come out of the great tribulation;** they have washed their robes and **made them white in the blood of the Lamb.** Therefore **are they before the throne of God,** and serve him day and night within his temple; and he who sits upon the throne will shelter them with his presence. They shall hunger no more, neither thirst any more; the sun shall not strike them, nor any scorching heat. For the Lamb in the midst of the throne will be their shepherd, and he **will guide them to springs of living water; and God will wipe away every tear from their eyes."* Rev. 7:14-17.

In *Revelation* (Chapters 1 through 3) Jesus says:
1. Maintain *patient endurance* and *discernment; express with the* LOVE *of first love.*

2. Have no fear; having "died" to the carnal, **death cannot hurt you.**

3. You will **receive "hidden strength" that is pure,** with your nature written on it.

4. **You will receive in keeping with your heart and mind;** those who take charge of themselves will receive the *morning star,* that which brings light to the world.

5. **Be of the "living,"** knowing you are a part of the living God.

6. Nothing can keep you from going through the open door. You are free from the trials of the world. You are essential to the expression of the whole. **On you is "written"** the nature of God and the nature of that which expresses God, **the new Jerusalem** – that of which my "new" nature is a part.

7. As such, you represent "gold" refined by fire. You are clothed in purity, and you can "see." All you have to do is **"answer"** my knock, and we will *be nourished* and *celebrate* **together!**

---

[57] The 'second death' is the physical death. The 'first death' is the death of the carnal mind. The mindset represented here has undergone the 'first death' and shall not be hurt by the 'second death.'

The Four Horsemen of the Apocalypse by Albrecht Dürer.

Let's look at ourselves for a moment. How are we dealing with the changes that are taking place in our lives and the world around us? Are we welcoming the chatisement of our LORD? Or do we see the world's changes as negative? Possibly it is a human characteristic to "see" doom and gloom. Consider the amount of money spent on the portrayal of violence and mayhem. Check out your television offerings. Mankind's mindset is at the level of the world.[58] Yet mankind can be more than what is presently being expressed.

Mankind can express in keeping with the sons of Israel. And we're told that the harm to earth and sea shall not take place, "...'til we have sealed the servants of our God upon their foreheads." *And I heard the number of the sealed, a hundred and forty-four thousand sealed, out of every tribe of the sons of Israel, twelve thousand sealed out of the tribe of Judah,... of Reuben,...of Gad,... of Asher, ... of Naphtali, ... of Manasseh,... of Simeon,... of Levi, ... of Issachar,... of Zebulun,... of Joseph, twelve thousand sealed out of the tribe of Benjamin. Rev. 7:3-8.*

Do you notice anything different in this list? Check page 108. Do you notice that the tribe of Dan has been replaced by the tribe of Manasseh? "Righteous judgment" has been replaced by "causing to forget." The Kingdom of Heaven has no more judgment at all, not even righteous judgment; for "righteous" means "seeing the relationship" correctly, i.e., making no judgment at all.[59]

The only judgment that will be expressed is the judgment of the **LAW.** To those of you who are willing to try another "symbolic" experiment, let's hang loose again! Take several different (in composition) wine glasses, and wet your middle finger with either water or wine. Now rub your finger around the rim of the glass (you will have to experiment to get

---

[58] The Ancient Wisdom Traditions teach that mankind is a hybrid between primitive humanity and the Sons of God. Genesis presents it with the enigmatic:*When men began to multiply on the face of the ground, and daughters were born to them, the sons of God saw that the daughters of men were fair; and they took to wife such of them as they chose. Then the LORD said, "My spirit shall not abide in man for ever, for he is flesh, but his days shall be a hundred and twenty years." (12 x 10 or 6 x 20) Gen.6:1-3.*

But as hybrids, we're not always guaranteed what will be produced. It may be primitive humanity (which operates at a lower vibration); it may be a *son of man* (which has the potential to operate at the higher vibration); or it may be the (*son of God*) which has the potential to go to a higher plane. We have to be very careful here not to sound like elitists or science-fiction "freaks." [As a point of interest, I invite you to observe the understanding presented by the work of Arthur C. Clarke and Stanley Kubrick in the film *2001* and its sequels.]

[59] The only judgment that is made in the end times is that **all is in divine completion. All is in divine perfection;** it is **12** times **12** times the cosmic level **000,** i.e., **144,000.**

a good tone).[60] Do you see how the LORD works? Do you see what we are supposed to be learning?

Despite the temptation to "sound" at the level of common men, John "resonates" at the level of finest crystal and finest wine. With Chapter 11 he says: *Then I was given a measuring rod like a staff, and I was told: "Rise and measure the temple of God and the altar and those who worship there, but do not measure the court outside the temple; leave that out, for it is given over to the nations, and they will trample over the holy city for forty-two months.* Rev. 11:1,2.

Believe it or not, we are back at the **LAW**. What we "measure" is what we get. But we are cautioned to **measure only the temple and the altar and those who worship there!** Everything else is the outer world, and it will be trampled for forty-two months. Now we are given a chance to see if we have learned to "measure" properly. *Forty-two months* is significant. Forty-two is the product of **6** times **7**. It is **3 + 3**, i.e., ✡ (not standing for Judaism, but for **two times equilibrium**) multiplied by **physical completion**. Forty-two is the equivalent of saying ½ **is finished.**[61] And *months* is something which simply makes up the year; it is not the whole thing. And the lesser portion is 1,260 days, 3½ years, i.e., ½ of **7**.

Tribulation is just *part* of our lives if we "measure"as does the temple, the altar, and those who worship there. And remember that the only *one* who can enter into the *holy of holies* is the dedicated, sanctified, *priest-king.* **As such, we will be delivered.**

---

[60] Since I do not want to bring into effect the postulate that *the scientist finds what he expects to find*, I'm putting my conclusion in this footnote. If you use water, you get a tone, but not of the density and clarity produced by having put your finger in wine. The density and tone, i.e., **the vibration**, will depend on the quality of the crystal used for the wine glass. Notice "plastic" produces no tone. Moreover, eventually, as the finger loses its moisture, even the finest wine and the finest crystal cease producing tone. Now, take your lessons to heart!

[61] Notice that two times 42 is 84, which, when added together (8+4) is 12.

428

*And a great **portent** appeared in heaven, **a woman clothed with the sun, with the moon under her feet, and on her head a crown of twelve stars;** she was with child and she cried out in her pangs of birth, in anguish for delivery. And **another portent** appeared in heaven; behold, a **great red dragon, with seven heads and ten horns, and seven diadems upon his heads.** His tail swept down a third of the stars of heaven, and cast them to the earth. And the dragon stood before the woman who was about to bear a child, that he might devour her child when she brought it forth; she brought forth a male child, one who is to rule all the nations with a rod of iron, but her child was caught up to God and to his throne, and **the woman fled into the wilderness, where she has a place prepared by God, in which to be nourished for one thousand two hundred and sixty days.** Rev. 12:1-6.*

Tribulation appears to continue as a "beast" (with ten horns and seven heads) rises out of the sea. And to it the "dragon" gave its power. [62] For a period of time evil reigns, but finally it comes to an end. As with all mystical literature, the spiritual triumphs and evil disappears. The original paradigm is in effect.

John says it nicely: *Then I saw a new heaven and a new earth; for the **first heaven and the first earth had passed away, and the sea was no more.** And I saw the holy city, **new Jerusalem, coming down out of heaven from God, prepared as a bride adorned for her husband;** and I heard a loud voice from the throne saying, **"Behold, the dwelling of God is with men.** He will dwell with them, and they shall be his people, and God himself will be with them; he will wipe away every tear from their eyes, and **death shall be no more, neither shall there be mourning nor crying nor pain any more, for the former things have passed away."** And he who sat upon the throne said, "Behold, **I make all things new."** Also he said, "Write this, for these words are trustworthy and true." And he said to me, **"It is done! I am the Alpha and the Omega, the beginning and the end.** To the thirsty I will give from the fountain of the water of life without payment. **He who conquers shall have this heritage, and I will be his God and he shall be my son.** But as for the **cowardly,** the **faithless,** the **polluted,** as for **murderers, fornicators, sorcerers,** idolaters, and all liars, their lot shall be in the lake that burns with fire and sulphur, which is the second death." Rev. 21:1-8.*[63]

---

[62] Of all of the symbols in *Revelation*, the "beast" most clearly seems to represent Rome, resting on 7 "hills" and carrying the power of the world, "10." *The Jerusalem Bible* says the 7 represents the 7 successive emperors and that 10 represents 10 subject kings. Some see the second "beast" as Caesar Nero in Hebrew letters, which add up to 666 or in Greek "Caesar-God" adds up to 616 (found in some ancient texts. (See *The Jerusalem Bible*, fn. p. 443 #h). Also see *Revelation* 17:8-14.

[63] Interestingly, I found a note that I had made in the margin of my old Bible. It says that those who fit in these categories will be subject to the *second death* and *fire and sulfur* because they will again be born into earthly life. The point of *The Tibetan Book of the Dead* is that failure to recognize "perfection" results in rebirth.

It will be as Jesus said: *"Truly, I say to you, in the new world, when the Son of man shall sit on his glorious throne, **you who have followed me will also sit** on twelve thrones, **judging the twelve tribes of Israel.** And every one who has left houses or brothers or sisters or father or mother or children or lands, for my name's sake, will receive a hundredfold, and inherit eternal life. But many that are first will be last, and the last first.* Mt. 19:28-30. [64]

What worldly eyes may call 500 years of Roman rule, might more properly be seen as 500 years of growing decay, beginning long before the time of Jesus. By the time that John is writing the *Revelation*, decadence is only too apparent. Although the Republic (ruled by "honest" and "moral" senators) had some positive characteristics, the Empire (filled with in-fighting, assassinations, moral licentiousness, brutality and the lowest expressions of mankind) has practically none. By A.D. 95 when John is supposedly writing on Patmos, the decency of Rome is gone; but it takes it 400 years to die.

Those who keep the teachings of Jesus in mind are able to endure. Paul writes to the Romans: *I consider that the sufferings of this present time are not worth comparing with the glory that is to be revealed to us. For **the creation waits with eager longing for the revealing of the sons of God;** for the creation was subjected to futility, not of its own will but by the will of him who subjected it in hope; because **the creation itself will be set free from its bondage to decay and obtain the glorious liberty of the children of God.** Rm. 8:18-21.

---

[64] Jesus continues: *"For **the kingdom of heaven is like a householder who went out early in the morning to hire laborers for his vineyard.** After agreeing with the laborers for a denarius a day, he sent them into his vineyard. And going out about the third hour he saw others standing idle in the market place; and to them he said, **'You go into the vineyard too, and whatever is right I will give you.'** So they went. Going out again about the sixth hour and the ninth hour, he did the same. And about the eleventh hour he went out and found others standing; and he said to them, 'Why do you stand here idle all day?' They said to him, 'Because no one has hired us.' He said to them, **'You go into the vineyard too.'** And when evening came, the owner of the vineyard said to his steward, **'Call the laborers and pay them their wages, beginning with the last, up to the first.'** And when those hired about the eleventh hour came, each of them received a denarius. **Now when the first came, they thought they would receive more; but each of them also received a denarius.** And on receiving it they grumbled at the householder, saying, 'These last worked only one hour, and you have made them equal to us who have borne the burden of the day and the scorching heat.' But he replied to one of them, 'Friend, I am doing you no wrong; did you not agree with me for a denarius? **Take what belongs to you, and go; I choose to give to this last as I give to you. Am I not allowed to do what I choose with what belongs to me? Or do you begrudge my generosity?'** So the last will be first, and the first last."* Mt. 20:1-16.

430

Traditionally, all of the apostles died as martyrs, except John.[65] Peter made up for his denial. According to

---

[65] For those of you who desire a chronology, I would begin – for those who know their world history – that the Republic died after **Julius Caesar** defeated Pompey in 48 B.C. and appropriated all power in Rome. Julius Caesar was **assassinated in 44 B.C.**. It took nearly ten years for Octavian to defeat Antony and Cleopatra – both of whom commit suicide in 30 B.C. – and after consolidating his power, **Octavian was renamed Augustus in 27 B.C.**. At least Augustus had some redeeming attributes, but Augustus dies August 19, A.D. 14 and is succeeded by his conniving step-son Tiberius. **Tiberius (14 thru 37)**, a moral degenerate, enjoyed absolute power. It is during the reign of Tiberius that Jesus is crucified.

Jesus is crucified in A.D. 30, and fifty days after Passover, the disciples experience the Pentecost and the presence of the Holy Ghost. Immediately they go out to preach. See Acts 2. But within seven (7) years the political climate becomes even more degenerated. **Stephen is stoned** in the winter of 36-37, and Jewish opposition to the teachings is quite strong, partially in the form of Saul of Tarsus. But shortly after Stephen's death, Saul is converted and becomes "Paul."

The ultimate "evil" is sitting on the throne in Rome. **Caligula becomes Emperor in A.D. 37** and declares himself a god, ordering the erection of his statue in the Temple. Before that can be accomplished, he even murders his own wife (sister), adding to the numerous murders and gross immoralities he had performed. Finally, in the year 41 he is assassinated, and **Claudius** (his uncle and grandson of Augustus) becomes **Emperor**. Although Claudius (a cripple) is an intellectual and a scrupulous man, he is forced by circumstances into appointing unscrupulous persons. He makes Agrippa I king of Judaea and Samaria; and shortly before his death in the spring of 44, Agrippa I **beheads James the Great (brother of John) and imprisons Peter.** In keeping with the "last days," Judaea experiences famines and false prophets and harassment and corrupt appointees to the office of High Priest.

During the twenty years since the crucifixion, the teachings of **the Nazarene** have been spreading. Peter has been active in Samaria and Judaea. Traditionally, **Thomas** has gone as far as India, and **Cornelius**, the centurion, has made converts along the Mediterranean. **Paul** and **Barnabas** have established the major hellenistic center in Antioch, and by A.D. 48-49 the council in Jerusalem declares that "converts from paganism" are exempt from Jewish Law, i.e., circumcision and dietary laws. And we know that John has been busy in Asia Minor.

According to *The Jerusalem Bible*, in **A.D. 50** the Aramaic **Matthew** and **complementary collections** are placed **in written form**. But most of the now canonical material comes in the letters being sent through the Mediterranean.

Of all canonical material, my favorite is the book of James, written either in 49 or 58. To me it reveals the most complete understanding of the teachings of Jesus. **James is the brother of Jesus, and becomes the head of the Judeo-Christian community in Jerusalem**, and in his epistle I think we see early Christianity apart from Paulian theology. Nevertheless, **James the brother of Jesus is stoned to death in 62,** at the insistence of the High Priest, Anan; and **Mary (sister-in-law of the mother of Jesus) suceeds James as head of the church of Jerusalem.**

Meanwhile, things in Rome have become more difficult. Claudius wasn't friendly to this new sect, but his successor **Nero** finds them to be an easy scapegoat. Social peace is uneasy in Rome. Too many of the wheat farmers from the provinces

(continued...)

John, the resurrected Jesus gave Peter three admonitions to replace the three denials. *When they had finished breakfast, Jesus said to Simon Peter, "Simon, son of John,* ***do you love me more than these?"*** *He said to him, "Yes, Lord; you know that I love you." He said to him,* ***"Feed my lambs."*** *A second time he said to him, "Simon, son of John, do you love me?" He said to him, "Yes, Lord; you know that I love you." He said to him,* ***"Tend my sheep."*** *He said to him the third time, "Simon, son of John, do you love me?" Peter was grieved because he said to him the third time, "Do you love me?" And he said to him, "Lord, you know everything; you know that I love you." Jesus said to him,* ***"Feed my sheep.*** *Truly, truly, I say to you, when you were young, you girded yourself and walked where you would; but* ***when you are old, you will stretch out your hands, and another will gird you and carry you where you do not wish to go."*** Jn.21:15-19.

Each of the apostles follows his own path. Peter does as he was admonished by the Christ. He **"feeds" the lambs;** he teaches those who had not been given the understanding of

---

[65](...continued)

are moving to the city and becoming not only a source of possible agitation, but an added cost to keeping the peace – because of providing them food. In addition, the shortage of yeoman farmers providing food had "upped" the cost of provisioning the legions that protect the borders; with fewer legions, the borders get more attacks.

To placate the masses, the games at the Coliseum become more important, and are utilized by the government. Consequently, the "Christians," too, become more important. When for some reason Rome catches fire in A. D. 64 (history has questioned if Nero set the fires himself), the perfect way to cement dissident movements is to unify them against an obviously different group. The tactics of Rome are no different than those of any totalitarianism. Ask Hitler; ask Machiavelli.

Peter is martyred in Rome (c. 64), reputedly insisting that he be crucified up-side-down; and **Paul is beheaded** three years later (c.67). Unrest is growing in Rome; unrest is rampant in Judea. Jerusalem is beseiged, and the community at Qumrân (site of the Dead Sea Scrolls, located between Jerusalem and the Dead Sea) is destroyed in 68. Nero is losing power and his mind. He "commits suicide" in June of 68, but things continue to deteriorate. By 69 Vespasian is emperor, and he gives Titus (son of Nero) the opportunity to bring Jerusalem under control. The *sicarii* (organized rebels) hold out in Jerusalem, in the Herodion, Masada and Machaerus.

Passover, A.D. 70, Titus lays seige to Jerusalem with four legions. By August, sacrifices cease because of famine. By August 29th (the **10th** day of the **5th month** (Loos) the Inner Court is penetrated and the **Temple is burned**. The Temple of Herod is burned on the same day that Nebuchadrezzar had set fire to Solomon's Temple in 587 B.C., 657 years later. And the Temple vessels are taken to Rome. Three years later the *sicarii* remaining at Masada will commit suicide rather than yield to those Romans surrounding them.

Despite of the chaos around them, the Church continues to grow and becomes more highly organized. Supposedly about A.D. 95 John is exiled to Patmos, and here *Revelation* is put together (some say from portions that had been composed at different times). Traditionally, **John dies in Ephesus in the year A.D. 100.**

432

the inner teachings. He **"tends" the sheep**; he holds the Church together, finally even giving in to the demands of Paul, (who began as an enemy of the Church) and easing the Jewish ritual-requirements that originally had also applied to Gentiles.[66] And he **"feeds" the sheep.** He remains as the most illumined of the apostles, leading the movement from Jerusalem until he moves on with it established and in the strong hands of Jesus' brother, James. Despite his "falling asleep" and then "running away" and "denying" the Christ, Peter follows Jesus' teachings, and he gains the strength he lacked before.

But what is revealed to John is a *different reality* than what the world sees. This is the vision of the mystic, and John takes us to the understanding of mysticism. John writes: *And I saw **no temple** in the city, for **its temple is the Lord God the Almighty and the Lamb.** And the city has **no need of sun or moon to shine upon it, for the glory of God is its light, and its lamp is the Lamb.** By its light shall the nations walk; and the kings of the earth shall bring their glory into it, and **its gates shall never be shut by day** -- and there shall be no night there; ... nothing unclean shall enter it, nor any one who practices abomination or falsehood, but **only those who are written in the Lamb's book of life.*** Rev. 21:22-27.

And John concludes: *Then he showed me the **river of the water of life, bright as crystal, flowing from the throne** of God and of the Lamb through the middle of the street of the city; also, **on either side of the river, the tree of life with its twelve kinds of fruit, yielding its fruit each month; and the leaves of the tree were for the healing of the nations.** There shall **no more be anything accursed,** but the throne of God and of the Lamb shall be in it, and **his servants** shall worship him; they **shall see his face, and his name shall be on their foreheads.** And **night shall be no more;** they need no light of lamp or sun, for the Lord God **will be their light,** and they shall reign for ever and ever.*

*And he said to me, "These words are trustworthy and true. And the Lord, the God of the spirits of the prophets, has sent his angel to show his servants what must soon take place. And **behold, I am coming soon." Blessed is he who keeps the words of the prophecy of this book.*** Rev. 22:1-7.

Just what are the "words" of this *Revelation*? Isn't it that mankind will reach a *different reality*, that mankind will *awaken* to find himself/herself living in the Kingdom of Heaven? Isn't it that mankind must climb the Mountain?

---

[66] Admittedly, this took place after an impressive "night vision" in which Peter is clearly shown that none of God's creatures are unclean.

The *esoteric* message of the Bible is that in the New Jerusalem, there is **only ONE tree** *– there is only the tree of life.* That old tree that we ate from so long ago is gone. The Christ is crucified on that which has come full circle. The *paradigm* is restored.

La Vision de Saint Jean by Vitrail de Lyon.

Yet, I think we have oversimplified the task of following Jesus. We often say that the requirement is only to **love** as Jesus loved. But the difficulty lies in what we see as **love.** The difficulty with "love" is that it always implies an "object." My intuition now tells me that our requirement is to reach the place where we ***are love.*** We are to reach a vibration

434

that is the same as *love*. In so doing, we *become* as Jesus was; we become the embodiment of the Christ, and we finish *Climbing the Mountain*.

This study of the Bible is concluded, yet, I suspect that as with the book of Deuteronomy, one last message has been saved for us.[67] It is the *Gospel According to Thomas* that will finish this study. Remember, Thomas didn't pretend to understand. He doubted; and to these doubts, Jesus said: *Have you believed because you have seen me? Blessed are those who have not seen and yet believe.* Jn. 20:29.

According to Thomas, Jesus says: *"You test the face of the sky and of the earth, and him who is before your face you have not known, and you do not know to test this moment."* ... Jesus said: *"Whoever seeks will find, and whoever knocks, it will be opened to him.* ... *Whoever does not hate his father and his mother in My way will not be able to be a disciple to me. And whoever does not love his father and his mother in My way will not be able to be a disciple to me, for My mother [bore me] but My true Mother gave me the LIFE."* ... Jesus said: *"Whoever knows father and mother shall be called the son of a harlot. When you make the two one, you shall become sons of Man, and when you say: Mountain, be moved, it will be moved."* Gospel of Thomas (92 - 107).

In many ways aren't we the harlot? We continually deal with the world, even though we have a greater understanding than the world has. But the Bible told us that despite our sins, we can proceed from being the *harlot* or the *son of the harlot* to being the *enlightened woman*, the "true" Mother, the mother of the Christ.

Our scriptural sources reflect the understanding of those who followed Jesus. Thomas probably was not the most spiritual of the disciples, but the *Gospel of Thomas* nicely finishes our study. In the last lines of his text, Thomas says something that I find nowhere else. Remember that there was

---

[67] As we saw with Deuteronomy, scripture that was too advanced for the Hebrews of Joshua's time was not found until the time of Ezra – until the time when mankind had advanced. So it is with the Gospel according to Thomas. It is not a part of the canon. *The Gospel According to Thomas* is a Coptic (Egyptian Christian Church which did not undergo the changes experienced by the remainder of Christendom) text discovered in 1945 in a ruined tomb near Nag Hamâdi, in Upper Egypt. Translated by A. Guillaumont, H.C. Puech, G. Quispel, W. Till, and Yassah 'Abd Al Masîh. Harper and Row, Pub., NY, 1959.

jealousy among the apostles. Remember John and James demanding the best seats in the Kingdom of Heaven? Well, Peter, the apostle most similar to the way we are, is also protective of his position. And Peter complains to Jesus that Mary Magdalene is accompanying the select few. Peter says:

"Let Mary go out from among us, because women are not worthy of the Life."

Jesus puts Peter in his place. *Jesus said: "See, I shall lead her, so that I will make her male, that she too may become a living spirit, resembling you males. For every woman who makes herself male will enter the Kingdom of Heaven."* Gospel of Thomas (114).

Let those who have ears, hear! Our feminine side, our gentle side, our Christ-mind, is that which becomes the Mother and produces the child. But, as in Michelangelo's sculpture of Madonna and Child, which we have here, what will come from our heightened selves is not ***clearly defined***.

And so it is!
April 22, 1996

Index

SYMBOLS
    blue - higher mental plane
    purple - wisdom and KING
    scarlet- energy (as with blood)
    hair - faith, strength
    hand - directive activity; divine action in the soul
    right hand - positive outgoing energy
    left hand - passive or incoming energy
    thigh - power to advance
    thirteen - lunar months; symbol of woman; denotes the soul
    twelve - solar months; denotes the spirit
    marriage - union of wisdom (fem.) + love (masc.); truth (masc.)+ love (fem.) or on the lower level - mind (masc.) +
        emotions (fem.); or union of Lower Self (heightened fem.) + Higher Self (heightened masc.)
    water into wine - transmutation from lower soul expression to higher Divine Spirit
    Shechinah - Holy Spirit, functioning on lower plane; same as #10

Sephiroth (numerations)

1 = Kethe - crown	6 = Tiphereth - beauty
2 = Chokmah - wisdom	7 = Neteach · victory
3 = Binah - understanding	8 = Hod - glory
4 = Chesed - mercy	9 = Yesod - foundation
5 = Geburah - judgment	10 =Malkuth - **The Kingdom brings transmutation of the lower into the higher.**